B6
6.95

W9-CZY-934

21.092

JK
1083
.K6
1977

Kofmehl
Professional
staffs of
Congress

DATE DUE

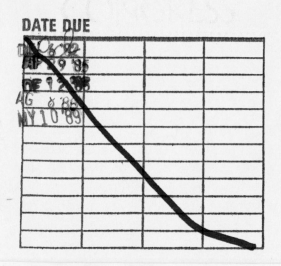

Professional staffs of Congress
JK1083.K6 1977   21092

Kofmehl, Kenneth Theodore
VRJC/WRIGHT LIBRARY

PROFESSIONAL STAFFS OF CONGRESS

by Kenneth Kofmehl

The Purdue University Press
West Lafayette, Indiana
1977

© 1962 by the Purdue Research Foundation
© 1977 by the Purdue Research Foundation
Library of Congress Card Catalog Number 62-63211
International Standard Book Number 0-911198-03-2
Printed in the United States of America
Third Edition

PREFACE TO THE THIRD EDITION

From May to July, 1976, nationwide attention was riveted on congressional staffing by lurid revelations of the Liz Ray-Wayne Hays affair and allegations of other sex scandals on Capitol Hill. Interest of the general public in congressional employees probably reached an all-time high. The otherwise rather dull subject of their qualifications and job requirements was livened. Representative Hays was deposed as chairman of the House Administration Committee. Marginal reforms involving staffs and other perquisites of House members were adopted, and yet another commission was created to study administrative services of the House. However, this was but a minor episode on the overall congressional staff scene. Although receiving relatively less media coverage, far more important developments have occurred since the second edition of this book was completed in April, 1969.

The Legislative Reorganization Act of 1970, the antecedents of which are discussed in the Preface to the Second Edition, has been enacted. Two major central staff agencies, the Office of Technology Assessment and the Congressional Budget Office, have been instituted by subsequent statutes. Along with the latter, two standing committees on the budget with large staffs have been set up in the House and Senate. Reforms of party structure and procedures in both chambers have modified the seniority system and stimulated additional efforts to reorganize the House and Senate. A House Select Committee on Committees conducted a comprehensive study that eventuated in the Committee Reform Amendments of 1974. A House Commission on Information and Facilities and a Commission on the Operation of the Senate have been created. S. Res. 60 of the 94th Congress has authorized a new kind of personal committee staff for Senators. And a Select Committee to Study the Senate Committee System has been established.

In no other seven-year period have there been as many occurrences directly and indirectly affecting the professional staffs of Congress. Adequate treatment of them would require a lengthy volume. These introductory remarks essay the more modest task of highlighting developments that primarily concern aspects of congressional staffing on which the rest of this book is focused. The approach is of necessity selective and summary. But the hope is that even this limited an endeavor will afford some understanding of major respects in which the environment and provisions for professional staffs of Congress have undergone change since April, 1969. Accordingly, let us resume the history of the Legislative Reorganization Act of 1970 where it left off in the Preface to the Second Edition.[1]

The Legislative Reorganization Act of 1970

On May 23, 1969, S. 844 was reported favorably by the Senate Government Operations Committee. With one major exception, omission of the section on regulation of lobbying, and some minor technical revisions, S. 844 incorporated the provisions of S. 355 of the 90th Congress, which the Senate had passed but which died in the House Rules Committee at the close of the 90th Congress on October 14, 1968. In view of that experience, the Senate was not expected to proceed further with S. 844 until the House had approved a legislative reorganization measure.[2]

Meanwhile, numerous House bills on that subject had been referred to the House Rules Committee. On April 22, 1969, Rules Committee Chairman William Colmer (D.-Miss.) appointed a Special Subcommittee on Legislative Reorganization to consider them. Representative B.F. Sisk (D.-Calif.) was chairman; and the other members were Richard Bolling (D.-Mo.), John Young (D.-Tex.), H. Allen Smith (R.-Calif.), and Delbert Latta (R.-Ohio).

In sixteen executive sessions between May 14 and October 30, 1969, the Sisk Subcommittee drafted its own version of a reorganization measure. At eight days of hearings in October, November, and December, 1969, the subcommittee compiled 453 printed pages of testimony and materials submitted for the record by seventy-six Congressmen and a dozen other persons. After the subcommittee and full committee had further reworked the draft bill, Chairman Colmer introduced the end result, H.R. 17654, which was sponsored by all the members of the Rules Committee. On June 17, 1970, the Rules Committee reported H.R. 17654 to the House.[3] In the accompanying report, the committee attempted to avoid amendments aimed at the seniority system by observing:

> The Committee on Rules is aware of the sentiment for broad reform of Congress. Most of the proposals advanced under that heading, such as those dealing with seniority, relate to party practices and customs rather than to the formal rules, structure, and resources of Congress. H.R. 17654 deals with the latter, and is therefore properly titled a legislative reorganization bill. Your committee believes that a joint reorganization measure is not an appropriate vehicle for dealing with party activities in Congress.[4]

Nevertheless, the committee brought H.R. 17654 to the floor under an open rule that allowed all germane amendments except those having the effect of altering the jurisdiction of any House standing committee. Between July 13 and September 17, 1970, the House considered H.R. 17654 on eleven days, which was probably the longest debate held by the House on a single measure for fifty years. During this marathon floor consideration of H.R. 17654, the House took several actions that affected congressional staffing. It adopted an amendment guaranteeing the minority on House committees not less than one-third of the funds for specially-authorized staffs and an amendment defining and expanding the functions of the House Office of the Legislative Counsel. It sustained a point of order against an amendment to create an Office of Technology Assessment. And it rejected several amendments to modify or abolish the seniority system on the grounds that such changes could be effected more properly by the party caucuses.[5]

On September 17, 1970, the House approved H.R. 17654 by a vote of 326 to 19. In two days of Senate debate on October 5 and 6, sixteen amendments were adopted. Nearly all of them added to H.R. 17654 provisions of S. 844 that dealt with Senate rules and procedures. Amendments to eliminate the seniority system were defeated by large margins for essentially the same reasons as in the House. On October 6, the Senate passed H.R. 17654, as amended, by a vote of 59 to 5. The House concurred in the Senate amendments on October 8, and the President signed the Legislative Reorganization Act of 1970 (Public Law 91-510) on October 26, 1970. Most of its provisions were to become effective at the start of the 92d Congress.[6]

As had been the case from its inception, Public Law 91-510 comprised moderate reforms. It revised committee and floor procedures in both chambers to expedite proceedings and make them more open to the public—probably the most important change being the provision for recorded teller votes in the House. It modified committee procedures in both houses to give the majority on a committee greater control over the chairman and the minority a larger role in committee operations. It altered somewhat jurisdictions and limitations on memberships and chairmanships of Senate committees. And it improved fiscal controls, staffing, research resources, bill-drafting facilities, and housekeeping services of Congress.[7]

In the Senate, the 1970 Act created a Committee on Veterans' Affairs and added urban affairs to the jurisdiction of the renamed Committee on Banking, Housing, and Urban Affairs. Continuing party practices expressed in the Johnson and Javits Rules, Public Law 91-510 restricted a Senator to membership on no more than two major committees (only one of which might be Appropriations, Armed Services, Finance, or Foreign Relations) and one minor committee (with exceptions for certain joint and temporary committees). Likewise, it limited each Senator to one committee chairmanship (with exceptions for certain joint and temporary committees) and to no more than one subcommittee chairmanship on any single major committee. Appropriately placed "grandfather clauses" safeguarded incumbents.

The 1970 Act significantly expanded the responsibilities of the General Accounting Office (GAO) for developing fiscal and budgetary data, reviewing administration of existing laws, assisting congressional committees by analyzing or conducting cost benefit studies of programs within their jurisdictions, and helping them in their consideration of proposed legislation—including requests for appropriations. It prescribed procedures designed to broaden the distribution and utilization of GAO reports. It prohibited detailing a GAO employee full time to any congressional committee for a period longer than a year. And the accompanying committee report directed the GAO to hire the requisite additional staff to fulfill these new duties within five years.[8]

Public Law 91-510 revamped the Legislative Reference Service even more thoroughly, retitling it the Congressional Research Service (CRS) to reflect the alteration of status and function. The 1970 Act substantially enlarged the responsibilities of the CRS to assist the committees and members of Congress, with particular emphasis on performing policy analysis for the committees and assisting them in planning their legislative activities. To supplement the in-house expertise of the CRS, it authorized the CRS to hire temporarily (not to exceed one year) individual consultants and research organizations. And the accompanying committee report encouraged the CRS to triple in size by 1975.[9]

In similar fashion, Public Law 91-510 comprehensively revised the statutory basis for the House Office of the Legislative Counsel. It defined the purpose and duties of the office and indicated priorities to be followed in carrying them out. And the House debate on this provision of the 1970 Act (which was offered initially as a floor amendment) revealed an intent to enlarge the office.[10]

To perform new functions involving Congress as an institution, Public Law 91-510 established a Joint Committee on Congressional Operations and an Office of Placement and Office Management. It directed the joint committee to make a continuing study of the organization and operation of Congress and recommendations for their improvement, to identify and call attention to court proceedings or actions of vital interest to Congress, and to supervise the Office of Placement and Office Management. Stipulating that use of this office would be optional, the 1970 Act gave it the duty of helping committees, members, and officers of the Congress to obtain qualified employees and of furnishing advice on office management procedures.

With the exception of eliminating the questionable position of review specialist for each standing committee, Public Law 91-510 carried over substantially unchanged the committee staffing provisions from S. 355 of the 90th Congress.[11] For the regular staffs of Senate committees, the language was almost identical. It increased the quota of professional staff members for each standing committee (other than Appropriations) from four to six (in addition to any other extra staff previously granted to a specific committee) and retained the requirements in the existing law that they be appointed on a permanent, merit, and nonpartisan basis and be assigned no other work than committee business. It provided that a majority of the minority members on a committee might, if they desired, select two of the six professional staff members and one of the six clerical employees for appointment. These appointees would be assigned such committee business as the minority members deemed advisable and would be dismissed upon request by a majority of the minority members. The rest of the professional and clerical staff would continue to be hired and fired by a majority vote of the committee.

Also, for specially-authorized staffs of Senate committees, the language was similar. It required each standing committee to consolidate all requests for funding them into a single annual authorization resolution that specified the amount for every subcommittee to be funded. And it admonished that "the minority shall receive fair consideration" in their appointment.

Likewise, the 1970 Act authorized each standing committee of the Senate to hire temporarily (not to exceed one year) consultants and consultative organizations to be selected by the chairman and ranking minority member acting jointly. And it had the same provisions as S. 355 empowering standing committees in both chambers to help their professional staffs obtain specialized training.

Because Public Law 91-510 treated Senate and House committee staffs separately in most respects, with the language for the latter directly amending the rules of the House, the phrasing of the provisions for House committee staffs differed appreciably from that in S. 355. However, they were in essence the same except for these differences. Concerning regular staffs, on each House standing committee (other than Appropriations and Standards of Official Conduct) the two professional and one clerical staff members that a majority of the minority party members could, if they desired, select for appointment had to be approved and could be dismissed by a majority vote of the committee. Regarding specially-authorized staffs, the minority party members on each House standing committee were entitled, upon request, to not less than one-third of the funds for such employees. With respect to hiring consultants and consultative organizations, their selection would be made by the House standing committee involved rather than by its chairman and ranking minority member acting jointly.

Three of the changes from provisions in S. 355—dropping the review specialist post and modifying the procedures for hiring minority staff and consultants—appeared to be improvements. As noted before, the proposal for a review specialist was dubious. One person could hardly handle all the oversight responsibilities of a standing committee and would have difficulty avoiding absorption into the rest of its staff. Vesting in a majority of each House standing committee the authority to appoint and dismiss the entire regular staff, including any minority components, and to select consultants and consultative organizations would seem desirable for two reasons. First, this was consonant with the philosophy expressed elsewhere in the 1970 Act of placing ultimate control over a committee in a majority of its members. Second, since 1946, under both Democratic and Republican chairmen, there had been enough instances in which a bipartisan majority of a committee had to invoke its formal power over hiring and firing to correct or prevent staffing abuses, to warrant retention of this safeguard.

On the other hand, the desirability of awarding not less than one-third of the funds for specially-authorized employees on each standing committee to the minority party members was debatable. During House consideration of H.R. 17654, several committee and subcommittee chairmen argued in vain against adopting the amendment containing this provision. However, before it could be put into effect, it was repealed.

On January 22, 1971, the House by a vote of 226 to 156 approved a rules change restoring the original language of H.R. 17654 that the minority party on each House standing committee "shall receive fair consideration" in the appointment of specially-authorized staff personnel. Previously, the House Democratic Caucus had bound its members to support this action. Many House Republicans were outraged.[12] During the next three years, they introduced a series of House resolutions that would grant the minority party on a House standing committee up to one-third of the funds for specially-authorized staff and filled pages of the *Congressional Record* with statements pleading their cause.

House Party Reforms

Paralleling the effort to reorganize Congress that culminated in the 1970 Act was a movement to reform the seniority system and other party practices in both chambers. These two endeavors, which had overlapping leadership inside and outside the Congress, were interrelated. Successful implementation of procedures prescribed by Public Law 91-510 to restrain committee chairmen depended on the willingness of committee members to insist upon their observance. With the backing or even the acquiescence of a majority on a committee, the chairman could disregard such rules. Modifying the seniority system to provide methods for removing chairmen who acted arbitrarily might very well make them defer more to their committee memberships. Party actions to decentralize power within committees would distribute among more members the means to exercise their rights. Moreover, revitalizing caucuses and other party organs would afford additional institutional bases from which to press the continuing struggle to reorganize Congress.

This party reform movement, which began earlier and had more dramatic successes in the House, originated on the Republican side. With the transformation of their Policy Committee in 1959, House Republicans embarked on a remarkable course of developing new policy formulating bodies and of reinvigorating the House GOP Conference. By 1967, in the judgment of Charles O. Jones, the House GOP Conference had become "more significant than any conference or caucus for either the majority or the minority since the majority party caucus in the 63rd Congress." And he characterized organizational changes in the House Republican Party since 1959 as "the most important developments in the role of the minority party in policy making in this century."[13]

These striking achievements resulted from a combination of circumstances. During this period, junior GOP members (those who had served no more than three terms), who constituted a majority of the House Republicans, became aware of their strength. The serious GOP losses in the 1958 and 1964 elections prompted junior House Republicans to overthrow their existing leadership and reshape their party structure. The expanded roles of the House GOP Policy Committee and Conference, involving the use of task forces and other subsidiary units, increased their opportunities for asserting themselves.[14]

In 1965, the House GOP Conference reduced the concentration of power in senior House Republicans somewhat by adopting a rule that prohibited GOP party leaders from serving as the ranking Republican on any House standing committee. However, direct assault on the seniority system did not begin in earnest until 1970 after House Democrats had taken some significant steps in that direction.

During the mid-1960s, House Democrats led by Democratic Study Group (DSG) members began laying the foundation for reform of the seniority system. In January, 1965, they established a precedent of exercising the power of the Democratic Caucus over committee assignments to strip seniority from two House Democrats, John Bell Williams (Miss.) and Albert W. Watson (S.C.), as punishment for supporting the GOP presidential candidate in 1964. In January, 1967, the House Democratic Caucus removed Adam Clayton Powell (N.Y.) from the chairmanship of the Education and Labor Committee for misconduct in office. In January, 1969, again the House Democratic

Caucus took seniority away from a member, John R. Rarick (La.), for having bolted the presidential ticket in 1968. More importantly, the caucus approved a DSG-backed proposal for monthly meetings of the caucus at which members could speak out on an equal basis on party procedures and public issues.[15]

At such a meeting on March 18, 1970, the Democratic Caucus approved a resolution, which had been instigated by DSG members, to set up a caucus committee to make a thorough study of party practices concerning the organization of House committees and report its findings and recommendations to the caucus in January, 1971. On March 26, 1970, the caucus chairman appointed a Committee on Organization, Study and Review, which had a membership broadly representative of House Democrats and was chaired by Julia B. Hansen (Wash.).[16]

On December 16, 1970, the Hansen Committee issued its report. In summary, it recommended these procedures for making committee appointments. Nominations by the Democratic Committee on Committees for the chairman and membership of each committee need not follow seniority and were to be made to the Democratic Caucus one committee at a time. Upon the request of ten or more members, a separate vote would be taken on the nomination of any chairman or member of a committee. If an appointment were rejected, the committee list involved would be recommitted to the Committee on Committees. By obtaining a letter signed by a majority of his or her state Democratic delegation, including himself or herself, a member could ensure that the Committee on Committees would consider him or her for nomination to a particular committee.

With respect to committee assignments and operations, it proposed the following. No member could serve on more than two legislative committees. The chairman of a committee could not head more than one of its subcommittees. No member could be chairman of more than one legislative subcommittee. Committee chairmen should permit subcommittee chairmen to handle on the House floor legislation reported from their subcommittees. The chairman of a subcommittee should be allowed to hire at least one staff member for it, subject to approval by a majority of the Democrats on the parent committee.

Also, it recommended that the Caucus Committee on Organization, Study and Review be continued, that the Select Committee on Small Business be made a permanent House committee, and that joint committees and minor housekeeping committees be exempt from the rules limiting subcommittee chairmanships and service on legislative committees.[17]

On January 20, 1971, the House Democratic Caucus approved all the recommendations of the Hansen Committee unchanged. At a meeting on

February 3, 1971, the new rule on selection of committee chairmen was invoked to try to unseat John McMillan (S.C.) as chairman of the House District Committee. Although the challenge was defeated by a vote of 126 to 98, a shift of but fifteen votes would have resulted in removing McMillan from his chairmanship. This demonstrated that the new procedure was not an empty formality but a potent reserve clause that could be invoked with some likelihood of success. Moreover, a month later the Hansen Committee frustrated an attempt to circumvent the rule prohibiting a member from chairing more than one legislative subcommittee. Chet Holifield (D.-Calif.), chairman of the House Government Operations Committee, declared that five of its subcommittees were investigative and that consequently their chairmen, who also headed other subcommittees, were not covered by this rule. When the Hansen Committee stated that this was an erroneous interpretation, Holifield promptly backed down. Implementation of this rule opened about thirty subcommittee chairmanships to junior House Democrats.[18]

Meanwhile, House Republicans had been taking similar actions. On March 17, 1970, House Minority Leader Gerald Ford (Mich.) announced the appointment of a Task Force on Seniority. This study group, which was balanced in composition as to seniority, geography, and ideology, was headed by Barber Conable (N.Y.). Over a period of several months, it sought the views of all House GOP members and held numerous meetings to consider alternative ways of selecting committee leaders.

In September, 1970, the Conable Task Force made public its recommendations. In essence, they were as follows. At the start of every Congress, the GOP Committee on Committees would nominate a candidate for the top GOP post on each committee (chairman or ranking minority member depending on which party controlled the House). The nominee need not be the most senior Republican on the committee. The GOP Conference would vote separately by secret ballot on each nomination. If a nominee were rejected, the Committee on Committees would submit another name until one had been approved.[19]

On January 20, 1971, the House GOP Conference adopted the procedures recommended by the Conable Task Force. When they were put into effect at a subsequent meeting, all the nominees were approved, but several received some negative votes. Two years later, at the start of the 93rd Congress, a serious challenge was mounted against the Committee on Committees' choice for ranking minority member of the Government Operations Committee. At the urging of GOP Whip Leslie Arends (Ill.), who argued against "splintering the seniority system," it was defeated by a vote of 100 to 36. Also, some votes were cast against all but seven of the twenty-one ranking minority members nominated.[20]

During the 92d Congress, House Democrats became dissatisfied with their new procedure for selecting committee chairmen. There was substantial discontent with the "kamikaze" requirement of ten members having to demand a separate vote on a committee chairman by the caucus and of having public votes on such occasions. Individuals who initiated a challenge or even voted against a chairman were subject to reprisal. Hence, a renewed drive for party reforms began gathering momentum inside and outside Congress in late 1972. An intensive lobbying campaign was mounted by Common Cause, Americans for Democratic Action, and a loosely-knit coalition of fifty national organized interest groups called the Committee for Congressional Reform. The Democratic Study Group put together a package of reform proposals. And in January, 1973, the Hansen Committee prepared another set of recommendations.[21]

At meetings on January 22-23, 1973, the House Democratic Caucus adopted several more rules weakening the grip of the seniority system. It amended the procedure for electing committee chairmen to require a separate vote on each nominee at the start of every Congress, which would be by secret ballot if requested by one-fifth of those present. From the initial application of this rule on January 22-23, 1973, the provision for secret ballot has invariably been invoked. On this occasion, each nominee received some negative votes, and six of the twenty-one were opposed by between 20 and 31 percent of those voting. One, Chet Holifield, against whom a formal campaign had been waged, was confirmed in office by a vote of 172 to 46.

Although not attracting as much public notice at the time, two other Hansen Committee recommendations approved by the caucus significantly affected seniority. The first established a House analogue of the Johnson Rule in the Senate. It entitled every House Democrat to one exclusive or major committee assignment. It prohibited any Democratic member of an exclusive committee from serving on any other committee (with a grandfather clause to protect incumbents) and any House Democrat from serving on more than one major and one nonmajor or two nonmajor committees. The second prescribed a set of procedures dubbed the "Subcommittee Bill of Rights." These provided that the Democrats on each standing committee should constitute a "Democratic Caucus" with authority to determine the subcommittee structure, to select subcommittee chairmen, and to control the budgets, staffing, and other aspects of administering the subcommittees.[22]

On February 22, 1973, the House Democratic Caucus adopted a DSG-originated proposal to create a Steering and Policy Committee. Superseding the rather inactive Steering Committee, this new body was designed to assist the House Democratic leadership in formulating party legislative programs and in scheduling matters for House or caucus consideration. It was to consist of the Speaker, Majority Leader, and caucus chairman, eight members to be appointed by the Speaker, and twelve members to be elected by House Democrats assembled in twelve regional groupings set up for that purpose. The Speaker was to serve as chairman, the Majority Leader as vice chairman, and the caucus chairman as second vice chairman. To encourage wider distribution of power, regional representatives were limited to two terms—four years—of service. In a related action, the caucus imposed a limit of two consecutive terms on its chairman, secretary, and assistant secretary.[23]

Initiating a role for the Steering and Policy Committee in making committee assignments on July 24, 1974, the Democratic Caucus empowered it to nominate seven of the fourteen Democrats on the newly-created House Budget Committee. Then in organizational meetings on December 2-5, 1974, the caucus transferred the Committee-on-Committees function entirely to the Steering and Policy Committee. On that historic occasion, the caucus further undermined the seniority system by providing for competitive nominations for committee chairmen from the floor if the original choice of the Committee on Committees were rejected, by requiring that nominations of all Appropriations Subcommittee chairmen be approved by caucus vote, by authorizing the Speaker to name all the Democratic members of the Rules Committee (subject to ratification by the caucus), and by strengthening the Subcommittee Bill of Rights.[24]

In January, 1975, the Democratic Caucus climaxed a six-year assault on the seniority system by deposing the chairmen of three standing committees: W.R. Poage (Tex.) of Agriculture, Edward Hebert (La.) of Armed Services, and Wright Patman (Tex.) of Banking and Currency. In the face of almost certain removal, a fourth chairman, Wilbur Mills (Ark.) of Ways and Means, had abdicated. The efficacy of the new procedure for selecting committee chairmen was resoundingly demonstrated.[25]

Concurrently with serving as an instrumentality of party reform, the Democratic Caucus was actively involved in the consideration of public policy issues and proposals for reorganization of the House. It adopted resolutions on the SST, the Vietnamese war, price controls, social service legislation, revenue measures, opening up House committee meetings, limiting the use of closed rules, and a wide variety of other substantive and procedural matters. On several occasions, it directed standing committees to report out legislation accomplishing certain purposes. Almost immediately after being established, the Steering and Policy Committee assumed an active role in recommending issues for consideration by the caucus. In addition, sometimes the Steering and Policy Committee set up *ad hoc* committees to formulate programs to deal with problems cutting across the jurisdictions of numerous House committees, such as its Task Force on Energy in the 94th Congress.[26]

What was responsible for these remarkable achievements by House Democratic party reformers? As had been the case with similar accomplishments by House Republicans earlier, a combination of circumstances interacted, among which was a relatively large influx of junior members. By the start of the 94th Congress in January, 1975, 42 percent of the House Democrats had but four years or less of service. The role of the seventy-five freshmen Democrats in spurring the memorable actions of the caucus in December, 1974, and in unseating senior committee chairmen in January, 1975, was widely noted. However, a more basic cause of these structural and procedural reforms of the House Democratic Party was the changing factional composition of its membership. There was a secular trend toward a larger proportion of northern and western Democrats and relatively fewer conservatives among the southern Democrats, and there was an increasing number of issue-oriented Democrats from all regions. In turn, these developments reflected underlying economic, demographic, and social changes and political changes giving expression to them, such as the growth of a nationwide economy, industrialization of the South, urbanization, large-scale migrations among sections and to suburbs, implementation of the United States Supreme Court reapportionment decisions, and enforcement of the civil rights and voting rights acts of the 1960s.

There were also gifted leaders in the House, such as Richard Bolling, who foresaw the potentialities of the Democratic Caucus as an instrument of reform and who devised appropriate strategies to exploit them. The DSG, to which many of these leaders belonged, afforded an institutional base for their efforts within the House. And external reinforcement came from organized interest groups who pushed for procedural changes they believed would facilitate policy outcomes they favored.

Senate Party Reform

Although subject to essentially the same generational and factional pressures for change, Senate Democrats began a similar course of party reforms somewhat later than House Democrats. Possibly, they may have felt a less intense need for modification of the seniority system. The operation of the Johnson Rule for a decade and a half had mitigated its effects somewhat. After adoption of the limitations on committee and subcommittee chairmanships in Public Law 91-510, most Democratic Senators became subcommittee chairmen during their first term, some upon receiving their initial committee assignments (as did four of the five elected in 1970). In any event, once underway, Senate Democrats proceeded more cautiously in tackling the seniority system but almost as aggressively in revitalizing their Conference and Policy Committee for taking stands on issues as House Democrats.

In May, 1969, the Senate Democratic Conference approved rules providing for regular meetings of the Policy Committee to consider issues on which the party might adopt a position. On November 30, 1970, a few liberal Democratic Senators began pressing for broader party reforms. Among other things, they proposed that the conference meet in open sessions monthly to discuss party policy and legislation and that it conduct a study of the seniority system. In January and February, 1971, the conference established the precedent that Democratic Steering Committee appointments of chairmen and members of Senate committees must be confirmed by the conference. Although this time the nominations were approved *en bloc,* shortly afterward the conference adopted a procedure subjecting each nominee for committee chairman to separate ratification. Also, the conference approved a rule that no Democrat could be ranking minority member on more than one standing committee whenever the Republicans controlled the Senate. It appointed a committee to study proposed changes in the seniority system. And the conference agreed to meet henceforth at the request of any Democratic Senator.[27]

When the new procedure for approving nominations for committee chairmen was applied at the start of the 93rd Congress in 1973, conference ratification was by voice vote. Majority Leader Mike Mansfield (D.-Mont.) stated that a secret ballot on a nominee for chairman could be had on the demand of any Senator. However, some Senate Democrats feared that asking for a secret ballot would expose them to retribution. Hence, on January 17, 1975, the conference adopted a rule providing for a secret ballot on a nominee for chairman whenever one-fifth of the Senate Democrats demanded it through a process designed to protect their anonymity by having them submit unsigned written requests. But this rule was not to go into effect until after committee chairmen had been selected for the 94th Congress.[28]

During this period, like their House counterparts, the Senate Democratic Conference and Policy Committee were actively engaged in the consideration of policy issues and proposals for reorganization of the Senate. They approved resolutions on economic stabilization, reduction of United States troops in Europe, the Indo-China war, freedom of the press, executive privilege, open committee hearings, increased Senate staffing, and a wide range of other matters. And occasionally the Policy Committee established *ad hoc* subcommittees to deal with complex problems, such as drafting a comprehensive energy and economic program in the 94th Congress.[29]

Concurrently, Senate Republicans were also proceeding against the seniority system. On January 26, 1971, the Senate GOP Conference adopted a rule that no GOP Senator could serve as ranking minority member on more than one standing committee, and it set up a committee to study seniority reform. In February, 1971, the conference temporarily replaced Karl E. Mundt (S. Dak.), who had been convalescing at home from a stroke since November, 1969, as ranking minority member on the Government Operations Committee and two of its subcommittees. On February 3, 1972, after an additional year of his absence, the conference stripped him of his committee assignments—an apparently unprecedented action for either party.[30]

On January 9, 1973, the Senate GOP Conference adopted a rule significantly modifying the seniority system. It provided that the GOP members of each standing committee should nominate which of them would be its ranking Republican, that they not use seniority as the exclusive criterion in making their selection, that their nominee must be approved by the conference, and that all the votes be recorded and made public. If their choice were rejected, the conference could recommit to them the nomination with instructions to name someone else. A grandfather clause exempted incumbent ranking minority members. Hence, in 1973, this new procedure applied only to filling five vacant ranking minority posts on committees.[31]

The Office of Technology Assessment

Meanwhile, another central staff agency to serve both the House and Senate had been established. Public Law 92-484, which was approved on October 13, 1972, created an Office of Technology Assessment. The OTA consisted of a Technology Assessment Board which formulated its overall policies, a director and other employees who carried them out, and a Technology Assessment Advisory Council. The board was in essence a joint committee of Congress, being made up of six Senators and six Representatives along with the director as a non-voting member. Its chairman and vice chairman alternated between the Senate and the House with each Congress. The advisory council was composed of ten public members appointed by the board and two ex officio members—the United States Comptroller General and the director of the Congressional Research Service. Besides being authorized to make full use of outside experts, the OTA was specifically entitled to assistance by the CRS and GAO.

The primary function of the OTA was "to provide early indications of the probable beneficial and adverse impacts of the applications of technology and to develop other coordinate information which may assist the Congress." In other words, the OTA was intended to provide an early warning service for Congress on the effects of technological advances. In carrying out its mission, the OTA utilized panels of experts, citizen advisory committees, consultants, contractors, and OTA staff members in variable combinations.

Because the first Technology Assessment Board, which was not organized until April, 1973, did not appoint a director or obtain funding until November, 1973, the OTA had been operational only a little over two years and was still in a shakedown stage in July, 1976. It was engaged in the process of developing methodology, refining its internal structure and procedures, and striking an appropriate balance in the use of outside experts and in-house staff to perform the emerging function of technology assessment—for which a universally accepted definition did not yet exist.[32]

The Committee Reform Amendments of 1974

At the start of the 93rd Congress, the House launched a comprehensive reorganization effort at the instance of Speaker Carl Albert (D.-Okla.) and Minority Leader Gerald Ford. On January 31, 1973, it approved a resolution creating a select committee to study the organization and operation of House committees. Considerable pains were taken to encourage a completely bipartisan endeavor. The membership and funds for staff of the select committee were evenly divided between Democrats and Republicans. Richard Bolling was chairman and Dave Martin (R.-Nebr.) was vice chairman. And the majority and minority leadership of the House agreed that the House Democratic Caucus and GOP Conference would each have to approve any recommendations of the select committee before the House would be allowed to act on them.

The Bolling Committee carried out its assignment with great thoroughness. Besides having several major studies done by its staff, the GAO, and outside consultants, it had thirty-five scholarly experts on Congress prepare special papers. Between May 2 and October 11, 1973, it held thirty-seven days of hearings and panel discussions in which House members, academic specialists on Congress, and organized interest group representatives participated. Including appendixes, the printed record of these activities totaled more than twenty-one hundred pages. On December 7, 1973, the Bolling Committee publicly released a working draft of its report on reorganization of the House committee system and solicited the reactions of all House members. The most controversial portion was a set of recommendations for rather drastic rearrangement of House committee jurisdictions. In a series of seventeen open sessions between February 4 and March 13, 1974, the Bolling Committee marked up a resolution incorporating proposals from its draft report. It unanimously approved and cosponsored the end product, H. Res. 988, which Chairman Bolling introduced on March 19, 1974. In this revision, some of the proposed changes in committee jurisdictions had been moderated, but H. Res. 988 still included a controversial requirement that each House member could serve on only one of the fifteen standing committees that would be "exclusive."[33]

Early in May, H. Res. 988 received the requisite approval by the House GOP Conference although many of its members were lukewarm in their support. However, among House Democrats, H. Res. 988 encountered severe opposition not only by committee chairmen, as might be expected, but also by some of the most ardent reformers in the DSG and their organized interest group allies. They felt that it would impair majority party control of the House, reduce their influence considerably, and affect their interests adversely in other ways. On May 9, after three days of divisive debate, the House Democratic Caucus voted 111-95 to refer H. Res. 988 to the Hansen Committee for further study with instructions to report back to the caucus by July 17, 1974.[34]

Working assiduously for two months, the Hansen Committee developed an alternative to H. Res. 988, which it presented to the Democratic Caucus on July 17, 1974. On July 23, the caucus adopted a motion instructing the Democratic members of the House Rules Committee to report an open rule that would permit the Hansen Committee proposal (H. Res. 1248) to be offered as a substitute for H. Res. 988, which the Rules Committee did on September 25. After six days of debate beginning September 30, the House approved an amended version of H. Res. 988, the Committee Reform Amendments of 1974, on October 8, 1974.[35]

Although the Bolling Committee had originally recommended abolishing several standing committees, H. Res. 988, as passed, retained all of them. It still made numerous committee jurisdictional changes, but some had been further reduced in scope. It dropped the controversial provision limiting each House member to one major committee assignment, thus leaving any such restrictions to the party caucuses as before. It imposed a new requirement that each standing committee (except Budget) with more than fifteen members must establish at least four subcommittees, and it made major changes in committee staffing provisions.

H. Res. 988 increased the standard allotment of professional staff members from six to eighteen and of clerical employees from six to twelve for each House standing committee (except Appropriations and Budget). If they desired, a majority of the minority party members on a standing committee (except Standards of Official Conduct) might select six of the professional and four of the clerical staff persons for appointment subject to approval of their character and qualifications by a majority of the committee. If the committee rejected any of these minority party choices, a majority of the minority party members might select others until the appointments were made. This minority staff would work on committee business assigned by the minority party members. The rest of the staff would be appointed solely and all staff members could be dismissed by a majority vote of the committee. Every staff person was to be hired without regard to race, creed, sex, or age.

H. Res. 988 retained the language of the existing House rule that professional staff members should be appointed on a permanent and merit basis and should not be assigned any work other than committee business. Significantly, it deleted the requirement that they be appointed without regard to political affiliation. However, H. Res. 988 did permit a committee to employ nonpartisan staff, in lieu of or in addition to staff designated exclusively for the majority or minority party, if a majority of the members of each party on that committee voted to do so.

H. Res. 988 granted the minority party members on each standing committee, upon request by a majority of them, one-third of the funds for specially-authorized staff. From these funds for the minority, it specified, the ranking minority member of the full committtee should provide the ranking minority member of each subcommittee with money to hire at least one professional staff person. All specially-authorized staff selected for appointment by the minority party had to be acceptable to a majority of the committee. If the committee disapproved any of the minority party choices, a majority of the minority party members might select others until the appointments were made.[36]

However, this provision was never to go into effect. History repeated itself. On January 13, 1975, the House Democratic Caucus decided to rescind the allocation of one-third of the specially-authorized staff funds to the minority party members on each standing committee. It incorporated in H. Res. 5, which the House adopted the next day by an almost straight party-line vote, an amendment to the House rules substituting this arrangement. On each standing committee, from the funds provided for specially-authorized staff, the chairman and ranking minority member of each standing subcommittee (up to a maximum of six except for the Appropriations Committee) were authorized to appoint one staff person apiece to serve at their pleasure. These staff positions would be taken from the quota of permanent professional staff for the committee if specially-authorized funds were not made available for them.[37]

These changes made by H. Res. 988 in staffing provisions for the House standing committees have almost completely eliminated the principle of nonpartisanship. Certainly the presumption now is that partisan professional staffs will be the rule. And a rather high obstacle has to be surmounted—getting affirmative action by a majority of the members of each party on a committee—to invoke the escape clause permitting an exception. Nevertheless, there is sufficient flexibility to accommodate strongly held preferences for a nonpartisan committee staff. Moreover, these new staffing arrangements reflect changes that have occurred in the underlying power structures of the committees and of the House. The accelerating development of party government in the House, described at some length above, has substantially increased partisan cleavages on policy issues and has been superseding dominance by a bipartisan coalition with majority party control in the House.

H. Res. 988 also contained a number of procedural and substantive provisions to facilitate the functioning and to strengthen the oversight capabilities of the House. Among these were two new central staff agencies, the Legislative Classification Office and the Office of the Law Revision Counsel, and a temporary study group, the Commission on Information and Facilities. Both the new central staff agencies were patterned after the House Office of the Legislative Counsel. They were to be small, professional, nonpartisan, and under the authority of the Speaker.

The main function of the Legislative Classification Office would be to develop and maintain a system linking federal programs and expenditures to the authorizing statutes and showing each committee jurisdiction for every authorization. In developing this cross-reference service, the office was to coordinate with the GAO and the CRS.

The principal duty of the Office of the Law Revision Counsel would be to develop and keep current an official and positive codification of all federal statutes. Also, the office was charged with making recommendations to the House Judiciary Committee for the repeal of obsolete, superfluous, or superseded provisions of public laws. And the office was to prepare and publish periodically a new edition of the United States Code, with annual cumulative supplements.

The Commission on Information and Facilities, which was to make its final report within two years, consisted of nine House members, five of whom came from the Joint Committee on Congressional Operations, appointed by the Speaker from both parties. Urged to utilize the staff of the joint committee wherever possible, the commission was directed to study and make recommendations on the information and space needs of the House and additional staffing for the House Legislative Counsel.[38]

The Congressional Budget Office

While H. Res. 988 was under consideration, Congress enacted the Congressional Budget Act of 1974 that created another central staff agency to serve the House and Senate, the Congressional Budget Office (CBO), and a standing committee on the budget in each chamber. In fact, H. Res. 988 had to be amended on the floor to include provisions for the House Committee on the Budget. Like the appropriations committees, the House Budget Committee was not restricted to a prescribed number of regular staff members. Also, both budget committees were given oversight responsibility for the CBO.

The CBO was established to provide Congress with budgetary and economic expertise independent of the executive branch. Its director was appointed by the Speaker and President *pro tem* of the Senate, acting jointly on recommendations of both budget committees, to a four-year term but could be removed at any time by either house by a resolution. In turn, the director appointed the other CBO personnel. All, including the director, were to be hired on a nonpartisan and merit basis. Besides being allowed to employ temporarily outside experts and consultative organizations, the director was authorized (upon agreement with them) to utilize the services, facilities, and personnel of executive and regulatory agencies, the GAO, Library of Congress, and the OTA. And the CBO was directed to coordinate its activities with those of the GAO, Library of Congress, and OTA.

The primary duty of the CBO was to provide the two budget committees information with respect to all matters within their jurisdictions. The CBO was to supply similar service to the appropriations and revenue committees of both houses upon request. And when asked by other committees or members of Congress, the CBO was to furnish them with information compiled for the foregoing committees and, to the extent practicable, additional related information. The functions and employees of the Joint Committee on Reduction of Federal Expenditures were transferred to the CBO, and that joint committee was abolished.

By April 1 of each year, the CBO was to submit to the budget committees a report on fiscal policy and national budget priorities. This report was to set forth alternative budget strategies that Congress might follow for the next fiscal year and to discuss their respective impacts on major national needs and balanced national growth. The CBO was also to present the budget committees with reports containing information, data, and analyses at appropriate times for their use.

Although the first director of the CBO, Dr. Alice M. Rivlin, was not appointed until February 24, 1975, she promptly recruited a large and well-qualified professional staff. By June 30, 1975, the CBO had begun issuing reports and within a few months was fully operational. During 1976, however, the CBO was still in a shakedown stage and experiencing some organizational growing pains.[39]

Senate Generational Uprising

At the start of the 94th Congress, junior Senators led a three-pronged attack on inequities and inefficiencies in the structure and functioning of the Senate. They initiated resolutions providing for extra "committee-related" staff for Senators, a select committee to study the Senate committee system, and a commission on the operation of the Senate. These resolutions, which had been endorsed by both the Democratic and GOP Conferences and had fifty or more co-sponsors apiece, originated from discussions among Senators first elected since 1967. Informally organized with Senators Lloyd Bentsen (D.-Tex.) and Bill Brock (R.-Tenn.) as co-chairmen, this group, which comprised nearly half the Senate membership, was bipartisan and represented the whole ideological spectrum in the Senate.

The primary goal of these junior Senators was comprehensive reorganization of the sprawling Senate standing committee structure, which by 1975 had 126 supcommittees, highly overlapping jurisdictions, and great disparities in workloads and access to staff by their members. In the preceding Congress, two of them, Senators Brock and Adlai Stevenson (D.-Ill.), had introduced resolutions authorizing select committee studies of the problem. However, because the most optimistic estimate was that at least two years would be required for a complete overhaul of the Senate committee system, they decided to press immediately for extra staff as a stopgap measure to help them cope with the existing situation.[40]

Hence, on February 5, 1975, Senator Mike Gravel (D.-Alaska) introduced S. Res. 60 to authorize additional "committee-related" personal staff for Senators to assist them on committee work. After a tortuous course involving complicated parliamentary maneuvers, several versions that prescribed differing degrees of control by committee chairmen over this new type of employee, and resort to cloture, S. Res. 60 was approved on June 12, 1975. As passed, S. Res. 60, in effect, allowed every Senator to hire a maximum of three committee assistants at near the top professional staff salary. It entitled each Senator to a staff allowance of $33,975 apiece for up to two major committee assignments and another $33,975 for one minor, select, or joint committee assignments. If a Senator were not on a minor, select, or joint committee but served on more than two major committees, he or she could receive $33,975 for a third major committee. However, this staff allowance would be reduced by an amount equal to the total annual basic pay of committee employees whose appointments were made, recommended, or approved by a Senator if they were assigned to assist with duties on a committee for which an allowance was received. In other words, a Senator with no committee staff could receive as much as $101,925; but a Senator with control over at least one staff member each on two major and one minor or three major committees could receive nothing. Any employee hired under this provision was to be certified by the Senator who made the appointment to the chairman and ranking minority member of the committee with which he or she was designated to work, and was to be accorded all privileges of a professional staff member of that committee. In short, under the prescribed conditions, a Senator could appoint several personal legislative assistants who would have all the privileges of professional staff members of the committees with which they worked.[41]

On March 11, 1975, Senator Stevenson introduced for himself, Senator

Brock, and fifty other co-sponsors, S. Res. 109 to establish a temporary select committee to study the Senate committee system. It was referred to the Rules and Administration Committee, where it languished for nearly a year. On February 5, 1976, a Rules and Administration subcommittee held a brief hearing on S. Res. 109, at which Senators Brock and Frank E. Moss (D.-Utah) testified in its behalf. Almost two months later, the Rules and Administration Committee reported out S. Res. 109, which was approved by the Senate on March 31, 1976.[42]

S. Res. 109 created a select committee of twelve members, evenly divided between the two parties. It authorized this select committee to conduct a thorough study of the structure, jurisdiction, number, and optimum size of Senate committees; committee rules and procedures; staffing; and other committee facilities. And S. Res. 109 stipulated that the select committee was to make a final report of its findings and recommendations not later than February 28, 1977.[43]

In April, 1976, the Temporary Select Committee to Study the Senate Committee System was organized. Senators Stevenson and Brock were elected chairman and co-chairman respectively. The other members were Frank Moss, Lee Metcalf (D.-Mont.), Gaylord Nelson (D.-Wis.), Lloyd Bentsen, Lawton Chiles (D.-Fla.), Clifford Hansen (R.-Wyo.), Barry Goldwater (R.-Ariz.), Bob Packwood (R.-Oreg.), Pete Domenici (R.-N. Mex.), and Jesse Helms (R.-N.C.). This was a very well-balanced and knowledgeable group. It comprised four of the five Senate members of the Joint Committee on Congressional Operations, including Metcalf, who alternated as chairman of that body and who had played an instrumental role in the enactment of the Legislative Reorganization Act of 1970. Its members represented twelve of the fourteen major standing committees in the Senate. They covered the ideological spectrum and ranged from three to seventeen years of experience in the Senate. Two were chairmen and two were ranking minority members of Senate committees. All were either chairmen or ranking minority members of subcommittees.

Proceeding promptly, the select committee engaged the services of a top-notch professional staff, some of whom had worked for the Bolling Committee. On July 20, 1976, it began a series of well-organized hearings. Although admirably qualified, the select committee was undertaking a truly formidable project if past experience were any guide.

To get the maximum value from any additional staff personnel provided by S. Res. 60 or subsequent measures, it would be necessary to improve their working conditions and the administrative support services of the Senate, which were unsatisfactory in many respects. Less than four months after entering the Senate, John Culver (D.-Iowa) proposed to the Democratic Conference that a commission of private citizens be set up to study this problem. Favorably impressed by the idea, which was unanimously endorsed by the Democratic and GOP Conferences, Majority Leader Mansfield worked together with Minority Leader Hugh Scott (Pa.) to give it concrete expression in the form of S. Res. 227. Bypassing the Rules and Administration Committee, Mansfield brought S. Res. 227 directly to the Senate floor where it was approved on July 29, 1975.[44]

S. Res. 227 created a temporary Commission on the Operation of the Senate composed of nine members chosen from private life and two ex officio nonvoting members who were Senate employees. They were appointed by the President of the Senate on the recommendations of the Majority and Minority Leaders. The commission was authorized to make a comprehensive study covering such Senate matters as office facilities, information resources, staffing requirements, administrative services, pay and allowances, conflicts in scheduling of business, and improving relations with the House and the other branches of government. However, Senate rules and committee jurisdictions were specifically excluded from its scope. The commission was directed to submit to the Majority and Minority Leaders a final report of its findings and recommendations by September 30, 1976 (later extended to December 31, 1976).[45]

At its first meeting on October 24, 1975, the commission elected former Senator Harold Hughes as chairman and Archie Dykes, chancellor of the University of Kansas, as vice chairman. On March 31, 1976, the commission issued an interim report focused on the administration of Senate-wide supporting services, in which it observed that there was a need to organize and consolidate housekeeping functions systematically and suggested that the Senate consider establishing a single administrative office for the management of all such services. And it outlined a broad program of studies in progress covering the whole range of tasks set forth in S. Res. 227.[46]

Concluding Comments

It may take years to discover, much less evaluate, all the effects of these manifold reform and reorganization efforts. However, one consequence was immediately evident: an acceleration in the already rapid growth of congressional staffs. As mandated by the Legislative Reorganization Act of 1970, the CRS more than doubled its staff positions, going from 323 to 778, between 1970 and 1976. By March, 1976, the CBO numbered 190 employees, and the OTA had an in-house staff of 90.[47]

Between 1966 and the end of 1974, House committee employees (regular and special) increased from 566 to 1046. As a result of the Committee Reform Amendments of 1974, House committees hired an additional 218 regular staff members in 1975. A major reason why that measure substantially raised the quota of regular staff for each standing committee was to reduce the need for specially-authorized staff. But there did not appear to be much of an effect in that direction. During 1975, House committees also added 191 more specially-authorized staff personnel than the year before. By December 31, 1975, House committee employees (regular and special) totaled 1531.[48]

Likewise, between 1966 and January 31, 1975, Senate committee employees (regular and special) grew from 642 to 1038. In the nine months after the adoption of S. Res. 60, 90 Senators took advantage of its provisions to hire 291 additional staff members. The Rules and Administration Committee made a vigorous effort to cut back the funds for specially-authorized committee employees to compensate for this increase. Even if completely successful, however, this endeavor would not have reduced the total amount of staff working with the Senate committees but only the portion on their payrolls. And during the rest of 1975, Senate committees hired 411 more employees to raise their number to 1449.[49]

A similar situation obtained with respect to the office staffs of Representatives and Senators. Between 1966 and the end of 1974, they increased from 3795 to 6114 in the House and from 1803 to 2935 in the Senate.[50]

In both chambers, a growing number of members have expressed concern about overstaffing. Even some of the most reform-minded junior Congressmen have begun to realize that continuing enlargement of the congressional staff may have dysfunctional consequences. For example, in introducing S. Res. 109, Senator Brock said:

> The most popular remedy for staffing problems is more of the same. . . . It is argued, plausibly, that additional staff would help junior Members to keep up with subcommittee and committee chairmen and the Senate to keep up with the executive branch. The opposite result is conceivable, however, and the better solution may be less partisan, less personal committee staffs.[51]

Again, in the July 22, 1976, hearings before the Select Committee to Study the Senate Committee System, Co-chairman Brock urged consideration of the idea of selecting committee staff on an entirely nonpartisan basis.[52]

Such remarks may indicate renewed interest in staffing principles of the Legislative Reorganization Act of 1946. If so, that affords additional justification for keeping in print the main body of this book, which describes conditions and practices with respect to professional staffs of Congress when the intent of the 1946 Act was fresh and enthusiasm for its objectives was high.

West Lafayette, Indiana   KENNETH KOFMEHL
August 7, 1976

NOTES

[1] See pp. xxxv to xl.

[2] *Congressional Quarterly Weekly Report,* XXVII, No. 23 (June 6, 1969), pp. 937-38.

[3] *Ibid.,* No. 24 (June 13, 1969), pp. 1031-33; Walter Kravitz, *The Legislative Reorganization Act of 1970: A Brief History and Summary of Its Provisions* (Washington: Library of Congress, CRS, 1972), pp. 6-8.

[4] House Report No. 91-1215, 91st Cong., 2d Sess., June 17, 1970, p. 3.

[5] *National Journal,* II, No. 30 (July 25, 1970), pp. 1607-14; *Congressional Quarterly Weekly Report,* XXVIII, No. 29 (July 17, 1970), pp. 1775-76; *ibid.,* No. 31 (July 31, 1970), pp. 1931-32; *ibid.,* No. 38 (Sept. 18, 1970), p. 2241; Kravitz, *The Legislative Reorganization Act of 1970,* pp. 8-10.

[6] *Ibid.,* pp. 11-12; *Congressional Quarterly Weekly Report,* XXVIII, No. 39 (Sept. 25, 1970), pp. 2321-26; *ibid.,* No. 41 (Oct. 9, 1970), pp. 2461-63; *ibid.,* No. 53 (Dec. 25, 1970), pp. 3061-64.

[7] Public Law 91-510, 91st Cong., 2d Sess., Oct. 26, 1970, 84 *Stat.* 1140; Kravitz, *The Legislative Reorganization Act of 1970,* pp. 12-23.

[8] House Report No. 91-1215, 91st Cong., 2d Sess., June 17, 1970, p. 19.

[9] *Ibid.*

[10] U.S., *Congressional Record,* 91st Cong., 2d Sess., Sept. 17, 1970, CXVI (daily ed.), p. H8891.

[11] For earlier analysis of these provisions, see pp. xl to xliii.

[12] U.S., *Congressional Record,* 92d Cong., 1st Sess., Jan. 22, 1971, CXVII, Part 1, pp. 135-44; *Congressional Quarterly Weekly Report,* XXIX, No. 5 (Jan. 29, 1971), p. 258.

[13] See Charles O. Jones, *The Minority Party in Congress* (Boston: Little, Brown, and Co., 1970), pp. 36, 160.

[14] *Ibid.,* pp. 194-95.

[15] *Congressional Quarterly Weekly Report,* XXVII, No. 1 (Jan. 3, 1969), p. 2; For an excellent account of seniority reforms through early 1971, see John F. Bibby and Roger H. Davidson, *On Capitol Hill,* 2d ed., (Hinsdale, Ill.: Dryden Press, 1972), pp. 168-77.

[16] *Congressional Quarterly Weekly Report,* XXVIII, No. 9 (Feb. 27, 1970), pp. 642-43; *ibid.,* No. 12 (Mar. 20, 1970), p. 783; *ibid.,* No. 14 (Apr. 3, 1970), p. 920.

[17] Committee on Organization, Study and Review, "Recommendations," dated Dec. 16, 1970, pp. 1-2; *National Journal,* III, No. 1 (Jan. 2, 1971), pp. 16-24; *Congressional Quarterly Weekly Report,* XXIX, No. 3 (Jan. 15, 1971), pp. 134-37.

[18] *Ibid.,* No. 4 (Jan. 22, 1971), pp. 177, 179; *ibid.,* No. 7 (Feb. 12, 1971), p. 365; *ibid.,* No. 10 (Mar. 5, 1971), pp. 520-21; "Committee Reform in House Periled by Holifield's Move," *The Washington Post,* Feb. 23, 1971, p. A-3; "House Clarifies Chairmen Rule," *ibid.,* Mar. 12, 1971, p. A-2.

[19] "House GOP Considering Seniority Reform," *ibid.,* Sept. 28, 1970, p. A-2.

[20] *Congressional Quarterly Weekly Report,* XXIX, No. 4 (Jan. 22, 1971), p. 179; "Rep. Erlenborn Loses Bid as Ranking GOP Member," *The Washington Post,* Jan. 19, 1973, p. A-2; "Old Guard House Republicans Beat Back 'Young Turks'," *ibid.,* Jan. 24, 1973, p. A-23.

[21] "Coalition to Fight House Seniority," *ibid.*, Dec. 14, 1972, p. A-2; *Congressional Quarterly Weekly Report*, XXX, No. 48 (Nov. 25, 1972), p. 3070; *ibid.*, XXXI, No. 3 (Jan. 20, 1973), pp. 69-71.

[22] *Ibid.*, No. 4 (Jan. 27, 1973), pp. 136-38; "Democratic Caucus to Vote on Chairmen," *The Washington Post*, Jan. 10, 1973, p. A-2; "Democrats in House Vote Reforms," *ibid.*, Jan. 23, 1973, p. A-1; "Seniority Survives Votes in House," *ibid.*, Jan. 24, 1973, p. A-4.

[23] "Panel on Policy Voted in House By Democrats," *ibid.*, Feb. 23, 1973, p. A-6; *Congressional Quarterly Weekly Report*, XXXI, No. 8 (Feb. 24, 1973), p. 419.

[24] "Democrats Nominate 14 for Budget Seats," *The Washington Post*, July 30, 1974, p. A-3; *Congressional Quarterly Weekly Report*, XXXII, No. 48 (Nov. 30, 1974), pp. 3199-3201; *ibid.*, No. 49 (Dec. 7, 1974), pp. 3247-52.

[25] *Ibid.*, XXXIII, No. 3 (Jan. 18, 1975), pp. 114-16; *ibid.*, No. 4 (Jan. 25, 1975), pp. 210-12.

[26] *Ibid.*, No. 18 (May 3, 1975), pp. 911-15; "Impoundment Tactics Talked by Nixon Foes," *The Washington Post*, Apr. 6, 1973, p. A-12; "Albert Backs House Vote on Bombing Halt," *ibid.*, May 4, 1973, p. A-1; "Democrats Frame Plan on Economy," *ibid.*, Jan. 5, 1975, p. A-1; "Energy Task Force Eyeing Economy Car Incentives," *ibid.*, Feb. 15, 1975, p. A-2.

[27] *Congressional Quarterly Weekly Report*, XXVIII, No. 50 (Dec. 4, 1970), p. 2916; *ibid.*, XXXI, No. 1 (Jan. 6, 1973), p. 12; *National Journal*, III, No. 10 (Mar. 6, 1971), pp. 500-501.

[28] *Congressional Quarterly Weekly Report*, XXXIII, No. 4 (Jan. 25, 1975), p. 213.

[29] U.S., *Congressional Record*, 92d Cong., 1st Sess., Feb. 24, 1971, CXVII (daily ed.), pp. S1802-S1803; *ibid.*, 93rd Cong., 1st Sess., Dec. 20, 1973, CXIX (daily ed.), p. S23489; "Senate Democrats Assert Limits to Executive Privilege," *The Washington Post*, Jan. 17, 1973, p. A-1; "Senate Democratic Caucus Votes to Open Panel Meetings," *ibid.*, Jan. 16, 1975, p. A-1; "Democrats' Economy Plan Gains," *ibid.*, Feb. 19, 1975, p. A-7.

[30] *Congressional Quarterly Weekly Report*, XXIX, No. 5 (Jan. 29, 1971), p. 257; *ibid.*, XXX, No. 7 (Feb. 12, 1972), pp. 306-307; "GOP Lifts Some Power of Ailing Mundt," *The Evening Star* (Washington), Feb. 4, 1971, p. A-2; "Mundt is Stripped of Senate Jobs," *ibid.*, Feb. 3, 1972, p. A-1.

[31] *Congressional Quarterly Weekly Report*, XXXI, No. 2 (Jan. 13, 1973), pp. 57-58; "Senate Republicans Alter Seniority Rule," *The Washington Post*, Jan. 10, 1973, p. A-2.

[32] Office of Technology Assessment, *Annual Report to the Congress, 1975*, (Washington: U.S. Government Printing Office, 1975), pp. 1-5; House Commission on Information and Facilities, *The Office of Technology Assessment: A Study of Its Organizational Effectiveness*, House Document No. 94-538, 94th Cong., 2d Sess., June 18, 1976, pp. 1-10.

[33] U.S., Congress, House, Select Committee on Committees, *Committee Reform Amendments of 1974*, House Report No. 93-916 (to accompany H. Res. 988), 93rd Cong., 2d Sess., Mar. 21, 1974, pp. 14-18; *Congressional Quarterly Weekly Report*, XXXI, No. 50 (Dec. 15, 1973), p. 3314; *ibid.*, XXXII, No. 11 (Mar. 16, 1974), p. 688; *National Journal*, VI, No. 12 (Mar. 23, 1974), pp. 419-30; For an insightful analysis of the Bolling Committee's actions by two political scientists who served on its staff, see Roger H. Davidson and Walter

J. Oleszek, "Adaptation and Consolidation: Structural Innovation in the U.S. House of Representatives," *Legislative Studies Quarterly,* I, No. 1 (Feb., 1976), pp. 37-65.

[34] *Congressional Quarterly Weekly Report,* XXXII, No. 17 (Apr. 27, 1974), pp. 1026-28; *ibid.,* No. 18 (May 4, 1974), pp. 1146-47; *ibid.,* No. 19 (May 11, 1974), p. 1256.

[35] *Ibid.,* No. 29 (July 20, 1974), p. 1889; *ibid.,* No. 30 (July 27, 1974), p. 1974; *ibid.,* No. 40 (Oct. 5, 1974), pp. 2655-57; *ibid.,* No. 41 (Oct. 12, 1974), pp. 2896-98; *National Journal,* VI, No. 43 (Oct. 26, 1974), pp. 1616-19.

[36] U.S., Congress, House, Committee Reform Amendments of 1974, H. Res. 988, 93rd Cong., 2d Sess., Oct. 8, 1974, pp. 84-94.

[37] U.S., *Congressional Record,* 94th Cong., 1st Sess., Jan. 14, 1975, CXXI (daily ed.), pp. H5-H18; *Congressional Quarterly Weekly Report,* XXXIII, No. 3 (Jan. 18, 1975), p. 118.

[38] H. Res. 988, 93rd Cong., 2d Sess., Oct. 8, 1974, pp. 46-55.

[39] U.S., Congress, Congressional Budget Act of 1974, Public Law 93-344, 93rd Cong., 2d Sess., July 12, 1974, pp. 3-9; *National Journal,* VII, No. 46 (Nov. 15, 1975), pp. 1575-77; *Congressional Quarterly Weekly Report,* XXXIV, No. 23 (June 5, 1976), pp. 1430-32.

[40] *National Journal,* VII, No. 18 (May 3, 1975), pp. 647-51.

[41] *Congressional Quarterly Weekly Report,* XXXIII, No. 11 (Mar. 15, 1975), pp. 541-42; *ibid.,* No. 12 (Mar. 22, 1975), p. 627; *ibid.,* No. 24 (June 14, 1975), pp. 1235-36; *ibid.,* No. 25 (June 21, 1975), p. 1294; U.S., *Congressional Record,* 94th Cong., 1st Sess., June 12, 1975, CXXI (daily ed.), pp. S10519-S10527, D703.

The Senate inserted in the Legislative Branch Appropriations Act for 1976 language establishing a legislative assistance fund that contained the provisions of S. Res. 60 and became effective on July 1, 1975. In doing so, the Senate added a provision permitting Senators to aggregate the monies received for service on different committees. This enabled a Senator to hire any number of committee-related assistants as long as their combined salaries did not exceed the staff allowance made available to the Senator under the provisions of S. Res. 60 (Public Law 94-59, 94th Cong., 1st Sess., July 25, 1975, sec. 108, 89 *Stat.* 276-78; U.S., Congress, Senate, Committee on Appropriations, *Legislative Branch Appropriation, 1976,* Senate Report No. 94-262, 94th Cong., 1st Sess., June 27, 1975, pp. 13-15).

[42] U.S., *Congressional Record,* 94th Cong., 1st Sess., Mar. 11, 1975, CXXI (daily ed.), pp. S3590-S3595; "Brock Asks Review of Committees," *The Washington Post,* Feb. 6, 1976, p. A-3; U.S., *Congressional Record,* 94th Cong., 2d Sess., Mar. 31, 1976, CXXII (daily ed.), pp. S4735-S4737.

[43] U.S., Congress, Senate, To Establish a Temporary Select Committee to Study the Senate Committee System, S. Res. 109, 94th Cong., 2d Sess., Mar. 31, 1976, pp. 1-5.

[44] *Congressional Quarterly Weekly Report,* XXXIII, No. 31 (Aug. 2, 1975), p. 1682; *ibid.,* No. 50 (Dec. 13, 1975), pp. 2715-21.

[45] U.S., *Congressional Record,* 94th Cong., 1st Sess., July 29, 1975, CXXI (daily ed.), pp. S14127-S14130.

[46] U.S., Congress, Senate, Commission on the Operation of the Senate,

Interim Report, Senate Document No. 94-165, 94th Cong., 2d Sess., Mar. 31, 1976, pp. vii, 1-17.

[47] U.S., Congress, Senate, Committee on Appropriations, *Hearings before a Subcommittee on the Legislative Branch Appropriations for 1976,* 94th Cong., 1st Sess., Apr. 17, 1975, p. 479; U.S., Congress, House, Committee on Appropriations, *Hearings before a Subcommittee on Legislative Branch Appropriations for 1977,* 94th Cong., 2d Sess., Feb. 5, 1976, p. 190; *ibid.,* Mar. 1, 1976, p. 1078; *ibid.,* Feb. 26, 1976, p. 963.

Between 1970 and 1975, the professional staff of the GAO grew from 2906 to 3800 persons, an increase of 894. However, according to an estimate by the Comptroller General in 1973, only about 30 percent of the work of the professional staff was classified as being of "direct assistance to the Congress." (*The GAO Review* [Winter 1973], p. 1; staff figures were taken from the *Annual Reports* of the Comptroller General of the U.S. for fiscal years 1970 and 1975).

[48] U.S., Congress, House, Committee on Appropriations, *Hearings before a Subcommittee on Legislative Branch Appropriations for 1967,* 89th Cong., 2d Sess., May 12, 1966, pp. 392-93; *ibid., Hearings before a Subcommittee on Legislative Branch Appropriations for 1976,* 94th Cong., 1st Sess., Mar. 6, 1975, pp. 865-66, 893; *ibid., Hearings before a Subcommittee on Legislative Branch Appropriations for 1977,* 94th Cong., 2d Sess., Feb. 19, 1976, pp. 646, 676.

Included in the Dec. 31,1975, total were seventy-six additional employees of the Appropriations and Budget Committees that were not affected by the Committee Reform Amendments of 1974 because of being already empowered to hire ·as many regular staff members as needed. The reason for specifying the date for a staff statistic wherever possible is that the number of committee employees fluctuates during a year.

[49] U.S., *Congressional Record,* 94th Cong., 2d Sess., Mar. 30, 1976, CXXII (daily ed.), p. S4567; Paul Rundquist, "Legislative Branch Employment Levels for Selected Years," CRS typed report dated Feb. 11, 1976; U.S., Congress, Senate, Committee on Appropriations, *Hearings before a Subcommittee on Legislative Branch Appropriations for 1977,* 94th Cong., 2d Sess., Apr. 6, 1976, p. 744; "Senate Panel Acts to Bar Staff Increase," *The Washington Post,* July 18, 1975, p. A-1; "Growth in Senate Staff is Opposed as Costly," *ibid.,* Feb. 4, 1976, p. A-8; Appendix D "Summary Data on Committee Staffing," First Staff Report to the Temporary Select Committee to Study the Senate Committee System, dated July 15, 1976, p. D-7.

The above totals for House and Senate committee employees do not include the figures for joint committee staff personnel, who numbered about 140 in 1975.

[50] U.S., Congress, House, Committee on Appropriations, *Hearings before a Subcommittee on Legislative Branch Appropriations for 1967,* 89th Cong., 2d Sess., May 12, 1966, p. 404; *ibid., Hearings before a Subcommittee on Legislative Branch Appropriations for 1976,* 94th Cong., 1st Sess., Mar. 6, 1975, p. 878; Rundquist, "Legislative Branch Employment Levels for Selected Years."

[51] U.S., *Congressional Record,* 94th Cong., 1st Sess., Mar. 11, 1975, CXXI (daily ed.), p. S3595.

[52] "Summary of Hearings of Thursday, July 22, 1976," prepared by staff for the Temporary Select Committee to Study the Senate Committee System, p. 2.

PREFACE TO THE SECOND EDITION

To paraphrase a popular saying from the comic strip *Peanuts*, "Happiness is sustained demand for a book seven years after publication." Besides occasioning such expressions of joy, the second edition of this work affords an opportunity to comment on some relevant developments that have occurred since the study was originally completed in January, 1962.

On January 12, 1965, the Senate Republican Conference adopted a rule relaxing adherence to seniority in the making of committee assignments. It provides that no Republican Senator already on one of four committees designated "exclusive"—Appropriations, Armed Services, Finance, and Foreign Relations—may be assigned to another of these four until every other Republican Senator has had an opportunity to go on one of them. However, the force of the rule was weakened by stipulations that Republican Senators currently holding assignments on two "exclusive" committees could continue to do so and that at any time a Republican Senator could transfer from one exclusive committee to another on which a vacancy existed. Because Senator Jacob Javits (R.-N.Y.) had advocated such a change for many years and chaired the subcommittee of the Republican Committee on Committees that formulated the specific proposal adopted by the Republican Conference, this modification in procedure has been appropriately nicknamed the "Javits Rule."[1]

In the 90th Congress, the number of standing committees in the House of Representatives was increased to twenty-one. On April 3, 1968, the House established the Committee on Standards of Official Conduct as a permanent standing committee.[2] This action carried out a recommendation of the Joint Committee on the Organization of the Congress, a brief history of which will be included below.

More recently, another House standing committee was transformed but retained the same membership. After an acrimonious debate on February 18,

1969, the House approved a resolution changing the name of the Un-American Activities Committee to the Internal Security Committee and redefining its jurisdiction. Opponents of the change unsuccessfully attempted to amend the resolution to abolish the Un-American Activities Committee and transfer its functions to the House Judiciary Committee.[3]

A few months earlier, however, a twenty-year-old congressional agency, the House Coordinator of Information, was eliminated. In the Legislative Branch Appropriation Act, 1968, the House cut off funds for this office "not later than October 1, 1967." The accompanying House report noted that the Joint Committee on the Organization of the Congress had recommended abolishing it.[4]

Perhaps even more importantly, since preventing is easier than correcting mistakes, Congress has avoided adopting inappropriate forms of staffing that could have had untoward effects on the whole legislative process. During the spring and summer of 1963 when Congress reached a new high in concern about science policy issues, several bills were introduced to establish a Congressional Science Advisory Staff. While well-intentioned, these proposals were based on faulty assumptions about the nature of science policy questions and the requirements for a congressional staff to handle them.[5] Congress wisely rejected them in favor of expanding and refining extant arrangements for obtaining advice on science-related issues.

Beginning with the Legislative Branch Appropriation Act, 1965, Congress has provided substantial funds for the Legislative Reference Service to hire additional high-grade specialists in science and technology. And a number of congressional committees have imaginatively experimented with the use of consultants, advisory panels, and the National Academy of Sciences for advice on science policy issues.[6]

Both chambers have made it possible for each member of Congress to hire a legislative assistant at a professional staff salary level. On May 26, 1966, the House adopted a resolution authorizing an additional clerk and an increase in the basic clerk-hire allowance of $7,000 ($19,220 in gross salary then) for every member of the House of Representatives.[7] On July 10, 1967, the Senate amended the Legislative Branch Appropriation Act, 1968, to provide an additional $23,400 (gross salary) in clerk-hire allowance for each Senator. When introducing this amendment, Senator Joseph Tydings (D.-Md.) stressed that its purpose was to enable every Senator to hire the legislative assistant authorized by the proposed Legislative Reorganization Act of 1967, S. 355, which had been passed by the Senate on March 7, 1967, but which he felt had poor prospects for speedy approval by the House.[8] Unfortunately, Senator Tydings' forebodings proved justified; for fifteen months later, S. 355 died at the close of the 90th Congress still incarcerated in the House Rules Committee.

As indicated at several places above, the most momentous factor influencing congressional structure and procedures since January, 1962, has been the creation of a Joint Committee on the Organization of the Congress and the continuing efforts to enact measures embodying its recommendations. This action was in response to a demand that had been mounting for a number of years. Increasingly, journalists, political scientists, and members of Congress had voiced the need for a thorough review of congressional structure and functioning. During the early 1960's, numerous resolutions to authorize studies of congressional reform were introduced. On September 19, 1963, one of them, S. Con. Res. 1, was reported favorably by the Senate Rules and Administration Committee but was not voted upon by the Senate. The 1964 election results strengthened elements in Congress pressing for reform, prominent among which was the House Democratic Study Group, an organization of liberal Democratic Congressmen.[9] House DSG leaders won the crucial support of Speaker John McCormack (D.-Mass.). On March 11, 1965, Congress approved S. Con. Res. 2 establishing a Joint Committee on the Organization of the Congress to conduct a comprehensive study of the organization and operation of Congress.[10]

Closely intertwined with this endeavor was the campaign for minority staffing, the beginnings of which are discussed in Chapter XIV "Postscript" (pp. 210-17). In 1962 Representative Fred Schwengel (R.-Iowa) joined Representative Thomas B. Curtis (R.-Mo.) and Senator Carl Curtis (R.-Nebr.) as leading proponents of minority staffing, and during that year they concerted their efforts rather informally. On January 24, 1963, then House Republican Conference Chairman Gerald Ford (R.-Mich.) appointed a Subcommittee on Increased Minority Staffing, headed by Representative Schwengel and including Representatives Curtis and Robert Griffin (R.-Mich.) among others. The Schwengel Subcommittee propagandized vigorously and coordinated a drive by Republican members of House committees for more minority staff members, which, according to them, enjoyed significant success.[11] In 1964 Representative Schwengel was defeated for re-election, but the organized effort by House Republicans continued. On March 30, 1965, the House Republican Conference Committee on Planning and Research appointed a Task Force on Congressional Reform and Minority Staffing, with Representative James Cleveland (R.-N.H.) as chairman. House Minority Leader Gerald Ford later explained that this task force "was created in part to assure that every significant aspect of the operation of the House of Representatives would be studied and to serve as a reservoir of recommendations should the Joint Committee [on the Organization of the Congress] fail to report out a comprehensive set of proposals for modernizing the machinery and strengthening the role of Congress in the twentieth century."[12]

At its first meeting on March 17, 1965, the Joint Committee on the Organization of the Congress elected as co-chairmen Senator Mike Monroney (D.-Okla.), who, as a young member of the House, had been vice-chairman of a similar joint committee that produced the Legislative Reorganization Act of 1946, and Representative Ray Madden (D.-Ind.), a member of the House Rules Committee, to which any bill emanating from the Joint Committee would be referred. The other Democratic members of the Joint Committee, which was evenly divided between the parties and the two chambers, were Senators John Sparkman (Ala.) and Lee Metcalf (Mont.) and Representatives Jack Brooks (Tex.) and Ken Hechler (W. Va.). The ranking minority member from the Senate was Karl Mundt (R.-S. Dak.) and from the House was Thomas B. Curtis. Republican Senators Clifford Case (N. J.) and J. Caleb Boggs (Del.) and Republican Representatives Durward Hall (Mo.) and Robert Griffin rounded out the committee roster.[13] In May, 1966, when Representative Griffin was appointed to the Senate, he was replaced by Representative James Cleveland.

Although many of the Republicans on the Joint Committee had been identified as crusaders for more minority staffing, the Joint Committee launched its undertaking in an aura of bipartisanship. It adopted a rule that forbade making any recommendation that had not been endorsed by a bipartisan majority of the members from each house. The staffs of the Democratic Study Group, the Republican Task Force on Congressional Reform and Minority Staffing, and the Joint Committee cooperated harmoniously in their research efforts.[14] In its *Second Interim Report,* the Joint Committee acknowledged: "The research and presentations of members of the Democratic Study Group and the Republican Task Force, as well as other Senators and Representatives, have been most helpful to the Joint Committee on Organization."[15]

Between May 10 and September 23, 1965, the Joint Committee held forty days of public hearings. The testimony, together with statements submitted for the record and supporting documents, totalled 2,322 printed pages. Along with this material and studies prepared by its own staff (including a computer analysis of the demands made by the committee system on members' time in the 88th Congress), the Joint Committee utilized reports of other committees and state legislatures, published and unpublished works by political scientists, and studies of congressional organization by foundations and other private institutions. All in all, Co-chairman Monroney was able to claim "that no proposal for congressional reform made in recent years—irrespective of source or media—escaped the attention of the joint committee." From January through July, 1966, the Joint Committee met in more than fifty executive sessions to consider what recommendations to make.[16]

On July 28, 1966, the co-chairmen filed the final report of the Joint Committee in their respective chambers. Essentially moderate in the scope of its reforms, this report contained over 100 proposals concerning the committee system, fiscal controls, staffing, research facilities, ethics, housekeeping functions, and the lobby regulation act. In what turned out to be among the most controversial portions, the report recommended a "bill of rights" for committee members to give the majority more control over the chairman and the minority a larger role in committee operations, increased staffing, and realignment of some committee jurisdictions. This last recommendation entailed creating a Senate Committee on Veterans' Affairs and committees on education in both houses with a corresponding redefinition of other committees' jurisdictions, redesignation of the Aeronautical and Space Sciences Committee as the Science and Astronautics Committee in the Senate, expanding the jurisdiction of both science committees, and renaming the banking and currency committees as the committees on banking, housing, and urban affairs with appropriate additions to their jurisdictions.[17]

On August 26, 1966, the Senate established a Special Committee on the Organization of the Congress (consisting of the Senate members of the Joint Committee) to receive, consider, and report a bill carrying out the recommendations of the Joint Committee. The authorizing resolution stipulated, however, that the Special Committee was not to report any bill until it had given the chairman and ranking minority member of each Senate standing committee an opportunity to appear before it and present their views.[18] At hearings of the Senate Special Committee on August 31 and September 8, 1966, three committee chairmen testified in person while three others and a ranking minority member submitted written statements for the record. In some cases vehemently, they criticized certain recommendations of the Joint Committee and the corresponding provisions of a proposed bill—mostly those involving changes in the jurisdictions of their respective committees.[19] Despite this adverse reaction, on September 21, 1966, the Senate Special Committee reported a bill, S. 3848, incorporating the Joint Committee's recommendations virtually unchanged. On September 29, 1966, Senate Majority Leader Mike Mansfield (D.-Mont.) announced that this bill would not be considered by the Senate prior to adjournment because of the heavy legislative workload but that it would be reintroduced and taken up early in the 90th Congress.[20]

Accordingly, on January 16, 1967, the Senate Special Committee reported out S. 355, the proposed Legislative Reorganization Act of 1967, which had been carefully revised to remove all the Senate committee jurisdictional changes except for the creation of a Committee on Veterans' Affairs and for adding urban affairs to the jurisdiction of the renamed Committee on Banking, Housing, and Urban Affairs. However, S. 355 retained all the recommended modifications in the jurisdictions of the House committees. The accompanying committee report rather plaintively stated:

> The Joint Committee on the Organization of Congress recommended two additional Senate jurisdictional changes which have not been included in this bill. . . . The hearings held by the Senate Committee following the publication of the Joint Committee's Final Report indicated wide opposition to these proposals and a view that sufficient consideration had not been given to potentially detrimental effects on the existing committee operations. After receiving this testimony, the Committee has concluded that these realignments should not be proposed at this time.[21]

After eighteen days of debate between January 25 and March 7, 1967, the Senate approved S. 355 by a vote of 75 to 9. Although forty amendments were adopted, efforts to delete the Senate Committee on Veterans' Affairs and the whole portion on the lobby regulation act were defeated. More importantly, the staffing provisions emerged almost intact with only minor amendments clarifying the status of a proposed legislative review specialist for each standing committee and adjusting the salaries of Senate staff members.[22]

On March 9, 1967, the Senate messaged S. 355 to the House where it was referred to the Rules Committee. Except for a short hearing on April 11, 1967, the Rules Committee took no further public action. Purportedly, strong opposition to the measure centered around the projected changes in House committee jurisdictions and the provisions on committee procedures, staffing, and regulation of lobbying. Through 1967 to the end of June, 1968, various versions of S. 355, revised to remove certain of these objections, were introduced in the House. Besides the House members of the Joint Commitee, two members of the House Rules Committee, Richard Bolling (D.-Mo.), longtime articulate advocate of congressional reform and prominent member of the Democratic Study Group, and H. Allen Smith (R.-Calif.), the ranking Republican on the Rules Committee, participated in this endeavor to produce an acceptable bill. On December 31, 1967, after having received several renewals of authorization, the Joint Committee on the Organization of the Congress expired. Likewise, the Senate Special Committee on the Organization of the Congress went out of existence on June 30, 1968.[23]

Meanwhile, in addition to those proposals already mentioned as having been accomplished (legislative assistants for Senators, creation of a House ethics committee, and discontinuance of the House Coordinator of Information), Congress continued to enact particular recommendations of the Joint Committee, such as increased travel allowances for Congressmen, separately in other legislation. This led to widespread speculation that the popular provisions of S. 355 would be extracted in this fashion, leaving the mutilated remains buried in the House Rules Committee.[24]

Periodically between October, 1966 and August, 1968, the House Republican Policy Committee, House Republican Conference, and House Minority Leader Ford issued statements urging favorable action on congressional reorganization bills. The 1968 Republican Platform exhorted:

> Congress itself must be reorganized and modernized in order to function efficiently as a co-equal branch of government. Democrats in control of Congress have opposed Republican efforts for Congressional reform and killed legislation embodying the recommendations of a special bipartisan committee. We will again press for enactment of this measure.[25]

On September 11, 1968, a group of thirteen Republican Representatives led by Donald Rumsfeld (Ill.) and including Thomas B. Curtis and James Cleveland delayed proceedings in the House for over two hours by engaging in dilatory parliamentary maneuvers. Their avowed purpose was "to dramatize the need for House consideration, and hopefully, House action" on S. 355 and a campaign spending reform bill (H.R. 11233). Thirteen days later, Representative Rumsfeld made public a letter to Speaker McCormack, signed by 134 of the 187 House Republicans, urging him to schedule the two bills for floor action.[26]

Also in September, 1968, five liberal House Democrats headed by Representative Thomas Rees (Calif.) tried to extricate S. 355 from the House Rules Committee by resorting to a discharge petition, but they failed to get the requisite 218 signatures of House members.

On October 8-9, 1968, the Rumsfeld group again impeded the conduct of House business. By means of forty-five roll calls and other delaying tactics, they kept the House in continuous session for more than thirty-two hours. Although Democrats accused the Republicans of trying to defeat the bill before the House to allow television debates between the presidential candidates, Rumsfeld maintained they were trying to influence the House Democratic leadership to bring S. 355 and H.R. 11233 to the House floor. House Minority Leader Ford publicly endorsed their actions and promised that these bills would have high priority on a Republican agenda for the 91st Congress.[27]

Inescapably, these events gave a partisan coloration to the struggle for House consideration of S. 355, which had been developed under such thoroughly bipartisan auspices. With the adjournment of Congress on October 14, 1968, all pending legislation died. On November 5, 1968, the prospects for congressional reform were further worsened when Senator Monroney was defeated for re-election and Representative Thomas B. Curtis left the House in his unsuccessful bid for a Senate seat.

In the months immediately preceding the 91st Congress, some liberal House Democrats continued to advocate congressional reorganization. On January 23, 1969, Speaker McCormack, who the preceding year had steadfastly contended that he was for congressional reform, said he would like to see the House Rules Committee hold hearings on it soon. And House Minority Leader Ford reiterated his desire that Congress take up the subject early in the session.[28]

On February 4, 1969, Senator Mundt introduced S. 844, a proposed Legislative Reorganization Act of 1969, with the four other remaining members of the defunct Senate Special Committee on the Organization of the Congress as co-sponsors. The next day in the House, Representative Rumsfeld introduced a similar bill, H.R. 6278. Both were essentially variations on S. 355 of the 90th Congress. On March 4, 1969, the House Republican Policy Committee again urged enactment of legislation reorganizing Congress. About a week later, Representative Rees announced his intention to introduce a congressional reform bill, which also would be a revised reincarnation of S. 355.[29] By April 3, 1969, when he had aggregated 103 Republican House members as co-sponsors of his bill, Representative Rumsfeld asserted that the chances of obtaining early floor consideration of such a measure by the House were greater than any time in the preceding twenty years.[30]

Whether or not this is an accurate forecast and if so, whether or not that would mean enactment of a comprehensive congressional reorganization bill is difficult to say at the time of writing (April 12, 1969). The loss of Senator Monroney's leadership is an incalculable handicap to moving another omnibus reform bill through the Senate. The extent to which the adoption of various attractive features of the measure as originally proposed has diminished the appeal of the remainder and the amount of bipartisan support that can be mustered in the House are hard to assess.

Whatever the outcome, however, the provisions on committee staffing in S. 355, as approved by the Senate in the 90th Congress, warrant examination. For they have been carried over substantially unchanged in most successive versions of the bill and hence should foreshadow any legislation amending the existing law on committee staffs.

S. 355 adheres to the original philosophy of the Legislative Reorganization Act of 1946 of keeping the permanent professional staffs of the standing committees small in size. It increases the quota for each standing committee (except the appropriations committees) from four to six, with the proviso that the two more professional staff members would be in addition to any other extra staff previously authorized for a specific committee and to a legislative review specialist which all the standing committees (except the appropriations and House ethics committees) would be allowed to hire.

Officially recognizing the practice of supplementing the regular staff with specially-authorized employees, S. 355 requires each standing committee to consolidate all such requests into a single annual authorization resolution that specifies by name and amount every subcommittee to be funded for that year. This has the twofold purpose of enabling the committees to gain greater control over their subcommittees and each chamber to evaluate better the overall requests for such extra staff.

After redesignating "legislative oversight" as "legislative review," S. 355 states in some detail the legislative review responsibilities of each standing committee and requires it to submit an annual report on their performance. Then S. 355 authorizes a review specialist for each standing committee, to be appointed by the chairman with the prior approval of the ranking minority member, to assist the committee in carrying out its legislative review duties.

To permit access to outside experts on a part-time basis, S. 355 authorizes each standing committee to hire temporarily (not to exceed one year) consultants and consultative organizations to be selected by the chairman and ranking minority member acting jointly. Likewise, S. 355 encourages improving the skills of the permanent employees by authorizing each standing committee to provide assistance to professional staff members in obtaining specialized training. In each instance, the committee must get the approval of the administration committee and of a resolution in the House or Senate, as the case may be, supplying the requisite funds.

With respect to the controversial demands for minority staffing, S. 355 makes the following concessions. In the case of specially-authorized staff personnel, it admonishes that "the minority shall receive fair consideration" in their appointment. For the regular staff of each standing committee, it provides that a majority of the minority members may, if they desire, select two of the six professional staff members for appointment, that these appointees "shall be assigned to such committee business as the minority members deem advisable," and that they shall be dismissed upon request by a majority of the minority members. The rest of the professional staff continues to be hired and fired by a majority vote of the committee. S. 355 retains the language of the existing law assigning the professional staff members "to the chairman and the ranking minority member . . . as the committee may deem advisable" (except where the minority exercises the option to select its own), requiring appointment of all professional staff members "on a permanent basis without regard to political affiliations and solely on the basis of fitness to perform the duties of the office," and prohibiting the assignment to them of any work other than committee business.

Likewise, S. 355 provides that a majority of the minority members may, if they desire, select one of the six clerical staff members for appointment. Further, it stipulates that all minority staff members shall be accorded equitable treatment on salary rates, the assignment of facilities, and accessibility of committee records. And S. 355 makes clear that it does not authorize minority members of a committee to select staff members for appointment in any case in which two or more professional staff members or one or more clerical staff members, who are satisfactory to a majority of the minority members, have already been assigned to assist them.

Relatedly, S. 355 establishes an Office of Placement and Office Management, which, upon request, shall assist committees as well as members and officers of the Congress in obtaining qualified staff and shall furnish advice with respect to office management procedures. By placing the use of this office on a purely voluntary basis, S. 355 has removed the principal objections to the creation of such a facility in the past.[31]

For the most part, the committee staffing provisions of S. 355, as passed by the Senate in the 90th Congress, embody the lessons of twenty years experience with professional staffs and probably unavoidable compromises with forces challenging principles incorporated in the Legislative Reorganization Act of 1946. Confining expansion largely to specially-authorized staffs, making possible more effective checks by the House and Senate on their growth, helping to combat the centrifugal tendencies of subcommittees, encouraging resort to outside expertise, and facilitating professional growth of the permanent staffs of committees are all laudable objectives.

The desirability of a review specialist for each standing committee is less obvious. In the process of passage by the Senate, an amendment vesting legislative review functions in the committee rather than in the proposed review specialist helped clarify that he would work under the control of the committee and within its existing staff structure.[32] However, there still remains a potential for conducting legislative review through a more or less independent staff operation, with all the bad effects that could produce (See p. 146).

The procedure of having the chairman and ranking minority member act jointly not only in appointing the review specialist but also in selecting consultants and consultative organizations is questionable. Although in most instances these two individuals might have the main say in making such choices, it would be prudent to retain the safeguard of requiring approval by a majority vote of the committee. Also, this would be more consonant with the pervading philosophy of S. 355, expressed in the "committee bill of rights" and elsewhere, of placing ultimate control over the committee in a majority of the membership.

The departures from the principle of nonpartisanship for committee staffs in S. 355 probably represent the minimum concessions acceptable to the proponents of increased minority staffing, who have constituted such a major element of support for the congressional reform movement in the 1960's. The exhortatory language on according the minority fair consideration in the appointment of specially-authorized staffs merely recognizes prevalent practices, which reflect the results of a more than decade-long crusade. By being couched in permissive rather than mandatory language, the provisions authorizing the minority of each standing committee to select part of the permanent staff as a matter of right, if they so desire, allow the maintenance of nonpartisanship in committee staffs wherever possible while taking care of situations where the minority might otherwise be denied adequate staff assistance. Moreover, the procedure for selection by a majority of the minority members is responsive to a basic desire of many advocates of more minority staffing: that on each committee there be more staff to assist the minority as such and not just the ranking minority member. For to some extent this cause, like many other aspects of the congressional reorganization movement, is but another manifestation of the generation gap, with junior members of Congress assailing the bastions of power manned by their elders.

West Lafayette, Indiana   KENNETH KOFMEHL
April 12, 1969

NOTES

[1] *Congressional Quarterly Weekly Report,* XXIII, No. 3 (Jan. 15, 1965), 86; U.S., Congress, Joint Committee on the Organization of the Congress, *Hearings,* 89th Cong., 1st Sess., May 27, 1965, pp. 497-500, 504.

[2] U.S., *Congressional Record,* 90th Cong., 2d Sess., April 3, 1968, CXIV (daily ed.), pp. H2510-45.

[3] *Ibid.,* 91st Cong., 1st Sess., Feb. 18, 1969, CXV (daily ed.), pp. H958-80.

[4] Public Law 57, 90th Cong., 1st Sess., July 28, 1967, 81 *Stat.* 132; U.S., Congress, House, Committee on Appropriations, *Legislative Branch Appropriation Bill, 1968,* House Report No. 323 (to accompany H.R. 10368), 90th Cong., 1st Sess., May 25, 1967, p. 9.

[5] For analyses of defects in these proposals, see Clinton P. Anderson, "Scientific Advice for Congress," *Science,* CXLIV, No. 3614 (Apr. 3, 1964), pp. 29-32, and U.S., Congress, House, Committee on Science and Astronautics, *Scientific-Technical Advice for Congress: Needs and Sources,* committee print, Government and Science No. 3, 88th Cong., 2d Sess., Aug. 10, 1964, pp. 11-61, 71-86.

[6] See Kenneth Kofmehl, "COSPUP, Congress, and Scientific Advice," *Journal of Politics,* XXVIII, No. 1 (Feb., 1966), 100-20.

[7] U.S., *Congressional Record,* 89th Cong., 2d Sess., May 26, 1966, CXII, Part 9, p. 11654.

[8] *Ibid.,* 90th Cong., 1st Sess., July 10, 1967, CXIII, Part 14, pp. 18164-76.

[9] For an account of the genesis and nature of the House DSG, see Kenneth Kofmehl, "The Institutionalization of a Voting Bloc," *Western Political Quarterly,* XVII, No. 2 (June, 1964), 256-72.

[10] *Congressional Quarterly Weekly Report,* XXIII, No. 26 (June 25, 1965), 1239-40.

[11] *Ibid.,* XXI, No. 6 (Feb. 8, 1963), 151-56; *ibid.,* No. 9 (Mar. 1, 1963), 239-40.

[12] U.S., *Congressional Record,* 90th Cong., 2d Sess., Sept. 10, 1968, CXIV (daily ed.), p. H8474.

[13] U.S., Congress, Joint Committee on the Organization of the Congress, *Interim Report,* Senate Report No. 426, 89th Cong., 1st Sess., July 8, 1965, pp. 3-4, 7.

[14] James C. Cleveland and others, *We Propose: A Modern Congress* (New York: McGraw-Hill Co., 1966), p. xii.

[15] Senate Report No. 948, 89th Cong., 2d Sess., Jan. 19, 1966, p. 6.

[16] U.S., *Congressional Record,* 90th Cong., 1st Sess., Jan. 25, 1967, CXIII, Part 2, p. 1558.

[17] Senate Report No. 1414, 89th Cong., 2d Sess., July 28, 1966, 97 pp.

[18] U.S., Congress, Senate, A Resolution to Create a Special Committee on the Organization of the Congress, S. Res. 293, 89th Cong., 2d Sess., Aug. 26, 1966, p. 2.

[19] U.S., Congress, Senate, Special Committee on the Organization of the Congress, *Hearings,* 89th Cong., 2d Sess., Aug. 31 and Sept. 8, 1966, pp. 2-64.

[20] U.S., *Congressional Record,* 90th Cong., 2d Sess., Oct. 11, 1968, CXIV (daily ed.), H9879.

21 Senate Report No. 1, 90th Cong., 1st Sess., Jan. 16, 1967, p. 4.

22 U.S., Congress, Joint Committee on the Organization of the Congress, *Tabulation of Senate Amendments to S. 355 (Jan. 25-Mar. 7, 1967)*, joint committee print, 90th Cong., 1st Sess., Apr. 18, 1967, p. 2.

23 *Congressional Quarterly Weekly Report*, XXV, No. 23 (June 9, 1967), pp. 975-78; *ibid.*, XXVI, No. 33 (Aug. 16, 1968), pp. 2200-3; U.S., *Congressional Record*, 90th Cong., 2d Sess., Oct. 11, 1968, CXIV (daily ed.), pp. H9877, H9880; Walter Kravitz, *The Joint Committee on the Organization of the Congress: A Chronological and Legislative History*, (Washington: Library of Congress, LRS, GGR 186, multilithed, July 17, 1968), 29 pp.

24 Robert K. Walsh, "House Boosts Phone Funds," *The Evening Star* (Washington), May 12, 1967, p. B-4; "Shabby 'Ho-Dag'," *The Washington Post*, May 12, 1967, p. A-24.

25 U.S., *Congressional Record*, 90th Cong., 2d Sess., Sept. 10, 1968, CXIV (daily ed.), p. H8474.

26 *Ibid.*, p. H8472; *ibid.*, Sept. 24, 1968, pp. E8166-67; *Congressional Quarterly Weekly Report*, XXVI, No. 38 (Sept. 20, 1968), 2471-72.

27 *Ibid.*, No. 41 (Oct. 11, 1968), 2726-27; U.S., *Congressional Record*, 90th Cong., 2d Sess., Oct. 10, 1968, CXIV (daily ed.), pp. H9804-5.

28 "Hill 'Reform'," *The Washington Post*, Jan. 24, 1969, p. A-5.

29 A letter addressed to "Dear Colleague," House of Representatives, Washington, D.C., dated Mar. 13, 1969. According to informed sources, plans were to introduce this bill the week of Apr. 14, 1969, and it was estimated that possibly as many as thirty Democrats might co-sponsor it (telephone interviews, Apr. 8 and 10, 1969).

30 "Reorganization Drive Success Predicted," *Roll Call*, Apr. 3, 1969, p. 6.

31 U.S., Congress, House, Legislative Reorganization Act of 1967, S. 355, 90th Cong., 1st Sess., March 9, 1967, pp. 10-11, 16-20, 59-68, 91-92.

32 U.S., *Congressional Record*, 90th Cong., 1st Sess., Feb. 15, 1967, CXIII, Part 3, pp. 3400-1.

PREFACE TO THE FIRST EDITION

The Legislative Reorganization Act of 1946 made an ambitious attempt to expand the existing and introduce new elements of a professional staff for Congress. The main body of this book is an analytical, descriptive study of that staff during the first three Congresses, 80th through 82d, the Act was put into effect. This was the formative period for most of the professional staff of Congress. That is the principal justification for publishing this work now. Knowledge of the initial stages of any institution is helpful to understanding its subsequent development and in appraising the soundness of the principles it embodies. The wish here is to acquaint the reader with conditions, practices, and ideas about the professional staffing of Congress that were prevalent when the intent of the Act was fresh and enthusiasm for its objectives was high. Then he will have some basis for judging at any later date whether the staffing goals of the Act have gained greater acceptance or a reaction has set in against them.

Because considerable time has elapsed since the close of the period covered, a lengthy "postscript" chapter has been added that discusses significant developments in congressional staffing through 1961. Also, at the suggestion of Professor Charles S. Hyneman, a chapter on the nature of the standing committees of Congress has been inserted ahead of the portion on committee staffing. In this chapter, emphasis is placed on aspects of the operation and internal power structures of these committees not usually stressed in textbooks. This has been done in the hope of giving the general reader a better appreciation of the context in which the committee staffs operate and the resulting requirements of their situation.

West Lafayette, Indiana   KENNETH KOFMEHL
March 17, 1962

CONTENTS

PART FIVE

LIST OF TABLES

ACKNOWLEDGMENTS

My debt of gratitude to Boyd Crawford and Professor Charles S. Hyneman is particularly great. They gave vital encouragement to the publication of this work and most helpful suggestions for improving the manuscript. Also, I am heavily indebted to Francis O. Wilcox, who supplied inspiration as well as much information for this study. A special word of appreciation is due the many members of the congressional staff who were generous with both their time and knowledge. In particular, I wish to thank Floyd M. Riddick, Assistant Parliamentarian of the Senate, and Alice Sattgast from the Disbursing Office of the House of Representatives. They aided immeasurably in unraveling some technicalities in the operation of Congress. I appreciate very much the study facilities and other assistance provided by the Library of Congress—especially by many friends in the Legislative Reference Service. And I gratefully acknowledge the generous financial support from the Purdue Research Foundation for this study.

In recognizing the contributions of others, I wish to absolve them of any responsibility for the views expressed. That responsibility is solely mine.

PART ONE

CHAPTER I

SETTING THE STAGE

The Background

Prior to the middle of the 19th century, clerks were provided for congressional committees on a temporary basis by special resolutions adopted by each house every session. In 1856, the House Ways and Means and the Senate Finance Committees were the first committees to secure regular appropriations for full-time clerks. Rather slowly at first but at an accelerating tempo, other important committees followed suit until by 1900 the legislative branch appropriations acts were carrying funds for the employment of clerical staffs for the standing committees in both chambers. Similarly, since the early 1900's, legislative branch appropriations acts have contained allowances for clerk hire for both Representatives and Senators.[1] The Legislative Reference Service in the Library of Congress was instituted in the latter half of 1914 with funds provided in a Senate amendment to the legislative branch appropriations bill for fiscal year 1915.[2] The Office of the Legislative Counsel was created in 1919 by sec. 1303 of the Revenue Act of 1918.[3] And the technical staff of the Joint Committee on Internal Revenue Taxation was set up under the provisions of the statute establishing the joint committee in 1926.[4]

Before the advent of the Legislative Reorganization Act of 1946, the Senate and House Appropriations Committees and the Joint Committee on Internal Revenue Taxation were the only standing committees that had consistently employed well-trained, technically-qualified staffs with continuity of tenure.[5] Occasionally, select investigating committees had included economists, lawyers, accountants, and other expert personnel among their staffs.[6] And the practice of borrowing specialists from administrative agencies to assist the committees for rather lengthy periods—sometimes extending through several Congresses— was quite prevalent.[7] However, most of the regular employees of the standing committees on legislation were under the patronage system with their positions "contingent upon changes of political party or the defeat, death, or resignation of a particular Congressman who has been the committee's chairman."[8] Exclusive of the appropriations committees, in 1941 the Senate committees had an average complement of around five or six clerks and assistant clerks (including the portion of the chairman's office force which was officially integrated into the committee staff); and the House committees averaged between two and three employees apiece.[9] Committee staffs and the office staffs of the chairman were intermingled in practice on the House and by law on the Senate side. Representatives who were the chairmen of relatively inactive House committees utilized the committee clerks to supplement their office forces. Under the express provisions of the Legislative Pay Act of 1929, when a Senator assumed the chairmanship of a committee, the three senior clerks on his office staff became ex officio clerk and assistant clerks of that committee.[10] Further, the Act stipulated that "where a Senator is the chairman of a committee the clerical force attached to that committee is his secretarial organization as well as the force for the transaction of the committee business."[11] The legislative draftsmen in the Office of the Legislative Counsel were recruited and retained their positions under a merit system and would qualify as professional staff members by any criteria.[12] Although located in the legislative branch, the Library of Congress was under the Classification Act of 1923, as amended; and its employees had permanence of tenure. A considerable portion of the Legislative Reference Service personnel was classified in the professional and scientific service. However, as late as 1944 the top grade for subject specialists was fixed at P-4 (GS-11), and most of the research positions were allocated at P-2 (GS-7) and P-3 (GS-9). And the Service was quite small, with its appropriations averaging but $145,816 annually during the five years from fiscal 1941 through fiscal 1945.[13]

In early 1941 the movement which culminated in the Legislative Reorganization Act of 1946[14] first became manifest. During the five and a half year germinal period of that measure, one of the main themes was the need for improving the staff facilities of Congress. Many and various ideas were abroad, both inside and outside of Congress, on how that should be accomplished: on the character, locus, size, and functions of any new increments of staff to be added. Almost all the voluminous literature on legislative reform endorsed expanding one or more forms of congressional staffing, and the many bills and resolutions introduced during this interval reflected the diversity of those proposals. Much of the testimony at the hearings of the Joint Committee on the Organization of Congress was devoted to some aspect of legislative staffing.[15] All this bore fruit in the staffing provisions of the Legislative Reorganization Act of 1946, which constitute one of the most significant—if not the major—lasting achievements of that legislation.

These staffing provisions were wisely made flexible to accommodate the diverse needs of Congress. As a result, competing organizational patterns and procedures have developed—each of which has its enthusiastic, and often vociferous, advocates. Moreover, several of the fundamental principles (like that of having nonpartisan, professional aides to the committees) incorporated in the LaFollette-Monroney Act, are increasingly being challenged.

Most importantly, capitalizing on the favorable climate of opinion toward increased technical assistance for Congress generated by the legislative reorganization movement, a number of elements in Congress have been pushing greatly expanded staffing—sometimes in forms not contemplated or even specifically disapproved by the authors of the Legislative Reorganization Act, such as the specially-authorized staffs for subcommittees and for select committees. The impulse responsible for some of the most constructive accomplishments of the Legislative Reorganization Act threatens to be carried too far or to be diverted into unanticipated directions. Having become persuaded of the utility of professional aides, Congress like many a religious convert threatens to become overzealous. Among numerous Congressmen, including ironically enough a few of the initial opponents of the LaFollette-Monroney Act, there is a growing tendency to regard staffing as a panacea. If Congress only had a larger staff, they assert, it could legislate in detailed instead of broad terms and halt the trend toward delegation of increasing amounts of authority to the administrative establishment. With enough staff, they believe, Congress could exercise minute supervision of the executive branch and really make its weight felt.[16]

Many of these are highly dubious propositions both as to ends and means. If a little staffing is good, it does not necessarily follow that a whole lot more is better. Too much staffing for the right purposes contains the threat of overinstitutionalizing the legislators and of impeding the operations of the whole staff. And any—much less a great deal of—staff for the wrong purposes not only interferes with the functioning of the part of the staff engaged in desirable work but also has adverse repercussions on the entire system of government. Similar considerations apply to the types of staff personnel Congress should or should not employ.

The only adequate test of the comparative validity of the many diverse—and often conflicting—ideas on congressional staffing, is how they have worked in practice. Since Congress now has been operating with a sizable professional staff for some time, it is desirable to examine the nature and working of this staff. That is what this study proposes to do.

Scope of the Study

Congress is but a part of our over-all system of government. Consequently, it cannot be considered in isolation as a self-contained entity. Any attempt to describe and appraise its staffing must take into account its relationships with the executive branch, political parties, organized and unorganized interest groups, and other official and unofficial constituents of the governmental system. The congressional staff operates in close conjunction with their staffs. To a large extent, the various segments of the congressional staff are a conduit of services to and from other staffs within and outside the legislative branch. Even a congressional facility like the Office of the Legislative Counsel, which performs the highly specialized task of bill drafting, acts as an intermediary to other sources of staff assistance on the technical as well as the substantive aspects of its work. The legislative counsel work closely with other congressional employees, administrative agency personnel, representatives of interest groups, or whomever else the committee or individual Congressman for whom they are executing a particular assignment directs.

Moreover, the various components of the congressional staff constitute a system, each part of which interacts with the others. For instance, the provision of enlarged and more competent committee staffs pursuant to the Legislative Reorganization Act has enabled the Office of the Legislative Counsel to concentrate more exclusively on bill drafting and hence to afford proportionately more of that vital service with a given amount of personnel. The new committee staffs not only have facilitated the work of the legislative counsel directly in numerous ways but also have divested them of much of the staff work on committee reports and other auxiliary tasks the latter used to do for the committees. Furthermore, not only do changes in any portion of this system have repercussions on the remainder but also proposals that threaten to gain acceptance sometimes do. For example, since the enactment of the Legislative Reorganization Act, the appropriations committees have been authorized to appoint an unlimited number of staff members. Until the spring of 1952, these committees had not evinced any desire to effect a large-scale expansion of their permanent staffs. However, in July, 1952, after S. 913 (a bill to create a Joint Committee on the Budget [which was intended to be primarily a means of affording a joint staff for the appropriations committee]) had been passed by the Senate and it appeared likely that the House might approve its companion measure, H.R. 7888, the House Appropriations Committee sought a sizable increase in appropriations for additional staff—obviously as a preclusive move.[17]

Finally, the various aspects—qualifications, nature of work, concept of role, tenure, size, recruitment, organization, and the like—of each component of the congressional staff are interrelated and could hardly be intelligently appraised apart from one another. For instance, the qualifications of the committee staffs are profoundly influenced, if not determined, by the nature of their work and the conditions under which they must operate. Concept of role affects the kind of tenure that is feasible and vice versa. The linkage between manner of recruitment and qualifications is almost too obvious to mention. Less apparent, but equally important, is the connection between the qualifications and organization of a committee staff. Permanent assignment of individual staff members to virtually autonomous subcommittees minimizes the short-comings of a conglomerate staff of mixed quality; the same structural arrangement, however, prevents a homogeneous staff of uniformly high quality from achieving maximum effectiveness. This is only a partial listing of the many complex patterns of interaction. All these factors point to the need for comprehensiveness in any study of the congressional staff.

On the other hand, there are equally cogent reasons for a particularized approach. Firstly, while there may be some universals in staffing, the context of their application in Congress is markedly different from what it is in the other branches of government or in private organizations. Secondly, there is great diversity within Congress. Conditions of staff work vary not only between the two houses and among their committees but in the same committee from time to time. Finally, the factors responsible for the success or failure of certain kinds of staffing are highly specific to their respective situations. For example, any realistic evaluation of the practicability of a device like the staff of the Joint Committee on Internal Revenue Taxation must take into account such relevant details as: the personality and unusual capacity of Colin Stam, long-time chief of that staff; the comparative homogeneity in policy views of the membership of the Senate Finance and House Ways and Means Committees during the establishment and most of the span of operation of that facility; and the technicality of revenue legislation.

These two sets of competing considerations clearly indicate the necessity for a compromise between an extensive and an intensive treatment of this subject. This study endeavors to find a middle ground by concentrating on the three primary components of the congressional staff under the immediate control of Congress: the committee staffs, office staffs, and Office of the Legislative Counsel. The three main parts of the study (Parts Two, Three, and Four) are devoted to them respectively; and their relationships with one another and with the other congressional, the executive branch, and nongovernmental staffs are dealt with collaterally in each of these parts. This manner of handling the subject brings out the systematic nature of the congressional staff and its interaction with staffs outside the legislative branch while still permitting a consideration of these three major segments of that staff detailed enough for a realistic appraisal of them. They are the most closely interknit elements of the congressional staff, perform the bulk of the staff work on legislation and in connection with oversight of administration, and comprise the largest share of the professional staff members.

Part Two (Chapters III-X) is concerned principally with the professional staffs of the standing committees on legislation in both the House and Senate. The aides to the Joint Committee on Internal Revenue Taxation are considered because they serve as the professional staff of the Senate Finance and House Ways and Means Committees on revenue measures. The Joint Committe on the Economic Report staff is also included because of its relationships with the aides to various legislative committees and because of the germaneness of much of the information on its organization and administration. The appropriations committee aides are excluded for the following reasons. Although the appropriating function is part of the over-all legislative process, work on appropriation bills differs markedly from that on other legislative measures and is confined to the two appropriations committees. The staffing provisions in the Legislative Reorganization Act for the appropriations committees are different from those for the other standing committees. With the succession of bills to establish a Joint Committee on the Budget under consideration in recent Congresses, the whole question of equipping the appropriations committees for the more effective discharge of their rather singular function is in a ferment. And that entire subject would lend itself admirably to a separate study.

Part Three (Chapter XI) is confined to the senatorial office staffs for several reasons. Firstly, during the period covered, only the Senators had administrative assistants, the class of office personnel that corresponds to the professional staff of a committee. A survey of experience with them will provide some basis for judging the desirability of equipping the Representatives with that type of aide—especially since their use by the Senators has developed in directions unanticipated by the sponsors of the Legislative Reorganization Act. Secondly, because the legislative process is more individualized in the Senate than in the House, the top-ranking office employees of Senators play a much larger role in the preparation of legislation than do those of Representatives. Also, as mentioned at the beginning, prior to 1946 the office forces of the senatorial chairmen were more thoroughly merged with the committee staffs than their counterparts on the House side. Consequently, the senatorial office staffs afford a more fertile source of data for studying the patterns of relations among office and committee aides and for ascertaining the extent to which the Legislative Reorganization Act's objective of separating these two forms of staffing has been attained. Thirdly, the general office staff work, such as handling departmental business and correspondence, is substantially the same in both houses—the only difference being one of magnitude rather than of kind. Hence, a description of such duties on the Senate side suffices for the House side also. Finally, because of the smaller number of Senators and the prominence of their views, factional affiliations, and other attributes, it was much easier to construct a representative sample of persons to interview from their office staffs. By covering thirty-two of the ninety-six Senators' offices, it was possible to secure data from a large cross section of all the senatorial aides. To make a comparable coverage of the office staffs of the 435 Representatives, many of whom were relatively obscure, was not practicable in the time available for interviewing.

Part Four (Chapter XII) includes both the House and Senate branches of the Office of the Legislative Counsel in order to bring out their relationships with each other as well as to afford a more complete description of that remarkable facility. For it was the most thoroughly accepted portion of the professional staff during the period covered by this study.

Part Five (Chapters XIII-XIV) rounds out the study. Chapter XIII summarizes the findings. Chapter XIV is a postscript on major trends in congressional staffing through 1961.

Although the Legislative Reference Service of the Library of Congress contains a sizable number of professional personnel (over fifty members of its research staff were in the grades of GS-9 or above in the fall of 1951),[18] none of the main divisions of this study is devoted to that organization because it is a peripheral element in the congressional staff both in location and function. The LRS is not under the immediate control of any officer or subordinate unit of Congress. Congress cannot hire or fire its director or any of its personnel. Congress can only control its administration indirectly through the medium of legislation or appropriations—principally the latter. And the relations between the LRS and the appropriations committees are analogous to those between any relatively autonomous administrative agency and the latter—with the exception that the LRS's budgetary requests are not screened by the Bureau of the Budget. The LRS is a department of the Library of Congress. The Director is appointed by the Librarian of Congress, who is a presidential appointee himself with substantially life tenure; and the remainder of the LRS staff is appointed by the Librarian upon the recommendation of the Director. Although the LRS enjoys considerable autonomy as a department of the Library, it is under the rules and regulations of the Library. Along with the other employees of the Library of Congress, those of the LRS are subject to the provisions of the Classification Act of 1949 and of the civil service retirement laws. All in all, the LRS occupies a rather anomalous position. In its organization and procedures, the LRS partakes of the nature of an executive agency except that instead of administering an action program it affords various services to Congress and is located in the legislative rather than the executive branch. Certain advantages and disadvantages inhere in this status. Often they are the same attributes regarded from a different perspective. For instance, another term which might be applied to the highly prized "independence" of the LRS is "remoteness." Because of its location and other organizational characteristics, the LRS almost inevitably is destined for the most part to be on the circumference rather than in the center of congressional staff activity.

Aside from the top-level senior specialists, the LRS analysts do not have much face-to-face contact with the members and committees of Congress or—as far as that goes—even with their aides. Most of their time is spent in working on requests which have been relayed to them through the front office in typewritten form on inquiry slips or which less frequently have been received over the telephone directly from congressional office or committee staff members. On occasion, LRS personnel—generally at the senior specialist level—have been detailed to the staffs of committees for varying lengths of time. However, in a number of such cases, the LRS researcher concerned has been employed exclusively on preparing a staff study, has remained physically located over at the Library, and has had only sporadic contacts with the committee staff or chairman to discuss that project with them. In a few others, LRS analysts who have found the atmosphere of particular committees very congenial have permanently transferred to their staffs.

More importantly, the LRS serves fundamentally as a supplement to the congressional office and committee staffs. It performs a large amount of reference and routine research work for them. Increasingly in the past few years the functions of a constituent service bureau have been thrust upon the LRS by the office staffs referring a large proportion of the growing number of constituent inquiries over to it. The demand from congressional offices for speech-writing assistance has developed at a comparable rate. The LRS provides a number of other services like publishing the *Digest of Public General Bills,* which the office staffs in particular find very useful. As might be expected, the most significant work of the LRS researchers consists of staff studies and compilations of data derived primarily from publications in the Library's collections. The average quality of these is very high, and they often receive wide circulation outside as well as inside Congress.

Finally, during the period covered by this study, there were several reorganizations and considerable shifting of titles and positions among key personnel of the LRS. Under such conditions, to describe even the well-established functions of the LRS would require a large number of pages. And many of the hypotheses about the present and prospective roles of the LRS could be properly evaluated only by taking into account the exact nature of the instances on which such generalizations have been based. To go into all these matters—much less to afford them adequate consideration—would unduly prolong this book and digress from its main focus. Hence, although exhaustive data were collected on the LRS, it has been treated by discussing its relations with the three primary components of the professional staff under the immediate control of Congress.

The Period Covered by the Study

This study covers the three Congresses from the start of the 80th on January 3, 1947, when the Legislative Reorganization Act of 1946 first became fully operative, through the expiration of the 82d six years later. In a very few cases, the terminal limit has been extended into the early part of the 83d Congress (which began on January 3, 1953) to include the effect of another change in the control of Congress on certain aspects of committee staffing. This period is most appropriate. During it, the staffing provisions of the Legislative Reorganization Act were institutionalized. Professional staffs authorized by other measures were established. The control of Congress switched from the Democrats to the Republicans with the 80th Congress, from the Republicans to the Democrats with the 81st Congress, and from the Democrats to the Republicans at the outset of the 83d Congress—with all the implications these changes might have for nonpartisanship and continuity in committee staffing.

For such a dynamic complex of institutions as that comprised in Congress, the underlying conditions were relatively stable during this interval. The factional groupings within the two major political parties and their interparty alliances followed a fairly consistent pattern—with the exception of the celebrated bolt by Senator Wayne Morse (Oreg.) from the Republican Party toward the close of the 82d Congress. And Harry S. Truman was President throughout these three Congresses with whatever repercussions that might have had on relations among the diverse parts of the executive branch, various elements in Congress, and their respective employees.

Research and Writing

Only through interviewing could sufficient data be acquired for an adequate description and understanding of a subject as variable, as personalized, and as cloaked with anonymity as the professional staff of Congress. Hence, the heart of the research effort for this study was the collection of firsthand information from congressional staff members. Approximately 180 congressional employees were questioned in controlled interviews averaging over an hour in length. An attempt was made to select a representative sample of persons to interview from each component of the congressional staff investigated.[19]

The style in which this study is written has been profoundly influenced by the fact that it is based primarily on interview data. Frequently information was made available on the condition that, if used, it be disguised in such a fashion that the incidents or individuals concerned could not be identified. As a result, many of the examples are described in abstract terms. Also, there are discernible over-all differences in the degree of specificity among the three main parts of the study. Part Two on committee staffs contains a much higher proportion of explicit material than either Part Three on senatorial office staffs or Part Four on the Office of the Legislative Counsel.

These differences were caused largely by the following conditions. Firstly, there were more published sources on committee staffs than on the other two. The activities reports of numerous committees gave brief case histories of the major projects handled by them. Similarly, the committee reports to accompany bills often contained portions describing the staff's contribution to their preparation. In the *Congressional Record* and committee hearings there were more frequent allusions to committee aides than to members of other segments of the congressional staff. And a few books like *Economics in the Public Service: Administrative Aspects of the Employment Act* by Dr. Edwin G. Nourse mention names in committee staffing incidents that occurred during the period covered by this study.[20]   When a published reference has revealed the participants in such cases, there is no breach of ethics in supplementing its account with background material obtained from interviews.

Secondly, information about committee staffs was more widespread among other parts of the congressional staff than knowledge of senatorial office staffs or the Office of the Legislative Counsel. Individual aides to members of a committee often had firsthand information on the administration and operations of its staff. Hence, frequently interview data on specific committee staffs were gained from persons external to them, who did not ask that the material be kept confidential as long as the source was not revealed. In contrast, few individuals outside a particular office force knew much of its internal workings. Consequently, for data on senatorial office staffs, reliance had to be placed principally on their members.

Finally, in general, senatorial office personnel imposed more restrictions on the use of the information they supplied than committee aides did. Although everyone knows that Senators rely on their office staffs for assistance in speechwriting, handling press relations, and other such services, many of them are sensitive about acknowledging it. Similarly, because of the adverse connotations widely associated with certain "pressure groups," senatorial aides often were concerned lest their bosses be identified with them. In contrast, committee aides, who worked for a committee as an entity with a shifting composition during the interval under consideration, usually had fewer apprehensions in that regard. On this whole score, the Office of the Legislative Counsel, as a central staff agency serving committees and individual members and their staffs in both houses, had to be particularly circumspect. Consequently, although the senatorial assistants and the Office of the Legislative Counsel were as generous as the committee aides in supplying particulars on their work, a much higher percentage of the information from them had to remain "off-the-record."

Besides the greater availability of concrete illustrative material on the committee staffs, there are other reasons why Part Two is much larger than Part Three or Part Four. In the main, the provisions for the committee staffs are more controversial than those for the office staffs or the congressional legislative counsel. It is more necessary to go into detail where considering conflicting theories of staff organization and operation than when describing prevalent practices of a noncontroversial character. Also, many aspects of committee and office staff work (for example, the services rendered by committee and senatorial aides at hearings) are very analogous.

After they have been discussed in Part Two, it is almost impossible to treat them in Part Three—although it is based on entirely separate data—without sounding very repetitious. Hence, many points of similarity between the committee and office staffs are disposed of summarily in Part Three by the use of "ditto phrases."

Premises—Inarticulate and Otherwise

Although this study was not undertaken to prove any predetermined hypotheses about congressional staffing, inevitably it is based upon a number of fundamental assumptions about our governmental process. Manifestly, value judgments on different aspects of congressional staffing are related to underlying theories about the nature not only of Congress but also of the executive branch, political parties, interest groups, and other official and unofficial constituents of our political system. Assuming that all the necessary materials for the formulation of such theories were available—and they are not—a comprehensive exposition of those would require a whole series of books by itself. Hence, instead of endeavoring to preface the text of this study with even a summary statement of such "first principles," fundamental premises about the character of the legislative process, of congressional-administrative-executive relations, and of political parties, are discussed throughout the study wherever they are especially relevant to the specific points under consideration.

However, to avoid a possible misunderstanding with regard to several of the most pervasive elements in the frame of reference for this study, they might appropriately be mentioned now. Firstly, the designations "Congress" and "executive branch" are employed solely as sort of shorthand terms to refer to the complexes of institutions and phenomena which they comprise. And it is constantly borne in mind that there are many subgroups within both Congress and the executive branch with widely disparate views on policy which ally with one another and with comparable groupings of organized interests to form coalitions of shifting composition on different issues. Secondly, it is postulated that the activities of interest groups are not pathological but are an intrinsic part of our process of government. By "interest groups" is meant unorganized, potential groups—including those widely held expectations known as the "rules of the game" or the "democratic mold"—as well as organized interest groups, which in popular parlance usually are referred to somewhat invidiously as "pressure groups."[21] In this connection it should be noted that, as elsewhere in governmental institutions, there are a number of interest groups within the congressional staff itself—some of which are partially organized, at least to the extent of having elected officials. A few of the latter like the Senate Secretaries Association, are briefly described. However, in general, no attempt has been made in this study to analyze staffing phenomena specifically in terms of the interest groups involved.[22] Thirdly, it is assumed that the peaceful adjustment of interests, both organized and unorganized, is the basic function of our system of government. Fourthly, it is posited that the politician is an essential mechanism in that process. Also, in that respect, the politician is recognized to be a two-directional and far from passive instrument. Besides detecting, gauging, and synthesizing social forces into programs acceptable to his electorate, he often serves as their leader. And his skill and preferences enter into the final syntheses he achieves. Fifthly, although politicians in every branch of the government, in political parties, and in organized interest groups all effect an adjustment of interests both inside and outside the formal institutions of government, that is the principal business of the legislator-politician. There is a separate stream of representation running from the popularly-elected President down through the executive branch. There is responsiveness built into various parts of the administrative establishment by means of advisory committees, methods of selecting policy-making officials, "virtual" representation of clientele groups by the administrators assigned to cope with their problems, and numerous other devices. But the members of Congress are—as the name of the lower house indicates—primarily representatives. Not only are the latter spokesmen for different clusters of interests than those finding ready expression through the presidency but also their agency for their constituencies is expected to be more intimate and insistent. In short, there is a difference of degree between the job of the legislator-politician and that of his counterparts elsewhere in the governmental system. That is the source of the oft-repeated warning about the danger of overinstitutionalizing the members of Congress and the two corollary admonitions about the necessity for: (1) keeping the various components of the congressional staff as small as possible and (2) holding them immediately responsible to their respective principals. To the extent that the relatively unique contribution of the legislator inheres in bringing a non-specialized, lay mind in close touch with his constituents' needs and preferences to bear on legislative problems and in the oversight of administration, that is jeopardized by the addition of either an excessive amount or the wrong kind of staff.[23]   As Professor V. O. Key, Jr., has observed with his characteristic facility of expression:

> The contribution of the lawmaker in the governmental process is not in the exercise of professional expertness. If he merely mouths what his experts tell him, we lose important values of representative government.[24]

In addition, ease of access to the members of Congress is essential if it is to continue to perform its vital function of maturing and perfecting legislation.[25] Finally, from preoccupation with staffing throughout, this study does not want inadvertently to exaggerate the importance of the congressional staff. Members of Congress are susceptible to many other influences besides that of the various segments of the congressional staff. And it is a fundamental postulate of this study that they must remain so if they are to continue to fulfill their special role in the over-all process of government.

Documentation and Usages

Because most of the persons interviewed requested that any information they furnished not be attributed specifically to them, footnote references have not been made to interview sources unless an individual has been directly quoted in the text. Throughout this study, all terms like "politician," "interest group," and "bureaucracy" are employed in a strictly neutral sense without any of the invidious connotations frequently attached to them in popular usage. If anything, they are freighted with favorable associations as applying to essential mechanisms in our governmental process. Similarly, there are no heroes or villains. No organized interest group is considered to be more pernicious or beneficial, selfish or altruistic, disreputable or respectable than any other. The different factions in the two major political parties are regarded as equally authentic and legitimate expositors of Republicanism or Democracy, as the case may be.

After certain lengthy titles have been introduced and used several times, they have been abbreviated. For example, Legislative Reference Service has often been contracted to LRS. Commonly accepted abbreviations for governmental agencies or national organizations, such as FBI and AMA, are employed without special explanation. Also, except in quotations, the designation "Congressman" is used in its generic sense to include members of both the House and Senate. In accordance with congressional usage, the same form of the word "counsel" is employed for both singular and plural.

The Road Ahead

Before we get to the main body of the study, Chapter II follows as an introduction to Part Two on committee staffing. The aim is to give the general reader a better understanding of aspects of the standing committees that strongly influence the nature and functioning of their professional staffs. This chapter is not confined to the period covered by the main body for these reasons. Since then, much useful literature on the standing committees has become available. More data on this subject were gathered through interviewing congressional staff members in the summer of 1961. It seemed unwise to exclude highly informative material that extended beyond the initial time limits—particularly since the "postscript" chapter would discuss trends through 1961.

CHAPTER II

THE STANDING COMMITTEES

Scope of Literature

Since the advent of *Congressional Government* by Woodrow Wilson in 1885, the importance of the standing committees of Congress has been accepted as an article of faith. But this belief did not stimulate much literature devoted to the systematic study of their exact nature and functioning for sixty-five years. There was a treatise on the origin and development of the committee system and a few monographs on specific committees. These were largely historical in treatment and did not delve very deeply into the composition, internal workings, and relationships among the chairmen and other members of the standing committees. There were several studies on the development of congressional investigative power. These and more general works on Congress discussed the purposes served by committee hearings and investigations and their limitations as fact-finding techniques.[1]

Increasingly since 1950, the standing committees have been subjected to more intensive scrutiny. Besides a growing number of case studies that have made penetrating analyses of their operations, books on policy formulation in certain fields, such as taxation or foreign relations, have afforded many insights into the relationships within and among committees. And there have been several periodical articles that have perceptively examined the operation of the seniority system, assignment of members, and other aspects of committee administration. But all these excellent materials have been fragmentary in approach, concentrating on a specific function or but part of the standing committees. A comprehensive exposition of the theory and practice of the standing committees in both chambers remains to be published.[2]

The accomplishment of such a work would require a lengthy volume. This chapter essays the more modest task of discussing features of the standing committees which have particular bearing on their staffs. The approach is perforce selective, summary, and impressionistic. But the hope is that even this limited an effort will convey some appreciation of the context in which the committee staffs operate and the resulting requirements of their situation.

Diversity and Changeability

The standing committees of Congress are characterized by great diversity and changeability. There are differences in vital particulars not only between House and Senate committees but also among the committees in the same chamber. Further, there are differences on a given committee from time to time and during the same period when considering various kinds of subject matter. Besides the obvious differences in attributes, functions, authority, and jurisdiction, there are great variations in organization and operation. Some committees have no standing subcommittees; others, standing subcommittees with well-defined jurisdictions. Some committees service subcommittees with their regular staffs; others permit subcommittees to establish separate specially-authorized staffs greatly exceeding their own in size. Some committees are the essence of informality in their proceedings, cheerfully reconsidering a decision at the request of any member. Others proceed strictly in accordance with parliamentary order, with anyone irrevocably forfeiting his chance if he does not make a motion in the proper form at the appropriate time. Some committees permit proxy voting; others do not, and so on. Moreover, alterations are continually being made in all aspects of committee functioning. Basically, this mutability reflects underlying conditions.

The circumstances of the committees are constantly changing. For example, between 1953 and 1961, amelioration of the seniority system by the "Johnson Rule"[3] in making Democratic committee assignments in the Senate had marked repercussions on the internal power structures of not only the committees but also the Senate. Newly-elected members more rapidly acceded to positions of influence on important committees. The long-unbroken homogeneity of some committees was disrupted. Failure of the Senate Republicans to adopt a comparable practice had additional—and sometimes untoward—effects on the operation of the committees. Greatly augmented strength of the Democrats and growing restiveness with Lyndon Johnson's leadership eventuated in modification of the method of selecting the Democratic policy and steering committees (the latter of which slates the standing committees) in the Senate. Presidential ambitions of some Senators affected committee and subcommittee assignments, organization, and staffing. Promotion to positions in the leadership structure altered not only the attitudes and actions of Senators but also their influence within the committees of which they remained members. Supersession of House Minority Leader Joe Martin (R.-Mass.) by an ambitious and energetic rival upset understandings between the Speaker of the House and the Minority Leader upon which control of the House Rules Committee hinged. The ensuing need to modify the effective majority of the Rules Committee had an aftermath on House committee assignments. The political debts of various committee chairmen to Speaker Sam Rayburn (D.-Tex.) were cancelled with

his death. And some of these chairmen may have placed Speaker John Mc-
Cormack (D.-Mass.) under obligation through having supported his candidacy.

Variation in Size

One of the most apparent differences among the standing committees is in
size. In 1961, the average membership of the standing committees in the
House was twenty-nine and in the Senate was fifteen. Although the House
committees ran almost twice as big as the Senate committees, there were substantial disparities in size among the standing committees in either chamber.
The House Appropriations Committee with fifty members was five and one-half
times as large as the House Committee on Un-American Activities with nine
members. The Senate Appropriations Committee with twenty-seven members
was nearly four times bigger than the Senate Committee on the District of
Columbia with seven members.[4]

Moreover, in both chambers the size of the committees is susceptible to
frequent change. For example, between January, 1953, and January, 1959, the
number of members on all fifteen of the standing committees in the Senate was
altered (on ten of them more than once), and a sixteenth standing committee
was added. During this interval, the membership was increased on ten committees, decreased on four, and fluctuated on two. The number of members
on the Senate Committee on Public Works was enlarged twice in one eight-
month period in 1959 and had been raised or lowered on three previous
occasions since January, 1953. The House standing committees underwent
similar changes. Roughly two thirds of them were increased in size, and a new
one was added.[5]

Differential Status

The Legislative Reorganization Act of 1946 sought to create a system of
major standing committees in each chamber. This goal was not fully achieved.
Some committees like the District of Columbia or government operations (originally named expenditures in the executive departments) have been considered
minor right from the outset.[6] Furthermore, there are substantial differences
among the other standing committees in prestige and popularity. However,
ranking the committees with exactitude according to their relative status in
either house is difficult for several reasons. Firstly, the positions of committees
within the "pecking order" of each chamber are constantly changing. Secondly,
there are differential perceptions of the attractiveness of various committees.
And thirdly, there are no precise, objective measures of prestige.

Some have attempted to rate the desirability of the committees by analyzing

VERNON REGIONAL
JUNIOR COLLEGE LIBRARY

the transfers of members to and from them. Dr. George Goodwin made such a ranking of the Senate standing committees for the 81st through the 85th Congresses; Dr. Donald Matthews, for the 80th through the 84th Congresses. Although both are highly knowledgeable observers covering essentially the same time span, the order of preference they assigned ten of the fifteen committees differed—in some cases by as much as four places. In part, the discrepancies in their findings could be attributed to the fact that Goodwin used the net transfers per committee weighted for the size of the committee as his index of desirability; whereas, Matthews considered for each committee the net gains from, or losses to, every other committee.[7]

Of course, any such listing reflects only the transfers made. It does not take into account what requests were refused. Also, at least in the House, the committee seat sought by a member often represents not his first choice but his estimate of the best assignment he is likely to receive and what the dean of his state delegation is willing to help him get.[8] Hence, this sort of classification affords at best but an approximation of committee popularity.

Moreover, any ranking based on preferences does not necessarily gauge the relative prestige or power of the committees. A member may transfer to a less influential committee like Interior and Insular Affairs to serve his constituency better. Other factors cause Congressmen to seek assignment to a committee of low prestige. For instance, to minimize Negro influence on the District of Columbia government, Southern Congressmen consistently endeavor to control the House District Committee.[9] As a consequence, any list based on transfers of members gives an exaggerated impression of the esteem with which most Representatives regard that committee. Further, because of the backing of powerful organized interest groups, a committee may regularly exert more influence on the floor than another on which seats are coveted by a much larger number of Congressmen.

Though no agreement appears possible on the exact order in which the standing committees should be ranked according to their prestige and popularity, there is a consensus on which are major and which are minor committees. Since 1947, on the Senate side, Foreign Relations, Finance, Interstate and Foreign Commerce, Appropriations, Armed Services, Judiciary, and Agriculture and Forestry have been generally regarded as important committees; Government Operations, Rules and Administration, Post Office and Civil Service, and District of Columbia, as lesser committees. On the House side, Rules, Ways and Means, Appropriations, Armed Services, Foreign Affairs, Interstate and Foreign Commerce, Agriculture, and Judiciary have been among the top committees; Government Operations, Post Office and Civil Service, and Veterans' Affairs, among the bottom committees.

This differential status of the standing committees has pronounced effects on their composition and functioning. Minor committees have an even more rapid turnover than the average. Unless having decided to try for the chairmanship or having some other special reason, most members of a minor committee strive to move as promptly as possible to a more important committee. Except in the Senate since the advent of the Johnson Rule (which applies only to Senate Democrats), very few freshmen have been assigned to major committees in either chamber.[10] This means that the lesser committees contain a disproportionate number of first-termers. As a result, in the House they are particularly vulnerable to loss of members from electoral defeat. For example, in 1960, six of the sixteen Democrats on the House Post Office and Civil Service Committee were election casualties. All six were freshmen.[11] Occasionally, minor House committees go understrength for protracted periods because enough Congressmen are not willing to forfeit more attractive committee posts to serve on them. With a large segment of their memberships inexperienced, lacking in parliamentary skill, and unenthusiastic about their assignments, the performance of minor committees often suffers in comparison with that of the major committees to which the influential members gravitate. In turn, this further widens the disparity in prestige and popularity between them.[12]

Changing Composition

There is a surprisingly high turnover in the memberships of the standing committees in the Senate and the House. On the average only 21.3 per cent of the members of the Senate standing committees (except Aeronautical and Space Sciences) in 1961 had been on them in 1952. The corresponding figure for the House standing committees (except Science and Astronautics) was 25.3 per cent. And this situation applied to major as well as minor committees. For example, in the Senate the proportion of the membership that had served on the committee since 1952 was: four out of seventeen on Foreign Relations (two Democrats and two Republicans), three out of seventeen on Finance (two Democrats and one Republican), one out of seventeen on Interstate and Foreign Commerce (a Democrat), five out of seventeen on Armed Services (three Democrats and two Republicans), and three out of fifteen on Judiciary (two Democrats and one Republican). On the House side, the ratios were: eight out of twenty-five on Ways and Means (six Democrats and two Republicans), eight out of thirty-three on Foreign Affairs (four Democrats and four Republicans), seven out of thirty-three on Interstate and Foreign Commerce (six Democrats and one Republican), fourteen out of thirty-seven on Armed Services (nine Democrats and five Republicans), and twelve out of thirty-five on Judiciary (ten Democrats and two Republicans).[13]

Several significant consequences flow from this rather rapid turnover. The complexion of a committee can be—and sometimes is—drastically modified within a brief span. The replacement or addition of but a few members can alter the effective majority of a committee in which the ultimate power of decision reposes. At the start of the 87th Congress, Senator Joseph Clark (D.-Pa.) unsuccessfully urged a modest enlargement of the Judiciary and Finance Committees for that very purpose.[14] Even one or two new members with a pronouncedly different ideological orientation from the rest can have noticeable effects on the functioning of a committee. For instance, since 1957, the presence of Senators Paul Douglas (D.-Ill.) and Albert Gore (D.-Tenn.) has been felt on the Finance Committee. Growing numbers of record votes have been taken on matters which customarily had been decided by consensus. Committee reports have no longer been unanimous but have included individual dissents and minority views. An increased divisiveness has intruded into the deliberations of the committee and sometimes has carried over to the floor consideration of a measure.

Such developments have made heavy demands on the adaptability of the committee staffs which have had to accommodate to the shifts in the internal power structures of their committees and, to a lesser extent, of other committees with which theirs might become involved. The changing composition of the committees has enhanced the prestige and influence of many staffs whose tenure soon antedated that of most members of their committees. Also, it has magnified the importance of the staffs both as custodians of the procedures and institutional practices on which continuity of operations depends and as repositories of information about substantive matters within the jurisdictions of their respective committees.

Multiple Committee Assignments

One of the principal problems the Legislative Reorganization Act of 1946 tried to solve was the excessive number of committee assignments many members had. As the accompanying Senate report stated:

> Today no Senator serves on less than 3 committees; and one sits on 10 committees, not counting the service on subcommittees, of which there are 67 in the Senate. In short, the committee work load of United States Senators today is too heavy to bear. Many Senators have so many committee assignments that they find it impossible to attend their meetings because of conflicts and are present by proxy or not at all.[15]

The remedy adopted was to consolidate the thirty-three standing committees of the Senate into fifteen and the forty-eight standing committees of the House into nineteen. Each Senator was limited to two standing committee assignments and each Representative to one (with exceptions for specified committees like District of Columbia). The original version of the law would have prohibited special committees, but this provision was eliminated in the process of enactment.[16]

In the 80th Congress, when the Legislative Reorganization Act was put into effect, there was a proliferation of subcommittees. Although fluctuating from year to year, the total has remained high. Then and in every succeeding Congress there have been varying numbers of special and select committees—including the Senate and House Small Business Committees, which Dr. George B. Galloway has characterized as "standing committees in everything but name."[17] Besides several standing joint committees, there have been a variety of special joint committees, boards, and commissions of greatly differing longevity. And in the 85th Congress, two new standing committees were established.

In 1961, for example, there were thirty-six standing committees, three special and select committees, eleven joint committees, and 253 subcommittees for a total of 303 committees of all types. For the Senate alone there were 151 committee units consisting of sixteen standing committees, two special and select committees, 109 subcommittees, and the eleven joint committees with their thirteen subcommittees. In addition, there were numerous *ad hoc* subcommittees and twenty-six commissions and boards.[18]

Besides serving on between two and six standing, select, and joint committees, Senators have as many as fourteen subcommittee assignments (exclusive of *ad hoc* subcommittees). Some of the more autonomous subcommittees with specially-authorized staffs are virtually separate committees. Appropriations subcommittees entail a heavy burden of work, and each member of the Senate Appropriations Committee is on between four and six of them. Also, a Senator of the majority party may hold several chairmanships. For instance, in 1961, Senator John McClellan (D.-Ark.) was chairman of: the Government Operations Committee, its Permanent Subcommittee on Investigations, the Subcommittee on Departments of State and Justice and the Judiciary and Related Agencies of the Appropriations Committee, and the Subcommittee on Patents, Trademarks, and Copyrights of the Judiciary Committee. He was a member of nine other subcommittees—including the Subcommittee on Internal Security of the Judiciary Committee—and of the Joint Committee on Immigration and Nationality Policy.

Along with their committee assignments, a number of Senators occupy responsible positions in their political party organizations within the Senate. For example, in 1959, Senator Lyndon B. Johnson (D.-Tex.) was Majority Floor

Leader and chairman of the Democratic Conference, of the Democratic Policy Committee, and of the Democratic Steering Committee. Concurrently, he was chairman of the Aeronautical and Space Sciences Committee, chairman of the Subcommittee on Departments of State and Justice and the Judiciary and Related Agencies of the Appropriations Committee, chairman of the Preparedness Investigating Subcommittee of the Armed Services Committee, and a member of five other subcommittees and of the Senate Office Building Commission.[19]

Although the situation is appreciably less acute in the House, Representatives are members of between one and four committees and as many as eight subcommittees. The restriction of each Representative to service on but one standing committee (with the exception of four minor committees) survived only through the 82d Congress. On January 13, 1953, the House rules were amended so that thenceforth there has been no limitation on the number of standing committees to which a Representative might be elected.[20] By 1961, 107 members of the House had two standing committee assignments. Thirty of the others were on at least one select or joint committee in addition to one standing committee apiece. And some Representatives from the majority party held several chairmanships. For example, Representative Wright Patman (D.-Tex.) was chairman of: the Joint Economic Committee, its Subcommittee on Economic Stabilization, Automation, and Energy Resources, the Select Committee on Small Business, and Subcommittee No. 2 of the Banking and Currency Committee. He also was vice-chairman of the Joint Committee on Defense Production and a member of the Defense Procurement Subcommittee of the Joint Economic Committee.[21]

These multiple committee responsibilities create numerous problems—particularly in the Senate. On many occasions several of the committees and subcommittees to which a Senator belongs are meeting simultaneously. As an expedient, he frequently divides his attendance among them. Like the eyes of a spectator at a three-ring circus, he darts back and forth trying to follow what is occurring several places at once. Needless to observe, this not only is distracting for him but sometimes disrupts committee proceedings. Along with the absenteeism induced by the numerous other duties of Senators, this practice rather often makes it hard for committees and subcommittees to get or retain a quorum. Because of this difficulty in convening, committees sometimes have to conduct their business by circularizing materials among the members and polling them individually. Often the accessibility of members—especially on the lesser committees—to committee aides is very limited. In the case of some of the more heavily-burdened Senators, even their office employees have to communicate with them largely through memoranda or by consulting them on the floor of the Senate.

This places a premium on the initiative of the committee staffs in planning and carrying out committee activities. When a committee aide conceives a creative innovation in committee or staff operations, he has to catch the ear of the chairman and/or other key members to sell them the idea. Preoccupied with many competing demands on his time, the chairman often leaves to the committee staff the responsibility for arranging meetings to suit the convenience of the members, keeping track of their availability and interests for various assignments, and so on. Occasionally, even a very able chairman of a major Senate committee walks into a meeting and asks the staff what is on the agenda.

Of course, manifold committee assignments have some results that are beneficial and others that are not necessarily adverse. In the Senate, overlapping membership of committees facilitates coordination of their work and integration of policy in important areas. Major committees like Foreign Relations habitually contain a goodly number of chairmen and ranking minority members from other important committees as well as Senators high in the over-all leadership structure of the Senate.

In both the House and Senate, a member often pursues interests through his secondary rather than his primary committee assignments. Although conjectural, his reasons for doing this are not always obscure. Perhaps he is able to get specially-authorized funds to conduct a study from one committee but not the other to which the subject is more relevant. For example, in 1949, when but a freshman on the House Armed Services Committee, Representative Porter Hardy, Jr., (D.-Va.) was chairman of the Government Operations Subcommittee of the House Expenditures Committee, with which he could vent any desires to investigate the military establishment. Possibly a Congressman can obtain a subcommittee with a membership more to his liking from one committee rather than the other. Or the approach of the one committee with emphasis on broad principles may be more congenial with the purposes he seeks to achieve than that of the other which stresses technicalities. In any event, there are numerous instances of this sort.

Similarly, once in a while, members use the staff from one of their committees as a supplementary or alternative source of assistance on matters falling primarily within the jurisdiction of another. Sometimes they do this to reinforce an understrength staff. For example, during the 82d Congress, when chairman of the Joint Economic Committee, Senator Joseph O'Mahoney (D.-Wyo.) occasionally utilized part of its staff to help the clerk of the appropriations subcommittee which he also chaired. In other cases, members turn to another staff because of insufficient access to the staff of the principal committee concerned.

Policy Specialists

Some members of Congress are recognized as authorities on particular subjects. Many of them have acquired their expertness from long service on committees or cognate bodies within whose jurisdiction such matters fall. From attending hearings at which eminent specialists appeared as witnesses, doing their home work on staff studies, self-directed reading, and availing themselves of the opportunity to consult leading experts inside and outside the government, they have got an advanced education in certain areas. For example, from his stint as chairman of the TNEC and of numerous congressional committees dealing with economic issues, Senator Joseph O'Mahoney (D.-Wyo.) developed a formidable reputation as a lay economist. Similarly, the vast knowledge of military affairs possessed by Representative Carl Vinson (D.-Ga.), who has served on House Armed Services and the predecessor Naval Affairs Committee since 1917, is legendary. There are myriad anecdotes about instances in which he has demonstrated a grasp of the intricacies of the defense establishment surpassing that of the Joint Chiefs of Staff, some of whom were in kneepants when he entered Congress. Other members bring to Congress an impressive background of education and experience in specific fields. For instance, with a Ph.D. from Columbia University and having taught economics at the University of Chicago for almost thirty years, Senator Paul Douglas (D.-Ill.) gained ready acceptance as a "policy specialist" (a designation applied to Congressmen with a high order of subject-matter competence).

Committee Influence

For any standing committee, impressive statistics can be compiled on the number of measures it reports that the parent chamber routinely approves. But the bulk of them would be noncontroversial and rather minor in nature. In the case of major, controversial matters, there is wide variation in the effectiveness of the standing committees in getting their recommendations adopted by their own house. Sometimes they suffer the humiliation of having proposals rejected outright. On other occasions, bills they report are mutilated almost beyond recognition by floor amendments. Various factors are responsible for this differential performance. Among them are how well the committee has designed a measure to gain ready approbation, how skillful the chairman is as a floor manager, and how cohesive the committee is on a given proposal.

To a considerable extent, the outcome on the floor reflects how accurately a committee has anticipated the preferences of the chamber. As numerous case studies have detailed, committees shape measures in accordance with their estimate of the political situation inside and outside Congress. Provisions are inserted, deleted, or changed to gain the support or reduce the opposition of influential legislators and of powerful interest groups. The scope of a bill is often adjusted to an appraisal of the temper of the whole country as well as of both houses. Committees take into account views of their opposite numbers in the other chamber and the probable attitude of committees handling cognate subjects in their own house—some of whom may be expected to conduct guerrilla warfare against a proposal or to try to siphon off jurisdiction over key features.[22] Even when bringing a measure to the floor under a closed rule, the Ways and Means Committee gauges the sentiment of the House about disputed provisions and modifies them accordingly so that adverse reaction to any portion will not cause defeat of the whole thing. Besides taking their own soundings, the Ways and Means Committee sometimes calls on the House leadership to poll the members for this purpose.

A crucial ingredient of success is the quality of the legislative generalship displayed by the chairman in managing a bill on the floor. Although getting a bill passed is a team operation, the floor manager is the quarterback. He controls the time and selection of supporting speakers in the debate. To cope with unexpected emergencies, he has to remain on the floor constantly. At critical junctures, he calls the signals. His adroitness in parliamentary maneuvering, quick-wittedness, judgment of where to yield and when to press for advantage, and his forensic ability all influence the final results. A closely-related consideration is how he is regarded by his colleagues. On occasion, the prestige of the chairman and of other prominent committeemen has compensated for the opposition of influential organized groups or of the Administration.

How united a committee is in backing a bill is critically important. If a committee reports a measure unanimously, ratification by the parent chamber is virtually assured. In fact, Donald Matthews found that during the 84th Congress any motion favored by more than eighty per cent of the reporting committee's members was invariably approved by the Senate.[23] Where there is division within the committee, not only the size but also the attitude of the dissident minority has a vital bearing on the floor action. If those who have voted against a bill in committee indicate that the compromise worked out is tenable though not entirely to their liking, the prospects for passage are still good. However, if they complain that the bill has been railroaded through over their objections, the committee proposal is vulnerable to being defeated or thoroughly rewritten on the floor.

The main determinant of the cohesiveness achieved by a committee on a particular measure is the chairman. He is largely responsible whether disputes are satisfactorily resolved within the committee or carried to the floor. Chairmen differ markedly in their appreciation of the need for taking as united a committee as possible on the floor and in their ability to develop the requisite consensuses. Many of the very capable chairmen go to great lengths to reach unanimity where attainable and to placate the minority on any issue always.

Importance of the Chairman

The chairman is the focal point of the committee. He presides at hearings, executive sessions, and other committee functions. As the main spokesman for the committee to the press, he is featured in publicity about the committee. Formal communications with the executive branch are transmitted through him. The President and cabinet officials consult him about matters within the province of the committee. Much of the committee work is done in his name. Committee publications are accompanied by a letter of transmittal or contain a preface by him. Replies to correspondence addressed to the committee go out over his signature. As administrative head of the committee, he signs the vouchers and is responsible for accounting for committee monies. He fixes the salaries of the committee employees and sets other personnel policies. By precept or pre-emption, he largely determines the availability of the staff (with the exception of some minority aides) to the other members of the committee. Customarily, he is allowed wide discretion over the organization and procedures of the committee. Normally, he appoints any subcommittees, handles the referral of bills and other assignments to them, and decides the program of committee business. He is the principal manager (and designates any alternates) of committee measures on the floor and in conference committees.

The degree to which a chairman dominates his committee varies appreciably with his personal characteristics and the composition of the committee. For he does not exercise his powers independently of the rest of the committee. He is but the center of one of many systems of power among which there is interaction. The sway exerted by the chairman and other members inside the committee is affected by their positions in power structures outside the committee. And there are complex, shifting patterns of influence within any committee.

The Effective Majority

On every standing committee, the formal majority consists of the chairman and the other members from the party controlling Congress. On the bulk of the committees in either chamber, however, few disputes over substantive policies or even the internal administration of a committee are decided by a straight party-line vote. Rather, most issues are resolved by a bipartisan majority. The size and composition of this majority varies from issue to issue. Once in a great while, it may not include the chairman as is evidenced by his signing the minority views or submitting an individual dissent in the report to accompany a committee measure. Nevertheless, during a given Congress there usually is enough consistency in voting patterns to identify the principal members of the "effective majority" on any committee.

Because of the sharp ideological cleavages within each political party, sometimes the real minority on a committee consists of members of the majority party. For example, during the 86th Congress—as had been true for many years—the Senate Government Operations Committee was controlled by a conservative Southern Democratic-Republican coalition. On any matter involving a split along liberal and conservative lines, Democratic Senators Henry Jackson (Wash.), Hubert Humphrey (Minn.), Ernest Gruening (Alaska), and Edmund Muskie (Maine) were outvoted by Chairman John McClellan (D.-Ark.), Sam Ervin (D.-N.C.), Karl Mundt (R.-S.Dak.), Carl Curtis (R.-Nebr.), and Homer Capehart (R.-Ind.).

A change in the effective majority of a committee may occur through the normal course of events. In the 87th Congress, the replacement of Senator Homer Capehart (R.-Ind.) by Senator Jacob Javits (R.-N.Y.) on the Government Operations Committee switched control to a liberal Democratic-Republican coalition consisting of Jackson, Humphrey, Gruening, Muskie, and Javits. Sometimes the size or composition of a committee is deliberately altered to modify its effective majority. Perhaps the most publicized recent instance is the "packing" of the House Rules Committee at the start of the 87th Congress. The addition of two more liberal Democrats along with another Republican compensated for the consistent alignment of Chairman Howard Smith (D.-Va.) and his fellow Dixiecrat, William Colmer (D.-Miss.), with the Republican members.

Occasionally, happenings are erroneously construed as efforts to reconstitute a committee. For example, at the outset of the 87th Congress, there was protracted delay in filling two Democratic positions on the House Post Office and Civil Service Committee. Several news columnists speculated that the conservative Democratic Chairman, Tom Murray (Tenn.), had persuaded the leadership to leave these posts permanently vacant to hold down the size of the liberal majority on that committee. It turned out, however, that no such Machiavellian ploy was involved. There simply were not enough Democrats willing to accept a seat on the Post Office and Civil Service Committee at the expense of giving up more attractive assignments.[24]

The Efficient Part

While ultimate control of a committee reposes in the effective majority, most of the impetus and supporting efforts for the committee work come from a smaller, bipartisan group which Holbert Carroll has felicitously dubbed the "efficient part."[25] Varying somewhat in composition with the subject under consideration, the efficient part of a committee rarely contains more than a third of the members and on some matters but one or two. The members in the efficient part play a dominant role in formulating and conducting the program of committee business. They instigate action on various measures. They participate actively in the hearings. They shape the contents of bills and accompanying reports. In the decision of points at issue within the committee, they mobilize additional members from both parties to constitute the effective majority. They take the lead in planning and executing the strategy for obtaining approval of the committee's handiwork by the parent chamber. They bear the brunt of the floor debate. They are the most interested, energetic, able, and informed individuals on the subjects with which they are dealing. And usually they make the heaviest demands on the committee staff.

On most committees junior members are readily admitted into the efficient part and considerable scope is given their abilities. Although they sometimes have to defer to their elders in public at hearings or on the floor in the case of a few prerogative-conscious committees, talented freshmen carry substantial weight in the deliberations during executive sessions on even the most tradition-bound units. Influence tends to gravitate to those with competence regardless of seniority. Any "policy specialists" are always in the efficient part. Of course, from long service on the committee, many times senior members have the greatest substantive knowledge as well as skill in parliamentary maneuvering. The chairman is always included because of the great power he can exercise irrespective of his ability. However, occasionally other members of the efficient part overshadow him, as Representative John Vorys (R.-Ohio) did both Representatives Charles Eaton (R.-N.J.) and Robert Chiperfield (R.-Ill.) when they were chairmen of the House Foreign Affairs Committee in the 80th and 83d Congresses respectively. According to Carroll, "Vorys wielded, with their tacit consent, many of the prerogatives of the chairman."[26] In the 80th Congress, this occurred to such an extent on the House Select Committee on Foreign Aid that it was nicknamed the "Herter Committee" although Eaton was chairman and Representative Christian Herter (R.-Mass.) was but vice-chairman.

Subcommittee Structures

Subcommittees exhibit an even more bewildering diversity than their parent committees. There are standing, special (sometimes called *ad hoc*), legislative, consultative, investigative (or legislative oversight), administrative (or house-keeping), "mixed," and joint subcommittees. Naturally, these categories are not mutually exclusive. A legislative subcommittee may be either standing or special. An investigative subcommittee may also have legislative authority. Sometimes a consultative subcommittee conducts an investigation, and so forth.

Standing subcommittees are continued until superseded or abolished by re-organization of their parent committee. Special subcommittees are supposed to expire upon the completion of the study or whatever other task they were created to perform. However, through obtaining successive renewals of their authorizations, some special subcommittees persist through several Congresses. Consultative subcommittees have the primary function of facilitating communications with executive branch officials administering programs within their jurisdictions. Investigative subcommittees discharge varying amounts of the legislative oversight responsibilities of their parent committees. Most administrative subcommittees are concerned with internal housekeeping matters, such as committee staffing. However, sometimes executive subcommittees are established to plan and supervise a study being conducted by the full committee. "Mixed" subcommittees (found only in the Senate) are subcommittees augmented by members from the Senate at large appointed by the Vice President. The distinction between them and joint subcommittees becomes blurred when the authorizing resolution specifies from which committees the supernumerary Senators are to be picked. Joint subcommittees may be drawn from committees in one or both chambers.

The standing committees vary widely in their practices regarding subcommittees. Some use them hardly at all. Others are characterized as but holding companies for their subcommittees. Some maintain only consultative standing subcommittees, handling nearly all legislative matters themselves or with *ad hoc* subcommittees. Other committees that have elaborate systems of standing legislative subcommittees assign them only minor bills and divide the rest between themselves and special subcommittees. Likewise, some committees with standing investigative subcommittees conduct particular investigations themselves and create *ad hoc* subcommittees for certain other inquiries. A few have no standing subcommittees and specifically deny legislative authority to the special subcommittees they infrequently establish. Some standing legislative subcommittees are designated only by number and have no prescriptive right to any class of bill. Others have distinctive titles and well-defined jurisdictions. Some legislative subcommittees make only oral reports to their parent committees; others prepare printed reports which the full committees almost invariably adopt, and so on through an almost infinite array of relationships.

In all this apparent chaos, there is an inner logic. Subcommittees are employed for far more than the achievement of a convenient division of labor. Subcommittees are created to serve many purposes—some of them external to Congress. For example, on February 28, 1961, the House Interstate and Foreign Commerce Committee set up a permanent Subcommittee on Regulatory Agencies. This action could be attributed partly at least to a desire to assert the primacy of Congress in overseeing these agencies and to discourage establishment of the proposed Office of Regulatory Agencies within the Executive Office of the President. Similarly, sometimes a committee resorts to a "mixed" subcommittee to broaden the base of support in Congress for the program to be studied. Occasionally, executive subcommittees are set up primarily to provide more vigorous leadership for an important project than the committee chairman can because of personal incapacity or distraction with other pressing matters. Personnel subcommittees often are created to put a layer of insulation between the chairman and the recruiting process. Rather frequently—particularly on the lesser Senate committees—a chairman uses subcommittees to stimulate participation by the membership. Through appointing individuals as subcommittee chairmen with the attendant publicity and other fringe benefits, he can induce them to do routine stints they otherwise would shun in favor of their more glamorous committee assignments.[27] Conversely, once in a while, a committee chairman grudgingly accedes to the demands of an influential member for his own subcommittee as the price of retaining his good will.

The subcommittee structure of a committee is truly an "organizational precipitate." In large measure, it represents the resultant of the centrifugal and centripetal forces within a committee. Although some chairmen voluntarily decentralize their committees to reduce the burden on themselves, most strive to consolidate their control and to preserve the integrity of the committee. Usually a chairman is backed in this endeavor by senior members who, being next in line of succession, have an obvious interest in keeping the committee intact and the authority of the chairmanship undiluted. As might be expected, junior committeemen are the strongest proponents of subcommittees with their own staffs. A member's views on this score often undergo a startling metamorphosis as he nears the main seat of power. On nearly every committee, the chairman has to resist pressures to divide its jurisdiction among standing subcommittees with their own staffs. To yield, results at best in aggravating the problem of coordinating committee activities, at worst in fragmenting the committee into a congeries of what amounts to separate committees with each going its own way. Every year when resolutions authorizing special funds for the committees are presented, bitter battles are waged within many committees over the issue of more subcommittees with special staffs. The outcome is reflected in their subcommittee structures, which normally represent a compromise between what is best in the abstract and multiple other considerations.

Efficacy of Formal Rules

Both House and Senate rules, as well as provisions in laws like the Legislative Reorganization Act of 1946, prescribe various committee procedures. Numerous committees in both chambers have adopted supplementary regulations. Many times, however, these formal rules exert but a marginal influence on the operation of a committee. Whether or not they are observed depends to a large degree on the informal power structures inside and outside the committee. With the backing of a majority, the chairman can disregard them. Even a majority is often reluctant to oppose the chairman under the rules on procedural matters. Dependent on him for favors in the conduct of committee business, they do not wish to incur his displeasure. Conversely, a chairman frequently is inclined to be complaisant by a desire to develop solidarity on a measure as a prerequisite for success on the floor. Sometimes a chairman has to defer to certain members because of the great influence they exert in the parent chamber as deans of state delegations, chairmen of other committees, or leaders in their party organizations.[28] Factors of this sort along with the ability, personality, energy, and experience of the chairman affect the way in which a committee is run far more than the formal procedures.

Personalized Nature of Relations

Relations among committee members are highly personalized. The replacement of even one key individual can drastically alter not only the method of functioning but also the spirit pervading a committee. For example, one House committee, whose chairman and ranking minority member were congenial, operated on a substantially nonpartisan basis through five Congresses. When the ranking minority member retired, his successor—who had been on the committee all this time—was a very partisan person and hated the vice-chairman. As a consequence, the committee became rent by a deep partisan cleavage, and cooperation between the majority and minority leaders virtually disappeared. Attitudes of committee members toward one another sometimes influence the positions they take. On one Senate committee many of the members are loath to oppose the chairman because of his skillful use of ridicule and invective in debate. They do not wish to be subjected to the verbal laceration sure to ensue from antagonizing him. Once in a while, personal friendships cutting across party affiliations have prevailed over institutional loyalties. Some time back a Senate committee of which the Majority Leader was a member favorably reported the nomination of an executive official. A minority member of that committee who habitually had breakfast with the Majority Leader had some reservations about the nominee. Although the Majority Leader had voted in committee for approval of the candidate, he blocked his confirmation by the Senate until the apprehensions of his breakfast companion had been allayed by further investigation. Although present in every institution, the interaction among personality, structure, and procedures is operative to an extraordinary degree in the standing committees and their parent chambers.

These are characteristics of the standing committees that profoundly affect the nature and functioning of their professional staffs. Against this background, let us examine how the committees proceeded to carry out the staffing provisions of the Legislative Reorganization Act of 1946 during the first three Congresses, 80th through 82d, that law was put into effect—the period covered (1947-1953) by the main body of this study.

PART TWO

CHAPTER III

PATTERNS OF
STAFF ORGANIZATION

Nomenclature

In the Legislative Reorganization Act of 1946, the only title used with respect to the professional aides of the committees is "professional staff member." The clerical employees are referred to simply as the "clerical staff" or as "clerks."[1] In a subsequent law prescribing the pay scale for the clerical staff of each Senate standing committee, authorization is provided for the two positions of "chief clerk" and of "assistant chief clerk"; and the other four members of the clerical staff are called "clerical assistants."[2] Utilizing only part of or ignoring completely this nomenclature incorporated in the organic legislation, the committee staffs have adopted a bewildering assortment of appellations.

Of the professional staff. During the period covered, over fifty different titles were applied to professional staff positions on various committees. Among those were:

> Research specialist, minority representative, expert, aviation and engineering specialist, consultant, assistant specialist, staff director, investigator, chief investigator, professional aide, chief of staff, director of studies and investigations, technical staff director, director of research, counsel, chief counsel, general counsel, legal counsel, law revision counsel, minority counsel, professional staff counsel, special counsel, assistant counsel, associate counsel, technical consultant, economic consultant, engineering consultant, tax adviser, tariff expert, executive officer, commodity and research specialist, professional staff member, minority clerk, professional consultant, minority staff member, legislative assistant, social security adviser, research analyst, senior investigator, technical expert, agent, staff adviser, minority professional assistant, legislative professional staff, special social security expert, staff associate, statistician, staff member to the minority, staff consultant, claims specialist, investigator to the minority, staff assistant.[3]

Furthermore, diverse meanings were attached to some of these titles. For instance, generally the designation "counsel" connoted the performance of specialized legal services for the committee. However, on several committees (for example, House Armed Services and Senate Banking and Currency), every lawyer on the staff, whatever his duties, was called "counsel." Likewise, the title "chief counsel" often denoted the head of a staff. But there was a staff director in addition to a chief counsel on a number of committees.

Of the clerical staff. The nomenclature of the clerical employees exhibited similar diversity. Among the more than half a hundred titles borne by them were:

> Clerk, assistant clerk, chief clerk, assistant chief clerk, staff assistant, clerical aid, clerk-stenographer, messenger, page, clerk to minority, legal clerk, clerk to majority, janitor-messenger, secretary, clerical staff, deputy clerk, executive secretary (clerk), special employee, clerk-stenographer minority, assistant to the clerk, assistant to the minority clerk, clerk-typist, clerk for research and coordination, clerk and administrative officer, staff administrator and clerk, assistant clerk and stenographer, assistant to the chairman, clerical assistant, assistant clerk-stenotypist, file chief, research clerk, secretary to clerk, chief of reference section, administrative assistant, staff assistant to the minority, minority stenographer, fiscal officer, document clerk, clerical staff (minority), clerk (stenographic), clerk (secretary), chief clerk and executive secretary, associate clerk, special clerk, staff member.[4]

There was the additional complication that no particular level of position was associated with most of these designations. The title "clerk" might be applied to anyone from the top to the bottom of the clerical staff of a committee. "Assistant clerk" might designate any employee from the second-in-command on down. Some of the titles most commonly used to indicate the head of the clerical staff of a committee were: "the clerk," "committee clerk," and "chief clerk."

Significance. Much of this "nomenclature run riot" undoubtedly stemmed from the omnipresent drive for greater prestige. There was more psychic return from being termed a "stationary engineer" instead of a "furnace man." Some of it represented nothing more than fortuity or fancy. For example, John Graham, the minority professional aide to the House Education and Labor Committee during the 81st and 82d Congresses, said that he could have adopted a title like "minority investigator" or "minority research specialist" but preferred to retain that of "minority clerk" which had already been established for that position in the 80th Congress.[5]

In other instances, however, the particular designations selected had considerable significance in the adjustment of intrastaff relationships. For example, on the House Foreign Affairs Committee, one of the professional aides complained that it was humiliating to be subject to the direction of the clerk.

But he withdrew his objections to the staff setup when the clerk's title was changed to "staff administrator." Likewise, on the House Armed Services Committee, the title conferred upon the staff director contributed materially to consolidating his authority over the entire staff.[6]

Organization and Assignment

Of the direction. During the period covered, there were four main patterns of organization for the management of committee staffs. In the first and most prevalent, there was no director of the professional staff, but a chief clerk was in charge of the clerical force. In the second, a director of the professional staff and a chief clerk, of roughly coordinate status, headed their respective components of the staff. In the third, the professional staff director—generally bearing the title "chief of staff"—supervised the entire staff; and the chief clerk served in a subordinate capacity as his administrative assistant. In the fourth, the positions of chief clerk and of staff director were consolidated. Since under this last structural arrangement, the combination chief clerk-staff director usually delegated most of the duties of the chief clerkship to an assistant clerk, the third and fourth categories were in essence the same. In fact, there were a number of variations on each of these basic types which could be classified equally well under two or more of them.

Of the clerical staff. On most committees, the routine tasks that constituted the bulk of the clerical staff work were distributed among the assistant clerks in a fairly uniform fashion. Usually one clerical assistant was made responsible for keeping the committee calendar up to date; another, for processing the hearings and other committee publications; another, for referring bills to the appropriate departments for their comments and for preparing the bill dockets; another, for maintaining the files; and another, for opening and sorting the mail. Although on some committees these various chores were permanently assigned to particular employees, they more often were rotated among the clerical assistants periodically—generally every session. This latter practice ensured that each assistant clerk was trained in all aspects of the work so that he could substitute for any of the others. Because the committee staffs desirably must remain small, such interchangeability is essential. Also, alternation of duties protects the members of a clerical force from the monotony of having to perform the same type of routine stint all the time.

In assigning the clerical employees to assist the professional aides in a stenographic and sometimes junior-grade research capacity, a committee usually followed one of two main systems. In the first, none of the assistant clerks was earmarked for the use of specific professional staff members. Rather, they were kept in a central pool and deployed flexibly in accordance with the ebbs and flows in the committee work. Then if necessary, several or all of them could be concentrated on helping a single professional aide who was rushed to meet a deadline on a high-priority project. In the second, each clerical employee had a relatively fixed assignment to one or two of the professional staff members. Under the latter arrangement, propinquity was often the determinant of the working relations that developed. Because of lack of sufficient office space, portions of a committee staff frequently were scattered over several widely separated locations—often on different floors and occasionally in other buildings. Under such circumstances, naturally a professional aide customarily relied for stenographic and research assistance on the clerical employees with whom he was housed. Of course, as with any competing principles of organization, these two were rarely found applied in their pure forms. Even on a committee where the services of an assistant clerk normally were reserved almost exclusively for a certain professional staff member, other professional aides occasionally called on him. And in emergency situations—for example, where on very short notice it was necessary to prepare numerous extra copies of a lengthy memorandum—the entire clerical staff pitched in together.

Whichever method of assigning the assistant clerks to professional staff members obtained, they were subject to a sort of modified "Taylorism" or dual supervision of their work.[7] When they were occupied with strictly clerical duties, the chief clerk acted as their overseer. When they were detailed to assist one of the professional aides, he superintended their performance of any quasi-professional tasks.

Of the professional staff. Likewise, there were two major alternative ways of organizing the professional staff of a committee. In the first, each professional aide had a clearly defined field of specialization covering certain classes of subjects considered by the committee. For example, during the 82d Congress, the four professional staff members of the House Committee on Interior and Insular Affairs specialized in the following fields respectively: irrigation and reclamation; territories and insular possessions; Indian affairs; and mines and mining.

In the second system, which was exemplified during the 82d Congress on the staffs of the two foreign relations committees among others, the professional aides were deemed equally qualified to handle any subject falling within the committee's jurisdiction. Measures were allotted among them in a flexible fashion depending chiefly upon their relative availability. Of course, other factors considered by the staff director (or chairman) in making assignments were the educational and experience backgrounds of the professional aides and their personal preferences. Also, once in a while, a subcommittee asked for the assistance of a certain professional staff member on a particular project. Such requests were almost always complied with.

Where a committee staff was organized in accordance with this second method, a professional aide usually followed through on major bills to handle any renewals of and amendments to that legislation or any related measures. Hence, the professional staff members were prone to develop on-the-job specializations in particular subjects. Conversely, on all but the most rigidly compartmentalized staffs, professional aides occasionally helped to prepare a portion of a report or handle a bill outside their provinces to relieve a colleague of an overload; and the staff directors assigned bills which were not within any of their fields to the professional staff members largely on the basis of their availability. As a result, between the two extremes of the highly-departmentalized professional staffs on the one hand and the nonspecialized on the other, there were varying combinations of the opposing considerations of flexibility and specialization in the organization of the committee staffs.

In addition, on staffs constituted along any of these lines, there was a cross current of professional specialization flowing from the need for legal, public relations, statistical, accounting, and other technical services. This was reflected in the structure of numerous committee staffs which contained such positions as counsel, statistical analyst, public relations consultant, or investigative accountant. The incumbents of those posts assisted and advised the other professional aides to those committees on the aspects of the latter's work that pertained to their specialties.[8] On committee staffs that did not have any technicians specifically designated to furnish such services, the professional aides often turned to any of their associates trained in law, accounting, journalism, or the other professions concerned. This tendency was most evident in connection with legal aid. Increasingly, on various committees when one of the professional employees wanted to check the legal implications of a measure or required some other specialized legal assistance, he went to the most experienced lawyer on the staff. As a consequence, several professional staff members developed into *de facto* committee counsel who divided their time between acting as ordinary professional aides and rendering legal services to their colleagues.

Intermixture of Clerical and Professional Staffs

On many committees there was considerable overlapping and blurring of the distinction between the clerical and professional aides. In practice, it was often difficult to distinguish the two classes of staff by the application of any criteria whether of educational and experience backgrounds or of the character of work performed. A number of committee clerks and assistant clerks possessed professional educational qualifications. For instance, during the 82d Congress, William Hallahan, clerk of the House Banking and Currency Committee, and Leo Irwin, clerk of the Ways and Means Committee, had LL.B.'s. John Lehman, clerk of the Joint Committee on the Economic Report; Pat

Holt, associate clerk of the Senate Foreign Relations Committee; and Frank Keenan, assistant clerk of the Senate Interstate and Foreign Commerce Committee, had master's degrees. And Ray Rodgers, assistant clerk of the Senate Labor and Public Welfare Committee, possessed a Ph.D. as well as an LL.B. Prior to becoming clerical staff members, several of them had occupied professional staff positions on the same committees or in governmental agencies. For example, during the 82d Congress, the chief clerks of the House Armed Services Committee, of the Senate Expenditures Committee, and of the House Ways and Means Committee had previously been professional aides to those committees. Jean Curtis, clerk of the House Select Committee on Small Business, had been a research analyst in the Legislative Reference Service of the Library of Congress as well as on the staff of that committee. John Lehman, clerk of the Joint Committee on the Economic Report, had been an assistant economist with the TVA, a regional consultant on public works with the National Resources Planning Board, and an economist and statistician with the Federal Reserve Bank of Chicago.

Moreover, on fourteen of the nineteen committee staffs from which interview data were collected,[9] clerical employees performed varying amounts of professional staff work. On three of those committees—Senate Expenditures, House Armed Services, and House Foreign Affairs—the positions of chief clerk and staff director were consolidated. On a few of them, an assistant clerk served full time in a professional staff capacity. For example, during the 82d Congress, Frank Keenan, assistant clerk of the Senate Interstate and Foreign Commerce Committee, served as an intermediate-grade professional assistant on domestic land and water transportation. And Pat Holt, associate clerk of the Senate Foreign Relations Committee, fulfilled the duties of public relations consultant for that unit. On the remainder of those committees, the clerks or assistant clerks served in a dual capacity, dividing their time between professional and clerical staff work.

Under this last type of arrangement, on some committees like House Banking and Currency or Senate Agriculture and Forestry, the clerks or assistant clerks collaborated on all major projects indistinguishably from the professional aides. On other committees, the clerks or assistant clerks specialized in certain kinds of legislation not covered by the regular professional staff members. For example, during the 81st and 82d Congresses, Ray Rodgers, assistant clerk of the Senate Labor and Public Welfare Committee, did the professional staff work on veterans' affairs and FEPC measures. On the Joint Committee on the Economic Report, John Lehman, the clerk, was the staff economist on regional studies. And in the case of a very few committees like Senate Foreign Relations, almost everyone of the regular clerical assistants[10] acted as a junior-grade professional staff member besides discharging his clerical duties.[11] Conversely, during this same period, one of the professional aides to the House Agriculture Committee, the executive officer,[12] was occupied mainly with administrative tasks normally classified as clerical: handling the processing of hearings and reports, assisting in recruiting and supervising the clerical force, and so on.

There are two main reasons for this widespread confusion of professional and clerical staff functions. The first is that a position is more than a job description and no two persons fill it in exactly the same way. Training, previous experience, capacity, temperament, and concept of role all affect the extent to which a clerical employee intrudes into the province of the professional staff. For instance, Jean Curtis's predecessor as clerk of the House Small Business Committee confined herself to serving as office manager. Mrs. Curtis, however, having been an economic analyst in the LRS, liked research and other creative work much more than the administrative management tasks of the committee clerkship and would have preferred to remain a full-time professional aide to the committee. As a result, when transferred to the position of clerk, she continued to operate at least half of the time in a professional staff capacity.[13]

The second reason is the imposition by the Legislative Reorganization Act of a fixed quota of four professional and six clerical staff members for each standing committee. To circumvent this rigid allocation of their staffs between clerical and professional employees, the committees ofttimes substituted one for the other. Committees with their full complement of professional staff, but desiring additional professional aides, appointed them to top-ranking positions on their clerical staffs and vice versa. In recognition of this problem in the 80th Congress, the Senate Expenditures Committee recommended that the committees be allowed to hire their ten staff members in any ratio of professional to clerical and added in explanation:

> The present arbitrary ratio of four professional staff members to six clerical does not fit all committees. Some need more professional members and fewer clerical; others require the opposite. It is our feeling that each committee should be permitted to allocate these positions according to its needs.[14]

In effect, this proposal would have legalized what now takes place in practice. However, it met the same fate as the many other excellent recommendations made by the Senate Expenditures Committee at that time. The bill embodying them was not enacted. Hence, the committees must continue to resort to their present extralegal and somewhat confusing means to accomplish the same end.

Need for Centralized Direction

Whether resulting from the formal designation of an individual as chief of staff or from evolution of the staff director's or chief clerk's office, centralized direction of the entire staff of a committee is necessary to achieve the most effective utilization of the personnel, because of the intermingling of clerical and professional staff duties, and for the convenience of the chairman and other committee members. The argument is frequently made that a staff director is not required because the assignment of work among the professional aides takes place almost automatically in accordance with their respective specializations and because persons of professional staff caliber ought to be able to work without supervision.

In many instances, however, clearly-defined jurisdictions over the different classes of subjects considered by a committee were not established for its professional aides during the period covered. And often that situation was aggravated by the tendency of many a chairman to disregard any rough division of labor the professional staff of his committee had effected and to give whatever task he wanted done to the first staff member he encountered. Even in the case of committee staffs on which the professional aides had fairly well-recognized fields of specialization, there was the problem of assigning bills and other projects which fell outside or which touched more than one of those. And on almost all the committees, there was the recurrent problem of equating the workload among the professional staff members. It did not arise from any inclination on their part to shirk. Quite the contrary, it consisted in preventing them from attempting to do more than their proportionate shares of the work. Because the professional staff function had not gained full acceptance on some committees and because of the consequent insecurity of tenure, professional staff members often displayed a propensity to try to handle too much work. In an effort to convince their committees of their indispensability, they were constantly reaching out for more things to do.

On several occasions, staff directors had to resort to threat of disciplinary action to get staff members to share the responsibility for performing particular assignments. And on the committees without staff directors, there frequently was fierce competition among the professional aides for the privilege of working on major measures which were likely to be of continuing interest to Congress through a number of sessions. On one such committee, a professional staff member confided:

> Art and I are engaged in a silent struggle for power and at present are contending for control over matters pertaining to oil. Art is a nice fellow, but it is imperative to me to keep this job.

Significantly enough, with the next change in the control of Congress, Art was dropped from the committee staff while the person making this comment was retained.

Where the latter sort of situation obtained, with individual staff members pre-empting large projects for themselves and acting in a mutually exclusive fashion, several of the professional aides to a committee occasionally had comparatively little to do while one of their colleagues was overburdened to the extent of working night and day. As a result of his overload, he might not be able to do justice to his work. Even where it was within his capacity, some of the other staff members might be subjected meanwhile to the demoralizing effects of having to occupy themselves with "make-work." Moreover, under such circumstances, no provision was made for one staff member to understudy another. Generally speaking, this practice of each professional staff member operating virtually autonomously in his own orbit was prevalent only on the committees without staff directors. And reciprocally, the more fruitful forms of intrastaff collaboration were confined almost exclusively to the committees with staff directors.[15]

Because of the mixture of clerical and professional staff functions, it is much more practicable to have a single head of the whole staff of a committee than to have a professional staff director and chief clerk of coordinate rank attempting to supervise their respective components of that staff. Further, it is more convenient for the chairman to have one person he can hold responsible for the performance of both the clerical and professional employees of the committee. Having a chief of staff through whom the chairman can transmit instructions and who keeps him informed on the operation of the staff economizes greatly on the time of both the chairman and the other aides to the committee, particularly where competing demands on the chairman render him relatively inaccessible to the committee employees. Also, this arrangement saves the time and energy of the other members of the committee. For a chief of staff can resolve in their early stages many of the intrastaff differences which otherwise would be referred back to the committee for settlement— generally after having assumed much more unmanageable proportions.

Chief Clerk's Function

Whatever other duties he might perform on different committees during the period covered, the chief clerk's main responsibility was taking care of the administrative management aspects of the committee staff work. He was a sort of combined administrative officer and executive secretary. He saw that the committee, its subcommittees, and staff were supplied with the various institutional services essential to their operating properly; took care of the routine details of organizing hearings; gave out information about the committee's activities; and handled the bulk of the committee correspondence. In addition to supervising the clerical staff in discharging the above and related duties, he took the minutes, conducted roll calls, and tallied the votes taken at committee meetings.

Office of Staff Director

Extent of use. During the 82d Congress, there were staff directors or chiefs of staff on about one third of the standing committees in both houses, on the two Senate policy committees, on most of the select committees and specially-authorized subcommittees in both chambers, and on almost every major joint committee.

Functions. Although different staff directors conceived and fulfilled their role variously, there was a definable cluster of duties common to the position. Firstly, the staff director usually served as the chairman's assistant and personal representative. In this capacity, he aided the chairman in planning the committee program and in organizing the committee to carry it out. He attended subcommittee sessions and conferences with departmental officials for the chairman. Anything he said or did on such occasions, in talking to newspaper reporters or in consulting with other members of Congress, was presumed to reflect the chairman's viewpoint. In fact, almost any action he took was generally construed to be either at the instance of or with the tacit approval of the chairman. When an important bill was up for floor consideration, the staff director sometimes acted as an intelligence officer for the chairman in scouting out potential areas of opposition and in determining whether it would be token or intransigent in nature. And when action on a major measure was imminent, the staff director often was sent out by the chairman to canvass Congressmen not on the committee.

Secondly, the staff director acted in a liaison capacity between the rest of the staff and the members of Congress. The extent to which a staff director canalized relations with the chairman and other Congressmen through himself varied markedly from committee to committee. In some cases the remainder of a staff was almost completely insulated from the members of Congress. For example, on the Joint Committee on Internal Revenue Taxation, about the only direct contact the professional aides had even with members of the revenue committees was in executive sessions or on the floor of Congress where the latter approached them for assistance—usually on something related to the topics under consideration then. And often in those instances the Congressmen had first gone to the chief of staff, Colin Stam, who had referred them over to the particular staff members most conversant with the matters involved. Almost all requests for staff work from individual members of Congress were addressed to Mr. Stam, and all written replies to inquiries and correspondence were prepared for his signature. In contrast, on other committees the staff directors encouraged the professional staff members to work directly with the Congressmen. A few even circulated notices of staff assignments among the committee members in order to facilitate their locating the professional aides handling the measures on which they wanted help. However, on most committees, the chairmen dealt with the professional staffs mostly through the staff directors. Often the other staff members worked directly with the chairmen only on the highly technical aspects of the subjects in which they specialized. In some cases, the staff directors took care of even such technical matters with the chairmen after having secured the requisite information to do so from the professional aides concerned. And generally, individual Congressmen not on a committee addressed their requests for assistance to the staff director with greater frequency than to the other members of the staff.

Thirdly, the staff director served as an interpreter of congressional attitudes to the other committee aides—especially where his length of service on the "Hill" greatly exceeded theirs. From his closer association with members of Congress over a longer period, the staff director had a more detailed and wider knowledge of their psychology and of the political context in which they make their decisions than the rest of the staff—particularly any technicians on it— usually possessed. As a result, the staff director generally could anticipate the congressional reaction to projected policy recommendations or to other con- templated action by the staff more accurately than the other committee aides. Frequently, he could discern aspects of a proposal which they had overlooked that would be distasteful to the Congressmen because not feasible politically. Similarly, he often could predict better than they what matters were most likely to receive congressional attention in view of the general political situa- tion. From such a perspective, he advised the other staff members on any major policy questions that arose in connection with their work or extra- curricular activities. On the same basis, he frequently recommended the priori- ties they should assign to the various projects they were handling.

Fourthly, likewise, the staff director usually made suggestions on the or- ganization and contents of reports, memoranda, and studies being prepared by the staff to maximize their acceptability to Congress. And he invariably reviewed all the written materials produced by the other committee aides from that standpoint as well as for technical competence. Frequently, he could sug- gest alternative ways of phrasing studies and reports to mitigate congressional opposition or to secure greater congressional approbation while saying essentially the same thing. If a study or report was destined for publication, he gave it an especially close scrutiny. And on some committees, no manuscript prepared by the staff went to the Government Printing Office until it had been approved by the staff director.

Fifthly, almost without exception, the staff director handled the assignment of work to the other professional staff members. Even more important than making the initial allocation of tasks among them was his related function of equalizing their workloads as discrepancies in those developed. Whenever a committee aide threatened to become snowed under, the staff director would reduce the burden on him to manageable size by redistributing part of his work among the rest of the staff. On some such occasions where all the other professional aides were fully occupied, the staff director pinch-hit for him on part of his assignments.

Aside from serving in this substitute capacity once in a while, different staff directors varied widely in the extent to which they performed regular professional staff work.[16] Some devoted most of their time to operating as an ordinary professional aide. Others divided their efforts almost equally between performing professional staff duties and acting as a staff director. A few felt that doing any routine professional staff work detracted from their supervisory ability. Hence, wherever possible, they assigned the tasks given them by their committees to the other staff members. On some committees, the position of staff director showed a tendency to undergo a metamorphosis in this respect as the staff grew in size and competency. In such instances, when the staff was understrength, the staff director worked preponderantly as a regular professional aide. Then as the staff acquired additional personnel and experience, he gave proportionately more of his time to serving as the chairman's personal representative and to the other unique functions of his office. However, because of the paramount consideration of keeping every committee staff small, there always will be a need for the staff director to double in brass as an ordinary professional aide on occasion.

Sixthly, to discharge his supervisory duties, the staff director had to keep informed on all the work being done by the rest of the professional staff. Some staff directors required the other professional aides to clear with them any lengthy projects requested by individual Congressmen before undertaking those. Others merely asked their subordinates to keep them apprised of all the assignments the latter were performing for individual members of Congress. A number of staff directors maintained excellent control records from which they could quickly ascertain exactly what each staff member was doing not only for the committee but also for individual Congressmen and the extent of his progress on each project. In addition, a staff director generally attended any interstaff conferences in which his subordinates were participating.

Lastly, the staff director usually consulted with the rest of the professional aides in making assignments and about other major aspects of the committee staff work. Whenever possible, decisions were made in common. However, when the members of a staff failed to agree after canvassing the alternatives thoroughly, the staff director was the final arbiter of matters still in dispute. For he bore the ultimate responsibility for the quality of the output and the performance of the entire professional staff. Exercising this power of final decision was perhaps the most crucial duty of the staff director and one which he could not delegate. Moreover, he had to apply it with great delicacy in order not to deprive himself of the counsel of his professional colleagues on problems confronting the staff but yet to be able to resolve them without inordinate delay.

Strife Between Staff Director and Clerk

From the above survey of their duties, it is not apparent that the chief clerk and professional staff director of a committee would experience much difficulty in delineating their respective spheres of authority. However, after the Legislative Reorganization Act was put into effect, a number of struggles for power between committee clerks and staff directors occurred, resulting frequently in the elimination of one or both of the principals from the staff and sometimes in the consolidation of the two positions. For example, during the 80th Congress, on the Senate Expenditures Committee, E. B. Van Horn, the staff director, and J. H. Macomber, the chief clerk, were almost continually engaged in jurisdictional disputes. Having observed this conflict firsthand from his vantage point as ranking minority member, Senator John McClellan (D.-Ark.) was determined to prevent a recurrence of that sort of situation when he became chairman. Hence, at the outset of the 81st Congress, he combined the two positions and elevated Walter Reynolds, one of the professional aides, to the consolidated post.[17]

Similarly, in the case of committees without a staff director, a comparable state of affairs developed when the committee clerk sought to extend his dominion over the professional staff. After the 80th Congress, the clerks on several committees made unsuccessful attempts to assume direction of the professional staffs. During the 82d Congress, on the House Armed Services Committee, after one of the professional aides had been made chief clerk, he tried to supervise the other professional staff members. Although he did not fully succeed in becoming a *de facto* staff director, his successor, also an erstwhile professional aide to that committee, did complete the process of converting the chief clerkship into the position of chief of staff. And on a few committees, despite the fact that the clerk had not made an overt bid to usurp control over the professional staff members, some of them feared that he might at any time. Hence, they regarded with hostility and suspicion even the most innocent requests from him for information about their work—which he had to have to answer inquiries about committee activities—as a step toward trying to assume direction of them.

What were the reasons for this propensity to conflict between the staff director and the chief clerk or to the analogous development of tension between the professional staff and the chief clerk? A basic cause was the previously-described need for centralized direction of the entire committee staff. Supplementing that was the factor of the personalities of the individuals concerned. When two aggressive and masterful persons occupied the positions of staff director and chief clerk of a committee, competition between them for recognition as head of the staff was almost inevitable. For instance, the internecine struggle between the clerk and staff director of the Senate Expenditures Committee in the 80th Congress was fundamentally the collision of two forceful personalities. Likewise, where there was no staff director and the clerk was a capable and ambitious individual, he was very likely to try to convert his position into that of chief of the committee staff.[18] That was particularly liable to happen where the clerk had previously served as a professional aide to the same committee. Generally in such cases he continued to operate in a quasi-professional capacity. And the temptation to utilize the administrative functions of his new post to assume direction of his professional colleagues was very strong.

Another significant consideration was how long both the clerk and staff director (or other professional aides) had been with the committee. Where the clerk's tenure antedated that of the entire professional staff, it was especially difficult for them to make an amicable division of labor. In such situations, the clerk had been organizing the hearings, drafting the committee reports, and discharging many of the other duties taken over by the professsional staff. And sometimes it was hard for him to relinquish control over those phases of the staff work. On several committees in which there was friction between the clerk and staff director (or other professional aides), the clerk was a carry-over from the pre-Legislative Reorganization Act period.

The members of a committee—particularly the chairman—constituted perhaps the single most important cause of strife between the staff director and chief clerk. For the members of a committee frequently wanted to turn to somebody as boss of the whole staff. Many of them were not aware of the precise distinctions between the administrative management and the substantive aspects of committee staff work. Possibly from chance, they initially called on one rather than the other of the occupants of these two top positions on the staff. Pleased with his work, they continued to rely on him—whether he were clerk or staff director—for everything. Naturally, the staff member they singled out in this fashion was not going to refer them to another employee of the committee—especially his main competitor for recognition as head of the staff— but jumped to do their bidding. Thus, the committee members unwittingly stimulated rivalry between the clerk and staff director and encouraged them to infringe upon each other's domain.

Undoubtedly, the decisive factor in any struggle for power between the clerk and staff director (or other professional aides) was which one received recognition from the chairman as head of the staff. In the aforementioned example on the House Armed Services Committee, the second professional aide to be made chief clerk succeeded in assimilating the duties of staff director to that position where his immediate predecessor had failed to do so, primarily because of receiving such recognition. The chairman had never explicitly stated that the first professional aide transferred to the clerkship would serve in a supervisory capacity over the professional staff; whereas, his successor insisted as a condition of accepting the position that the chairman clarify his status to the other professional aides by announcing that thereafter the clerk would also bear the title "chief counsel" and as such would be their director.

Moreover, the accessibility of the chairman to the staff vitally affected the relations between the clerk and the professional aides to a committee. An excellent illustration in this respect is afforded by the following experience of a committee which for obvious reasons must remain unidentified. During the 80th Congress, when the chairman of that committee was freely available to discuss committee business with any staff member, the clerk did not try to invade the sphere of the professional staff. However, in the 81st Congress, the new chairman was badly incapacitated physically by arthritis. To reduce the staff's demands on his time and energy, the professional aides allowed the clerk to convey most of the information about their work to and from the chairman. Using that conduit role as an excuse, the clerk made a definite effort to assume direction of the professional staff. Here as on other committees, the chief weapon used by the professional aides to contain the clerk's imperialism was renewed insistence upon exercising their privilege of reporting to and receiving their assignments directly from the chairman.

Finally, these factors did not operate in isolation but reinforced one another. In the above instance, the clerk had been on the committee staff for thirty years and apparently resented being divested of many of his duties by the professional aides. However, he made no attempt to achieve dominance over them until the favorable juncture afforded by the chairman's inaccessibility. Conversely, on committees characterized by cordial relations between the staff director and clerk, almost always a combination of propitious circumstances was responsible. For example, on the Senate Foreign Relations Committee the staff director, Dr. Francis Wilcox, joined the staff ahead of the contemporary committee clerk, C. C. O'Day. When Dr. Wilcox was first employed by that committee at the start of the 80th Congress, Chairman Arthur Vandenberg (R.-Mich.) conferred upon him a title, "chief of staff," which indicated that he was head of the entire committee staff. And Chairman Vandenberg's successor, Senator Tom Connally (D.-Tex.), followed the precedent of designating Dr. Wilcox as chief of staff. Similarly, on the Joint Committee on the Economic Report, the professional and clerical components of the staff were established concurrently at its inception in the 80th Congress. Although John Lehman, the clerk, performed some professional staff work and acted as assistant to the staff director, Dr. Grover Ensley, during the 81st and 82d Congresses, he did not covet Dr. Ensley's job but preferred his own where the emphasis was on the administrative management rather than the substantive aspects of the committee staff work. Also, Mr. Lehman and Dr. Ensley were very congenial.

CHAPTER IV

MAJORITY-MINORITY EARMARKING

Lack of Partisanship in Committee Proceedings

Every proposal for earmarking part of each committee staff for the minority must be appraised against the prevailingly nonpartisan operation of most committees. According to the staff members interviewed, there was little—if any—cleavage along party lines or interjection of partisan issues in the proceedings of an overwhelming majority of the committees during the period covered. The *Congressional Record* was replete with testimonials to the same effect from Representatives and Senators.[1] The minority on any measure before those committees almost always comprised both Republicans and Democrats and sometimes included the chairman. Occasionally, minority members even served as chairmen of subcommittees. For example, during the 80th Congress, on the Senate Foreign Relations Committee, Senator Elbert Thomas (D.-Utah) was chairman of the Subcommittee on Treaties of Friendship, Commerce, and Navigation with Italy. In the 81st Congress, Senator Edward Thye (R.-Minn.) was chairman of the Subcommittee on Foot-and-Mouth Disease, Senate Agriculture and Forestry Committee. During the 82d Congress, Senator Robert Hendrickson (R.-N.J.) was chairman of the Subcommittee on Taxation, Senate Select Committee on Small Business. And in both the 80th and 83d Congresses, Senator Harry Byrd (D.-Va.) continued as chairman of the Joint Committee on Reduction of Nonessential Federal Expenditures.

In most cases, this lack of partisanship in the functioning of the committees derives from the nonpartisan nature of the subject matter handled by them. Numerous studies of record votes have revealed that most of the legislation enacted by Congress has received substantial bipartisan support.[2] Moreover, this nonpartisanship permeates our entire governmental process and has deep roots in our polity and society. To a large degree it stems from our federal system and the separation of powers principle incorporated in the structure of our national government. And enduring social phenomena like the "Solid South" contribute to it.[3]

Even on the comparatively few committees that habitually deal with subjects fraught with partisan implications such as taxes, the memberships of those committees often are relatively homogeneous in their views on policy. For example, during the 82d Congress, Senator Robert Kerr (D.-Okla.) was the only professed liberal on the Senate Finance Committee; and his credentials in that regard were somewhat dubious. Although there was more of a distinction along party lines in the House Ways and Means Committee, the ranking members on both sides were very similar in their political orientations, being uniformly conservative.

Access of Minority Members to the Staffs

Similarly, the extent to which the services of the committee staffs are available to the minority committeemen is a highly relevant consideration. During the 82d Congress, on over two-thirds of the standing committees in both houses, the whole staff was accessible to every member of the committee for whatever assistance he might want on any aspect of committee work. A number of chairmen specifically directed the staffs of their committees to serve the majority and minority members without differentiation and publicly promised to correct any failure of the staffs to do so. For instance, during the debate on S. 913 (a bill to establish a Joint Committee on the Budget) in the 82d Congress, Senator John McClellan (D.-Ark.), chairman of the Senate Expenditures Committee, stated:

> My instructions to every member of the staff has [sic] been to serve every member of the committee irrespective of party. Every member of the committee is as free to go to a member of the staff and ask for service as I am.[4]

And Senator Walter George (D.-Ga.), chairman of the Joint Committee on Internal Revenue Taxation, declared in a similar vein:

> . . . anyone on the Republican side of the committee or on the Democratic side of the committee, as well as any Republican Member of the Senate or any Democratic Member of the Senate, can call on the committee for any information he wants, and he will get it. If he does not get it, a single complaint will correct any shortcomings on the part of the staff.[5]

During the 82d Congress, several committee staffs did as much work in the aggregate for the Republican as for the Democratic members of their committees. On the Senate Foreign Relations Committee, the member who made the most use of the staff was a Republican. And on many a committee, only the chairman received more staff assistance than the ranking minority member.

Statutory Basis of the Practice

Legislative history. In S. 2177, 79th Congress, as originally passed by the Senate, the section that ultimately became sec. 202(a) of the Legislative Reorganization Act of 1946 did not contain any provision for apportioning the professional staff of a committee between the chairman and ranking minority member. The phrase "and said staff members shall be assigned to the chairman and ranking minority member of such committee as the committee may deem advisable" first appeared in the House substitute bill in the form of an amendment, which was accepted *in toto* by the Senate because of the exigencies of the parliamentary situation. Hence, in the committee report to accompany S. 2177,[6] there was no explanation of that clause. There was no report to accompany the House bill and no conference report. And there was no discussion of that provision during the debate in either chamber to clarify the legislative intent concerning it.

In S. 2177 the section corresponding to sec. 202(c) of the Act made a fixed allocation of the six clerks authorized for each committee by assigning two to the chairman, two to the ranking minority member, and two to the professional staff. The House bill rendered that provision more flexible by specifying only that the clerks were "to be attached to the office of the chairman, to the ranking minority member, and to the professional staff, as the committee may deem advisable." Both the House and Senate versions of what became sec. 202(c) of the Act significantly omitted the requirement in sec. 202(a) for appointment of the professional staffs "on a permanent basis without regard to political affiliations and solely on the basis of fitness to perform the duties of the office."[7]

Variant interpretations. During the period covered, the committees that earmarked part of their staffs for the minority based that practice upon these somewhat contradictory and ambiguous passages in sec. 202(a) and sec. 202(c). Their interpretations were diverse. Some committees like Senate Agriculture and Forestry allotted part of the clerical staff to the minority but construed the language for selection of the professional staff members on a nonpartisan basis as prohibiting a similar division of the professional staff. Ironically, in that particular instance, the distinction was without a genuine difference; for the assistant clerk, who was the minority representative on that staff, acted in a quasi-professional capacity. Other committees like House Interior and Insular Affairs understood sec. 202 to mean that the minority was entitled to one clerical and one professional staff member. And during the 81st Congress, the Senate Labor and Public Welfare Committee gave the minority two of the professional staff positions as well as the assistant chief clerkship. Moreover, the quota of minority employees for a given committee sometimes fluctuated from

Congress to Congress, depending upon the generosity of the chairmen. For example, upon becoming chairman of the Senate Labor and Public Welfare Committee in the 82d Congress, Senator James Murray (D.-Mont.) reduced the number of regular professional staff members allowed the minority to one.[8]

The uncertainty among the members of Congress themselves about the situation with respect to minority staffing for the committees is revealed in the following colloquy between Senator Robert Taft (R.-Ohio) and Senator Allen Ellender (D.-La.) that occurred during a discussion of the need for additional funds for the Minority Policy Committee staff for fiscal year 1952:

> SENATOR TAFT. If you get a first-class minority legislative expert on the committee, he can do the job for you. But, as a rule, a good many committees do not have anybody particularly assigned to the minority, and there are a good many who have some who are not really experts particularly in the job they are in there for.
>
> Take this minority committee on labor—Schroyer [sic] is an expert on labor. But we also have questions of hospitalization and health, as you know, and also questions on education, of which he does not know anything. So we have one man there who covers labor, but we do not have other things covered.
>
> SENATOR ELLENDER. As a matter of fact, each committee is supposed to have four experts.
>
> SENATOR TAFT. Yes; that is right, and one of them is supposed to be for the minority, I think.
>
> SENATOR ELLENDER. Well, the minority, as I understand it, is supposed to name some of these persons.
>
> SENATOR TAFT. I have one on Labor, and I have one on the Joint Economic Committee. On Finance, there has never been anybody.[9]

Lack of Official Identification of Minority Staff

To compound the confusion, many minority aides to committees did not have their special status indicated by their titles. The Senate committees, in particular, were reluctant to designate officially as such the professional staff members allotted to the minority. In the 80th Congress, the only minority professional aides listed in the semiannual reports on committee employees in the *Congressional Record* were those to the House Education and Labor and House Ways and Means Committees.[10] In the 81st Congress, until June 30, 1949, Serge Benson was called "minority professional assistant" to the Senate Finance Committee.[11] Then for the remainder of the 81st and 82d Congresses, the word "minority" was dropped from his title; and he was listed merely as a "professional staff member."[12] During the 81st and 82d Congresses, the Senate Public Works, House Expenditures, and House Merchant Marine and Fisheries Committees applied minority appellations to their minority professional and clerical aides. And throughout the period covered, the House Committees on Appropriations, the District of Columbia, Education and Labor, Rules, and Ways and Means labelled their minority clerical employees.

Another complication was the lack of consistency about indicating minority staff members even on the same committee. For instance, during the 82d Congress, with one of the largest groups of minority employees of any committee in either house,[13] the Senate Labor and Public Welfare Committee singled out only the minority economist to its Subcommittee on Labor and Labor-Management Relations to be identified officially as working for the minority. Melvin Sneed, minority staff member of its Subcommittee on Health, was called "assistant staff director." During the 81st Congress, when he was on the full committee staff, he and Thomas Shroyer, another minority aide, were listed simply as "professional staff members." And Ray Rodgers, the minority clerk in the 81st and 82d Congresses, was termed just "assistant clerk." During the 83d Congress, his successor assumed the more honorific appellation "minority staff director." However, the remaining minority aides to that committee continued without any official avowal of their minority status.

Because of this absence of distinctive nomenclature for many minority staff members of committees in either chamber, numerous committee aides—including minority employees—did not know who were the minority representatives on the staffs of committees in their own house much less in the other one. And the members of Congress were even less well-informed in that respect. For example, in the above quotation, Senator Robert Taft, then the second-ranking minority member of the Finance Committee, asserted that the Finance Committee had never had a minority professional aide despite the fact that Serge Benson had been serving in that capacity for over two years.

Degree of Minority Affinity

Possibly resulting in part from this circumstance, there was an almost complete lack of special affinity among the minority aides of different committees and sometimes within the same committee during the period covered. When seeking assistance from another committee staff, they generally called on any personal acquaintances they might have on that staff regardless of whether those were minority aides or not. If they did not know any of a committee's employees, they usually asked for the staff member handling the matter on which they desired information or other help. In the 81st and 82d Congresses, even the Minority (Republican) Calendar Committee aide (who was part of the Minority [Republican] Policy Committee staff) did not always deal with the minority representatives on other committee staffs. Sometimes that was because they were so insulated from the rest of those staffs that they did not have the information he sought. But in at least one case, a contributing reason was that the minority staff man in question was an appointee of a Senator from the liberal wing of the Republican Party and consequently the object of greater distrust by the Minority Calendar Committee aide than the staff members appointed by Democratic Senators. Although both the Minority Policy Committee staff and the minority aides to the Labor and Public Welfare Committee were immediately responsible to Senator Robert Taft and presumably reflected his views, there were negligible relations between those two staffs aside from the latter's answering the Minority Calendar Committee aide's queries about bills pertaining to labor.

Similarly, during the 82d Congress, on the House Interior and Insular Affairs Committee, the minority clerk, Nancy Arnold, did not work for the minority professional staff member, William Hackett, but instead one of the other clerks was assigned to assist him. And though Thomas Shroyer, minority aide to the full Committee on Labor and Public Welfare, attended nearly all the hearings of its Subcommittee on Labor and Labor-Management Relations, interrogated some of the witnesses there, and assisted in drafting some of the minority reports, he did not have any contact with the minority economist on the subcommittee staff in connection with that work.

Mode of Selecting Minority Staff Members

Almost invariably, the minority aides to a committee were selected by the ranking minority member. In a very few cases, the chairman insisted that all minority staff members meet certain minimum standards. And in some instances, a committee went through the formality of approving the individuals named by the ranking minority member. Once in a while, the ranking minority member allowed a colleague to choose one of the minority stenographic assistants. However, the ranking minority member always in effect appointed any professional aides and the clerk for the minority. In none of the committees covered did the minority membership act as an entity in selecting the minority staff representatives.

Through the operation of the seniority system, accession to the position of ranking minority member was as much divorced from party control as becoming chairman was. Consequently, sometimes the ranking minority member was from a different wing of his party than most of the other minority members on the committee. In such situations, because of the sharp factional cleavages within each party, the minority aides picked out by him were distrusted by and occasionally their services were totally unacceptable to the latter. For example, during the 81st Congress, since the minority staff members of the Senate Banking and Currency Committee had been appointed by Senator Charles Tobey (R.-N.H.), they were regarded with some suspicion by Senators Homer

Capehart (R.-Ind.), Harry Cain (R.-Wash.), and John Bricker (R.-Ohio), who constituted three of the five minority members of that committee. Likewise, during the 82d Congress, on the Labor and Public Welfare Committee, Senators Wayne Morse (R.-Oreg.)[14] and Irving Ives (R.-N.Y.) would not rely for staff assistance on Thomas Shroyer, Senator Robert Taft's choice for minority professional aide.[15]

Nature of the Minority Staff Function

During the period covered, the nature of the function fulfilled by minority aides on different committees varied widely. In some cases, they were completely integrated into the staff and worked indistinguishably from the other staff members. For example, in the 82d Congress, Nancy Arnold, the minority clerk of the House Interior and Insular Affairs Committee, discharged the same duties as the other assistant clerks. In fact, having been a newspaperwoman and being gifted with a faculty for writing clearly and succinctly, she did most of the summary explanations of bills included in the reports to accompany those prepared by the rest of the clerical staff. And in the 83d Congress, she did not become chief clerk but continued as an assistant clerk. Similarly, William Hackett, the minority professional aide to that committee, served the majority and minority committeemen alike. On the Senate Interstate and Foreign Commerce Committee, the assistant chief clerk, Frank Keenan, did not expect to and did not switch places with the chief clerk upon the change in control that occurred with the 83d Congress. He had not executed any assignments of a partisan character for the minority members of the committee. Further, he had not functioned as an assistant chief clerk at all but instead had acted as an intermediate-grade professional staff member specializing in domestic land and water transportation. In such instances, formal designation or unofficial recognition of certain employees as minority representatives on a committee staff signified merely that they had been selected by the ranking minority member.

However, in other cases, the minority aides to a committee were almost completely insulated from the remainder of the staff and worked principally for the ranking minority member and his like-minded colleagues from both parties. In that type of setup, the minority staff members were under the direction of and responsible only to the ranking minority member. They handled the mail, wrote speeches, and prepared campaign materials besides doing staff work in connection with legislation, investigations, and other committee activities for their exclusive clientele. In the organization of some hearings they monitored the selection of witnesses by the majority staff to ensure that the record would not be loaded in favor of the majority point of view. Occasionally, they negotiated back and forth with the majority staff members over the language to be used in bills or reports to remove their principals' objections. Possibly the best example of this kind of arrangement was afforded by the Senate Labor and Public Welfare Committee staff in the 82d Congress. The majority and minority components of that staff were not only psychologically but also physically a considerable distance apart. The minority aides, Messrs. Rodgers, Shroyer, and Sneed, were isolated in a relatively inaccessible room in the Capitol well-removed from the main committee offices.

Between these two poles of complete integration and virtual insulation, there were many gradations of relationships between the minority employees and the other members of committee staffs. For example, on the Senate Banking and Currency Committee, the assistant clerk and one professional staff member were minority aides. When the control of Congress changed, they switched places with the chief clerk and staff director, becoming the majority staff. The bulk of the remainder of the staff was "nonpartisan." However, the entire staff collaborated in serving the committee as a whole and was accessible to all the members of the committee regardless of their political affiliations. The majority staff members assisted not only minority committeemen whose perspective was congenial with that of the chairman but also those whose viewpoint was diametrically opposed to his. The minority aides did likewise with the majority committeemen. About the only differences between this composite staff and a homogeneously nonpartisan one were: the majority and minority aides occupied positions of special confidence with the chairman and ranking minority member respectively; they would push the program and interests of their principals on their own initiative; they worked for committee members on the other side only upon request; and they were correspondingly not as susceptible to centralized direction as the members of a uniformly nonpartisan staff.

On the Senate Agriculture and Forestry Committee, the chief clerk and assistant chief clerk changed places at the outset of the 81st and 83d Congresses. However, during the 81st and 82d Congresses, there was no minority aspect to the work of the assistant chief [minority] clerk, James Kendall. He assisted committee members of both parties alike. And he continued to prepare bill analyses, organize hearings, and draft reports for the entire committee. In the 81st Congress, he was the only committee aide to accompany the Subcommittee on Foot-and-Mouth Disease to Mexico to inspect the work of the Mexican-United States Joint Commission for the Eradication of Foot-and-Mouth Disease in Mexico.[16]

A curious mutation of the common arrangement for alternating the majority and minority clerks with each change in the control of Congress occurred on the House Agriculture Committee. At the beginning of the 81st Congress, the chief clerk, George Reid, resumed his previous position as secretary on the office staff of the ranking minority member; and the chairman installed his sister and former secretary, Mrs. Mabel Downey, as the chief clerk. Then with the 83d Congress, Mr. Reid once more transferred from the ranking minority member's office force to the post of chief clerk; and Mrs. Downey became the assistant chief clerk. Aside from this rotation of the chief clerkship, the status of the other staff members of the House Agriculture Committee, including minority appointees, was not altered because of the shifts between Democratic and Republican Congresses. Every one of this committee's employees interviewed stressed the completely nonpartisan nature of his work.

In addition, the role of minority staff members varied not only from committee to committee and from Congress to Congress but also might be—and sometimes was—sharply modified within a given committee in the same Congress when the chairmanship changed hands. For example, during the 81st Congress, when Representative John Lesinski (D.-Mich.), a liberal Northern Democrat, was chairman of the House Education and Labor Committee, John Graham, the minority clerk, and his assistant were completely isolated from the rest of the committee staff. The main committee offices were practically foreign territory to Mr. Graham. Whenever he entered them, the majority staff members would turn papers upside down so that he could not see what they were doing. An exaggerated spirit of partisanship extended down through the clerical employees on both sides, with the stenographers shunning each other and arguing about which one would carry materials over to the other. John Forsythe, the general counsel of the committee, conformed to the dominant attitudes of the group and was as insulated from Mr. Graham as the other majority aides were.

After Representative Graham Barden (D.-N.C.), a conservative Southern Democrat, succeeded Mr. Lesinski as chairman during the latter half of the 81st Congress, he replaced the chief clerk and all of the majority professional staff members except Mr. Forsythe, who remained as general counsel, but retained most of the clerical assistants. A dramatic change occurred in the relations between the majority and minority components of the staff. An atmosphere of cooperativeness to the nth degree developed. Harmony prevailed among the erstwhile feuding stenographers. Mr. Graham collaborated with the remainder of the professional staff on almost every major committee undertaking like the investigation of the Wage Stabilization Board during the 82d Congress. On such assignments, Mr. Graham, Mr. Forsythe, and Mr. Derrickson, another professional aide to the committee, worked together as a team in a friendly and indistinguishable fashion. Mr. Graham participated fully in staff field investigations, in planning hearings, in screening witnesses, in formulating questions for Mr. Forsythe to ask, and in drafting the ensuing committee reports. Throughout, he worked on those projects at the direct request and under the supervision of the chairman rather than of the ranking minority member.

Of course, Mr. Graham continued to handle mail, assemble reference materials, and perform other special assignments for minority members both on and off the committee, of which the rest of the staff were not informed. However, this changed orientation of the staff, which reflected the underlying realities of the situation in which a Southern Democratic-Republican coalition controlled the committee, relieved him of a considerable amount of work. For the Republican committeemen could then utilize the bill analyses and other memoranda produced by the entire staff, whereas during the Lesinski regime, Mr. Graham had to prepare all such materials for them by himself. This example and similar experiences on other committees with divided staffs demonstrated that the relations between the minority aides and the other employees of a committee were in a state of unstable equilibrium and readjusted at a new level every time a shift took place in the internal power structure of the committee.

Adventitious Origin of Some Minority Posts

Occasionally, a minority staff position originated largely from accident rather than from partisan necessity. For instance, when the Joint Committee on the Economic Report began to assemble its staff in the spring of 1947, Senator Joseph O'Mahoney (D.-Wyo.), ranking minority member, recommended the appointment of Fred Berquist, who had worked for him on the staff of the TNEC. Accepting the suggestion, Chairman Robert Taft (R.-Ohio) hired Mr. Berquist in March, 1947, but apparently for the main committee staff rather than in a minority capacity. For at the end of the month when he announced the appointment of Mr. Berquist as assistant staff director and of his own choice, Dr. Charles Hardy, as staff director, Senator Taft explicitly stated that neither of them was to be regarded as a representative of either the majority or minority members of the committee.[17] And in his book *Economics in the Public Service,* Dr. Edwin Nourse relates that both these individuals expressed a desire to act as nonpartisan economists and that Chairman Taft and other members of the committee accepted that as an appropriate role for them.[18] As staff director, Dr. Hardy recruited the remainder of the staff.[19] And as assistant staff director, Mr. Berquist served as an employee of the entire committee throughout the 80th Congress.

Meanwhile, operating from the Legislative Reference Service of the Library of Congress where he was carried as a senior specialist in price economics, Dr.

Theodore Kreps, who had also been employed by Senator O'Mahoney on the TNEC staff, became increasingly involved in the activities of the Joint Committee on the Economic Report. From handling requests for individual members on both sides of the committee, he worked more and more for Senator O'Mahoney until he was functioning almost as a *de facto* minority staff member. For example, in March, 1948, he prepared the initial draft of the minority views in the annual report of the committee for 1948.[20] However, Senator O'Mahoney evidently did not contemplate replacing Dr. Hardy with Dr. Kreps as staff director in the event he became chairman. For when the 1948 election returns revealed that the chairmanship of the committee would change hands in the 81st Congress, Senator O'Mahoney wrote Dr. Hardy a letter stating that he desired to have Dr. Hardy remain on as staff director.

Then on November 15, 1948, Dr. Hardy died unexpectedly. No new staff director was named for nine months. Mr. Berquist was given the title "acting staff director," and undoubtedly he expected to be elevated to staff director. The remainder of the staff was continued on intact. And Dr. Kreps was borrowed from the LRS as an "economic consultant" to the committee.[21]

Now there had been a long-standing animosity—if not downright feud— between Dr. Kreps and Mr. Berquist dating from the days when both had served on the staff of the TNEC. It was exacerbated by the uncertainty of the situation with respect to the selection of Dr. Hardy's successor and the competition between them for the favor of Chairman O'Mahoney.[22] In this contest, Dr. Kreps had certain advantages. As a professor of economics at Stanford University, he had a more securely-established professional standing than Mr. Berquist, who had never completed his doctorate. Dr. Kreps possessed a dynamic and engaging personality that inspired the respect and admiration of his like-minded associates. And he was a militant proponent of certain economic views long cherished by Senator O'Mahoney; whereas, Mr. Berquist was somewhat more conservative than Senator O'Mahoney apparently had assumed when sponsoring him for his initial appointment to the staff.

Anyway, in the spring of 1949, Dr. Kreps won out. On June 15, 1949, Senator O'Mahoney appointed Dr. Kreps' choice, Dr. Grover Ensley,[23] as "associate staff director." Creation of that post was necessary to provide supervision of the staff during Dr. Kreps' absence, for he spent only part of each year in Washington, D.C., on leave from Stanford University. In August, 1949, Dr. Kreps was named staff director.[24] Meanwhile, according to Dr. Nourse's account of what took place, Mr. Berquist suggested to Senator Taft that he be designated as "economist for the minority." Consequently, Senator Taft wrote a letter to Chairman O'Mahoney asking that Mr. Berquist be given that status.[25] Thus, the position of minority economist came into being.

Although there were some overtones of differences in the basic economic philosophies of the protagonists in this drama, the root cause of the establishment of this minority staff post was the personal strife between Dr. Kreps and Mr. Berquist. Hence, there was the anomalous result that the individual originally hired by Chairman Taft upon the recommendation of ranking minority member O'Mahoney in the 80th Congress was made minority economist by Chairman O'Mahoney at the request of ranking minority member Taft in the 81st Congress. Further, the rest of the staff appointed while Senator Taft was chairman was carried over intact.[26] Having been on Senator Flanders' office staff, Dr. Ensley was certainly acceptable to the ranking minority members of the committee. And in April, 1951, Dr. Ensley became staff director when Dr. Kreps resumed his status as economic consultant on a per diem basis.[27] During the 81st and 82d Congresses, the economists added to the staff were nonpartisan technicians.[28] And the entire committee staff with the exception of Mr. Berquist was equally available to every member of the committee for whatever assistance he desired in connection with the committee's work.[29] Even after Mr. Berquist had been specially designated to assist the minority membership of the committee, the remainder of the staff continued to serve Senator Taft and other minority members freely, even helping to prepare individual dissents and minority reports.[30]

Consequently, on this committee there was no rational basis for a minority staff position per se. Had it not been for the unfortunate circumstances of Dr. Hardy's death and the feud between Mr. Berquist and Dr. Kreps, the principle of a unified staff for the Joint Committee on the Economic Report would not have been breached.

Dogmas about and Arguments for Earmarking

Against the background of this summary description of the situation with respect to the minority staffing of committees during the period covered, it is appropriate to examine some of the current dogmas about and arguments for allocating committee aides between the majority and minority.

Political nature of clerkship. One generalization frequently made was that the clerkship of a committee was a highly political position. And the corollary was usually added that the chief clerk and assistant chief clerk, therefore, had to trade places when the chairman and ranking minority member did. Firstly, the job of committee clerk was not intrinsically political. Quite the contrary, the administrative management duties which were the province of the chief clerk were susceptible to being more thoroughly divorced from partisanship than the substantive matters handled by the professional staff members. In the preparation of S. 2177 (Legislative Reorganization Act of

1946), 79th Congress, strategic considerations, rather than any allegedly political nature of the clerk's office, dictated omitting the requirement of selecting clerical staff members on a nonpartisan and merit basis. According to Senator Mike Monroney (D.-Okla.), coauthor of the Legislative Reorganization Act, the Joint Committee on the Organization of Congress desired to avoid engendering needless opposition to enactment of that measure by extending standards to the post of committee clerk which automatically would have necessitated supplanting most of the incumbents when the law went into effect. Instead, the Joint Committee left to the discretion of each committee whether or not to retain the extant committee clerks, who were predominantly patronage appointees. Also, since that was the case, the Joint Committee did not want to blanket in as permanent employees any of the less-qualified clerks who might be carried over.[31]

Secondly, the practice of alternating the chief clerk and assistant chief clerk of a committee with each change in the control of Congress was far from universal in either chamber, being more prevalent in the House than in the Senate. With the advent of the 83d Congress, it occurred on only four Senate committees: Agriculture and Forestry, Banking and Currency, Labor and Public Welfare, and Rules and Administration. Six Senate committees retained the same chief clerks: Appropriations, Government Operations, Finance, Foreign Relations, Interstate and Foreign Commerce, and Judiciary. And of the remaining five Senate committees that employed new chief clerks, three kept the same assistant chief clerks: Armed Services, Interior and Insular Affairs, and Public Works. On the House side, the chief clerks and assistant chief clerks swapped jobs on ten committees:[32] Agriculture, Education and Labor, Government Operations, House Administration, Merchant Marine and Fisheries, Public Works, Rules, Un-American Activities, Veterans' Affairs, and Ways and Means. However, six House committees retained the same chief clerks: Appropriations, Armed Services, Banking and Currency, District of Columbia, Foreign Affairs, and Interstate and Foreign Commerce. And though bringing in different chief clerks, two of the three remaining House committees kept the same assistant chief clerks: Judiciary and Post Office and Civil Service.[33]

To ensure access to staff. Proponents of allotting part of a committee staff to the minority members often claimed that such an arrangement was necessary to ensure the latter access to the committee staff. Significantly, to support their contention, they made only vague, unsubstantiated allegations of inability to secure the services of committee aides or indulged in hypothesizing about such contingencies in contrast to the numerous concrete examples to the contrary cited by other Congressmen in the *Congressional Record,* committee hearings, and elsewhere. For instance, in the 82d Congress, during the debate on S. 913

when urging division of the staff of the proposed Joint Committee on the Budget between the majority and the minority, Senator Styles Bridges (R.-N.H.) asserted:

> I have known occasions upon which I have asked members of a staff to help me, and they did not dare to do so. Sometimes I was told that they would have to take the work home and do it on Sunday, because they did not dare to do it in the committee room. Other Senators have faced similar situations. What we want is to have someone upon whom we can count, someone who dares to do what he is asked to do.[34]

And his colleague Senator Ferguson (R.-Mich.) supported him by saying:

> We know from personal experience that on occasion a member of the staff of a committee has advised some member of the minority, and has been criticized by the chairman of the committee for doing so. Let us be realistic about this matter. Do we not find at times that a member of the staff of a committee if he gives advice to a minority member, is criticized in the committee for giving such advice, or for making a suggestion to a witness on the witness stand? . . . The situation which I have described may happen only rarely, but it can happen.[35]

Such occurrences must have been rare indeed within Senator Ferguson's own immediate experience, for about six weeks later on the floor of the Senate he joined Chairman Pat McCarran (D.-Nev.) in lauding the staff of the Senate Judiciary Committee as follows:

> Mr. President, I wish to join in the remarks of the Senator from Nevada, and to say to the Senate that on all occasions the Senator from Michigan, a member of the minority on the Senate Committee on the Judiciary, has received the cooperation of Miss Johnson, Mr. Arens, and Mr. Blair. They have worked tirelessly, and have been of great aid and assistance in perfecting the bill which has been under consideration and which has just been passed by the Senate.[36]

And a little over a month later, he paid the following encomium to the majority staff of the Subcommittee on Defense Department Appropriations, Senate Appropriations Committee:

> I cannot too highly praise the work of the staff of the majority as well as the staff of the minority for the able assistance they rendered to me and to the subcommittee.[37]

To do special jobs. Another argument advanced was that occasionally there were special assignments which the minority members wanted done without the rest of the committee knowing about those. And to handle that sort of project, they needed to have a staff member of their own. In the first place, this line of reasoning disregards the fact that the entire professional staff of a committee was bound by the rule of safeguarding confidential assignments. Secondly, functionalization among the members of a committee staff cut across their status as majority or minority aides. On an earmarked committee staff, there usually was but one professional aide for the minority. Obviously, he could not possibly know the intimate details of all the numerous complicated measures on the committee calendar. Hence, for assistance on bills of a highly technical nature, the minority members of the committee often had to depend on one of the other professional staff members who had specialized in the subject matter concerned. Conversely, except on a committee staff where the minority representative was completely segregated from the other members, he sometimes was the only staff member conversant with certain classes of legislation. For example, during the 82d Congress, on the Senate Banking and Currency Committee, Robert L'Heureux, a minority aide, was the only professional staff member assigned to work on bills relating to slaughter quotas and allocation of livestock.

Since the committeemen of one party had to depend on the representative of the other party on the staff in situations of that sort—which occasionally involved highly controversial issues—the question might well be asked as to why they could not trust him to handle anything within the jurisdiction of the committee. Furthermore, in such cases, the fact that a staff member had a special responsibility to the minority (or majority, as the case might be) would subject his integrity to a greater strain than if he were expected to function as a neutral employee of the whole committee all the time. For he then would suffer to some degree an internal conflict between divided loyalties which otherwise would not exist.

Finally, the contention that the minority members of a committee needed to have their own employees for the performance of jobs which could not be entrusted to the rest of the staff founders on the reef which underlies the surface plausibility of the other arguments for earmarking part of the committee aides for the minority: the deep factional cleavages within each of the major parties. A basic condition which cannot be disregarded or exorcised is that the ideological differences between the liberal and conservative factions within either party were much greater than those between comparable factions of the two parties. During the period covered, one almost had to experience the attitudes of the Tobey-Ives-Morse and the Taft-Millikin-Bridges wings of the Republican Party and of their staff personnel toward each other to appreciate their enmity. The intemperateness of their language in discussing each other matched that of *Pravda* in tone. And the gulf between the New Deal-Fair Deal

Democrats and the conservative Southern Democrats was just as great. Reinforcing the hostility arising from disagreements over specific issues was an emotion akin to the fervor aroused by doctrinal disputes within a religion. Each of the contesting factions within either party regarded themselves as the apostles of the true faith and their opponents as heretics. It was repeatedly demonstrated not only that conservative Southern Democrats would rely on committee aides appointed by conservative Republicans in preference to committee staff members selected by liberal Democrats and that liberal Republicans eschewed the services of committee aides chosen by conservative Republicans but also that conservative Republicans were more prone to trust appointees of liberal Democrats than committee aides selected by their own liberal brethren.

To look after minority interests. The same consideration applies with even greater force to refute the contention that minority staff members were necessary to look after the interests of the minority on the committees. For under no circumstances during the 80th through the 82d Congresses, would a Taft-Republican have deemed a Tobey-Republican employee suitable for that purpose. Nor would a Lehman-Democrat have entrusted that responsibility to a McCarran-Democratic staff member. Moreover, implicit in this argument is an essentially erroneous concept of the role of the committee staff. It is not the function of the committee aides to promote particular policies but rather to facilitate the work of the entire committee by procuring information, by arranging for the services of other elements of the legislative and executive branch staffs, by pointing up relevant factors the committee should take into account when considering certain problems, by incorporating the committee's decisions in bills and reports, and by discharging the manifold other staff duties that conserve on the committee members' time and render less difficult the performance of their vital office. The members of a committee themselves, not the staff, should take care of the majority and minority interests and presumably, as politicians, should be well-qualified to do so.

To achieve continuity. Finally, advocates of apportioning staff members between the majority and minority often asserted that was the only way by which continuity in the committee staffs could be attained. In the first place, this argument ignores the evidence of the numerous nonearmarked staffs of committees like House Interstate and Foreign Commerce or Senate Foreign Relations which continued virtually intact from the 80th through the 82d Congresses. Secondly, only if the professional staff of a committee were evenly divided between the majority and minority could the whole staff survive a change in the control of Congress. In view of the relative workloads and responsibility borne by the majority and minority sides of a committee respectively, such an equal allocation of the professional staff between them would be unrealistic. Furthermore, most of the vigorous proponents of divided staffs openly espoused assigning a larger share of the committee aides to the majority than to the minority. For example, in a statement to the Senate Expenditures Committee in 1951, Senator James Murray (D.-Mont.) made the blanket recommendation that every committee be permitted to hire six professional staff members to be distributed in the ratio of two thirds to the majority and one third to the minority.[38]   And as previously mentioned, on an earmarked staff, generally not to exceed one of the four professional positions was allotted to the minority. Obviously, if one third to one half of the professional aides had to be discharged every time the chairmanships of the committees alternated between the Republicans and the Democrats, little would be left of permanency in the committee staffs.

Conclusion

This brief survey of the theory and practice of earmarking part of the committee aides for the minority leads almost inescapably to the conclusion that it is an undesirable principle of organization which should be avoided wherever possible.   If anything, experience with divided staffs has confirmed the validity of the original intent of the Legislative Reorganization Act to establish nonpartisan committee staffs.   During the period covered, great variety characterized and considerable misunderstanding surrounded the practice of allotting committee aides to the minority.   Sometimes it resulted from chance or from an erroneous interpretation of sec. 202 of the Legislative Reorganization Act.   The best that could be said for it was that in a very few cases it was necessitated by the attitudes of key committee members and of outside groups with whom they dealt.   At the worst, it was a cloak for patronage drives of the Congressmen and was extended to the staffs of committees where there was no justification in fact or logic for doing so.   Fortunately, in the latter instances, the good sense and moderation of the individual employees and the forces exerting an influence toward nonpartisanship in the work of those committees often mitigated some of the attendant disadvantages.   There was ample empirical evidence that most of the arguments advanced for majority-minority earmarking of committee staffs were inconsonant with the political realities of the situations to which they related.

Despite the undesirability of apportioning committee aides between the majority and minority, no attempt should be made to forbid that by law.   For any provisions on staffing must be flexible enough to allow the committees to accommodate their individual needs as they conceive those.   However, adoption of partisan representation on committee staffs where it is unnecessary should not be encouraged by the language of the law either.   As the provisions in sec. 202 of the Legislative Reorganization Act for assigning committee aides to the chairman and ranking minority member have occasionally been misconstrued to cause partition of committee staffs where that was not necessary, those passages might well be repealed.[39] And the enactment of any of the increasingly numerous proposals for mandatory allocation of committee staffs in prescribed ratios between the majority and minority should be vigorously resisted.[40] If the imposition of such statutory obstacles can be averted, the force of example of the advantages enjoyed by the committees with nonearmarked staffs and the dynamics toward nonpartisanship in the operation of the committees should ultimately bring about substantial realization of the Legislative Reorganization Act's goal of nonpartisan, professional staffs for the committees.

CHAPTER V

HIRING AND FIRING

Statutory Requirements

The Legislative Reorganization Act of 1946 makes the following express provision for appointment and dismissal of the professional staffs by the committees:

> SEC. 202. (a) Each standing committee of the Senate and the House of Representatives (other than the Appropriations Committees) is authorized to appoint by a majority vote of the committee not more than four professional staff members in addition to the clerical staffs on a permanent basis without regard to political affiliations and solely on the basis of fitness to perform the duties of the office; . . . Each such committee is further authorized to terminate the services by a majority vote of the committee of any such professional staff member as it may see fit.[1]

Similarly, it stipulates: "The clerical staff of each standing committee, which shall be appointed by a majority vote of the committee, shall consist of not more than six clerks. . . ."[2]

Powers of the Chairman

In view of this specific requirement of action by a majority of the committee, it is difficult to understand how some members of Congress and others could entertain the mistaken idea that the chairman had authority to hire and fire the staff without the consent of the committee. Of course, a committee might delegate that power to the chairman. During the period covered, some committees regularly passed resolutions conferring upon their chairmen authority to hire the staffs. Others by a sort of gentlemen's agreement left the selection of the staffs to the chairmen. However, such grants of power—whether explicit or tacit—could be rescinded at any time. And in at least one instance, a committee did withdraw such authorization from the chairman. At the beginning of the 81st Congress, the House Education and Labor Committee, outraged by Chairman John Lesinski's (D.-Mich.) attempted appointment of ex-Representative Frank Hook as committee counsel, decided to resume its prerogative of selecting replacements to its staff. The committee rejected Frank Hook by a vote of eighteen to seven (which meant that nine Democrats sided with the Republicans against him). Then it established a subcommittee on staffing comprised of Chairman Lesinski, ranking majority member Graham Barden (D.-N.C.), and ranking minority member Samuel McConnell (R.-Pa.) to recommend a nominee for the position of counsel. And it subsequently approved the subcommittee's choice, John Forsythe. After Mr. Barden succeeded Mr. Lesinski as chairman, the committee reverted to its previous practice of allowing the chairman to select the staff. However, this incident dramatically illustrated that this provision of the law was not an empty formality but a potent reserve clause which a majority of any committee could activate whenever it desired.[3]

Ratification by the Committee

Even where a committee delegated authority to the chairman to hire the staff, he often consulted with the senior members on both sides before adding a new employee. Similarly, where staff appointments were subjected to confirmation by the committees, the procedures followed in approving them varied widely. Occasionally, the process was quite perfunctory. In some instances, after having discussed a prospective staff member with the committee, the chairman took silence to mean assent. Of course, in such situations if any objections were raised to a candidate, the chairman usually submitted his appointment to a formal vote by the committee. In others, a slate of employees agreed upon in advance by the chairman and other key committeemen was accorded a largely *pro forma* ratification—customarily by unanimous consent. However, in many cases a committee seriously deliberated on the qualifications of nominees for staff positions before passing upon them. And in a few instances, the chairman or staffing subcommittee presented the names of the two or three top-ranking applicants to the committee, which then actually made the final choice among them by a majority vote.

Modes of Recruitment

By various committeemen. The methods of recruiting committee employees were very diverse. On some committees, individual members were allowed to name the appointees to particular staff positions. As previously mentioned, the ranking minority members usually picked any minority aides. Some committees parcelled out the selection of all their employees among their influential members.[4] Many subcommittees followed this practice in choosing their specially-authorized staffs. Occasionally, as the price of securing a special staff for a subcommittee, the chairman had to promise to allocate a

staff position to the chairman of the parent committee as well as one or more to the ranking minority members of both units.

Some very capable staff members were obtained through this mode of procurement. Nevertheless, any committee staff selected in this fashion was invariably conglomerate and nearly always of mixed quality. More importantly, this procedure was not conducive to staff discipline and efficiency. As long as his sponsor was on the committee, an employee was practically irremovable and could be very unsubmissive to control by the staff director or by other staff members whom he might be assigned to assist. Although a more or less satisfactory *modus operandi* generally was worked out under such conditions, there were several rather extreme cases where professional aides almost had to implore their clerical assistants, who were the patronage of powerful committee members, to get routine stenographic tasks done and frequently had their requests ignored with impunity.

Hence, this manner of choosing staff members was the least desirable of all those followed by the committees. Although probably no statutory prohibition of such "subcontracting out" of staff appointments could ever gain acceptance or be successfully enforced, numerous chairmen prevented adoption of the practice by their committees. And encouragingly, a few committees abandoned the procedure in favor of better methods of recruitment.

By the chairman. By far the most prevalent practice was for the chairman to recruit the entire staff. In an effort to secure nonpartisan employees, a number of chairmen habitually cleared all appointments with the ranking minority members of their committees. This was more than a gesture. On several committees where this procedure was followed, professional aides said that they had had at least one and sometimes a series of interviews with the ranking minority member in which he had subjected them to a searching inquiry as to their educational backgrounds, experience, and other qualifications before giving them his approval. And in a few cases, the chairman would discuss the top two or three candidates for a post with the ranking minority member, and the latter would assist in making the choice among them.

By staffing subcommittees. Going one step further, some committees institutionalized minority participation in the recruitment process by establishing subcommittees on staffing. Often they consisted of the chairman, ranking majority member, and ranking minority member. Occasionally, they included additional senior committeemen from both sides for a total of as many as nine members. In a few instances, staffing subcommittees contained neither the chairman nor the ranking minority member but were comprised of several majority and minority members of intermediate rank. This latter arrangement ensured the acceptability of the staff to a cross section of the committee as a

VERNON REGIONAL
JUNIOR COLLEGE LIBRARY

whole and protected the chairman from the imputation of having dominated its selection. Some committees resorted to staffing subcommittees only under unusual circumstances as in the aforementioned dispute over Chairman Lesinski's attempt to hire Frank Hook as counsel of the House Education and Labor Committee. Others habitually used them. Most committees appointed them on an *ad hoc* basis when additions were to be made to their staffs. But some like the House Armed Services Committee utilized a standing subcommittee for that purpose. Also, normally a staffing subcommittee merely screened the applicants and recommended appointees to the full committee for ratification. In a few instances, however, a staffing subcommittee was delegated the actual power of appointment.

Role of staff director. Whether the chairman or a subcommittee on staffing was primarily responsible for the recruitment of a committee's employees, the staff director (if there were one) usually played a large role in the process. Generally, the chairman had the staff director handle the initial phases of recruiting: screening the applicants in accordance with standards prescribed by the chairman, preparing any job descriptions, designing the questionnaires or other forms used, and taking care of related administrative details. Likewise, a staffing subcommittee usually consulted closely with the staff director at every stage of the proceedings. Moreover, on many specially-authorized subcommittees and a number of standing committees, the staff director was given a relatively free hand in selecting his subordinates. He hired the remainder of the staff subject to the approval of the chairman and sometimes of the ranking minority member. In most cases of that sort, the chairman and ranking minority member rarely rejected his recommendations of persons whose qualifications were obvious. In a few instances, individuals insisted upon being granted the right to hire the remainder of the staff as a condition of accepting the post of staff director. And where a staff director did not receive such authority, he often was given a veto power over appointments to the staff.

Clerk's contribution. On some committees, the chief clerk performed an analogous function in recruiting the clerical staff members. Occasionally, he selected them subject to approval by the chairman and/or the committee. Normally where a staff director was delegated authority to hire the staff, he picked out both the professional and clerical aides. However, sometimes he in turn allowed the chief clerk the main say-so in choosing the clerical employees. Occasionally where the chief clerk served in a quasi-professional capacity, the staff director consulted him about applicants for professional staff positions. On a few committees, the staff director integrated the rest of the staff into the recruitment process. In such cases, he generally introduced a prospective appointee to the other staff members individually and then sought their reaction to him. As a regular practice on one committee, the staff director had the leading candidates for a position meet with the assembled staff and let the present employees determine which one of those should be hired. Naturally, that procedure conduced to a high degree of compatibility between new increments to and the remainder of the staff.

Nonpartisanship in Selection

A gratifying number of the committees honestly endeavored to carry out the intent of the Legislative Reorganization Act that professional staff members be selected on a nonpartisan and merit basis. Many of them scrupulously avoided inquiring about the nominal political affiliations of candidates for staff posts and still did not know whether most of their employees were Republicans or Democrats.[5] Of course, some did explore in general terms the personal economic and political philosophies of applicants by asking such questions as: "What meaning they poured into an abstraction like the 'public interest?'" or "Whether they adhered to the mechanistic or the 'sociological jurisprudence' concept of the law?" Such action would seem not only unobjectionable but in accordance with the best practices of personnel administration.[6] For that sort of information would indicate whether a candidate possessed the requisite perspective to be able to accommodate himself to the policy benchmarks of the committee or not. And the intensity with which he espoused his views would afford a good clue to the nature of his temperament and personality, those all important determinants of his ability to work with the committee.

Steps in the Recruiting Process

Whether operating principally through the chairman, a staffing subcommittee, or the staff director in the preliminary phases of recruitment, many committees made a thoroughgoing effort to secure highly-qualified professional staffs. Some of the steps commonly taken by them in the recruiting process are described below.

Formulating standards. Before starting to search for competent professional aides, a number of these committees formulated general standards of experience, training, and capacity by which to judge the candidates. For example, the Senate Armed Services Committee wanted individuals who had held a series of high-ranking positions in the military forces and who were mature without being fuddy-duddies. The Senate Foreign Relations Committee sought generalists in the field of international relations with a Ph.D. degree or its equivalent in educational preparation and experience. The Senate Permanent Subcommittee on Investigations endeavored to get lawyers and accountants with extensive investigative experience—preferably in the FBI.[7] The House Interstate and Foreign Commerce Committee wanted staff members whose combined background of experience would cover the whole area of its jurisdiction but who were not excessively specialized. The Joint Committee on the Economic Report sought competent and objective economists from the outset and later added the qualification that they have certain specialties helpful in preparing its annual report.[8] Although it did not specifically require appointees to possess a doctorate, most of its professional staff members were Ph.D.'s as was the case with the Foreign Relations and Foreign Affairs Committees. With the exception of the statistical analysts on its staff, the Joint Committee on Internal Revenue Taxation followed the general rule of hiring lawyers and economists who were not specialists in particular areas of taxation.

Almost all these committees assigned considerable weight to the personality and temperament of the candidates. Particularly averse to crusaders, they sought individuals who would adopt a client-counsel attitude to serve willingly committee members of every political persuasion. Also, they especially looked for candidates possessing in generous measure the qualities of discretion, diligence, ability to work well under pressure, facility of expression both written and oral, a faculty for getting along well with diverse types of people, and an interest in making a career of committee staff work.

The committees rarely enunciated such criteria in the form of a written job specification. However, a few did outline staff duties and responsibilities in letters or memoranda that amounted to job descriptions, which they used to acquaint prospective applicants with the nature of the work and sent to a candidate's references as a guide in assessing his qualifications for the position in question.

Securing candidates. Most committees maintained a file of applicants for staff jobs. Whenever persons came around seeking employment with the committee, the clerk usually asked them to leave a resume of their educational and experience backgrounds. In most instances, there was no dearth of candidates. For example, at the beginning of the 80th Congress, the Senate Banking and Currency Committee alone had over 600 people apply for positions on its professional staff. Further, whenever the word got out that a committee was contemplating filling a vacancy in its staff—and such news would spread very rapidly—it received numerous additional applications. Hence, most committees customarily began their search for suitable candidates by going through the list of names in their personnel files. In some cases, because of the many high-caliber applicants available there, a committee did not deem it necessary to go outside that source. In others, where the files did not yield any especially promising candidates or the committees wished to broaden the recruitment base, the chairman or staff director resorted to personal acquaintances and other people in a position to know of qualified individuals. They asked administrators and technicians in the fields concerned on the staffs of major universities, of executive agencies, of the Library of Congress, of other committees, of private research organizations, and of interest groups to suggest likely prospects. Occasionally, they requested a professional association like the American Bar Association to submit a list of suitable candidates for staff posts to be filled with practitioners of that profession. And once in a while, they inserted a notice in the house organ of a group like the Society of Former Special Agents of the FBI that the committee was looking for trained investigators at a salary of $6,000 to $7,000 yearly—usually with a prompt and overwhelming response.

Requesting references. Ordinarily, committees asked applicants to give the names of several references who could appraise their qualifications from first-hand knowledge as their immediate superiors in the military service or in civilian employment. A few committee staffs prepared questionnaires covering the points on which information was sought from the references. Some of those were very well-designed. In accordance with the best principles of personnel management, each question was accompanied by a rating scale consisting of a series of statements setting forth various degrees of the trait being evaluated rather than of such ambiguous adjectives as satisfactory, very good, excellent, and superior.

Competitive examinations. During the 81st and 82d Congresses, the House Ways and Means Committee required applicants for stenographic jobs to take a competitive examination of a performance type administered by the chief clerk. None of the committees subjected candidates for professional staff positions to any sort of written achievement or aptitude tests. However, some of the committees requested applicants to submit samples of their published writings. Evaluation of those together with the other information on a candidate supplied by him, derived from his references, and gained during personal interviews by the committee and its staff constituted the main elements of an unassembled examination—which was the kind habitually used in selecting on a competitive basis employees of a comparable grade level in the classified service of the executive branch.

Interviewing. Because of the crucial importance of their temperaments and personalities, candidates for positions on the staff of a committee almost invariably where subjected to successive layers of interviews by the committee and its aides. After eliminating the obviously unfit through examination of their education and experience statements, the staff director and/or clerk screened the remaining applicants in interviews. If there were a staffing subcommittee, it interviewed the most promising candidates, and the chairman always did. Sometimes before approving an individual recommended by the staffing subcommittee or chairman, the entire committee met with the prospect to look him over. In this connection, a number of staff directors commented upon the almost uncanny ability of the members of their committees to "size up" persons accurately in a minimum time.

An Illustrative Case

In selecting two professional aides at the outset of the 82d Congress, the House Foreign Affairs Committee followed an excellent course which exemplified most of these steps in the recruiting process. It appointed a subcommittee on staffing composed of Representatives Mike Mansfield (D.-Mont.), chairman, Thomas Morgan (D.-Pa.), Laurie Battle (D.-Ala.), John Vorys (R.-Ohio), and Lawrence Smith (R.-Wis.). This subcommittee met on January 29, 1951, to plan its program. Pursuant to that, it mailed a request to every applicant for a sample of his writings and the names of five references. Then it sent to each reference a special questionnaire with a covering letter that described the position to be filled. And it invited all nearby applicants to appear before it for brief interviews.

At meetings on January 31 and February 19, 1951, the subcommittee interviewed nineteen candidates. Out of a total of thirty-three applications, it processed twenty-four. Nine aspirants either withdrew their applications or failed to answer the subcommittee's letters. On the basis of the personal interviews, returns from the questionnaires, and other data in its files, the subcommittee narrowed the field down to the four best-qualified candidates. In its last meeting on March 2, 1951, after further careful deliberation, the subcommittee made its final choice among these four. It unanimously voted to recommend the immediate appointment of Dr. Roy Bullock and the appointment of Dr. Albert Westphal "as soon as he is available and a place on the staff is available."[9] The full committee approved the recommendations made by the subcommittee. Throughout, the staff administrator worked very closely with the subcommittee and was in complete agreement with its conclusions. The validity of the process of selection and the skill with which it was applied was attested by the widely-recognized excellence of the House Foreign Affairs Committee staff.

De Facto Probationary Appointments

Inasmuch as no techniques of recruitment were infallible and the congressional environment was relatively unique, the only accurate measure of an individual's suitability for committee staff work was the pragmatic test of how he actually performed on the job. The principle incorporated in the Legislative Reorganization Act that there should be but a small number of highly-qualified professional aides for each standing committee was eminently sound. However, in attempting to ensure its observance, the Act prescribed a minimum salary for the professional staff positions that precluded the committees from filling any of those at the junior or intermediate grade level. As a result, the committees generally did not have an opportunity to try out professional aides in less responsible capacities before advancing them to the top rank or to make provision for training replacements. Further, because one to two years of experience on the "Hill" was required before an employee could become fully productive, it was very difficult to use probationary periods of any reasonable length.

In a few instances, however, an alternative means of checking a prospective staff member's performance on the job and of enabling him to serve a sort of apprenticeship was accidentally afforded by specially-authorized subcommittee staffs. When the liquidation of a special subcommittee staff and a vacancy on the full committee's staff occurred at approximately the same time, the committee had a chance to retain staff members whose abilities it had been able to appraise under actual working conditions. For example, during the 82d Congress, the Senate Expenditures Committee assimilated into its regular staff the counsel of its defunct Subcommittee on Relations with International Organizations. Similarly, the Joint Committee on the Economic Report kept a research assistant from the staff of its Subcommittee on Low-Income Families after the latter had gone out of existence. Although not the result of deliberate design in either case, the individual's employment on a special subcommittee staff fulfilled the function of a probationary appointment.

Effect of Salary Level

During hearings before the Senate Expenditures Committee in June, 1951, the chief of staff of the Senate Foreign Relations Committee testified that the present salary limitations in the law prevented recruiting the caliber professional aides he felt the committees of Congress should have.[10] However, provided that appropriate adjustments would be made for any major rises in the cost of living, most of the professional staff members interviewed considered the existing salary levels adequate to attract and retain the type of personnel contemplated in the Legislative Reorganization Act.[11] And they were rather philosophically resigned to the fact that an increase in congressional pay would be prerequisite to any sizable raise for them. Although the salary ranges authorized by law for the committee aides did not present any serious obstacle to securing qualified employees, sometimes the action of a chairman in fixing their compensation within those limits did. For instance, during the 81st and 82d Congresses, one parsimonious chairman of a House committee restricted the salaries of the staff well below the average paid by the other committees. His niggardliness resulted in a very high turnover in the committee employees and posed a severe problem in recruiting. At one time because of the low pay scale and other adverse working conditions arbitrarily imposed by the chairman, the chief clerk had to fill a vacancy in the clerical staff on an average of once every two months. And recruiting a professional aide then was largely a matter of finding a qualified person who would accept the salary allowed by the chairman. Fortunately, that situation was rectified with a change in chairmen.

Security Checks

During the post-World War II effort to discover and eliminate Communist infiltration of governmental agencies, the charges were frequently made that in the late 30's and early 40's a number of Communists and confirmed fellow travelers had been on the staffs of committees of Congress.[12] Prior to the 83d Congress, there was no provision for loyalty checks on congressional employees on a Senate-wide or House-wide basis. Each committee was a law unto itself in the safeguards it adopted against employing security risks. As a standard operating procedure, some committees like House Un-American Activities and House Foreign Affairs obtained an FBI report on all applicants before hiring them. Other committees used ex-FBI agents on their staffs to investigate every prospective employee for any interest in subversive organizations and for other indications of untrustworthiness securitywise.[13] And some committees apparently had taken few, if any, precautionary measures of that sort.

On March 6, 1953, the Senate passed Senate Resolution 16, which provided for a mild form of security check on all Senate employees.[14] It did not require any kind of clearance of senatorial staff personnel as a condition either of their appointment or of their continued employment. Also, under its terms, full field investigations by the FBI like those conducted into the backgrounds of persons in sensitive positions in the executive branch were not contemplated nor considered necessary. The resolution provided only for a name check with the FBI on present and prospective members of the senatorial staff. If the FBI reported that there were any adverse information on a senatorial aide in its possession, the action to be taken to clarify the loyalty and reliability for security purposes of that person was left entirely to the discretion of the Senator, committee, or Senate official, as the case might be, who had appointed him.[15]

Termination of Services

As was the case with the procedure prescribed for hiring professional aides, the provision for dismissing them by a majority vote of the committee was variously observed. On some committees, the chairmen customarily submitted the question of removing a professional staff member to a vote by the committee. But on many committees, the chairmen exercised virtually unfettered power to discharge committee employees. Often in such situations, the only effective check on a chairman was the understandings he had with the sponsors of particular staff members about retaining them. However, for the most part, chairmen displayed commendable self-restraint in removing professional aides. Generally, where their predecessors had made an honest attempt to appoint the staffs on a nonpartisan, merit basis and where the staff members had conducted themselves accordingly, the chairmen did not displace them for political reasons.

Conclusion

The present provision of the law for hiring committee staffs has proved admirably suited to the diverse needs of the committees. Under it during the period covered, the committees could, and some did, adopt refined processes of recruitment in accordance with sound principles of personnel administration. Three of the methods of recruiting followed were better than the others because they were more conducive to a homogeneous staff with a high degree of control, continuity of tenure, and willingness to serve all members of the committee alike. In descending order of their efficacy in this respect, they were: (1) delegation of authority to the staff director to choose the remainder of the staff subject to the approval of the chairman and/or committee; (2) use of a staffing subcommittee in conjunction with the staff director; and (3) clearance by the chairman of all prospective appointees with the ranking minority member. However, procedure as such should not be overemphasized. The important thing was the desire to obtain a qualified staff. Where a committee genuinely wanted to do that, it usually succeeded even when handicapped by faulty practices such as the allocation of staff positions among the committeemen. Also, recruiting and selecting staffs was not too great a burden on the committees. In the case of those that procured good staffs initially, the rate of attrition was very low, often necessitating the hiring of but one or two replacements in several Congresses.

Although not a major problem, the present statutory authorization for the chairman to fix the salaries of the committee staff members[16] confers upon him leverage over them apparently not contemplated in the other provisions on staffing in the Legislative Reorganization Act. At least it is not consistent with the philosophy of that measure which vests ultimate control over committee operation in a majority of the membership rather than in the chairman. Hence, some thought might be devoted to amending sec. 202(e) so that the annual compensation of the staff members would be determined by a majority vote of the committee. This would place control over the salaries on the same footing as that over hiring and firing the staff. And correspondingly it would afford a safeguard against their manipulation by the chairman for coercive purposes.

Finally, if the members of Congress are to be entrusted with deciding the many crucial substantive issues in their legislative and other work, they certainly should be capable of picking out competent committee aides—especially since they are generally acknowledged to be shrewd judges of men. Further, where Congressmen have disregarded the standards and procedures now stipulated in the law, they could with as great facility ignore any others that might be prescribed. For such requirements are exceedingly difficult, if not impossible, to enforce against them—particularly since they can always pass special resolutions exempting themselves from provisions of the law in specific cases. Hence, the primary reliance for attaining the staffing goals of the Legislative Reorganization Act must remain on gaining voluntary acceptance of them by the members of Congress. In this connection, undue significance should not be attached to the instances of poor staffing—which outside observers frequently have exaggerated by the use of defective criteria—but rather the encouraging number of committees that have honestly endeavored to comply with the intent of the Legislative Reorganization Act should be noted. The exhortatory language about selecting professional aides on a merit basis has exerted considerable influence on the conduct of many committees. Moreover, their need for capable staff assistance is so great that they cannot afford to employ incompetents with the amount of funds normally allowed them. In the long run, these factors plus the force of example of the well-staffed committees should result in raising the quality of the committee staffs to a uniformly high level.

Proposal for an Office of Congressional Personnel

As brought to the floor of the Senate, S. 2177 (the Legislative Reorganization Act), 79th Congress, contained a provision requiring the participation of a proposed Director of Congressional Personnel in the selection of the committee staffs. It provided for the creation of an Office of Congressional Personnel to be headed by a director, who was to be appointed by the majority and minority leaders of the Senate and House acting jointly. And it stipulated that no person was to be appointed to the staff of any committee in either house unless recommended by the director and certified by him to be qualified.[17] This feature was eliminated in the Senate and not included in the House substitute bill.

Unfortunately, the circumstances surrounding this action beclouded the basic issues involved. The move to delete this provision was led by several Southern Democratic committee chairmen. Because of the extravagant language some of them employed and because of their status, their opposition was easily stigmatized as being capricious and patronage-minded.[18] Nevertheless, there was considerable validity in some of their criticisms of the proposed scheme for a congressional personnel director. It was poorly conceived in a number of respects, containing several unresolved problems about such important matters as how the director could be dismissed.[19] It gave the director a veto power over appointments to the committee staffs. There is a legitimate doubt that such control over the selection of their staffs should be vested in an employee of Congress who would be no more directly responsible to the various committees than the proposed personnel director would have been. To do so would be to risk structuring a dangerous element of unresponsiveness into the committee staffs. This arrangement would have reduced by an indeterminate amount the ability of the committees to hold their staffs immediately accountable through the unrestricted power of dismissal. In that respect, it is subject to the objections against any attempt to strengthen the external safeguards of tenure for the committee aides.[20]

Exploring the merits of this proposal in detail would not seem warranted because it was a dead issue during the period covered and probably will remain so indefinitely in view of the widespread aversion to it, especially among the leadership, in Congress. However, there are reasonable grounds for believing that this provision for using a personnel director as a primary means of guaranteeing the quality and tenure of the committee staffs not only was politically infeasible but also was of dubious desirability. In rejecting it and substituting the method of appointment by a majority of each committee, Congress acted wisely. Under the present system, the objective of separating the committee staffs from the chairmen's office forces can be—and to a large extent has been—achieved. And the committees can obtain as good staffs on a merit basis without incurring the dangers inherent in vesting such control over their selection in a congressional personnel director.

CHAPTER VI

QUALIFICATIONS OF COMMITTEE AIDES

Educational Attainments

Of the fifty-eight committee staff members interviewed,[1] six were strictly clerical employees. Although nine of the others bore the nominal designation of clerical staff, they actually functioned part or full time as professional staff members. Of this roughly representative sample of fifty-two professional aides to committees in the 82d Congress, forty-four had B.A.'s or B.S.'s; thirteen, M.A.'s or M.S.'s; twenty-two, LL.B.'s; three, LL.M.'s; eight, Ph.D.'s; and one, a J.S.D. Two professional aides, E. R. Jelsma and Dr. Grover Ensley, possessed two master's degrees apiece. Dr. Francis Wilcox had two doctor's degrees. And two others with their doctorate, Dr. Ray Rodgers and Dr. Carl Marcy, also had LL.B.'s. In addition, five had taken some college courses but had not completed the requirements for a bachelor's degree; two had studied law, one of whom had qualified for the bar, without receiving an LL.B.; and nine had done some graduate work beyond their highest degrees. Nine of the B.A.'s or B.S.'s were in economics; eight, in political science; four, in business administration; two, in engineering; two, in history; two, in journalism; one each in classics, geology, liberal arts, military science, philosophy, and sociology; and eleven were unspecified. Seven of the M.A.'s or M.S.'s were in political science; three, in economics; three, in business administration; one, in history; and one in Romance languages. Four of the Ph.D.'s were in political science; and four were in economics.

Experience Backgrounds

Thirty-two of these professional staff members had been employed in the executive branch;[2] twenty-six, in the same general field as their committee work. Sixteen had been on the staff of more than one administrative agency. Eleven had had more than six years of experience in the administrative establishment. And employment in the executive branch had constituted the principal previous occupation of seventeen. Twenty-five had had prior congressional staff experience. Fourteen of those had served on the office staffs of members of Congress, seven of whom were chairmen of the committees by which they were employed. Seven had worked for Senators; six, for Representatives; and one, for both a Senator and a Representative. Five had been on the office force of more than one Senator or Representative. Nine had served on the staffs of other committees; two, on the staffs of committees in both houses. Three had been employees of the LRS, and one had been an assistant counsel in the Office of the Senate Legislative Counsel. Eighteen had spent more than six years as members of the congressional staff. And working on the "Hill" had been the primary vocation of nine before occupying their present positions. Three had been employees of the judiciary. One of those had been clerk to a U.S. District Court; another, law secretary to a U.S. District Court judge; and the third, a court reporter and research assistant to a circuit court judge.

Eleven had had experience as state and local government employees. One had been on the staff of a state legislature. All eleven had worked in different capacities for state and local administrative agencies. One had been a city manager; another, an assistant city manager. Three had been in state and county treasurers' offices. One had been a state director of finance. And two had been staff members of municipal research bureaus. Working for state or local units of government had previously been the chief pursuit of three.

Seven had been newspapermen. Two of them had subsequently gone into public relations work. Ten had been practicing lawyers. Ten had held responsible positions in private business concerns. Two of them had had their own businesses. Three had been accountants. One had been an office manager, and one had been a secretary. Three had been employed by more than one business firm. And working for private business concerns had constituted the principal previous occupation of one. Thirteen had taught in college or law school, and one had taught in junior college and high school. Seven continued part-time teaching in local universities while on the committee staffs. Seven had been members of college faculties for more than six years. And the primary prior vocation of seven had consisted of teaching at the university level. Three had been on the staffs of private research organizations. Three had been employees of organized interest groups. Two had been on the Hoover Commission staff. One was a retired major general in the U.S. Army, and one was an ex-Congressman.[3]

Appraisal of Training

From the above survey it is evident that the educational qualifications of these professional aides to committees in the 82d Congress compared favorably with those of corresponding employees in the executive branch or in other segments of the congressional staff—even in a scholarly organization like the

Legislative Reference Service which encouraged formal academic accomplishments by awarding points in its promotional system for each advanced degree or year of graduate work completed. For example, during the 82d Congress in the LRS, although most of them had taken additional graduate courses beyond their highest degrees, one third of the nonlegal analysts in grades GS-12 and GS-13 who were not section chiefs had only a B.A. or B.S.; and less than a fourth were Ph.D.'s.[4]

The recipient of a college education is presumed to have a certain level of intellectual ability and training. However, too much significance should not be attached to the major field in which he took his degree. To do so ignores the versatility of the average college graduate. In a number of cases during the period covered, the subjects in which committee staff members had majored as undergraduates were not very relevant to their duties. For example, the chief counsel of the House Armed Services Committee had majored in geology for his B.S.; whereas, the professional aide to the Senate Interior and Insular Affairs Committee who handled matters pertaining to mineral resources and tidelands oil—and who might, therefore, have been expected to be a geologist—had taken his A.B. in the classics. Similarly, the specialist in air transportation on the staff of the Senate Interstate and Foreign Commerce Committee had majored in philosophy as an undergraduate. And, of course, exaggerated emphasis should not be placed on the possession of academic degrees. During the 82d Congress, two committee staff directors—one in the House and the other in the Senate—generally acknowledged to be highly competent did not have even a B.A.; and one of them had no college training at all.

Beyond the bachelor degree level, each additional increment of graduate study decreases in value as compared with the equivalent amount of on-the-job experience. For committee aides are concerned primarily with utilizing the research findings of others rather than with doing lengthy research projects themselves. Among the different types of graduate training, those leading to degrees such as the M.I.A. which lay stress on broad preparation for staff and managerial posts in government or business are more adapted to the peculiar needs of committee staff work than those culminating in a regular M.A. or Ph.D. degree with their more intensive specialization and emphasis on original research.

A legal education is advantageous for a committee aide. Most importantly, it inculcates him with a propensity to adopt a client-counsel attitude. It equips him to be a generalist.[5] It is helpful in preparing bill analyses, briefs, opinions, and other legal memoranda. It is almost a prerequisite to acquiring skill in the art of bill drafting. It facilitates learning parliamentary procedure with its analogous paraphernalia of precedents, rulings, and maneuvers. It is very useful in handling casework and other kinds of legislative oversight duties involving technical points of law. Being of the same profession and knowing the vocabulary and mindset of legal practitioners is an asset in dealing with the large number of congressional liaison officials from the executive agencies and from organized interest groups that are lawyers. The committees operate in a legal context. Many of the measures with which they deal relate to modifying the effects of administrative or judicial interpretation of statutes rather than to abstract principles of economics or of political science. Moreover, with the increasing reliance of the courts on the committee reports to accompany bills and on the record of the hearings as well as of the floor debate in construing the resulting legislation, the need for checking the legal implications of those grows correspondingly. A number of committee aides—including several graduate economists—expressed a feeling of inadequacy because of a lack of legal training. And an ex-employee of the Joint Committee on Internal Revenue Taxation, Dr. E. E. Oakes, said that had he decided to remain in committee staff work as a permanent career, he would have deemed it imperative to acquire a law degree not only for the technical training and background knowledge he would derive thereby but also to afford him the status to deal with the legal staffs of the agencies.[6]

For personnel on special investigating staffs or for standing committee aides who handle budgetary and fiscal measures, educational preparation in accounting is useful. Also, training as an accountant conduces to the adoption of a client-counsel attitude. Several of the committee aides interviewed had the very propitious combination of an undergraduate major in accounting and a law degree. Another advantageous union of specialties is that of law and journalism. Three of the professional staff members interviewed had both an LL.B. and either extensive experience as newspapermen or a degree in journalism.

Value of Previous Employment

Obviously, previous congressional staff experience is very valuable to a committee aide. It familiarizes him with the unique environment on the "Hill." From working on the staff of a Congressman or of another committee, he acquires an understanding of the legislative process—particularly of the importance of the strategy and tactics followed, both on and off the floor of Congress, in effecting the defeat or passage of a measure. He gains an appreciation of the political factors that members of Congress have to take into account in performing their special function and learns the other items comprehended in the term "political savvy." He discovers procedural and mechanical devices like annotated conference committee prints that facilitate the Congressmen's consideration of complex measures. He becomes acquainted with the central staff agencies like the Office of the Legislative Counsel, the LRS, and the House Coordinator of Information and with the other facilities—both official and unofficial—available to the committee staffs, their capabilities, and how to utilize them most effectively.

In numerous instances, employment in some other segment of the congressional staff had contributed to a committee aide's knowledge of the subject matter he handled, acquainted the committee members with his abilities, or conduced to his obtaining a position with the committee in other ways. For example, for four years prior to becoming counsel to the Senate Agriculture and Forestry Committee, Harker Stanton had specialized in drafting agricultural legislation in the Office of the Senate Legislative Counsel. While they were senior specialists in international affairs in the LRS, both Dr. Francis Wilcox and Dr. Thorsten Kalijarvi, professional aides to the Senate Foreign Relations Committee, performed many assignments for and were detailed part or full time to that committee. And as previously mentioned, service on specially-authorized subcommittee staffs led to subsequent employment by the parent committees for several individuals.

Similarly, prior employment in the executive branch conferred many advantages on a committee aide. Firstly, it often had been a primary source of his substantive knowledge of his specialty on the committee staff. As noted above, eighty per cent of the professional aides interviewed with previous experience in administrative agencies had been working in the same general field as their principal committee staff assignments. For instance, in the 82d Congress, James Carr, consultant on irrigation and reclamation to the House Interior and Insular Affairs Committee, had been a career employee in the Bureau of Reclamation for fifteen years; Herman Loeffler, Senate Expenditures Committee staff specialist on budgetary and fiscal legislation, had served eleven years in the Bureau of the Budget—for the last few as assistant chief of the fiscal division; and A. E. Stockburger, aviation consultant to the House Interstate and Foreign Commerce Committee, had been in the Civil Aeronautics Authority for seven years. Secondly, such prior executive branch service frequently had equipped a committee staff member with essential skills. For example, former FBI agents were thoroughly trained in the fundamentals of investigative techniques. And several committee aides who had been in the OSS during World War II commented on the value of the instruction they had received there in methods of investigation and in report writing. Thirdly, in a number of cases the chairman and other committee members first became acquainted with a committee staff member's abilities through his having been sent up from an administrative agency to assist the committee. For instance, during World War II when John Courtney was with the Navy Department, he worked closely with the old House Naval Affairs Committee, of which Representative Carl Vinson (D.-Ga.) was then chairman. Several years later in the 82d Congress when chairman of the House Armed Services Committee, Representative Vinson hired Mr. Courtney as special counsel to head the staff of its Procurement Subcommittee. Finally, from previous employment in the executive branch a committee aide gained an understanding of how the administrative agencies operate, a knowledge of where and how to obtain most readily various kinds of services, and usually a network of personal acquaintances that made securing such assistance easier.

For the most part, the committee aides interviewed had very good backgrounds of experience. However, as with their educational attainments, the importance of their previous employment should not be exaggerated. In particular, the qualifications of professional staff members should not be evaluated solely on the basis of their educational and experience backgrounds. To do so disregards their personalities and other attributes essential to success in committee staff work. In a number of instances during the period covered, persons with highly impressive academic and experience records proved unsatisfactory as committee aides. The only adequate measure of an individual's suitability for committee staff work is how he performs on the job. Moreover, if a professional staff member possesses the intelligence, temperament, and other requisites for his position, he can readily acquire sufficient knowledge of the subjects handled by the committee as he goes along.

In any event, he will have to learn some things about the committee work on the job. Numerous committee aides observed that an individual without previous congressional staff experience must spend a year or more as a committee employee to become fully productive. Naturally, that apprenticeship period can be materially reduced for a person who has served on the staff of another committee or in the office of a Congressman. Nevertheless, because of the differences among the committees, even a veteran "Hill" employee needs a short "shakedown cruise" when he joins a new committee staff. He has to become acquainted with the internal power structure and procedures of that committee, the preferences of each of its members for staff work, and its special clientele of interest groups. Hence, beyond a certain point, the background of experience—no matter how germane and impressive—an individual brings with him has less marginal utility than the equivalent amount of time devoted to work for that committee in equipping him for a position on its staff.

Essential Attributes

As mentioned above, neither educational nor experience backgrounds are as important qualifications for a committee aide as the possession of certain abilities and other characteristics. In the first place, a committee staff member must be fundamentally a generalist. A committee considers such a diversity of subjects that he could not possibly be a specialist in more than a fraction of them. Even if he were an expert on some aspects of the committee work, he would have to justify his continued existence on the staff by functioning as a generalist in other areas. The changing emphases of congressional attention and the small size of the staff would require him to deal with multiple matters outside his specialty. Consequently, he must have a faculty for rapidly acquiring and grasping the essential details of a wide variety of complicated measures sufficiently to handle them intelligently. And he must be able to visualize all the significant ramifications of a proposal with respect to the existing structure of law and practice. It is the broad-gauged individual with an active intellectual curiosity, ability to see interrelationships, quick apperceptiveness, and mental agility who best fulfills that role.

Flexibility is a prime requisite for a committee aide. Where an office staff member has to accommodate to the predilections of but one boss, a committee aide has to adjust to those of the entire membership of the committee. And especially on the minor House committees, there is a fairly high turnover in members. In effect—at least so long as he can command the tacit support of a majority of the committee—the chairman controls the organization and administration of the committee and its staff. Whether standing or special subcommittees are used; their composition, jurisdiction, and functions; the scheduling of committee activities; and the assignment of the staff, are left almost entirely to his discretion. With each change in chairmen, those may be altered—sometimes drastically. And during the tenure of some chairmen, there are no standard practices with regard to referring bills either to subcommittees or to the full committees and little systematization of other key internal procedures.

Even on a committee where the work is highly organized, there still is a lack of predictability about its program because of factors beyond its control. When a scandal in an administrative agency or some other emergency requiring immediate investigation by that committee breaks, the staff has to postpone work on major measures with which it may have been occupied for weeks to assist on th probe. Furthermore, ordinarily a committee staff member is handling several major bills and numerous other assignments concurrently. He must be able to discontinue and then to resume work on any of them after a protracted interruption during which many different matters have competed for his attention.

Manning one of the main communication centers in the Congress, a committee aide must be able to express himself with facility in speaking and writing. There is a heavy two-way traffic of verbal messages delivered through him. Much of the information relevant to his work is acquired and dispensed orally both within and outside the committee. Particularly desirable is the faculty some professional staff members have for elucidating complicated measures such as proposals for taxing life insurance companies which involve technical actuarial formulas in a way the Congressmen can readily understand without sacrificing the accuracy of the explanation in the process. Articulateness was one of the outstanding characteristics of the committee aides interviewed. While being interrogated, many of them displayed an almost uncanny ability to divine precisely the points on which information was desired; and all of them spoke on those in a rapid and well-organized fashion.

Similarly, a professional aide must be able to write clearly and succinctly. The individual members of Congress not on a committee depend largely on its reports and documents to acquaint them quickly with the matters treated by the committee. With the voluminous processed materials and publications received by the committees, their staffs must be skillful digesters. To conserve the time and energy of the committee members, the staffs often condense reports, legal opinions, and bill analyses prepared by executive departments, the Legislative Reference Service, or other outside agencies. And sometimes they even abridge lengthy letters. There is a premium on brevity in any sort of staff memoranda to the committee members. Among the professional aides interviewed, there was a consensus that such memoranda should not exceed a page or two in length and should cover the points of greatest interest to the committeemen as tersely as possible.

The companion factors of temperament and personality are very important determinants of how successful a committee staff member will be. A suitable temperament is prerequisite to his acceptance and fulfillment of the proper concept of his role. He must be willing to serve committee members of all gradations along the political spectrum and to supply material to support a position directly contrary to his own on any issue. Above all else, he must not be a crusader who cannot resist attempting to influence the committeemen in the direction of his personal views. With each shift in the chairmanship and in the effective majority of the committee, he must be temperamentally capable of effecting a corresponding change in the orientation of his staff work and a complete transfer of loyalty to his new bosses. He must be able to appreciate that the large influence that political factors exert on the decisions of the committee members is an inevitable concomitant of their essential function as politicians. And he must not experience frustration because such considerations prevent their taking action he deems desirable or shape the contents of measures differently from his own preferences. He must cheerfully accept the fact that as a result of the fundamentally facilitative nature of his role, the committee members ordinarily will not turn to him for policy guidance but rather will ask him to make a case on the side they have already adopted. He must be willing to work anonymously and to have the committee members take credit for what he has done. Because of the frequent short deadlines occasioned by the erratic and unpredictable character of committee staff work, he must be able to operate well under pressure. And the ability to think on his feet in a fast-moving situation is a decided asset in his occupation.

The significance of an appropriate personality for a committee aide can hardly be overemphasized. His relationships not only with the members of the committee but also with employees in other segments of the congressional staff and in the executive branch are highly personalized. No matter how qualified he may be in other respects, if he is not compatible with the chairman and ranking members of the committee, he cannot survive long in his job. And to an appreciable extent, the level of efficiency which he can achieve depends upon his ability to develop and maintain friendships with key personnel in the congressional staff and administrative establishment. Such connections greatly facilitate obtaining information and other services essential in his work and sometimes make possible the procurement of assistance of a sort that otherwise would not be forthcoming.

Because of the marked variations among the committees, there probably is no uniform personality pattern that would be equally suitable for all the professional staff members. However, there are certain traits that it is desirable—if not imperative—for every committee aide to possess. Perhaps the most crucial of those is the ability to inspire trust in his integrity and fidelity. For the committee members must have complete faith that he will not disclose to other Congressmen—especially their partisan opponents—secret assignments or information which they have entrusted to him. And they must have absolute confidence in his word when he assures them that there are no jokers in highly technical measures or that the organization of a hearing is not being loaded against their position on the issues concerned. An aptitude for getting along well with diverse types of people is almost indispensable to him. He must possess good judgment, tact, and common sense. And because of the protracted periods of overtime he habitually has to work—especially toward the end of a session when numerous important measures are coming to fruition concurrently—he must have a sturdy constitution.

In addition, there were certain other qualities common to most of the committee aides interviewed. Nearly all of them derived considerable psychic income from the instrumental role they were playing in the legislative process by servicing the "workshops of Congress." Yet they were refreshingly free from an exaggerated sense of their own importance. A number of them seemed to thrive on the unsystematic, crisis atmosphere and lack of normalcy intrinsic to committee staff work. Almost without exception, they were very accommodating, pleasant, and frank. And many of them were blessed with an excellent sense of humor.

Alleged Excess of Lawyers

Some political scientists have made the criticism that there are too many lawyers and not enough social scientists on the professional staffs of the committees. For example, Dr. Gladys Kammerer wrote in 1951:

Preponderance of Lawyers. The preponderance of lawyers or persons trained in the law among committee professional staffs is discouraging to the social scientist. Congress itself, of course, is made up largely of lawyers; and since few attorneys are at all aware of the usefulness of social science analysis to the legislative process, perhaps it is to be expected that many committee chairmen fail to turn to persons trained in any discipline other than the law for committee work. Of a total of forty-two professional staff members on Senate committees in 1948, twelve were lawyers, but in 1950, of a total of forty-nine, twenty-one were lawyers. On the House side, of a total of fifty-one professional staff members in 1948, eighteen were lawyers; in 1950, of a total of sixty-three, thirty-four were lawyers. The number of social scientists remained constant in the two Congresses, standing at nine on the Senate side and nine on the House side in 1948, and at eight on the Senate side and ten on the House side in 1950. The failure to increase the total number of social scientists after Congress became Democratic in 1949 may seem inconsistent in view of the Fair Deal advocacy of more social legislation than was pushed by the Republicans.

One reason for employment of lawyers advanced by some committees is that they are helpful in bill drafting. This argument, however, is fallacious in the light of the existence of the Legislative Counsel's office on each side of the Capitol. This office is well staffed and exists primarily to render bill-drafting services. On the other hand, the great danger in overemphasis of legal training for professional committee work is that lawyers are too seldom exposed in their training to social, economic, and political problems. They bring to committee work the same narrow, technical, legalistic background already characteristic of so many legislators. In other words, "nothing new has been added" to the making of the legislative product.[7]

In his book *Congress: Its Contemporary Role,* Dr. Ernest Griffith, director of the LRS, expressed similar views in more guarded language. When discussing the quality of the committee staffs, he said:

The staffs of the standing committees present a less clear picture. . . . Lawyers and journalists have been employed in considerable numbers, economists and subject specialists perhaps somewhat less so than would have been anticipated.[8]

First of all, with respect to this charge that there is an excessive number of lawyers on the committee staffs, a question may properly be raised as to what constitutes a lawyer. Does the possession of a law degree automatically make an individual a lawyer? For instance, take the case of John Heimburger, professional aide to the House Agriculture Committee. Before he joined that committee staff, almost all his gainful employment had been in newspaper or public relations work. Both before and after securing his LL.B., he had worked on newspapers. When he was employed by various administrative agencies, he did not serve on their legal staffs but was in their public and press relations sections. He had never engaged in private law practice. Yet Dr. Kammerer included him in her summary totals of the number of lawyers on House committee staffs in 1948.[9] Likewise, should Dr. Carl Marcy, professional staff member of the Senate Foreign Relations Committee, be classified as a lawyer because he has an LL.B.? In addition to having an M.A. and a Ph.D. in political science, he was performing the duties of an ordinary professional aide to that committee. And most of his experience in the executive branch was concerned with the substantive aspects of international relations. However, he might more appropriately be placed in the category of lawyers on committee staffs than Mr. Heimburger. For Dr. Marcy did serve for a while in the Office of the Legal Adviser of the State Department. There were numerous other committee aides with LL.B.'s who had never practiced law—some of whom had not even qualified for the bar, who had never functioned as legal technicians on administrative agency or committee staffs, and whose principal previous occupations had been in college teaching or in some other field than law. Should they be used to support the contention that there are too many lawyers on the committee staffs?

Similarly, the designation "social scientist" is a very elastic one. Although the cynical aphorism: "In Washington, D.C., an economist is a guy who calls himself an economist" is somewhat of an overstatement, it contains a large kernel of truth. As has just been noted in connection with evaluating the educational attainments of the committee staff members interviewed, the highest academic degree possessed by many of the economists and other species of social scientists in the upper grades of the classified service in the Legislative Reference Service was a B.A. or B.S. Nineteen of the twenty-two committee aides interviewed who had law degrees also had a B.A. or B.S. Three of those had an M.A. or M.S., and two had Ph.D.'s. One of the remaining three had two years, and the other two had three years of college work. The one practicing lawyer who did not have an LL.B. had a B.S. degree. A large proportion of those bachelor's degrees were in political science or economics. And a goodly number were in business administration and history. This data clearly contradicts the assertion that most of the lawyers on the committee staffs were not trained in any other discipline than the law and had not been sufficiently exposed to economic, political, and social sciences in their educational backgrounds. Having taken supplementary training in law as graduate students certainly did not nullify the knowledge of the concepts, methods of analysis, literature, and research tools in the social studies they had previously acquired in working for their bachelor's degrees.

Moreover, many of the top subject specialists in the executive branch and in other segments of the congressional staff were lawyers or persons with a legal education who had gained their expertness through on-the-job specialization. For example, in the executive branch, Leon H. Keyserling, vice-chairman of the Council of Economic Advisers from its inception in 1946 to 1950 and chairman of that high-level presidential staff agency from 1950 to 1953, was recognized as a "heavyweight" economist by his professional colleagues. Yet the only graduate degree he had was an LL.B. Another lawyer, Berchmans T. Fitzpatrick, deputy administrator and general counsel of the Housing and Home Finance Agency, who had been with the HHFA and its predecessors since 1938, was generally acknowledged to be one of the foremost experts on public housing in the federal government during the period covered.[10] Similarly, in the Legislative Reference Service, Raymond E. Manning, senior specialist in taxation and fiscal policy, had a J.D. (equivalent to an LL.B.) as his highest academic degree. He had acquired his advanced knowledge of taxation and economics through digesting laws, preparing reports, and doing other work in those fields in the LRS. Also, the senior specialist in social welfare from 1947 to 1951, Fedele F. Fauri, was a lawyer who became an expert on social security matters largely through having served on the staff and as director of the Michigan State Department of Welfare.[11]

Sixteen of the twenty-two committee aides interviewed who had law degrees had been employed in executive agencies, thirteen in the same fields as their committee work. Nine had had previous congressional staff experience, six as employees of committees handling the same types of subject matter as their present committees. And three had been on the staffs of state or local units of government. Thus, it is apparent that on the basis of their nonlegal educational preparations and of their experience backgrounds, a large majority of these committee aides with law degrees could with equal facility—and with greater accuracy in many instances—be classified as social scientists or subject specialists instead of as lawyers.

Similar considerations apply to the characterization of lawyers as narrow, technical, and legalistic in their viewpoints. Firstly, this stereotype has no more validity than that concerning any other profession. There are lawyers and lawyers. Some of the most creative staff work on the social legislation of the New Deal was done by lawyers like Benjamin V. Cohen, Thomas J. Corcoran, and William O. Douglas. Secondly, the stricture that lawyers are preoccupied with technicalities and argue over every comma in a proposed law may reflect the failure of the person voicing that criticism to appreciate the necessity of prescribing certain procedures or the effect of the established legal connotations of the language used in a statute on its subsequent interpretation by executive agencies and the courts.

The argument that lawyers are not needed on committee staffs to do bill drafting because of the existence of the Office of the Legislative Counsel does not accord with the prevalent pattern of use of that most capable agency. During the period covered, there was a wide range in the extent to which different committees in the two chambers availed themselves of its services. Some like the appropriations committees rarely, if ever, called on it. Others like the revenue committees relied on it heavily. The scope and nature of the assistance requested from it varied not only among the committees but also from time to time and with different measures in the same committee.[12] Even the staffs of the committees which were the most consistent customers of the Office of the Legislative Counsel sometimes drafted amendments or minor bills. And on occasion where highly technical legislation of a controversial nature was involved, committees brought individuals onto their professional staffs expressly for the purpose of drafting the measures desired. For example, in the 80th Congress, the Senate Labor and Public Welfare Committee hired two labor lawyers, Gerard D. Reilly and Thomas E. Shroyer, to assist in preparing the bills which eventuated in the Taft-Hartley Act. Shortly after the enactment of that legislation, Gerard Reilly, who had done most of the drafting of the Senate version, left the committee staff to go back into private practice.[13] Mr. Shroyer remained in the employ of the Senate Labor and Public Welfare Committee or of its subsidiary Joint Committee on Labor-Management Relations until the 83d Congress.

If every committee depended on the Office of the Legislative Counsel to the degree that those making heaviest use of it do, it would have to be greatly enlarged—which would deprive it of certain advantages inhering in its small size. Thus, there are definite benefits in the present arrangement of having some personnel skilled in bill drafting organic to the committee staffs as well as in the Office of the Legislative Counsel.

Moreover, bill drafting is not the only legal service required by the committees. There are briefs, opinions, and other legal memoranda to be prepared. In an investigation which may well result in the bringing of perjury or other criminal charges against particular witnesses, the interrogation and cross-examination of them almost has to be conducted by a staff member who is a lawyer. Although the Office of the Legislative Counsel does turn out a limited number of legal memoranda, it endeavors to hold their production down to a minimum.[14] The American Law Section of the LRS does provide legal reference and research assistance to the committees. However, in the 82d Congress, there were only seven legal analysts in the grade of GS-9 or above in the American Law Section.[15] And not all of them were fully available to do research studies.

Several of them had continuing responsibilities such as compiling the *Digest of Public General Bills,* the State Law Index, and other research and reference tools which pre-empted a large share of their time. Also, most of them handled numerous routine inquiries and requests for legal data.

If the American Law Section were to be expected to supply the needs of all the committees for legal memoranda, it too would have to be expanded considerably. Furthermore, at present, committee aides often procure legal studies from the American Law Section or from the Office of the Legislative Counsel primarily as a check on those they have done themselves on the same subjects or as a tactical device to be able to insert a written opinion by an "independent central staff agency" in the record to support their committee's position on the issues involved.

Because of these committee staff functions necessitating the talents of an attorney, there ought to be at least one lawyer on each committee staff to act part or full time in the capacity of a legal technician. Employing the statutory quota of four professional staff positions for each legislative committee as the norm, this would mean that at least twenty-five per cent of the professional aides to committees would be lawyers. Also, some committees like Senate and House Judiciary whose work is predominantly of a technical legal nature ought to have several, if not all, lawyers on their professional staffs.[16] Finally, as mentioned above, many of the professional aides with law degrees were authentic subject specialists. In view of these considerations, slightly over forty per cent[17] does not seem an excessive proportion of the committee professional staff members to be lawyers or persons with some training in law.

Summary

In the main, the committee aides interviewed were well fitted for their posts by education, previous employment, and aptitude. They had as good educational and experience backgrounds as comparable groups of employees elsewhere in the government. More importantly, most of them possessed in generous measure the attributes of an adaptable, articulate generalist and had suitable personalities. Considering the committees' need for legal services and the fact that many of the professional aides with law degrees also were well versed in other subjects, the number of lawyers on the committee staffs was not excessive during the period covered.

CHAPTER VII

OTHER ASPECTS OF STAFF ADMINISTRATION

Optimum Size

Desirability of smallness. During the period covered, experience confirmed the philosophy of the Legislative Reorganization Act of having only a few well-qualified professional staff members for each standing committee. A rather severe limitation on the size of a committee staff proved necessary to confine it to its proper role. Where the number of aides to a committee was enlarged much above the minimum required to handle its normal workload, the more ambitious and industrious were prone to justify their existence by encroaching on the province of the executive branch.[1] When the staffs were kept small, the committees could not afford to hire incompetents because of the pressing need for staff services. However, undue expansion of the staffs removed that check. As a result, the incidence of purely patronage appointments was much higher among the supernumerary than among the regular professional aides. Office politics and intrigue were worse among the inflated staffs. And in some cases like that of the Senate Labor and Public Welfare Committee during the 81st and 82d Congresses, the excessive number of employees adversely affected the conduct of committee affairs. Finally, the professional staff of a committee could not be enlarged too greatly without exceeding the span of control of the chairman or of the staff director (if there were one) and without imposing other problems of administrative management. Not the least of those for the immediate future was the lack of sufficient office space to accommodate much more staff.

Adequacy of current quota. Although there was nothing sacrosanct about it, the statutory quota of four professional staff members for each standing committee of the House and Senate (other than the appropriations committees)[2] seemed sufficiently large for most committees. Three-fourths of the committee aides interviewed considered it adequate. Throughout the 82d Congress, seven Senate committees: Agriculture and Forestry, Armed Services, District of Columbia, Finance, Foreign Relations, Post Office and Civil Service, and Rules and Administration had less than their authorized complements of professional staff members.[3]   And ten House committees: Agriculture, Banking and Currency, District of Columbia, Foreign Affairs, House Administration, Post Office and Civil Service, Public Works, Rules, Veterans' Affairs, and Ways and Means did not fill all the positions on their regular professional staffs.[4]

Certainly with the successive crises in international affairs and the accompanying domestic problems of inflation, allocation of scarce materials, and defense production during the period covered, the two foreign relations committees and the two banking and currency committees handled as many—if not more—major legislative measures and investigations as any other committees did. Yet, three of them operated with less than their quotas of regular professional aides, and the fourth did not exceed its.

That the workload was not always the primary factor in determining the size of a committee's staff was illustrated by the history of the Senate Labor and Public Welfare Committee. In the 80th Congress, when it prepared the Taft-Hartley Act, it did not have all four of its professional staff posts permanently filled. Whereas, during the 82d Congress, when it did not process any major legislation in the fields of either labor or health, the full committee had one extra professional staff member for a total of five; its Subcommittee on Labor and Labor-Management Relations had a separate staff that contained as many as six professional aides at a time; and its Subcommittee on Health had still another special staff that comprised four more professional aides.[5]

On the basis of a disproportionately large workload, the Senate Judiciary Committee had the most legitimate claim to more than the standard allowance of professional staff members. For example, during the 82d Congress, the Senate Judiciary Committee received 47.1% of all the bills and resolutions introduced in the Senate and 59.3% of all those sent over from the House. It filed 57.8% of the 2,121 written committee reports submitted by all the Senate committees. It disposed of 9,361 individual immigration cases, of which 7,145 related to suspension of deportation under the Immigration Act of 1917 and 2,216 involved adjustment of status under sec. 4 of the Displaced Persons Act of 1948. And it processed 143 executive nominations.[6]

Nevertheless, in this case, additional staff personnel should be provided merely as a stopgap. The only permanent solution to the problem of the overload on the Senate Judiciary Committee lies in the direction of readjusting its jurisdiction and divesting it of its quasi-administrative duties. For instance, its Subcommittee on Internal Security might be reconstituted as a separate Senate committee or combined with the House Un-American Activities Committee to form a Joint Committee on Internal Security. And both the judiciary committees should be relieved of such essentially administrative functions as reviewing suspension of deportation cases.[7] At any rate, some fundamental remedies of this nature should be applied. Ever-increasing dosages of extra staff should not continue to be administered to relieve the symptoms while the basic cause of the disease remains untreated.

And certainly while such disparities in their workloads exist, the judiciary committees could not conceivably be used as the norm in establishing a new quota of professional aides for each standing committee. Similarly, it would be incongruous to employ an investigating or service committee like House Un-American Activities or Senate Small Business as the standard for judging the staffing needs of the legislative committees. For the former are more akin to an administrative agency than to the ordinary congressional committee. Any quota based on the size of their staffs would be too large for the average legislative committee. Conversely, any staffing allowance keyed to the requirements of the latter would not be adequate for them.

A further deterrent to providing even a modest increase in the statutory allotment of professional aides for each standing committee is that some would hire the authorized number irrespective of their needs. That was demonstrated in the 82d Congress by the fact that committees like Senate Public Works and House Merchant Marine and Fisheries had their full complements of professional staff members. It is improbable that these minor committees[8] needed more professional aides than many of the major committees had then.[9]

Conclusion. In view of these factors, it would be undesirable to enlarge the statutory quota of professional staff members for each standing committee. Rather, the present practice of requiring committees to secure the approval by their respective chambers of resolutions authorizing extra employees for them is a better approach. It enables the committees to accommodate flexibly to the fluctuations in their workloads. Under it, the committees are subjected to the check of having their requests for additional aides screened by the Committee on Rules and Administration in the Senate or by the Committee on House Administration in the House. And the necessity for such supplementary staffs is periodically reviewed when their authorizations have to be renewed. If anything, under this system, both the House and Senate and their respective administration committees have been too generous in allowing extra increments of staff. Hence, efforts might better be directed toward tightening up the present procedure rather than to remove the restraints it imposes. For overstaffing the committees is as bad as understaffing them and may prove a greater threat to the constitutional balance of our government. With the 82d Congress having expended over $5,500,000 (much of which went for staff salaries) of specially-authorized funds for investigations of various subjects, including big league baseball and pornographic literature,[10] the tendencies toward overexpansion of the congressional staff are readily discernible.

Pros and Cons on Permanence of Tenure

Advantages. The objective of the Legislative Reorganization Act of placing the tenure of the committee staffs on a more stable basis than under the patronage system is very commendable. There are decided advantages in continuity of employment for committee aides. They can reduce repetitive aspects of their work to a routine. They have more incentive to fill in their backgrounds. They acquire a detailed knowledge of the contents and legislative histories of measures that are carried over and reintroduced in several successive Congresses. Where the executive departments try to put through the same old bills—or modifications thereof—which the committees have previously rejected, they can detect those and save taking up the committees' time with needless reconsideration of such measures. Likewise, they become acquainted with shortcomings in the operation of laws within the jurisdictions of their committees. As a result, when those come up for re-enactment or amendment, they are better able to assist in improving them.

Paramountcy of responsibility. Despite these and other benefits of continuity in the committee employees, there is the overriding consideration of holding them responsible and of confining them to their proper role. If permanent tenure, like that of the classified service in the executive branch or in the Library of Congress, were to be provided by law for the committee staffs, there is a grave danger that the professional aides in particular would become less responsive to control by the committeemen and would attempt to exert undue influence on them. In his incisive little essay "Politics and Administration," Professor V. O. Key, Jr., points out how the discipline of professional conformity reinforces such propensities of career employees in the administrative establishment.[11] Tendencies of that sort among committee staff personnel would be encouraged by the rather high turnover in committee members—especially on the House side. Also, at various stages in the legislative process, there are opportunities for an unscrupulous committee aide to insert provisions in a law or to predispose its subsequent interpretation in a direction not intended by the Congressmen. Because of the great trust the committees perforce repose in their staffs, they must be able to enforce effective responsibility in the latter through the exercise of unobstructed power of dismissal.

Besides, the more staff positions are surrounded with statutory protections of tenure, the more difficult it becomes to eliminate incompetents from them. Since there is not any reliable means of predicting an individual's suitability for congressional staff work, this consideration assumes greater importance than in the executive branch. Also, the present situation, in which an employee's retention on the staff of a committee is dependent upon the continuing acceptability of his output to it, affords a good prophylactic against the syndrome picturesquely described as the "dead hand of bureaucracy." Hence, the perennial proposals for providing greater safeguards of tenure for committee aides by statutory stipulation that they could be discharged only for some ambiguous cause like malfeasance or inefficiency and/or by the institution of a congressional personnel director are incongruous.[12]

Determinants of continuity. The present provisions of the law go about as far as possible in promoting stability in the staffs without depriving the committees of the ability to hold them immediately accountable. The specific statement of intent in sec. 202(a) of the Legislative Reorganization Act that professional staff members are to be appointed on a permanent and merit basis markedly affected the behavior of many committees during the period covered. Continuity in their staffs was maintained through several changes in the control of Congress. In each case, a number of factors contributed to achieving that result. Some of those were: the nonpartisan nature of the subject matter handled by the committee, homogeneity of viewpoints among the ranking majority and minority members, and the establishment of sound precedents in the selection and conduct of the staff at the outset.

Of all these determinants of continuity, perhaps the most important was the manner in which the individual staff member conceived and fulfilled his role. If he adopted a client-counsel attitude to serve committee members of every persuasion without differentiation and was not tinctured with a tribune-of-the-people complex to influence committee actions in particular directions, he was likely to be retained by a chairman even with a personal economic and political philosophy radically divergent from that of his predecessor. In challenging the fundamental premise of the Legislative Reorganization Act on permanence of tenure, one critic posed the rhetorical question: "Would it be reasonable to expect . . . that Congressman Spence would keep the man selected by Congressman Wolcott on the Banking and Currency Committee?"[13] Well, as a matter of fact, when Representative Spence became chairman, he did retain both the professional staff member, Orman Fink, and the clerk, William Hallahan, who also functioned in a professional capacity. And six years later Mr. Fink and Mr. Hallahan were still on that committee staff in the same positions. In addition to being of recognized competence, both these individuals completely abstained from trying to affect the policy decisions of the committee; and they adapted their work to the views held by the Congressmen controlling the committee during any given period.

Of course, these factors did not operate in isolation but interacted and reinforced one another. For instance, where attempting to attain a bipartisan policy, as on the foreign affairs committees, chairmen were more inclined to clear appointments to the staffs with the ranking minority members and to make the staffs' services equally available to all the committee members.

Conclusion. There will always be a need for supplementing the regular committee staffs with temporary employees recruited on an *ad hoc* basis to assist on particular projects. However, there are certain fundamental forces in Congress that are conducive to the development of relatively permanent staffs for a majority of the committees. Among those are the nonpartisan character of most congressional business, the long maturation period of many measures, and the pressing need for experienced staff assistance in the technicalities of preparing complicated legislation. Catalyzed by and operating through the present provisions of the law, these forces should in time bring about the kind of tenure for committee staffs intended by the Legislative Reorganization Act without the dangers inherent in any attempt to accomplish that by further legislation.

Salaries

Sec. 202(e) of the Legislative Reorganization Act originally provided:

> The professional staff members of the standing committees shall receive annual compensation, to be fixed by the chairman, ranging from $5,000 to $8,000 and the clerical staff shall receive annual compensation ranging from $2,000 to $8,000.[14]

To make clear that these limits were intended to apply to basic rather than gross salary levels, the Supplemental Appropriation Act, 1948, amended this paragraph to read:

> The professional staff members of the standing committees shall receive basic annual compensation, to be fixed by the chairman, ranging from $5,000 to $8,000 and the clerical staff shall receive basic annual compensation up to $8,000.[15]

Meanwhile, Public Law 4, 80th Congress, prescribed the following pay scale for the clerical staff of each Senate standing committee:

> The annual rates of compensation for the clerical staff of each standing committee of the Senate (other than the Appropriations Committee) shall be $2,000 to $8,000 for one chief clerk and one assistant chief clerk; and $2,000 to $3,720 for not to exceed four other clerical assistants.[16]

The gross salary of a congressional employee was calculated from his basic annual rate of compensation by a complicated system of adding a number of percentage increases and flat sums authorized in a series of pay acts, three of which were enacted during the period covered.[17] Because the conversion formulas varied then, it is impossible to give a single set of corresponding gross and basic salary rates for that entire time. Table 1 shows the gross salaries received for selected basic annual rates of pay in the latter half of the 82d Congress.

TABLE 1

CORRESPONDING BASIC AND GROSS SALARIES IN 1952*

Base Pay	Gross Pay
$8,000.00	$11,646.00
5,000.00	8,492.02
3,720.00	6,481.67
2,000.00	3,741.36

*From information supplied by the Disbursing Office, U.S., House of Representatives.

In most cases, one or more (sometimes all) of the professional aides to a standing committee drew as much salary as the staff director. To reward him for his greater responsibility, to contribute to his prestige, and indirectly to strengthen his authority, the head of a staff should receive more salary than his highest-ranking subordinates. Hence, the Legislative Reorganization Act should be amended to permit staff directors of standing committees to be paid an additional amount, say $2,500 above the maximum salary authorized for the other professional staff members.[18]

Intrastaff Collaboration

Range in degree. During the period covered, the extent to which the professional aides to a committee customarily collaborated varied widely on different committees. On some like Senate Interstate and Foreign Commerce, each professional staff member functioned in isolation from his colleagues. Despite the fact that the different types of transportation—land, water, and air—constitute a system, regulation of any part of which affects the others, the professional aides specializing in them never consulted or worked together. On others like House Interior and Insular Affairs, each professional staff member operated independently in his own field such as Indian affairs or mines and mining—even on projects overlapping the provinces of two or more staff members. However, all of them turned to the committee counsel for assistance on bill drafting and other technical legal aspects of their work. On still others like Senate Banking and Currency, the professional aides handled minor bills within their respective specialties individually but collaborated on major measures. And on some like House Foreign Affairs, virtually every project was a joint enterprise of the staff. Even in the performance of rather minor assignments for which only one staff member was responsible, there was much informal discussion and review of one another's work by the professional aides.

Paradoxically, a few staffs, like that of the Senate Armed Services Committee, maintained that they could not afford to put more than one of their members to work on a single measure because of their small size; whereas, others, like the House Small Business Committee staff, advanced the same reason for having all their members cooperate on practically everything. Similarly, the almost universal assumption was that collaboration among the members of a professional staff was desirable per se. Yet at least one committee staff was vehemently opposed to the practice on principle. The professional aides to the House Armed Services Committee firmly believed that the responsibility for executing any assignment should not be shared.

Facilitative devices. A number of procedural and organizational devices were employed by various committee staffs to promote cooperation among their members. One was the routine circulation of drafts of staff studies and memoranda. For example, on the House Foreign Affairs Committee staff, an extra copy of each study or other important memorandum was automatically prepared on special green onionskin and passed around among the professional aides for criticism. Then the author of the memorandum made the final decision whether or not to accept any resulting recommendations for changes.

A second technique, which was an elaboration of the first, was for the staff to operate as a committee. In this method, of which the Joint Economic Committee staff was the chief exponent, the professional aides constituted a committee which acted in an advisory capacity on all aspects of the staff work. Together they deliberated on any major proposals for altering staff procedures and planned their program of activities. When an individual staff member or consultant was assigned to do a study, he would draw up and submit to them a summary statement of its contemplated scope and manner of treatment. Usually then they would meet to discuss that outline with him. While the study was in progress, they would consult with him periodically. After he had finished the first draft, they would convene to review it with him. Likewise, on joint projects such as the preparation of the staff materials section of the Joint Economic Committee's annual report, the professional aides conferred together throughout and made a group decision on what findings and recommendations to make. As a result, the staff director was able to say in his letter of transmittal that such materials represented the composite views of the committee's full time professional staff, thereby enhancing their authoritativeness.[19]

A third and more prevalent practice was that of making dual assignments. On numerous committees, two professional staff members customarily were put to work on any major measure, often with one of them having the primary responsibility for handling it and the other being designated more or less as his understudy. Occasionally on a really important bill, the staff director would detail additional professional aides to help those two—sometimes until the entire staff was concentrated on that measure during certain stages of its preparation.

And a fourth procedure, which was a refinement of the third, was the organization of staff subcommittees. This technique was developed and was used almost exclusively by the staff of the Joint Committee on Internal Revenue Taxation. It consisted of setting up subcommittees of professional staff members to prepare studies on various topics such as excise taxes or taxation of cooperatives which were likely to receive the attention of the House Ways and Means and Senate Finance Committees. Normally, these staff subcommittees were established well in advance of when the revenue committees were going to consider legislation on their subjects of study. Sometimes they were continued through several sessions of Congress, periodically being reconstituted. If the personnel were available, the chief of staff, Colin Stam, preferred to make these staff subcommittees interdisciplinary by appointing an attorney, accountant, and economist to each of them. Nearly always, a statistical analyst was pulled in at the conclusion of a study to prepare the statistical projections to be incorporated in it. And once in a while, a statistical analyst was assigned to a staff subcommittee at the outset as a regular member.[20]

In almost every case from the inception to the completion of a study, the entire staff subcommittee collaborated at every stage. The end product was not just a symposium of discrete contributions by different members on aspects of the topic falling within their respective specialties. Nor was it primarily the handiwork of but one or two members merely ratified by the others. Rather, each subcommittee member usually shared in producing every part of the study; and it represented a distillate of the group's thinking on the subject.

Although there was no prescribed procedure, generally a staff subcommittee started to work by having a series of generalized discussions on what already had been written on the subject such as: periodical articles, old bills, and previous committee reports. Then with that as a background, it turned to a consideration of the most recent data available from the executive agencies, from committee hearings, from correspondence with taxpayers, and sometimes from round-table conferences with affected parties. As its thinking began to crystallize, it composed a rough draft of the study. The practice in formulating that initial draft varied. Sometimes several members of the staff subcommittee wrote portions of it. More frequently, one member was delegated the task of reducing the group's views to writing. In either case, the first and successive drafts were subjected to an intensive review by the entire staff subcommittee.

And the final result was the same in that all the ideas embodied in the study together with the phraseology expressing them had been thoroughly discussed and approved by the whole group.

After the staff subcommittee had arrived at a draft of the study with which it was satisfied, it reported back to Mr. Stam. Meeting with the staff subcommittee members, Mr. Stam would go over the study with them to make the final revision of it. At these reporting sessions, Mr. Stam often was accompanied by one or more of the other professional aides to the Joint Tax Committee who had not served on that staff subcommittee. Again there was full participation by everybody in attendance. The members of the staff subcommittee, Mr. Stam, and any supernumerary professional aides present discussed the study freely and frankly.

Several distinctive advantages resulted from this system of establishing staff subcommittees on the Joint Tax Committee. Most importantly, the interaction among the accountants, lawyers, and economists produced a very significant fusion of the viewpoints and skills of their respective disciplines. They acquired a working knowledge of the concepts and terminology of one another's professions. Several Joint Tax Committee aides—including lawyers—observed that Russell Oram, an accountant, knew more tax law than most lawyers. Similarly, the economists readily acknowledged that the lawyers on the staff became good practical economists; and the lawyers commented on the economists' grasp of tax law. From this cross-blending of the different disciplines involved and from the interchange of ideas in attacking common problems, they often developed new perspectives and arrived at insights—especially in the twilight zones between each of their fields—that any one of them probably could not have achieved if working only with members of his own profession. In addition, the versatility of the entire Joint Tax Committee staff was increased; for the lawyers and economists could—and did—substitute for each other where only one could be spared for an assignment requiring the services of both.

Types of collaboration. Finally, there were several different kinds of collaboration. In the first, two or more staff members shared a common task such as screening witnesses. Or they divided a job along substantive lines, with each assuming the responsibility for preparing the portions with whose subject matter he was most conversant. In the second, an ordinary professional aide resorted to a technician on the staff like the committee counsel for help on aspects of his work relating to the latter's specialty. And in the third, two different types of technicians made complementary contributions to the performance of an assignment. The best illustration of that sort of mutual assistance was afforded by the collaboration between the economists and the statistical analysts on the Joint Tax Committee staff in making their annual estimates of anticipated revenues.

That undertaking was a joint effort from laying down the preliminary assumptions to arriving at the final figures. Firstly, they had to forecast the size of the aggregate corporate profits, individual incomes, and other constituents of the gross national product on which to base the specific estimates of the revenues to be derived from the different forms of taxation like the personal and corporate net income tax or excise taxes. To secure the data from which to prepare such forecasts, they would hold a series of panel discussions with economists from major industrial, banking, and other private business concerns. The Joint Tax Committee economists generally played the principal role in conducting these conferences. And the statistical analysts averaged and collated the predictions made by the different participants regarding the various indexes of economic activity on which their opinions were being sought.[21] Upon the conclusion of these conferences, the Joint Tax Committee economists accompanied by the statistical analysts would go around interviewing numerous governmental economists in various executive agencies and on the staff of the Joint Economic Committee on an individual basis to elicit essentially the same information from them. Again, the Joint Tax Committee economists bore the brunt of arranging and conducting the interviews.

After they had completed their collection of data from industrial and governmental economists, the two Joint Tax Committee economists would tentatively determine their forecasts of the gross national product, of individual and corporate income levels, and of other tax bases. Then they would meet with the two statistical analysts and Mr. Stam, the chief of staff, to discuss their combined estimates. At that conference, all of them would participate in making the final decision on what their forecasts of the various tax bases would be. From that point on, the statistical analysts would complete the project by applying the appropriate rate structures to those to arrive at specific figures for the partial and over-all estimates of annual revenue receipts.

Relations with Specially-Authorized Subcommittee Staffs

After the 81st Congress, when the procedure first became prevalent, some committees like Senate Labor and Public Welfare and House Expenditures habitually staffed their subcommittees with personnel hired under special resolutions. Others like House Agriculture rarely resorted to that practice but generally used their regular staffs to service their subcommittees—even those conducting special investigations. Similarly, some specially-authorized staffs like spawning salmon quietly expired after having accomplished the mission they were destined to perform. Others clung tenaciously to life, securing successive renewals of their authorizations until they achieved a sort of immortality or at least a semipermanent status. For instance, the staff of the Subcommittee on

Senate Investigations antedated that of the parent Senate Expenditures Committee by several years.

Likewise, the relations between the regular committee staffs and such more or less temporary adjuncts to them ran through a wide gamut. On some committees, there customarily was close association between them from the outset. For example, on the Joint Economic Committee, the chairmen of subcommittees usually invited the regular staff to participate in recruiting any specially-authorized aides. And the Joint Economic Committee staff almost always helped the latter in every phase of their work from the initial planning to the final reviewing of the studies they had been engaged to make. Also, the Joint Economic Committee staff generally supplied them with the requisite clerical assistance.

More typically, in particular where they were good-sized, the specially-authorized subcommittee staffs were organized and operated autonomously from the full committee staffs. For instance, the staffs of the Investigations Subcommittee of the Senate Expenditures Committee or of the Preparedness Subcommittee of the Senate Armed Services Committee constituted little *imperia in imperio.* The regular staffs of those committees had nothing to do with their recruitment or control. They were hired upon the recommendation of and worked under the immediate supervision of their own staff directors, who were the personal choices of the subcommittee chairmen. The relations between them and the aides to their respective parent committees were analogous to those between the staffs of two separate committees. Ordinarily, they maintained liaison with each other of varying degrees of effectiveness. And once in a while, a subcommittee staff consulted or borrowed the services of one of the full committee aides who was especially versed on a particular problem with which it was dealing or vice versa.

On a few committees, relations between members of the regular staffs and specially-authorized subcommittee employees were strained and occasionally erupted into open warfare. One factor conducing to such incompatibility was that often the staffs of a committee and of its subcommittees were selected by and were responsible to different groups of committee members. Consequently, there was no common center of authority for adjudicating disputes between them. A more fundamental cause of such dissension was rivalry. A few full committee aides were obsessed by the fear that specially-authorized subcommittee employees operating in their provinces would supersede them. Inasmuch as several committee professional staff members gained their positions via the route of first having served as specially-authorized subcommittee aides, perhaps the apprehensions on that score were not entirely unfounded.

On a number of committees, "investigative" subcommittees equipped with special staffs were established on a more or less continuing basis expressly to exercise a large share of their legislative oversight functions.[22] The staff directors of the Senate Expenditures and House Armed Services Committees heartily approved and advocated perpetuating this structural arrangement. They cited the following advantages of having an investigative adjunct to the staff separately organized under its own director and financed from supplementary funds. Firstly, it shielded the regular committee aides from identification with the probes highly fraught with political connotations or extremely embarrassing to the executive branch. Secondly, it enabled the full committee staff to be kept down to a more manageable size. And thirdly, the special investigative force could be expanded and contracted to accommodate to the ebbs and flows in the legislative oversight activities of the committee more easily than the regular staff with its fixed quota of positions could. Although these arguments may have contained some "virtue of necessity" rationalizations, there also was a large element of validity in them—especially in the last one.

CHAPTER VIII

WORK ON LEGISLATION

Planning and Conducting Hearings

Selection of witnesses. During the period covered, for all practical purposes on almost every committee, the staff selected the witnesses for hearings. Occasionally, committee members would name individuals whom they wished to have testify on particular subjects. And the staff generally cleared proposed lists of witnesses with the chairman and often with the ranking minority member. To supervise the planning of hearings on major bills—especially any on which there were deep cleavages among their members—a few committees would set up special "calendar subcommittees," which were bipartisan. Although the staff sometimes consulted it on touchy problems that arose, such a subcommittee usually did little more than ratify arrangements recommended by the staff and served chiefly as a device to reassure the remainder of the committee that the chairman was not having the staff load the hearings.

In most instances, making up the roster of witnesses was a routine task handled mainly by the chief clerk. The selection of witnesses from the executive branch was left almost entirely to the discretion of the agencies concerned. After a committee had announced in the newspapers and *Congressional Record* that hearings would be held on a certain subject, representatives of organized groups and other interested parties generally took the initiative in requesting an opportunity to testify. Securing witnesses then consisted merely of notifying such individuals when they could appear. Usually on noncontroversial measures, the committees—particularly the minor ones—would afford an audience to everyone desiring to be heard. Sometimes it was necessary to impose a time limit on the oral presentations or to restrict the witnesses to spokesmen for major organizations. But nearly all the committees would accept prepared statements for insertion in the record from well-nigh anyone who submitted them by the stipulated deadlines.

Once in a while, the chief clerk would seek the advice of the professional staff on which experts to invite to testify on highly technical aspects of a subject to supplement the presentations of volunteer witnesses. Also, on controversial measures where many more persons asked to testify than could be accommodated in the time available, the staff had the responsibility of protecting the committee against the charge of stacking the hearings. In such a situation, the professional staff would carefully check the tentative roster of witnesses to ensure that spokesmen for all the major viewpoints were included and that a rough balance between the pros and cons was maintained. Sometimes for that purpose or to eliminate repetitious testimony, the professional staff interviewed and screened prospective witnesses.

Preparation of questions.   Occasionally, a committee staff would compose and send to witnesses a questionnaire covering points on which their testimony was desired. On almost every committee, the staff customarily prepared lists of questions for the members to ask in the hearings. Those ranged from a generalized statement of problem areas on which additional information was required to an integrated set of precisely formulated questions typed on cards. In addition, all the committee aides interviewed—including some who doubted the utility of questions prepared beforehand—wrote out queries that occurred to them during hearings and passed them to the chairman or to other committee members especially interested in the topics involved.

Briefing committee members.   Practices among professional aides in supplementing written staff materials with oral explanations of subjects of committee action varied widely. In most instances, briefings before a hearing were given on an individual basis and were usually confined to the chairman. But nearly all the professional staffs willingly extended that service to other committee members on request. These individual briefings ran the gamut from a hurried attempt five minutes before the start of a hearing to acquaint the chairman with a list of questions prepared for him to going over a bill in detail with him for a whole afternoon or evening.

On some committees prior to hearings on a major measure, the professional staff habitually briefed the entire membership as a group. In such sessions, the staff typically summarized the provisions of the bill, pointed up its policy implications, described the departmental position on it—making certain that the committee was aware of the alternatives that the agencies had rejected and of considerations they were likely to minimize in their presentations—and indicated other relevant factors for which the members should be on the lookout during the hearings. Sometimes this process amounted in effect to the staff's testifying before the committee in executive session. For example, prior to the hearings on a bill for universal military training, the House Armed Services Committee met for eight days with the professional aide handling that measure and questioned him closely on every aspect of it.

Interrogation of witnesses.   On a majority of the standing committees— especially in the Senate—the professional staffs usually did not interrogate witnesses in public hearings of the full committees on legislative matters. Some chairmen forbade their staffs to do so—in at least one instance because of the indiscreet conduct of a staff director on that score. In any event, most of the professional aides interviewed customarily went through the committee members in asking questions of witnesses. And some did not approve even of passing notes or whispering suggested queries to the chairman because they felt that detracted from the dignity of the proceedings and because they did not wish to appear to be manipulating or trying to usurp the functions of the committee members.

However, a different situation existed in investigations—particularly those conducted by select committees or subcommittees with staffs recruited specially for that purpose. In the case of inquiries into complicated affairs like the intricate transactions surrounding the illegal sale of surplus government oil tankers where an excessive amount of time would have been required to familiarize the committee members with them, the staff generally did most of the interrogation. But even in a situation of that sort, if the committee were comprised of Congressmen with backgrounds as trial lawyers or as prosecuting attorneys skilled in the art of cross-examination, the committee members handled a large share of the questioning. And nearly always such interrogation was a collaborative enterprise of the professional staff and the committeemen. Ordinarily, either the staff laid the foundation of the case and the Congressmen built on that with their queries or after the committee members had completed their examination of the witnesses, the staff rounded out the record by asking about any points they had overlooked.

Similarly, committees invited their staffs to quiz witnesses more frequently on field trips than in Washington. And the professional aides usually participated more freely in questioning by a subcommittee than by a full committee. The main reason for that was the difference in size of the two units. At a session of a full committee in the House, thirty or so members who desired to take part in the interrogation might be present; whereas, at a subcommittee hearing, often but two or three members were in attendance.

Even where the professional aides were permitted to examine witnesses in legislative hearings, they exercised considerable discretion as to the time and mode of their intervention. For they were dealing with strong personalities who would have resented too frequent or officious interruptions. Generally, they confined themselves to asking only such questions as were necessary to clarify the record, to pin down an evasive witness, or to ensure that relevant factors were not being neglected. Some staff members would not interpose a query unless the situation were most urgent. And a few professional aides habitually requested "off-the-record" at any point where they felt impelled to quiz a witness. Significantly, with just one exception among the standing committee staffs interviewed, the professional aides who were generally considered the most capable and who achieved the greatest continuity of tenure were among the most circumspect about interrogating witnesses in public hearings on legislation.

Round-table discussions. During the period covered, a significant innovation in the hearings process occurred. In the study of broad economic or social problems—especially those of a highly technical nature—committees increasingly made use of round-table conferences in lieu of or as a supplement to the traditional type of hearing. Though differing in details, these panel discussions consisted in essence of a seminar-like procedure. Rather than testifying individually and then undergoing cross-examination by the committee members or staff, the participants jointly discussed prescribed topics, arguing back and forth among themselves. In doing so, they subjected one another's views to searching criticism and sometimes achieved a synthesis of their opinions acceptable to all of them. The chairman of the committee holding a round table acted as moderator of the group. For the most part, the rest of the committee present afforded a "studio audience" for the performance by the panel of experts. And the regular hearings reporters made a verbatim record of the proceedings.

Usually in advance of a round table, the committee staff would prepare and distribute to the individuals invited to take part a compilation of reference data and list of questions or of subjects upon which they would be asked to comment. Sometimes the panels were comprised of spokesmen for particular industries or for other elements of the economy like the National Petroleum Council of the Department of Interior or the Small Business Advisory Committee of the Department of Commerce. Often they consisted of economists or of other technicians from universities, private research institutions, organized interest groups, and similar sources. Some committees made use of round-table conferences only sporadically; others employed them regularly. Also, some held them ahead of formal hearings; others, after taking testimony in the customary manner. In the latter case, transcripts of the witnesses' statements were among the reference materials made available to the participants in the ensuing panel discussions.

One of the pioneers in developing the round-table procedure was the Joint Committee on the Economic Report. In 1949 when seeking a way to obviate the sterotyped presentations of interest group representatives, the Joint Economic Committee hit upon the idea of putting them around a table and having them comment in a group discussion on the President's Economic Report for 1949.[1] This initial experiment worked out rather well. The witnesses tended to debate the issues, and from the interaction among them, the committee gained more fruitful insights and a better development of opposing views than in the ordinary kind of hearing. The following year after the executive branch witnesses had testified on the President's Economic Report for 1950, the Joint Economic Committee held one round table with non-governmental economists and another with spokesmen for business, labor, agriculture, consumer organizations, and state and local governments.[2] In 1951 the Joint Economic Committee had panel discussions with nongovernmental technicians again; but instead of holding another with representatives of the major economic interest groups, it sent them a questionnaire covering the same ground and published their replies in the record of the hearings.[3] From that time on, the course followed by the Joint Economic Committee in gathering information and opinions on the President's Economic Report each year—and often in the study of other matters—contained the three steps of: (1) having the heads of appropriate administrative agencies testify in executive and public hearings; (2) sending questionnaires to major economic interest groups; and (3) conducting round tables with nongovernmental technicians.[4]

Favorably impressed by his experience with panel discussions on the Joint Economic Committee, Senator Joseph O'Mahoney (D.-Wyo.), who was chairman of both then, imported the round-table procedure into the operation of the Senate Interior and Insular Affairs Committee. After the passage of S. Res. 239 authorizing the Interior and Insular Affairs Committee to investigate the available fuel reserves and to formulate a national fuel policy,[5] Senator O'Mahoney directed the professional aide working on that investigation to organize panel discussions with leading experts on the subject "as the Joint Economic Committee staff does." Originally, the plan was to hold three round tables: one with representatives of the oil, natural gas, and coal industries; a second with specialists from the executive branch; and a third with nongovernmental consultants. The list of questions in the letter of transmittal and the main topics in the table of contents of the staff study *Basic Data Relating to Energy Resources*,[6] which had been compiled as a reference work for the participants, were to constitute the agenda for these conferences. The round table with the spokesmen for the fuel industries was held, and all who took part agreed that it was very successful.[7] However, a change in circumstances caused the investigation to be discontinued before the panel discussions with the technicians from administrative agencies and from private practice could be conducted.[8]

For the consideration of highly complex or controversial economic and social problems, this round-table procedure has several advantages over the ordinary hearings technique. Firstly, it enables the representatives of one interest to challenge the presentations of spokesmen for opposing interests directly. This spares the committee members and staff from exposing themselves to the danger of becoming identified with one side or the other in the capacity of proponent or opponent, prosecuting attorney or defense counsel, as sometimes happens in the regular-style hearings. Most importantly, by making it possible for expert witnesses to cross-examine one another and define their areas of agreement, the round-table procedure greatly extends the range of a generalist staff. Far less specialized substantive knowledge on the part of the staff is required to set up a panel comprising a representative sample of technicians in a given field than to attempt to evaluate their testimony and ascertain the limits of their consensuses. Besides, the interplay among the members of a round table conduces to developing their areas of agreement. Finally, this seminar approach enhances the educational value of the hearings process. Through participation in discussions by panels of experts, both the committee members and staff acquire increased subject-matter competence more rapidly than through the ordinary type of hearing.[9]

Staff hearings and round tables. Occasionally, ordinary hearings inadvertently were transformed into what amounted to staff hearings. Where all the committee members had to leave before individuals had finished testifying, the last one to go often allowed the hearings to continue in charge of the professional staff with—and sometimes without—the permission of the witnesses concerned. In addition, there were genuine staff hearings with no committeemen present at any stage of the proceedings. Those were conducted just as the regular hearings were, and the official reporters made verbatim transcripts of them. Generally, this procedure was followed only where committee members were unable to convene for hearings on rather urgent matters. Though there was no formal means of requiring individuals to appear before a staff hearing, usually they accepted with alacrity the option of presenting their testimony in that fashion rather than not at all. In situations involving legislative oversight of administration, many times after a staff hearing brought the complainants and agency representatives together, the problems were resolved without necessitating action by the committee.

For instance, in the 82d Congress, the export quota for secondary tin plate for the second quarter of 1952 was reduced from 75,000 to 62,500 tons although the steel exporters complained that their warehouses were bulging with secondary tin plate which they could not sell domestically. When approached about this problem by the counsel to the Joint Committee on Defense Production, the National Production Authority officials concerned asserted flatly that no such surplus existed. On April 21, 1952, the Joint Committee on Defense Production authorized a staff hearing on the matter. The staff met with fifteen steel exporters from all over the country and with officials from the National Production Authority, the Defense Production Administration, and the Office of International Trade. During the hearings, it was revealed that the agencies had not made a survey of the stocks of secondary tin plate in the possession of the exporters preliminary to fixing the export quota. As a consequence, the steel exporters agreed to survey the total store of tin plate in their industry and report the findings to the agencies. When that check revealed that they had a large supply of secondary tin plate on hand, the export quota was raised from 62,500 to 125,000 tons.[10]

The Joint Committee on Defense Production was one of the committees that employed staff hearings most frequently. During the 82d Congress, its staff held about a dozen such hearings. In conducting them, its counsel customarily functioned analogously to the chairman at regular committee hearings. After he had delivered an opening statement, the witnesses would testify. While they were making their presentations, the counsel and other staff members would interrogate them just as the committeemen ordinarily did. Then upon the completion of their testimony, the counsel would sum up the points at issue and throw the hearing open to a round-table discussion, over which he would preside.

Besides holding hearings to take testimony for the use of their committees, some staffs conducted panel discussions for their own information. For example, every year when forecasting revenue receipts, the staff of the Joint Committee on Internal Revenue Taxation would hold round tables with economists from private industry to obtain their views on the economic outlook. Representatives from Swift and Company, the United States Steel Corporation, and other major concerns were regular participants. In the letter inviting an individual to take part in these panel discussions, the Joint Tax Committee staff explained their purpose and the procedure followed in them. Also, it included a questionnaire covering the various indexes of business activity on which his predictions were being sought, such as the level of corporate profits, the size of the labor force, the amount of unemployment, the wholesale and retail price levels, and the size of the gross national product.

At the initial meeting of each round table, which nearly always was in the morning, the industrial economists would successively present and explain their forecasts on the different items covered in the questionnaire. Although occasionally some questions were asked at that time, the Joint Tax Committee staff endeavored to hold down such interruptions until all the panel members had finished giving their estimates. During the interval between the morning and afternoon sessions, the Joint Tax Committee staff would collate and average them. Then in the afternoon, utilizing the ranges of forecasts presented in the morning as the basis of discussion, the industrial economists would argue back and forth over one another's statistics and fundamental assumptions. The Joint Tax Committee aides would interject comments now and then to keep the debate going and to stimulate consideration of points which otherwise might have been overlooked. The entire proceedings were kept confidential, and no stenographic record was made of them. Also, the participants all recognized that the Joint Tax Committee staff was not bound by any specific estimates upon which the group might agree.

Sometimes, the Joint Tax Committee staff used the same method to gather data bearing on a particular measure—especially if it involved a complicated form of taxation. For instance, in 1951 when preparing excess profits tax legislation,[11] the Joint Tax Committee staff conducted panel discussions with representatives from more than twenty-five trade associations like the Machinery and Allied Products Institute and the Association of American Railroads. In this series of conferences, which extended over several weeks, the Joint Tax Committee staff acquired a great deal of detailed information about the impact of the World War II excess profits tax on those industries: its effects on their operations and the costs of compliance.

Similarly, when the Joint Economic Committee was holding its annual round tables on the President's Economic Report, its staff occasionally would invite the participant technicians to closed luncheon-conferences at which they would talk over a proposed program of staff work or other topics not immediately related to the subject of the panel discussions with the committee members. In addition, the process the Joint Economic Committee staff habitually went through in having agency specialists review its staff studies was in essence a round-table procedure.

Contribution to Bill Drafting

Committee counsel usually drafted at least some amendments and bills. In a few specialized fields like international law with which the nonlawyer members of a committee staff were much more familiar than the average attorney was, they occasionally wrote the actual language for portions of bills or treaties. However, in the majority of cases, the primary contribution made by professional aides to drafting legislation was acting in a liaison and/or mediating capacity. Their most important function in this regard was to convey to the legislative counsel or departmental draftsmen precisely what their committees wanted in bills and conversely to refer back to the committees for decision policy questions that developed as the drafting proceeded. Also, committee staff members helped the legislative counsel considerably by explaining technicalities in the subject matter and by describing the backgrounds of measures. And where the legislative counsel needed specialized assistance from the executive branch staff, the committee aides frequently made the arrangements for obtaining that.[12]

At various stages in the process of drafting and revising a bill, committee aides often negotiated at the staff level with representatives of the affected agencies and/or interest groups to remove their objections to it. Of course, in attempting to work out alterations in the contents and phraseology of a measure for that purpose, a committee staff member always operated within the guide lines of policy established by his committee. For example, during the 82d Congress, in the formative period of H.R. 7408 (a bill for the prevention of major disasters in coal mines) the drafting subcommittee of the House Education and Labor Committee adopted the two principles: (1) that the bill was to stay out of the general field of health and safety measures and to concentrate on removing the causes of the big disasters like fires, explosions, floods, and man-hoist accidents in mines; and (2) that the area of administrative discretion was to be circumscribed by spelling out the standards and the procedures to be followed in enforcing them. Having laid down these essentials of the bill, the subcommittee then sought to embody them in a form which would be acceptable to the Northern coal mine operators, United Mine Workers of America, and U.S. Bureau of Mines. The committee staff member and House legislative counsel assigned to this project collaborated closely with representatives of these groups in resolving the many problems that arose in connection with prescribing standards for safety equipment, administrative procedures, provisions for judicial review, and other details in successive drafts of the bill. After the subcommittee had finished with the measure, the committee aide continued to clear with them all amendments made by the full committee.

Preparing Reports to Accompany Bills

Significance of reports. The committee report to accompany a bill is a very important document of advocacy and interpretation. Its primary purpose is to afford the members of Congress sufficient information to evaluate the measure intelligently, with particular emphasis on the factors responsible for the committee's recommendations. During the period covered, members of Congress not on the committee concerned often relied largely on the report to accompany a bill for their knowledge of it. Generally, when explaining or justifying a measure on the floor of either house, its managers made heavy use of its report as a reference work.[13] Frequently, opponents as well as proponents of a bill quoted from its report to support their contentions.[14] And opponents of a measure were quick to exploit any defects—real or fancied—in the accompanying report. For example, in the 82d Congress, during the debate on H.R. 7405 (Defense Cataloging and Standardization Act), Representative Chet Holifield (D.-Calif.) made the following indictment of its report:

> The report is mischievous and faulty in its draftsmanship. It is deceptive in its failure to report accurately the history of cataloguing and if considered under regular rules of the House, would—in my opinion—be subject to a point of order for failing to substantially comply with the Ramseyer Rule.[15]

Even more important than the informational or tactical advantages in the debate conferred by a bill's report was its subsequent use by the courts, administrative agencies, and GAO as a guide to congressional intent in construing the resulting legislation. Awareness of this crucial interpretive function of the reports on bills was widespread among both the members of Congress and their staffs. In fact, some were concerned lest the courts and agencies extend that role to other committee documents as was evidenced by this disclaimer in the chairman's foreword to the activities report of the House Foreign Affairs Committee for the 82d Congress:

> This survey has been prepared, on my instructions, by the staff of the Committee on Foreign Affairs. Nothing contained in the survey should be interpreted as indicating legislative intent with respect to the legislative matters covered. This intent, where expressed, will be found in the appropriate hearings, reports, debate, and statutes.[16]

Format of reports. Although committee reports to accompany bills varied greatly in size—ranging from one or two pages to over a hundred pages long—and in organization, they usually comprised three basic ingredients: the main body, which was rather irreverently nicknamed the "guff" in some congressional staff circles;[17] the section-by-section analysis; and the portion required by the Ramseyer Rule in the House[18] or the Cordon Rule in the Senate.[19]

The guff displayed considerable diversity in the scope and arrangement of its contents. Generally, it included a statement of the purpose of the bill; a legislative history of the measure with special emphasis on the committee's role in that; an explanation of the need for the legislation; the reasons prompting the committee to adopt the policies incorporated in the bill; and a summary of the major provisions of the measure organized topically rather than under the section headings of the bill. Similarly, it expounded technical aspects of the programs authorized by the measure like infrastructure or offshore procurement. It set forth any amendments adopted by the committee. Frequently, alternative proposals were analyzed in the guff. It usually contained a discussion of the main arguments for and against the bill and occasionally listed the major interest groups on both sides. Where a renewal of the authorization for a program was involved, it ordinarily included a brief account of the progress made under that in the preceding year. Statements of the committee's intent and directives to the administrators of the proposed legislation were interspersed throughout the guff. Hence, despite its somewhat flippant sobriquet, the main body of a report often had very important legal implications.

A variety of titles were applied to the section-by-section analysis: "analysis of the bill," "analysis of provisions of the bill as reported," "analysis of the bill with explanation of changes," "explanation of the bill by sections," and "the provisions of the bill." But like the rose called by any other name, it was in essence the same. Proceeding through the entire bill in order, it attempted to explain each section in simplified language. Although the section-by-section analysis was sometimes nicknamed the "paraphrase,"[20] it was far more than that. Normally, it contained supplementary interpretive statements which gave the reasons for including certain provisions, defined terms used, and specifically construed particular requirements. For example, sec. 209(c) of H.R. 7408 (a bill for the prevention of major disasters in coal mines), 82d Congress, simply said:

> (c)   *Roof Support.*—The roof and ribs of all active underground roadways and travelways in a mine shall be adequately supported to protect persons from falls of roof or ribs.[21]

And the section-by-section analysis elaborated on that as follows:

> *Subsection (c)—Roof Support.*—This subsection provides that the roof and ribs of all active underground roadways and travelways in a mine shall be adequately supported to protect persons from falls of roof or ribs.
>
> The principal purpose of this subsection is to protect against man-trip accidents. Man-trips generally are the trips by which workmen are moved into and out of the underground areas of a mine at the beginning and ending of working shifts. On such trips many workmen often travel in a group in close proximity to each other. While so traveling they have no opportunity to examine the roof over, or the walls along the sides of, the roadway or travelway along which they travel, to ascertain if portions thereof are loose and likely to fall upon them. If the roof or ribs of the roadway or travelway along which they are traveling falls, it may kill or injure many of them. If such workmen are traveling on such roadways or travelways in a man-trip of cars traveling on rails and propelled by electricity, and a section of roof or rib falls upon them, it may not only kill or injure many persons, but it may also cause derailment and wrecking of cars, and mine fires ignited by sparks for [*sic*] short-circuited electric wires.
>
> Obviously this subsection does not apply to the support of roof and ribs everywhere throughout the underground areas of a mine. Nor does it apply to the roof and ribs of all underground roadways and travelways in a mine. It applies to the roof and ribs of *active* underground roadways and travelways. Active roadways and travelways means such roadways and travelways as are in use as distinguished from those which are not in use. The roof and ribs of such roadways and travelways must be adequately supported to protect persons from falls of such roof and ribs. The requirement of such adequate support should not be construed to require that such roof and ribs must necessarily be supported by artificial support. If the natural support of such roof and ribs is adequate to protect persons from falls of such roof and ribs, artificial support would not be required. Nor should this subsection be construed to authorize a Federal coal-mine inspector to require an operator of a mine to provide any particular kind or type of roof or rib support.[22]

Section-by-section analyses were not in all reports to accompany bills. During the period covered, some committees like Senate Post Office and Civil Service rarely, if ever, placed them in their reports. Other committees that habitually included them in their reports occasionally omitted them. And sometimes the section-by-section analysis was assimilated into the guff to form a sort of hybrid.[23] However, there were section-by-section analyses in most of the reports on major bills.

Both the Ramseyer and Cordon Rules provide in substance that the report to accompany any bill which repeals or amends a statute must include a comparative print of the two showing by appropriate typographical devices the changes to be made. But the two rules differ in three significant respects. Firstly, the Ramseyer Rule has been construed to apply to the bill as originally introduced regardless of committee amendments; whereas, the Cordon Rule explicitly states that it refers to the bill in the form recommended by the committee. Secondly, the Cordon Rule stipulates that the comparative print is to be prepared by the staff of the committee concerned. And thirdly, to release a House report from complying with the Ramseyer Rule requires specific exemption by a special order. But a Senate committee can dispense with the application of the Cordon Rule to any of its reports merely by declaring in them that such action is necessary to expedite the business of the Senate.[24]

Drafting of reports. During the period covered, committee reports to accompany bills were almost entirely a staff product. On a number of committees, the whole staff collaborated in preparing the report on a major measure. Jointly they would draw up the outline for it. Each staff member would write particular portions. Then after the draft of the report was completed, all would participate in revising it. In general, the professional aides to a committee collaborated on such reports to about the same extent as on other kinds of staff work.[25]

Before starting to do a report, the staff usually consulted the chairman on what to emphasize in it. Fairly often during the hearings and deliberations on a bill in executive sessions, individual committeemen would state that they wanted certain expository, qualifying, or other passages put in the accompanying report. And, of course, the reactions of the membership throughout the processing of a measure afforded a guide to the staff in deciding what the contents and emphases of the report should be. But for the most part, the staff drafted the reports on bills without much direct supervision from the committee.

Moreover, such reports were reviewed perfunctorily—if at all—by the committee as an entity. Rarely did a committee mark up reports the way it did the bills they accompanied. When a committee did meet to go over a report on a major bill, normally the clerk or staff director merely read eclectically from the guff, stressing any portions containing interpretive language. Most of the time, a committee did not collectively consider such a report at all. Instead, the staff would send a copy to each committee member to review individually. Rather often, the staff submitted a draft report to only the chairman and ranking minority member for revision. A prevalent practice was for the chairman alone to review the reports on unimportant measures. And sometimes in the case of a minor and uncomplicated bill, the staff threw the accompanying report in the hopper without having had any of the committee members go over it. Of course, where individual committeemen had requested that certain things be included in a report, the staff usually submitted the relevant sections to them for inspection.[26]

Occasionally, members of Congress complained about the lack of opportunity to review reports emanating from their committees. For example, in the 82d Congress, Representative Thomas A. Jenkins (R.-Ohio) charged:

> When the bill [H.R. 7800 (Social Security Act Amendment of 1952)] was reported out, it was accompanied by a beautiful big report. I daresay that nobody on the Ways and Means Committee wrote a line of that report, containing 51 pages of very illustrative tables and figures. And nobody saw that report as far as I know: I know I did not see it.[27]

And Representative Thomas B. Curtis (R.-Mo.) made the following accusations:

> I have constantly been embarrassed in my committee, for example, by refusing to approve a committee report on the ground that the first opportunity I have had to even look at a lengthy report was at the very minute the committee met for the purpose of adopting or rejecting the report. I should not have to state here the obvious fact that it should be routine procedure that lengthy written reports be furnished to the committee members at least a few hours before meeting time in order to give them an opportunity to study the report before the meeting. . . . In one instance, I might state, copies of the report which the committee was asked to approve were not even furnished or available to the committee at the time of the meeting; instead the written report was read by the clerk to the committee members. In the objection I raised to this procedure, I stated an even more obvious fact that it is impossible for a person to properly consider and weigh the words of a written report or [sic] an oral recitation. To my surprise the chairman overruled this objection.[28]

However, their strictures were but isolated voices of protest. Most of the members of Congress apparently were satisfied with the existing conditions. For instance, in the 82d Congress, when the staff of the House Education and Labor Committee suggested that it meet to go over a report on a bill, the members replied in astonishment, "Why should we? We never have in the past." With such complacency and the inertia of precedent on the side of current practices, it seemed unlikely that they would be changed on a widespread scale very soon.

In view of the important interpretive function of reports to accompany bills, the prevailing failure of the committees to review them more carefully was an Achilles heel of the legislative process. Frequently, the staffs had to divine the preferences of the effective majorities of their committees and incorporate those in the reports on bills without the benefit of a confirming check by the principals concerned. This state of affairs again stressed the necessity of having the staffs adhere strictly to their proper role and of holding them immediately responsible to their respective committees.

Participation in Executive Sessions

Almost invariably, a professional aide to a committee attended all its executive sessions at which a bill, report, or other item of committee business on which he had worked was under consideration. There he rendered a variety of services, ranging from acting as a reading clerk to drafting amendments. But for the most part, he was available to furnish additional information and explanation of whatever project he was handling. When a bill was being marked up, he would expound technical provisions, point up policy questions, analyze proposed changes, keep track of committee decisions, and incorporate them in successive revisions of the bill. The extent to which professional staff members participated in committee deliberations on their own initiative varied widely. Some rarely, if ever, volunteered any comments but preferred to go through the chairman or another member, slipping a note or whispering to him about any matter which should be brought to the committee's attention. Others participated in the discussions in executive sessions on almost the same basis as the committeemen. Generally, though, even where committees encouraged their staffs to take an active part in their proceedings, professional aides had to be very tactful in exercising that privilege. For they were dealing with groups of individuals who were very sensitive about their prerogatives. And all the staff members interviewed emphasized the importance of proper timing and of avoiding obtrusiveness when making comments at their own instance.

Preparing for and Assisting during Floor Action

Before a major bill came up for consideration on the floor of the House or Senate, the staff of the committee concerned usually took several preparatory steps. On the House side, where the chairman had to go before the Rules Committee to request a special order on a bill, the professional aide handling it normally assisted him in making his presentation. On the Senate side, if it were deemed necessary to bring up a bill under a motion to suspend the rules by a two-thirds vote of the Senate, the committee staff prepared the motion and filed it at the appropriate time. In both chambers, the committee staff nearly always drafted the statement with which the chairman (or other manager) opened the debate on a bill. Customarily, this introductory speech summarized the entire measure and set forth the committee's position on any controversial aspects of it. Frequently, the staff would make up a series of brief memoranda containing answers to certain arguments and questions that probably would be raised. Then when one of them came up, the staff could simply encircle the relevant portion of the "prefabricated" reply and hand it to the chairman to read right off in rejoinder. Generally, the staff assembled a file of reference materials for use during the floor action on the bill. And on a few committees after the first day of the debate, the staff indexed each issue of the *Congressional Record* with multicolored marginal tabs before the start of the next day's session.

Usually, the professional aide who had done the bulk of the staff work on the bill accompanied the chairman on the floor. There he assisted the chairman in many ways: locating references for him, obtaining additional information, analyzing proposals and arguments advanced then, and suggesting responses to them. Also, sometimes he reworked amendments offered there to make them acceptable to the committee or relayed the chairman's directions on that score to the legislative counsel, who often was present in the rear of the chamber. And frequently, he was responsible for editing the chairman's remarks in the transcript of the proceedings, primarily to ensure that no erroneous interpretation of the legislative intent could be derived from them.

While he was on the floor, other members of the committee often turned to him for assistance. And generally, a number of individual Congressmen not on the committee would come over to inquire about the bill. Occasionally, they requested him to draft amendments. And once in a while, they asked him for supporting data or for short statements they could deliver in behalf of the bill.

Staff Work for Conferences

Where a bill was sent to conference, again considerable staff preparation was necessary. For the convenience of the conferees, one of the committee staff members or legislative counsel who had worked on the bill would make up a conference committee print of it. That almost indispensable visual aid focused attention on the differences in the House and Senate versions of a bill by means of appropriate typographical devices. A few committee staffs annotated conference committee prints by pasting typewritten notes in the margins telling which member of Congress had sponsored each amendment and other background information. Nearly all the committee staffs prepared supplementary memoranda pointing up the discrepancies in the two versions of a bill.

If there were sufficient time before the initial session of a conference committee, the committee staffs and legislative counsel from both houses who would be present usually endeavored to meet in advance. At such preliminary staff consultations, they often decided which of them would make up the conference committee print. Where one of the legislative counsel had not been called in until then, the committee staffs and legislative counsel from the other chamber would brief him on the two versions of the bill. However, their primary purpose in getting together was to try to anticipate how the conferees would reconcile the differences in the House and Senate versions of the bill. Occasionally, they would draft amendments incorporating such prospective compromises. And once in a while, they would write part of the statement of the House managers.[29]

At the meetings of a conference committee, the staff members functioned much the same as at executive sessions of their respective committees. They explained variant provisions of the bill, kept track of the decisions made by the conferees, and collaborated with the legislative counsel in embodying those in amendments. One of the gravest concerns of the staff at this stage was to ensure that the conference committee acted on every difference in the two versions of the bill. Since the conferees frequently did not go through the bill taking up the disputed points in order but instead proceeded to dispose of the less controversial ones first, they rendered this task doubly difficult. Skipping around that way, they were far more likely to overlook some discrepancies. Operating in an atmosphere of urgency, the staff members had to work at high speed under conditions taxing their energy and endurance. When a conference committee meeting adjourned at midnight, they sometimes had to work until three or four o'clock in the morning getting ready for the next day's session.

After the conferees had reached agreement on all matters at issue, the staff drafted the conference report and the accompanying statement of the House managers. Generally, the preparation of these two documents was a combined operation by the staff members from both chambers. Often, the Senate committee aides and Senate legislative counsel even helped to write portions of the statement of the House managers, and ordinarily, all the staff members present reviewed the entire report and accompanying statement. From time to time when a particular point was being discussed, conferees would ask that a paragraph treating it in a certain fashion be put in the statement of the House managers. But aside from that, these two documents were mainly staff products. Rather often toward the end of a session, the conferees were unable to reassemble to review a conference report. In such cases, the committee aides or legislative counsel usually endeavored to check it with the ranking managers from both chambers and with any of the other conferees who had requested that specific passages be inserted in the statement of the House managers.

In at least one instance in the closing days of the 82d Congress, the preliminary work done by a Senate committee staff member made it unnecessary for a conference committee to convene at all. After the House had disagreed to the Senate amendments to H.R. 1739 (a bill authorizing an annual appropriation for the care of lepers in Hawaii) and conferees had been appointed, the Senate Interior and Insular Affairs Committee aide concerned contacted the House sponsor of H.R. 1739 and worked out with him changes in the language of the Senate version which would both preserve the Senate's intent and remove the House's objections. Upon securing approval by Senator Russell Long (D.-La.), ranking Senate conferee on H.R. 1739, of the compromise they had effected, this staff member drafted a conference report on the bill. Receiving Senator Long's permission to circulate the report among the conferees for their signatures, he carried it around to the other Senate managers. Then he sent the report over to his opposite number on the House Interior and Insular Affairs Committee staff, who did the same thing with the House managers. And the conference report, which was subsequently approved by both the House and Senate, was filed without the conference committee ever having met.

Although rather exceptional, this episode highlights the large amount of responsibility customarily delegated to the congressional aides servicing conference committees, the most crucial phase of the legislative process. In general, work on legislation illustrates—probably better than any of their other activities —the very complex facilitative job to be done by the professional staffs of committees, the advantages accruing from continuity of tenure in mastering the details of that job and in devising new techniques for its more effective performance, and the great trust habitually reposed in committee aides. These considerations, in turn, re-emphasize the need for having professional staff members who are competent, reliable, immediately accountable to their respective committees, and imbued with the proper concept of their role.

CHAPTER IX

OVERSIGHT OF ADMINISTRATION

Methods of Exercising

During the period covered, the committees exercised oversight of the administrative establishment in a number of different ways. Among those were: conferences with top departmental officials; investigations; handling casework; requiring periodic reports on the status of particular programs; and reviewing or passing upon discrete administrative actions in advance.

Conferences. At the beginning of every Congress, several committees like House Interstate and Foreign Commerce and House Interior and Insular Affairs would hold what might be termed "orientation seminars" on the administrative agencies within their respective provinces. In those, the head of each agency and his immediate assistants would describe its functions, give a short progress report on its current activities, outline its program for the coming year, and suggest directions in which its services could be expanded. Similarly, during the course of a Congress whenever they became concerned about some aspect of an agency's operations, most committees would summon its top officials and discuss that thoroughly with them.[1]

Such conferences were not always initiated by the committees. Sometimes they were held at the instance of the agency involved. And they were not invariably critiques of departmental policies but occasionally were convened so that an agency could seek a committee's advice during the formative stages of such policies.[2] For example, once in a while, the Bureau of Internal Revenue or the Treasury Department would ask to meet with the Joint Committee on Internal Revenue Taxation to consult it about prospective regulations or the settlement of particular tax deficiency cases.[3]

Ordinarily, most conferences of this sort did not entail too much committee staff work. For the orientation seminars, the committee aides generally just notified the agency officials when to appear and indicated in only the broadest terms what they were to cover. Frequently, departmental personnel went through the committee staff in requesting an opportunity to consult with a committee. Sometimes a committee staff suggested the need for such conferences to the committee and/or agency staff members. Occasionally, when a committee held a series of consultations with departmental officials about an agency's administrative problems, the staff formulated questions for the committee members to ask; and the distinction between such conferences and regular hearings in executive sessions became blurred.

Investigations. In a full-fledged committee investigation, the staff customarily participated at every stage from preparing the original resolution authorizing the inquiry to drafting the final report on it. Some committees like House Education and Labor and Senate Agriculture and Forestry usually had their staffs make preliminary investigations as a basis for deciding whether or not formal inquiries by them were warranted. And some committees occasionally relied on staff investigations in lieu of conducting inquiries themselves, dispatching staff members not only throughout the United States but all over the world for that purpose. For example, during the 82d Congress, the Subcommittee on Export Controls and Policies, Senate Interstate and Foreign Commerce Committee, sent a professional aide to West Germany and other European countries on two separate occasions to check on allegations that West Germany was a major channel of war goods going from the West to Russia.[4] And the Subcommittee on Territories and Insular Possessions, House Interior and Insular Affairs Committee, had its professional staff member, William H. Hackett, travel to Alaska in July, 1951, to collect information on the operation of the new tax program and on the economy of Alaska.[5]

Casework. The "service" or "watchdog" committees like the House and Senate Select Committees on Small Business or the Joint Committee on Defense Production encouraged all the members of Congress to refer constituent complaints and other departmental business falling within their respective spheres to them,[6] and their staffs justified their existence largely by the amount of casework they performed.[7] Similarly, all the legislative committees took care of some departmental business, which was handled almost entirely by their staffs. Except for the "service" or "watchdog" committee staffs,[8] casework did not constitute a major fraction of their over-all workloads, ten to fifteen per cent being the average estimate of the committee aides interviewed.

Periodic reports. Many agencies like the Mutual Security Agency were required by law to submit to Congress periodic reports on their operations under certain statutes.[9] The use made of those reports by the committees to which they were referred varied. Generally, they were filed and utilized by the committee staffs principally as reference works. Occasionally, professional aides prepared summaries of them for the members of their committees. And once in a while, such reports or excerpts from them were included in committee reports—generally as appendixes.

Reviewing individual actions. Several committees had statutory authority to review certain types of administrative transactions in advance. For example, sec. 3777 of the Internal Revenue Code stipulated that the Commissioner of Internal Revenue could not make a tax refund or credit in excess of $200,000 (in excess of $75,000 prior to August 27, 1949) until thirty days after he had submitted a written report to the Joint Committee on Internal Revenue Taxation, giving the name of the person to whom the refund or credit was to be made, the amount of such refund or credit, and a summary of the facts and decision of the Commissioner in each case. Although the Joint Committee on Internal Revenue Taxation had no formal power to disallow such refunds or credits, Dr. Roy Blough, former Director of Tax Research and Assistant to the Secretary of the Treasury, said that a refund or credit to which the Joint Tax Committee objected was not likely to be made unless the taxpayer concerned sued and won.[10]

This review by the Joint Tax Committee of refunds or credits in excess of $200,000 was exercised mainly through its staff. The staff examined all the refunds and credits reported by the Commissioner and made final disposition of most of them, referring only the cases about which it was undecided or to which it raised objections to the Joint Tax Committee for consideration. That this was a rather sizable operation was indicated by the fact that the Commissioner reported 616 cases aggregating $281,276,631.36 for the fiscal year 1949 and 369 cases totalling $485,122,283.66 for the fiscal year 1950.[11] A "branch office" of the Joint Tax Committee staff located at the Bureau of Internal Revenue was comprised of several attorneys who did nothing else but work on reviewing tax refunds and credits under the supervision of Gaston Chesteen, the assistant chief of staff of the Joint Tax Committee. The successive steps in the scrutiny of a refund or credit by the Joint Tax Committee and its staff were as follows.

After the attorneys in Mr. Chesteen's office had examined a refund, they would send the report on it to Colin Stam, chief of staff of the Joint Tax Committee, with an accompanying statement of their concurrence or disagreement with it. Where they opposed a refund, Mr. Stam had to decide whether or not to take their recommendation to the Joint Tax Committee.[12] In such instances, Mr. Stam generally arranged a meeting between the Joint Tax Committee staff and representatives of the Bureau of Internal Revenue (or of the Department of Justice, depending on which of those agencies was handling the tax case involved)[13] at which they would discuss the case thoroughly. After that, if Mr. Stam felt that there were substantial grounds for opposing the tax refund, he referred the case to the Joint Tax Committee. Then both the Joint Tax Committee staff and Bureau of Internal Revenue (or Department of Justice) personnel would argue the case before the Joint Tax Committee in executive session. Most of the time, the Joint Tax Committee upheld the recommendations of its staff to object to a refund.

Ratifying transactions. Further, a few committees were empowered to disapprove specific administrative actions in prescribed categories. For example, Title VI of Public Law 155, 82d Congress, required the Army, Navy, Air Force, and Federal Civil Defense Administration to come into agreement with the Armed Services Committees of the House and Senate with respect to the acquisition or disposal of real property for an amount estimated in excess of $25,000, including leases involving an annual rental in excess of $25,000 and transfers of real property with an estimated value in excess of $25,000 between the military departments, to other federal agencies, or to states—with certain minor exceptions.[14] Pursuant to this provision of the law, the miliary departments and Federal Civil Defense Administration submitted reports on all such proposed real-estate transactions, which in congressional parlance were called "projects," to the House and Senate Armed Services Committees. To handle those, each armed services committee established a special subcommittee. Both these subcommittees were serviced by professional aides from their parent committees, and they followed a generally similar course in dealing with agency real-estate transactions.

Normally about ten days after receiving the departmental report on a project, a copy of which was automatically distributed to every member of the full committee, the subcommittee would meet to consider it. Usually, the subcommittee held hearings at which officials from the military departments, members of the full committee, individual Congressmen not on the committee, and occasionally interested private parties testified. Then the subcommittee passed upon the project. At that point, there was a difference in the procedure of the two committees. The Senate Armed Services Committee authorized its Subcommittee on Real Estate and Military Construction to make final disposition of these projects; whereas, the House Subcommittee on Acquisitions and Disposals could only take tentative action which had to be confirmed by the full House Armed Services Committee in each instance. But actually this distinction was more one of form than of substance. Although occasionally the House Armed Services Committee examined a project very thoroughly, ninety per cent of the time it approved the recommendations of its Subcommittee on Acquisitions and Disposals almost automatically.

In any event, whether acting directly or through a subcommittee, each armed services committee could do one of three things with every project: approve it, disapprove it, or approve it conditionally. For example, in the 83d Congress, the Senate Subcommittee on Real Estate and Military Construction approved Air Force acquisition No. 121 with the stipulations that the Air Force was to purchase the property at a cost not to exceed five million dollars and if unable to do so, might initiate condemnation proceedings for acquisition of either a leasehold interest or fee simple title.[15] Either armed services committee could veto a project. Likewise, either committee could impose conditions on a project without the concurrence of the other. And if both committees placed similar qualifications on a project, the more stringent prevailed.

The professional aide assigned to each real-estate subcommittee assisted it materially by analyzing and making recommendations on all the projects reported by the military departments. Generally, any objections he raised to a project were based on technical considerations such as the undesirability of paying two thirds of the price of a piece of land for only an easement in it. Of course, he usually did not have a chance to go into the projects too thoroughly because servicing the real-estate subcommittee was but one of his duties.

Other forms of oversight. In addition to the ways just described, there were several other methods by which legislative committees supervised administration—one of which was available only to Senate committees.[16] When considering executive nominations, Senate committees often examined policies of the agencies involved. Finally, much of the congressional oversight of the executive branch was performed by the appropriations committee and their staffs,[17] which are outside the scope of this study.

Proportion of Workload

Generalizing about the extent to which the staffs of legislative committees were engaged in supervisory activities is difficult because those were so intermingled with other aspects of their work. For example, when amending or re-enacting statutes, the committees customarily reviewed the previous administration of those. Reciprocally, committee investigations and casework often eventuated in specific legislation. Furthermore, the amount of oversight of administration performed by a committee staff was not constant but varied widely in different periods. During Congresses when a committee did not handle any major legislation and during the intervals between sessions, its staff usually devoted proportionately more time to surveillance of the executive branch. Taking all these factors into account—exclusive of committees with special supervisory responsibilities like the Joint Tax Committee—the committee aides interviewed estimated that not to exceed twenty per cent of their time was spent on congressional oversight duties, the chief continuing element in which was casework.

Connection between Staffing and Oversight Problems

Although oversight of administration is an accepted function of Congress, there are some major unresolved problems concerning it. Among them are: How much and what kinds of supervisory activities should Congress undertake?

Where should the responsibility for their performance be placed? All such questions have obvious implications for congressional staffing—particularly its size and organization. Congress can exercise oversight of administration in detail and on a large scale only with the aid of staff. A desire to extend the supervisory activities of the standing committees is responsible for much of the demand for enlarging their staffs. Overexpansion is one of the gravest dangers confronting the committee staffs. In addition, any appraisal of staffing should take into account the validity of the purposes for which it is used. Therefore, the rest of this chapter is devoted mainly to some of the problems arising from oversight of administration by the standing committees.

Invasion of the Executive Branch Province

During the period covered, under the guise of supervising administration, some legislative committees and their staffs encroached on the executive branch province in a number of instances. Several of those were but isolated incidents of a debatable nature. However, others were repetitive and an undeniable invasion of the administrative process.

Improving management. In the first category fell the various efforts of committee staffs to improve the management of an agency or to catalyze and coordinate joint attempts by several agencies to improve certain common procedures. For example, in the 80th Congress, the Senate Expenditures Committee staff conducted a management survey of the U.S. Maritime Commission. Pursuant to the findings of that study, the Maritime Commission thoroughly revised its organization and operations.[18] Also during the 80th Congress, the Senate Expenditures Committee staff mediated among the GAO, Bureau of the Budget, and Treasury Department in an endeavor to effect improvements in the accounting system of the federal government. The Senate Expenditures Committee's activities report for the 81st Congress gives the following account of that staff undertaking:

> Conferences were held with representatives of the General Accounting Office, Bureau of the Budget, and Department of the Treasury, with a view of improving the accounting system at all levels of administration and to adopt business-type methods, procedures, and forms in order that a single monthly report could be prepared that would furnish the information necessary for agency management and at the same time fulfill the needs of the Bureau of the Budget and the General Accounting Office.

> At the conclusion of these conferences, the staff recommended that the Bureau of the Budget, General Accounting Office, and Treasury Department make a concerted drive to study the problems involved and work out improved methods and procedures for the purpose of streamlining the Federal accounting and reporting systems.

On January 6, 1948, the Comptroller General established an Accounting Systems Division in the General Accounting Office to deal with the administrative accounting system of the Federal Government, ... A cooperative agreement was signed by the Secretary of the Treasury, Director of the Bureau of the Budget, and the Comptroller General, whereby those three agencies would spearhead study and development of better accounting and reporting of fiscal affairs of the Government in collaboration with the departments and agencies concerned.[19]

Likewise, occasionally a committee hired a management engineering firm to make a study of the organization and procedures of an agency. For example, in the 82d Congress, the Senate Interstate and Foreign Commerce Committee employed the Wolf Management Engineering Company to conduct a management survey of the Interstate Commerce Commission.[20] If such a study were deemed desirable for an agency, it would seem more in accord with the concept of administrative responsibility to allow the agency head rather than a legislative committee the requisite funds to engage a management firm to do the job. And the more prevalent practice was for the department concerned to secure an appropriation for that purpose. For instance, in the 80th Congress, the Treasury Department was authorized to spend $100,000 for a management survey of the Bureau of Customs, which was performed by McKinsey and Company, management consultants.[21]

"Preauditing" specific acts. Intrinsic to our system of government based upon the separation of powers principle is some ambiguity about the rightful limits of congressional control over the administrative establishment. As a result, the extent to which the committees and their staffs exceeded the bounds of constitutional propriety in the above-cited instances is arguable. Also, there were many other marginal cases. However, where congressional committees made the final decisions on specific administrative acts as the armed services committees did on real-estate transactions under Title VI of Public Law 155, 82d Congress,[22] they unquestionably had assumed a purely administrative function. Where committees were empowered to review particular administrative actions but had no statutory authority to disallow those as was the case with the Joint Tax Committee regarding tax refunds or credits in excess of $200,000, the situation was less clear. But seeing that the Joint Tax Committee generally could in effect disapprove such refunds or credits,[23] that type of procedure probably should be considered the same as the preceding one.

This participation by congressional committees in the actual administration of laws is a very ominous development. Firstly, it deprives the agency heads and the President of effective responsibility for the manner in which that legislation is executed. Secondly, it has other undesirable repercussions on administration. It causes centralization in Washington, D.C., of the transactions subject to ratification by the committees, extra work for the departments, and delays in carrying out the programs involving those projects. Thirdly, it adversely affects the operations of the committees concerned. It diverts their attention from work on major legislation and other important business to passing upon the details of administrative acts. And usually it necessitates a sizable expansion of the committee staffs, with all the problems that entails.[24]

The main reasons the adverse effects of this usurpation of administrative functions by congressional committees were not more widely felt were that it had been on such a small scale and of fairly recent origin. However, the requirement of ratification by the appropriate congressional committees could be extended to a large variety of administrative actions.[25] And it was incorporated in laws with increasing frequency during the period covered. The first statute specifically vesting such power in congressional committees was Public Law 289,[26] 78th Congress, which provided:

> That prior to the acquisition or disposal, by lease or otherwise, of any land acquired for naval use under the authority of this, or any other Act, the Secretary of the Navy shall come into agreement with the Naval Affairs Committees of the Senate and of the House of Representatives with respect to the terms of such prospective acquisitions or disposals. . . .[27]

Next on May 1, 1951, Congress passed H.R. 3096 (a bill relating to land transfers by the military departments), which would have extended this procedure to the real-estate transactions of all the military departments and of the Federal Civil Defense Administration—with the qualification that only leases having an annual rental in excess of $10,000 were to be included. That bill was vetoed by the President on May 15, 1951; and the House promptly voted 312 to 68 to override his veto on May 17, 1951.[28] Although the Senate did not act on the veto, both chambers passed H.R. 4914 (Military and Naval Construction Act of 1951)—Title VI of which contained substantially the same provisions as H.R. 3096 except that it applied only to real-estate acquisitions, disposals, and annual rentals involving an amount in excess of $25,000—on September 18, 1951; and this bill was approved by the President on September 28, 1951, to become Public Law 155, 82d Congress.[29]

Title VI of Public Law 155 applied only to real property within the continental United States or its possessions. On July 14, 1952, Public Law 534, 82d Congress, was approved, Title IV of which contained a similar proviso with respect to certain classified military construction projects—including any real-estate transactions pertaining to those—in both the United States and foreign countries.[30] Also in July, 1952, Congress passed but the President pocket-vetoed H.R. 6839 (a bill authorizing the lease-purchase of property for postal purposes), which stipulated that all lease-purchase agreements made under that Act had to be approved by the House and Senate Post Office and Civil Service Committees.[31]

The most insidious aspect of this usurpation of administrative functions by congressional committees is that neither of the other two main branches of the federal government can effectively check such encroachment. If statutory provisions like Title VI of Public Law 155, 82d Congress, could be subjected to judicial review, they almost certainly would be declared unconstitutional invasions of the executive power in accordance with the doctrine enunciated in *Springer v. Philippine Islands,* 277 U.S. 189 (1928), which has generally been followed by the state courts in such cases as *People v. Tremaine,* 252 N.Y. 27 (1929). Essentially, this rule of law is that in a government based on the separation of powers principle, the legislature may not impose executive duties upon a legislative office.

In the Springer case, the Supreme Court held that statutes of the Philippine legislature vesting the voting power of the stock of the government-owned bank and coal company in a board comprised of the Governor General, President of the Senate, and Speaker of the House of Representatives of the Philippine Islands were invalid because they transgressed the "separation of powers" embodied in the Philippine Organic Act. In the majority opinion delivered by Justice Sutherland, the Court said:

> It may be stated then, as a general rule inherent in the American constitutional system, that, unless otherwise expressly provided or incidental to the powers conferred, the legislature cannot exercise either executive or judicial power; the executive cannot exercise either legislative or judicial power; the judiciary cannot exercise either executive or legislative power. . . .

> Legislative power, as distinguished from executive power, is the authority to make laws, but not to enforce them or appoint the agents charged with the duty of such enforcement. The latter are executive functions. . . .

> Not having the power of appointment, unless expressly granted or incidental to its powers, the legislature cannot engraft executive duties upon a legislative office, since that would be to usurp the power of appointment by indirection. . . .[32]

Applying this rule in the Tremaine case, the New York Court of Appeals invalidated statutory provisions which subjected the segregations made by department heads of lump sum appropriations for personal services to the approval of the chairmen of the finance committees of the legislature. In its opinion, the Court of Appeals declared:

> This is a clear and conspicuous instance of an attempt by the legislature to confer administrative power upon two of its own members. It may not engraft executive duties upon a legislative office and thus usurp the executive power by indirection. (*Springer v. Philippine Islands,* 277 U.S. 189.)[33]

However, the catch is that in all probability a measure like Title VI of Public Law 155, 82d Congress, will never be brought before the courts for a test of its constitutionality. It is difficult to envision how a justiciable issue could arise from its application. Conceivably, if the President wished to restore executive prerogatives in this area, he might order the heads of the military departments not to comply with this provision of the law.[34] But in view of the realities of the power structures of the executive and legislative branches, the President would not be prone to precipitate such a contest, which—if won—undoubtedly would prove to be a Pyrrhic victory for the military departments.

Likewise, lacking an item veto, the President is powerless to cope with that sort of proviso where it is incorporated in an essential statute. In any event, when the tide of sentiment in both houses is running strong for the imposition of such legislative controls on administration, Congress can readily override his veto. As the legislative history of H.R. 3096 and its successor measure, Title VI of Public Law 155, 82d Congress, graphically demonstrated, sometimes the President cannot even fight a creditable delaying action through the use of his veto.

Hence, the only ultimate safeguard against and remedy for such invasion of the executive power by Congress lies in the self-restraint of the individual legislators based upon an awareness of the constitutional limits of their proper sphere and of the adverse effects on efficient and responsible administration if they exceed those. During the debates on various proposals for requiring certain classes of transactions to be ratified by the appropriate congressional committees, numerous members of Congress displayed an acute appreciation of the conditions necessary for an effective administrative process.[35] Also, several legislators like Senator Everett Dirksen (R.-Ill.), who had not been noted for their solicitude for executive prerogatives in the past, revealed a penetrating grasp of the constitutional issues involved. But unfortunately, they did not constitute a majority then.

Oversight Provisions of the Legislative Reorganization Act

Against this background, it is appropriate to examine the express provisions and philosophy of the Legislative Reorganization Act of 1946 regarding supervision of administration by the standing committees. In its final report on March 4, 1946, the Joint Committee on the Organization of Congress recommended:

> That the standing committees of both Houses be directed and empowered to carry on continuing review and oversight of legislation and agencies within their jurisdiction; that the power of subpena be given

them; and that the practice of creating special investigating committees be abandoned.[36]

These three recommendations were incorporated in secs. 128, 125, and 126 of S. 2177, 79th Congress. Sec. 128 directed each standing committee of the Senate and House to exercise continuous surveillance of the execution by the administrative agencies concerned of laws within its jurisdiction. Sec. 125 extended the subpoena power, authority to investigate any matter within their respective provinces, and other procedural powers to the committees of both chambers. Sec. 126 provided that no bill, resolution, or amendment to establish or continue a special or select committee should be considered in either house.[37] And in the report to accompany S. 2177, there was the following commentary:

> A third group of provisions in the bill is designed to strengthen congressional surveillance of the execution of the laws by the executive branch. Congress has long lacked adequate facilities for the continuous inspection and review of administrative performance. We often delegate the rule-making power to administrative departments and commissions, without making any provision for follow-up to see if administrative rules and regulations are in accord with the intent of the law. Several of the postwar acts, for example, require certain agencies to submit quarterly reports to Congress, but assign the responsibility for scrutinizing these reports to no legislative committees.
>
> To remedy this situation, S. 2177 would authorize the standing committees of both Houses to exercise continuous surveillance of the execution of the laws by the administrative agencies within their jurisdiction. Armed with the power of subpena and staffed with qualified specialists in their respective provinces of public affairs, these committees would conduct a continuous review of the activities of the agencies administering laws originally reported by the legislative committees. . . .
>
> Under this arrangement, it will no longer be necessary to create special committees of investigation from time to time. Sporadic investigations of the conduct of public affairs in the past have often served a salutary purpose by exposing administrative incompetence or corruption and by improving the execution of the laws. But they have lacked continuity and have not provided the members of standing committees with direct knowledge of the information they have gathered. In cases where legislative action is indicated, standing committees find it necessary to do much of the work over again. S. 2177 proposes, therefore, to ban the use of special committees hereafter.[38]

These three sections of S. 2177 were approved by the Senate with only one slight modification. The word "watchfulness" was substituted for "surveillance" in sec. 128 because Senator Forrest Donnell (R.-Mo.) thought the latter connoted an unconstitutional control of administration by Congress.[39] However, in the House substitute for S. 2177, which was accepted *in toto* by the

Senate because of exigencies of the parliamentary situation, sec. 126 was eliminated; and the scope of sec. 125, which became sec. 134(a) of the law as enacted, was reduced to apply to just the Senate committees. Sec. 128 was carried over intact to emerge as sec. 136 of the Legislative Reorganization Act, which reads thusly:

> SEC. 136. To assist the Congress in appraising the administration of the laws and in developing such amendments or related legislation as it may deem necessary, each standing committee of the Senate and the House of Representatives shall exercise continuous watchfulness of the execution by the administrative agencies concerned of any laws, the subject matter of which is within the jurisdiction of such committee; and, for that purpose, shall study all pertinent reports and data submitted to the Congress by the agencies in the executive branch of the Government.[40]

This brief excerpt from the legislative history of the LaFollette-Monroney Act establishes the intent of its authors to focus supervision of administration in the standing committees. Inasmuch as the section prohibiting special committees was deleted, this design was imperfectly realized. Nevertheless, despite not having been approved, the proposed ban on select committees left a lingering radiation of effects. During the period covered, critics of special committees maintained that the creation or continuation of such committees was "contrary to the spirit" of the Legislative Reorganization Act. And they generally proceeded to argue that the standing committees should conduct every investigation because of having been expressly empowered[41] and equipped with professional staffs to do so.[42]

Also, according to Dr. George B. Galloway, former staff director of the Joint Committee on the Organization of Congress, the authors of the Act intended that the standing committees should take over much of the supervisory role of the individual members of Congress. In 1951 he wrote:

> Intervention of individual Members of Congress in the affairs of administrative agencies with a view to expediting or influencing agency decisions on behalf of constituents is considered improper, where the Congressman is not a member of the corresponding supervisory committee and is not merely seeking information or making a routine inquiry. It was the intention of the authors of the Legislative Reorganization Act that the oversight committees would serve as a clearing house to which Members would refer all such constituent complaints and inquiries and which would then bring them to the attention of the agencies concerned. The volume and character of such complaints would be a rough index of the performance and weakness of the agency. At the same time, as the Hoover Commission task force report on regulatory commissions remarked, "this method would shield both the Congressman and the Commission from the suspicion of influence inherent in direct approaches for constituents."[43]

Undesirability of Focusing Oversight Duty in Standing Committees

This objective of making the standing committees the principal, if not the exclusive, locus of congressional oversight (particularly of the detailed and continuous sort contemplated) of administration is undesirable for both philosophical and practical reasons. Firstly, it is lacking in balance and perspective because it does not take into account the totality of action of each chamber and of both chambers together in the over-all legislative process, which in turn is but a constituent of the comprehensive process of government. The whole concept of supervision by a standing committee of the execution of the laws within its jurisdiction ignores the fact that the congressional purpose imparted to each of them was determined by the combined action of the two houses. If the membership of the committee be substantially the same as when a law was enacted, the interests which the committeemen collectively represent probably have already exerted a disproportionate influence on its contents. Anyway, further distortion in the direction of the committee members' preferences should not be encouraged by making them the official interpreters of the "legislative intent" regarding that statute. After a measure has gone through successive compromises and emerged as the resultant of the conflicting forces in the two chambers, why should either standing committee that handled it be given an opportunity to warp its application toward the committee's undiluted version of that statute? This whole argument has been summed up very neatly: "The hazard is that a body like Congress, when it gets into detail, ceases to be itself; it acts through a fraction which may be a faction."[44]

Moreover, the executive branch's administration of a measure is yet another essential ingredient in the over-all governmental process. The executive agencies, presidency, and judiciary give expression to additional interests which contribute to the final synthesis in the law as enforced. These considerations assume even greater importance where passages in a statute have been left calculatedly ambiguous in the hope that the administrative agency concerned could work out a policy on a case-by-case basis that Congress was unable or unwilling to define precisely. In such situations, neither standing committee that worked on the measure should be placed in a position to influence the judgment of the agency in the direction it was unable to persuade its respective chamber or Congress as a whole to move.

Further, there is a relatively high turnover in the memberships of many standing committees—particularly on the House side. Several Congresses after the enactment of a statute, the committees that processed it may be—and often are—comprised of almost entirely different personnel, who would not have any firsthand knowledge of what the legislative intent was when it was passed.

All these shortcomings are accentuated to the utmost when congressional committees are empowered to disapprove specific administrative acts. Though sec. 136 does not authorize the standing committees to ratify individual administrative actions, it undeniably has contributed to the spread of the sentiment for enacting laws that do. The debates on such measures are studded with references to the supervisory duty imposed upon the standing committees by the Legislative Reorganization Act and with the corollary argument that they would enable the committees to discharge that responsibility better. Also, the growth of this climate of opinion favoring more intervention by Congress in administration weakens the only effective check on the enlarging encroachment by congressional committees on the executive branch province—the self-restraint of the legislators grounded in an appreciation of the bounds of their rightful orbit.

Fundamentally, nearly all these objections stem from concern about the danger of excessive meddling by congressional committees in administration. Paradoxically, some persons oppose focusing the oversight function in the standing committees for the almost exactly opposite reason that they may not perform it vigorously enough. Proponents of this viewpoint fear that the standing committees are prone to develop a paternalistic attitude toward the agencies within their respective jurisdictions and hence to become apologists for, rather than searching and impartial critics of, those. And on some committees like Senate Interstate and Foreign Commerce during the period covered, there was a discernible tendency in that direction. Even if an entire committee does not share such solicitude for the agencies within its province, so this argument runs, administration stalwarts among its members may block embarrassing probes or suppress revelations arising from those. Again, though not prevalent, there have been enough instances of that sort in the recent past to lend color to this charge. And at least, the rules of procedure adopted by several committees, requiring a majority vote (sometimes a unanimous vote in the case of a subcommittee) to initiate an inquiry or to release the findings of an investigation,[45] make that possible.

Relatedly, the proposals for concentrating the oversight function in the standing committees disregard the striking contributions that individual members of Congress have made in exposing deficiencies in the administration of particular agencies. The accomplishments of Senator John J. Williams (R.-Del.) in his one-man probe of the Bureau of Internal Revenue during the 81st and 82d Congresses afford an excellent case in point. If there be any substance to the apprehension that some standing committees may become "captives" of agencies within their jurisdictions, the independent check run by individual members of Congress—often in connection with handling casework—serves as an essential corrective to that contingency.

Furthermore, this emphasis on oversight of the executive branch by the standing committees raises the difficult practical question of how that responsibility is to be divided among them. What are to be the respective roles of the appropriations committees—which have done most of the congressional supervision of administration in the past and are not likely to relinquish any of their activities in that respect—and of the legislative committees? Among the legislative committees what is to be the line of demarcation in this area between the other committees and the expenditures committees,[46] which have what they consider to be a mandate to oversee the entire executive branch? For the expenditures committees construe their duty of "studying the operation of Government activities at all levels with a view to determining its economy and efficiency"[47] as authority for looking into the administration of agencies within the purview of any of the other legislative committees.

A proposed solution to this problem has been advanced by Dr. George B. Galloway. When testifying before the Senate Expenditures Committee on February 18, 1948, he said:

> Parenthetically, Mr. Chairman, I should like to comment upon the division of labor intended by the Legislative Reorganization Act and its authors in the performance of this oversight function. There has been some confusion in the public mind on this question. Some of the critics of the act have alleged that it provided, in effect, for duplicating and overlapping investigations of the executive branch of the Government by many committees. But it was the intention of the authors of this act and of the members of the Joint Committee on the Organization of Congress to effect a so-called three-way division of labor in the performance of the oversight function. Their thought was that the Appropriations Committees, on the one hand, would exercise financial control before expenditure through the scrutiny of the departmental estimates, and that the Expenditures Committees would undertake to supervise administrative practices and procedures of the executive agencies, on the other hand, while the legislative committees of the Congress would have the function of reviewing the operation of substantive legislation.[48]

Although this three-way division of oversight duties among the standing committees appears plausible, it will not stand up under analysis. To appraise departmental estimates intelligently, the appropriations committees require considerable knowledge of the performance of the agencies under the previous years' appropriations. Hence, the appropriations committees almost inevitably will go on doing a large share of the supervision of administrative management this formula would assign to the expenditures committees. Likewise, as some of the bitter struggles over the Brownlow Committee and Hoover Commission proposals have demonstrated, administrative procedures and organization are inextricably mingled with substantive policy.[49] Consequently, the expenditures committees could not go very far into structural or procedural matters without encroaching on the provinces of the other legislative committees.

And experience during the period covered, amply confirmed this analysis. The appropriations committees continued to engage in systematic oversight of administrative management in the executive branch.[50] The expenditures committees repeatedly conducted investigations of matters within the jurisdictions of other committees that were primarily concerned not with fraud, incompetence, or waste (which might conceivably be related to economy and efficiency of operations) but with substantive policies. For instance, during the 80th Congress, the Senate Expenditures Committee's Investigations Subcommittee inquired into the acquisition of Camp Beale, California, by the Air Force for use as a bombing range. There was no question of irregularities in procurement or of its suitability for that purpose. Rather, the former owners of that area, who were interested in farming it again, had objected to its retention by the military establishment. Clearly, this controversy was over an issue of substantive policy which was within the jurisdiction of the Senate Armed Services Committee.[51] This example, which was selected at random, could be multiplied many times for both the expenditures committees in the period covered.[52]

However, it is not necessary to cite a lengthy list of such instances to document the charge that the expenditures committees consistently invaded the bailiwicks of other committees. The Senate Expenditures Committee not only freely admitted such intrusions but aggressively maintained that it had concurrent jurisdiction in the congressional oversight field with every other standing committee of the Senate. In fact, proceeding from that assumption by rather inverse reasoning, it claimed that whenever other Senate committees obtained specially-authorized staffs to investigate subjects within their respective provinces, they were duplicating the existing facilities of its Permanent Subcommittee on Investigations—which it openly aspired to erect into a central investigative service for the entire Senate.[53]

A strong statement of this view was set forth in an article, "Jurisdictional Overlaps and Conflicts in Congressional Investigations with Special Reference to Senate Practice," prepared in 1951 by a professional aide to the Senate Expenditures Committee, Mr. E. E. Nobleman. In it, he wrote:

> As will subsequently appear, the Senate has repeatedly ignored the availability of this subcommittee, with its staff of trained and experienced attorneys, investigators and other experts, and has proceeded to conduct a variety of investigations through its other standing committees, subcommittees, or special committees in accordance with the authority granted by the Legislative Reorganization Act of 1946. This practice has resulted in a duplication of staffs and facilities with a consequent increase in expenditures.
> . . . .

Although one of the major objectives of the Legislative Reorganization

Act of 1946 was the elimination of duplication and jurisdictional overlapping, by specifically assigning jurisdiction over economy and efficiency
in the operation of the Government at all levels to the Committees on
Expenditures in the Executive Departments in each House, a new jurisdictional overlap was created.   A few examples should serve to illustrate the
problem, with particular reference to the Senate.[54]

After citing several instances in which other Senate committees purportedly
had duplicated the facilities of the Permanent Subcommittee on Investigations by
hiring specially-authorized staffs, Mr. Nobleman advanced his solution to this
problem of overlapping jurisdiction between the Senate Expenditures Committee on the one hand and the rest of the Senate standing committees on the
other.   In essence, it consisted of centralizing the bulk of the Senate investigations in the Permanent Subcommittee on Investigations.   Mr. Nobleman
divided investigations into three classes: (1) those which relate to legislation
pending before standing committees; (2) those which concern technical matters
within the jurisdiction of a particular standing committee but involve primarily the application of investigatory techniques; and (3) those which are
purely investigative in nature.   In the interests of economy and efficiency, he
would confine the other Senate committees to conducting only those inquiries
falling in the first category and would have the Permanent Subcommittee on
Investigations take care of the rest.   As a concession to the other standing committees, occasionally he would allow their staffs to collaborate on investigations
in the second category.[55]

On its face, this scheme of classification appeared confusing and did not
afford any intelligible standards for distinguishing the second and third categories from each other.   And that initial impression was verified by Mr. Nobleman's attempt to apply it to specially-authorized Senate investigations in the
81st Congress.   For instance, he placed the investigation of available fuel reserves
by the Senate Interior and Insular Affairs Committee under the authority of S.
Res. 239, 81st Congress, in category three as one "purely investigatory in nature"[56] although S. Res. 239 concomitantly directed the committee "to formulate
a national fuel policy to meet the needs of the United States in times of peace
and war, such policy to include the use of all fuels and energy resources except atomic energy. . . ."[57]   And ironically, the importers of residual fuel oil
and domestic natural gas and oil producers were very concerned at the time that
this inquiry would eventuate in legislation restricting the use of those fuels
in order to stimulate the soft coal industry—the chronically depressed state of
which had been the fundamental reason for initiating this investigation.   Several
other equally incongruous examples could be cited.

However, without further digression into the merits of Mr. Nobleman's
proposal, the following conclusions may reasonably be drawn.   Firstly, intrinsic

to sec. 136 and the other provisions for oversight of administration by the standing committees in the Legislative Reorganization Act, there is a major overlapping of jurisdictions. Secondly, the two formulas which have been advanced as guides for distributing this joint supervisory responsibility among the standing committees are not very useful. They are without substantial foundation in a natural breakdown of the work, incorporate ambiguous criteria, and consequently invite arbitrary application. Finally, after three Congresses, the question of how the standing committees were to divide the congressional oversight function among themselves was still unanswered. On a number of occasions, the resulting difficulties would have been much greater had it not been for the mutual accommodativeness of the chairmen involved and for the fact that many of the standing committees were principally occupied with handling legislation. In the future, to the extent that the standing committees devote increased attention to supervising administration, this practical problem of defining the respective roles of the appropriations, expenditures, and other legislative committees in that activity will become correspondingly harder.

Impracticability of Continuous Oversight

Similarly, the feasibility of directing the standing committees to exercise *continuous* surveillance of the executive branch is questionable. The idea that the standing committees can constantly supervise administration while concurrently discharging their other duties is rather like the myth of the omnivigilant citizen who incessantly participates in political affairs. By the very nature of things, the performance of both legislative and nonlegislative work by the standing committees is discontinuous. And there is a large empirical element in the programming of both. While engaged in preparing several important bills, a committee cannot simultaneously conduct a major investigation or vice versa. As the deadline for the expiration of a momentous measure like the Defense Production Act of 1950 approaches, the attention of the committee is fixed on that to the exclusion of handling casework and occasionally even correspondence. Reciprocally, when engrossed in a lengthy, full-time probe, a committee sometimes virtually suspends work on legislation. An urgent matter like the recall of General Douglas MacArthur from his commands in the Far East emerges and demands immediate investigation entailing weeks of day-long hearings. During such an interval, the preparation of even essential measures is held in abeyance.[58]

The extent to which a committee engages in supervision of administration varies markedly not only within a given session but from session to session. During Congresses when a committee does not have any major bills pending, it tends to occupy itself with surveillance of the executive branch. Likewise, in the interval between sessions, a committee is prone to make investigations, take overseas inspection trips, and perform other supervisory tasks which had been postponed during the preceding session because of the press of legislative duties. In other words, with the exception of dramatic developments like the riots in the Koje Island prisoner-of-war camps in May, 1952, that require attention at once, congressional oversight activities constitute an elastic element in the average committee's schedule with which it fills in the time not absorbed in working on legislation.

Undesirability of Providing Extra Regular Committee Aides for Supervisory Work

All these considerations should be taken into account in evaluating the persistent proposals for expanding the regular staffs of the standing committees to enable them better to perform their oversight duties under sec. 136 of the Legislative Reorganization Act. Generally, such recommendations are prefaced with the observation that the current "limited" staffs of the committees have been so engrossed in work on legislation that they have had little time to devote to supervision of administration. Usually, these proposals do not indicate in precise terms the amount of staff that should be added for this purpose. They range from simply recommending some enlargement of the professional staffs to urging that every standing committee be adequately equipped with investigators.[59]

Such recommendations should not be adopted. Whether or not the committees should attempt to carry out sec. 136 on a much larger scale, is questionable. As has been discussed at some length, the underlying theory of the Legislative Reorganization Act with respect to concentrating the congressional oversight function in the standing committees is faulty. During the period covered, some of its defects materialized. Also, the objectionable types of legislative oversight: reviewing or actually passing upon individual administrative acts, can only be exercised with staff assistance.[60] Further extension of those should not be encouraged by the provision of extra staff.

Assuming it were desirable for the standing committees to increase their supervisory activities greatly, their respective roles in that sphere are still undefined. Until that problem has been resolved, obviously all the standing committees should not be fully staffed with investigators. To do so would compound the present duplication of investigative staffs. Relatedly, another fundamental defect of such proposals is that they do not consider the oversight facilities of Congress as a whole. In a number of cases, one of the chief reasons that the regular professional staff of a committee devoted so little attention to surveillance of the executive branch was the existence of specially-authorized staffs for subcommittees and/or joint "watchdog" committees to which the committee had delegated many of its supervisory duties under sec.

136. If any increase in committee staffing for oversight purposes were deemed necessary, it would be better to have such expansion occur in temporary staffs of that sort. For when the missions that bring them into being are completed, they can be liquidated. Or at least their size can be adapted to the fluctuations in supervisory activities more readily than that of the permanent committee staffs.

Finally, another major reason why the regular professional staffs of the standing committees worked mostly on legislation during the period covered was that the committees were principally concerned with legislative matters then. Under no circumstances should the regular staffs of the standing committees be enlarged in an attempt to maintain continuous, detailed surveillance of administration through a more or less independent staff operation. To do so could easily result in setting up a competing bureaucracy which Congress—or rather more precisely, subordinate units of Congress—could completely control and which would aggravate extant shortcomings in our system of government. Such a legislative bureaucracy would not have the centripetal forces operative within it that the administrative establishment has. There would not be the unifying influence of the institutional focus of the presidency. No form of hierarchical organization is possible among the staffs of all the committees in one chamber, much less in both. The committee staffs are responsible to their respective committees, which often have widely disparate opinions on policy and have at best but partial views of the over-all program of governmental activities. Consequently, it would hardly be possible for them to coordinate their supervision of administration.[61]

Any attempt to build up a legislative bureaucracy of this sort would be self-defeating. The committee staffs could not possibly be expanded enough to oversee continually even the major transactions within the executive branch. And by establishing additional centers of direction for the various executive agencies, such a legislative bureaucracy would make the management tasks of the President much harder. Therefore, instead of pursuing this course, Congress would be better advised to strengthen the supervisory facilities and other internal controls of the administrative establishment and to utilize legislative oversight primarily as a means of stimulating them.

CHAPTER X

INTERSTAFF RELATIONS

Among Committee Staffs

In the same chamber. During the period covered, relations among committee staffs in the same house were characterized by infrequency, informality, and mainly by cooperation rather than collaboration. The legislative committee aides had very few dealings with the staffs of the corresponding appropriations subcommittees. Over two thirds of the committee aides interviewed had none; and most of the remainder, but one or two. Even the expenditures committee staffs had relatively little to do with the appropriations committee employees. On the Senate side, there was a prevalent attitude among the professional aides that overlapping in the memberships of the legislative committees and of the appropriations committee sufficed to take care of liaison between them at the principal level. On the House side, most legislative committee staff members felt that once the authorization legislation had been enacted, they had discharged their duty. If the appropriations committee aides sought information from them, they gladly furnished that; but the appropriations committee staffs rarely did.

Of course, the appropriations committee aides could and sometimes did utilize the hearings, reports, and other publications of the legislative committees.[1] Once in a great while, appropriations committee employees obtained staff memoranda or other unpublished materials from the legislative committee staffs.[2] And in one instance (the only such discovered) during the 81st Congress, the counsel of the Subcommittee on Relations with International Organizations, Senate Expenditures Committee, was asked to brief the clerk of the Subcommittee on the Departments of State, Justice, Commerce, and the Judiciary, Senate Appropriations Committee, on the findings of his study of the United States' participation in international organizations and then to attend that subcommittee's hearings on the budget requests of the Department of State for contributions to international organizations for fiscal 1951.

Likewise, relations among the staffs of legislative committees in the same chamber were practically confined to situations in which there were jurisdictional overlaps. In the majority of such cases, they discussed only matters of mutual interest. Sometimes, they procured from one another analyses of bills, staff studies, or other unpublished materials that were already prepared. Less frequently, one committee staff would ask another to make up a memorandum especially for it. And occasionally one committee staff would invite another to review those portions of a report or bill that impinged upon the jurisdiction of the latter's committee.

However, committee staffs rarely collaborated in the preparation of reports and legislation. Even where two or more committees engaged in a joint hearing or in some other combined undertaking, there usually was not much done in the way of joint staff work. Instead, as a rule, the aides to one of the participating committees rendered the bulk of the staff services entailed. For instance, during the 82d Congress, when subcommittees of the Senate Committees on Agriculture and Forestry, Interior and Insular Affairs, and Interstate and Foreign Commerce held joint hearings on three bills authorizing research into weather control and into increasing the supply of potable water, the chief clerk of the Interior and Insular Affairs Committee made the arrangements for the hearings and merely checked those with the staffs of the other two committees.[3] Similarly, when a joint subcommittee of the House Expenditures and Armed Services Committees under the chairmanship of Representative Porter Hardy, Jr., (D.-Va.) made an inspection tour of military construction projects in Europe and North Africa in November, 1951, two aides to the Government Operations Subcommittee, House Expenditures Committee, and one House Armed Services Committee staff member accompanied it.[4] But the Government Operations Subcommittee aides did all the staff work on the report which the joint subcommittee issued after returning to this country.[5]

Two exceptions to this general absence of joint staff work on a combined operation of two or more committees occurred in the Senate during the 82d Congress. Both when the Senate resolutions relative to sending United States ground troops to Europe under the North Atlantic Treaty[6] and when the bills which became the Mutual Security Act of 1951[7] were jointly referred to the Senate Armed Services and Foreign Relations Committees, their staffs collaborated thoroughly in preparing the reports to accompany those.[8]

Also, the only example discovered of continuing interstaff collaboration in one chamber involved the Senate Foreign Relations Committee staff. Whenever the Foreign Relations Committee was considering tax conventions, the Joint Tax Committee aides (who acted as the professional staff of the Senate Finance Committee on revenue measures) worked very closely with its staff. They analyzed the conventions in relation to the existing revenue laws of the United States. They participated in the hearings and executive sessions of the subcommittees on tax conventions of the Foreign Relations Committee. And they assisted its staff in drafting and reviewing the reports to accompany and any reservations to the tax conventions.[9]

But much more typically where aspects of a measure before one committee fell within the jurisdiction of another, their staffs did not refer to each other. For instance, the bills on Indian affairs touched on matters within the province of almost every other committee, yet the interior and insular affairs committees' aides who handled them had relatively few contacts with the other committee staffs in their respective houses. In a great many cases when seeking assistance in a particular field, a committee aide turned to the administrative agency rather than to the committee staff concerned. For example, in the 82d Congress, for the investigation into the sale of government-owned surplus tankers, the staff of the Permanent Subcommittee on Senate Investigations secured the requisite knowledge of merchant marine laws and regulations from the U. S. Maritime Commission, although it was an interested party to—if not an object of—that probe, rather than from the Senate Interstate and Foreign Commerce Committee aide who specialized in merchant marine measures—primarily because the latter did not have the information.

What were the factors responsible for this paucity of collaborative relations among the committee staffs intracamerally? One was the heavy workload of every major committee.[10] Because of that and the small size of each committee staff, the professional aides just did not have time very often to attend the hearings and executive sessions of other committees or to assist their staffs in the preparation of bills and reports—especially when those were of but marginal interest to them.[11] Likewise, the short deadlines under which they operated frequently prevented them from submitting reports or bills to other committee aides for review of the portions impinging upon the latter's sphere—even if those aides had been available to do so. Moreover, as a general rule, collaboration among the staffs could not greatly exceed that among their respective committees. For instance, in the second session of the 82d Congress, when the Senate Foreign Relations and Armed Services Committees discontinued jointly considering MSA bills, their staffs ceased their previous close collaboration on the reports to accompany those.[12]

And there were many obstacles to joint action by committees in the same chamber. One was the differential interest of the committees concerned in the subject under consideration. For example, the Senate Foreign Relations and Armed Services Committees quit acting jointly on MSA legislation mainly because of the declining participation of the Armed Services Committee members in the combined proceedings. Another was that in either house special permission had to be obtained for joint referral of a measure. But among the most important were the inertia of custom and precedent; personal incompatibilities of key committeemen; and strong senses of prerogative, institutional rivalries, and dissimilarities in corporate viewpoints and procedures of the committees involved.

Furthermore, these frequently reinforced one another. For example, during the 81st Congress, when Senator Joseph O'Mahoney (D.-Wyo.), chairman of the Joint Economic Committee, was urging enactment of an excess profits tax, he had the Joint Economic Committee staff prepare an excess profits tax bill, which he introduced. Not only was Senator Walter George (D.-Ga.), chairman of the Joint Tax Committee, opposed to the specific provisions of the O'Mahoney bill but also both the revenue committees and the Joint Tax Committee staff strongly resented this flagrant invasion of their province by the Joint Economic Committee staff. Under such circumstances, collaboration between the two joint committee staffs on that legislation was out of the question. Moreover, this incident placed considerable strain on the relations between even the personal friends on those two staffs and diminished ordinary cooperation between them for some time. For the above and related reasons, collaboration among the staffs of the committees in either chamber was not likely to increase very much in the near future.

Although there were not very many instances of joint staff work intracamerally, numerous committee aides stressed the spirit of cooperativeness pervading the committee staffs. Several chief clerks and staff directors related how they had been assisted by or had helped other chief clerks or staff directors to become oriented and to organize their work. Usually such assistance was extended individually. But sometimes it was provided on a group basis. For example, on February 12, 1952, the House Administration Committee staff held a meeting to which it had invited all the House committee clerks. There they discussed administrative problems and procedures in committee staff work; the House Journal Clerk explained the correct method of filing bills, amendments, and conference reports; and other useful information was disseminated.

Between the two houses. Likewise, relations between the staffs of the corresponding committees in the two chambers were predominantly sporadic, informal, and cooperative rather than collaborative in nature. About the only occasions on which most of them worked together—or even saw one another—were at conference committee sessions. As previously described, there usually was a genuinely shared effort among the staff members servicing a conference committee.[13] But even at the meetings of House and Senate conferees—especially where their positions were widely divergent—their respective staff assistants sometimes functioned quite apart.

In a few cases—generally not to exceed one or two a session for the staffs most addicted to the practice—the aides to companion House and Senate committees held joint staff meetings.[14] Those rarely were devoted to planning or conducting a combined operation. Rather, they usually either were primarily social gatherings or consisted of conferences between the two staffs and executive agency officials on the latter's pending presentations to their committees, on departmental policies, or on similar matters.

Sometimes, committee staff members attended hearings of the corresponding committee in the other chamber as observers. On rare occasions, they testified before a committee in the other house.[15] Less frequently still, a committee aide from one chamber performed staff work at hearings before a committee in the other. And once in a very great while, a committee staff member participated in the executive sessions of a committee in the other house.

However, conversations—principally over the telephone—constituted the bulk of the dealings between the staffs of committees in the two chambers. Several maintained a fairly systematic interchange of information. But most of them contacted each other only irregularly in connection with a specific matter of mutual interest. A number of the staffs of corresponding committees in the House and Senate automatically exchanged their publications—including confidential committee prints. Upon request and sometimes on their own initiative, they supplied each other with unpublished staff materials.

There were occasional references in committee hearings and in the *Congressional Record* to publications of committees in the other chamber.[16] Now and then, a committee staff would reprint a report prepared by its opposite number in the other house or incorporate portions of the latter's unpublished memoranda in a report—usually crediting the source. However, in isolated instances, one or two of the less qualified committee staffs were guilty of plagiarizing items of the output of their counterparts in the other chamber. This problem never assumed threatening proportions, and generally a vigorous complaint by the committee staff whose material had been pirated sufficed to put an end to the practice.

Very infrequently, a committee aide in one chamber would ask his opposite number in the other to review a report or staff study he had done. But, aside from the aforementioned exceptions at conference committee sessions, the staffs of corresponding committees in the House and Senate rarely collaborated on reports or legislation. As was the case with intracameral staff relations, even where there was a joint hearing, the aides to but one of the participating committees usually took care of most of the staff work involved. Only one instance was discovered where the staffs of parallel committees in the two houses shared the preparation of a staff study. In the 80th Congress, the Senate Foreign Relations and House Foreign Affairs Committee staffs collaborated on the staff report *The European Recovery Program: Basic Documents and Background Information.*[17]

The rarity of such projects was not surprising, for there were many obstacles to joint undertakings by the staffs of corresponding Senate and House committees. One of the most fundamental was the difference in the timetables of the two chambers. As several weeks or months often elapsed between the separate consideration of the same measure by the House and Senate committees, it would have been difficult for the staff of the one which would not be handling the matter until that much later to spare the time for a joint study of it when the other committee first took it up. Since the members of the committees not their staffs decided the order of business, it was not possible for the latter to integrate their work to any great extent. Also, various committees had sharply contrasting preferences in staff materials. For instance, the House Foreign Affairs Committee liked lengthy, detailed background studies; whereas, the Senate Foreign Relations Committee preferred succinct memoranda of but a page or two. And there were numerous discrepancies in the jurisdictions of the parallel committees in the two houses. For example, in the Senate all measures pertaining to "public health and quarantine" were referred to the Labor and Public Welfare Committee; in the House, to the Interstate and Foreign Commerce Committee.[18] Of equal or greater importance, there frequently were differences of interest within those jurisdictions. For instance, during the 80th Congress, the Senate Expenditures Committee held hearings on the operation of the Legislative Reorganization Act and reported out amendments to that statute.[19] But there was no indication that the House Expenditures Committee gave comparable organized consideration—if any at all—to that subject.

As in the case of intracameral staff relations, the staffs of corresponding committees in the House and Senate, because of their small size and heavy workloads, did not have time very often to attend the hearings and executive sessions of each other's committees or to engage in joint projects. Another adverse circumstance was geographical separation. Particularly where the two staffs involved were located in the Senate and House office buildings respectively, the intervening distance was a hindrance to collaboration between them. In a few instances, a widely divergent concept of role or a marked differential in the competence of the two staffs further deterred them from seeking each other's help. Interacting with all these elements were the personalities of the individuals concerned. In several cases there was considerable incompatibility—if not downright enmity—between opposite numbers on the staffs of Senate and House committees. Because of these factors, a professional aide, where assisting a committee in the other house, sometimes worked directly with the members of that committee rather than with its staff. And occasionally the dealings between parallel House and Senate committees were characterized by competition and friction rather than by cooperation.

Finally, as was true intracamerally, the relations between the corresponding

House and Senate committees largely determined the collaboration possible between their staffs. And the parallel committees in the two houses evinced little inclination toward joint action. Once more, there were numerous impediments such as the inertia of custom and precedent and the institutional rivalries, jealous regard for independence and prerogatives, and differences in perspective and procedures of both the committees and their parent chambers. And many of the major committees—including some that enjoyed the highest degree of intercameral comity—were strongly opposed to joint hearings with their counterparts in the other chamber.[20] As a result, collaboration between the staffs of the corresponding Senate and House committees was not likely to grow greatly in the next few years.

With Senate Policy Committee Staffs

During the 81st and 82d Congresses, most of the Senate committee staffs had hardly any dealings with the Majority (Democratic) Policy Committee staff aside from supplying it with information on the status and contents of bills before their committees. Likewise, except for their relations with the Minority Calendar Committee aide, neither the regular nor the minority members of the Senate committee staffs had much to do with the Minority (Republican) Policy Committee staff. Nearly all the minority aides interviewed were critical of the latter's failure to maintain effective liaison with them, lack of cooperativeness, and duplication of their work. None had used any of the processed materials turned out by the Minority Policy Committee staff on its own initiative.

With the Minority Calendar Committee aide, David Kammerman, the Senate committee staff members mainly discussed possible grounds for opposition by the Minority Calendar Committee to specific bills. Occasionally at Mr. Kammerman's instance, they would prepare amendatory language or an explanation of an ambiguous portion of a measure to remove prospective objections by the Minority Calendar Committee. Generally, Mr. Kammerman solicited their opinion or assistance on the bills in question. However, sometimes when they discovered a defect in a measure after their committee had reported it out, they would arrange with Mr. Kammerman to have the Minority Calendar Committee challenge the bill so that deficiency could be remedied. Also, once in a while on a comparatively important measure which was going to be brought up on the call of the calendar, a staff member of the committee concerned would contact Mr. Kammerman to inquire if any Senators had asked the Minority Calendar Committee to oppose it and if so, what their objections to the bill were. Among the Senate committee aides interviewed, there was a consensus that the Minority Calendar Committee—which operated largely through its staff—performed a very valuable function.

With House Coordinator of Information[21]

Exchange of information constituted the principal relations between the Office of House Coordinator of Information and the House committee staffs. For the most part, the House Coordinator's Office asked them about bills pending before their committees. And they called on the House Coordinator's Office mainly for data from administrative agencies outside the jurisdictions of their respective committees. In fact, they utilized that organization more or less as a liaison office for such executive agencies. The committee aides who had patronized the House Coordinator's Office praised the speediness of its service. But in general, the House Coordinator's Office made many more requests of the committee staffs than they did of it. Further, the over-all number of contacts between them was rather small. Several of the House committee aides interviewed had never dealt with the House Coordinator's Office at all.

With the Legislative Reference Service

A considerable proportion—and in some cases nearly all—of the requests that committee staffs made of the Legislative Reference Service were for help on assignments not immediately related to their primary duties. Where a member of a committee asked its staff to write a magazine article or speech for delivery outside Congress, to answer a constituent's inquiry, or to perform some other extraneous task, the staff often either sent over to the LRS for materials or routed the request over to the LRS and relayed the reply back to the Congressman—acting solely in a conduit capacity. Also, if an individual member of Congress not on the committee asked the staff to prepare a lengthy memorandum or to engage in some other sizable project, it nearly always tactfully referred him to the LRS.

In connection with their main work for their respective committees, most professional aides called on the LRS chiefly for routine reference and research assistance such as: searching for newspaper items; identifying or completing quotations; looking up the history of particular incidents; procuring government documents, interest group publications, magazines, books, or maps; making translations; photostating materials; compiling state or foreign laws on certain subjects, specialized bibliographies, or chronologies of events; preparing the legislative histories of bills; and making up tabulations of statistics from scattered published sources. Sometimes, committee staff members asked the LRS to index hearings and other publications. Once in a while, they had the LRS make a straight digest or an analytical summary of a set of hearings.

Occasionally, committee staff members had the American Law Section of the LRS prepare opinions, briefs, and other sorts of legal memoranda. Sometimes, they called on the other sections of the LRS for short, nonlegal, analytical reports.[22] Fairly often, a committee had an LRS specialist do a lengthy staff study.[23] And once in a while, committee aides had LRS analysts collaborate with them on staff reports.[24] On this last type of project, a committee staff member customarily served as editor.

Conversely, now and then, committee aides asked an LRS senior specialist to review their staff studies. Likewise, on occasion, they consulted with the top LRS analysts about matters pertaining to the latter's specialties. Usually, the committee staff members merely sought suggestions as to sources—especially in foreign literature. Sometimes, they discussed a point of law. And once in a great while, they obtained a briefing on some topic.

With the Executive Branch

Exchange of information. One of the most valuable—certainly the most heavily in demand—of the numerous services departmental staffs afforded the committee aides was the provision of information of various sorts. With their immense and well-equipped staffs, including field forces distributed not only throughout the United States but all over the world collecting statistics and other intelligence, the administrative agencies had amassed a vast reservoir of data that the committee staffs could never have hoped to duplicate. If the committee aides had been unable to obtain information in the possession of the executive branch, they could not have functioned successfully. Although sometimes committee staffs got supplementary factual materials from interest groups, private research institutes, and other organizations, the administrative establishment was their primary source of data.

Besides procuring statistics from departmental technicians, committee aides often consulted them to gain the benefit of their experience or general professional knowledge. Reciprocally, agency personnel frequently sought the advice of committee staffs—mainly concerning the attitudes and preferences of the members of their committees. Usually, committee aides and departmental personnel obtained information from and consulted each other on an *ad hoc* basis. However, occasionally arrangements were made for a more systematic exchange of data and advice between them.

(a) Semiformalized arrangements. For instance, during the summer of 1947, the staff of the House Select Committee on Foreign Aid promoted a series of meetings between itself[25] and the staffs of the Senate Foreign Relations, Harriman, Krug, and Nourse Committees.[26] Over a period of several months, they held weekly luncheon-conferences. At them the staffs of these congressional and presidential committees exchanged considerable information. Each was able to keep apprised of the other's progress. Occurring at mealtime, these meetings did not cut into their workday as much as consultations at other times. Nearly all the participants agreed that these interstaff luncheon-conferences were a useful device which might profitably be employed more often.

In the fall of 1947, the State Department invited the staffs of the foreign relations committees and of the House Select Committee on Foreign Aid to attend the Washington Conversations on the European Recovery Program as observers.[27] There they became acquainted with the latest data on European needs for economic assistance as the departmental representatives discussed those with the European governments' experts.

During the 80th through the 82d Congresses, there were a few other analogous cases in which a committee aide was present as an observer at meetings of an interdepartmental committee in the preliminary phases of developing an Administration program. But the number of such instances probably would remain small in the future. For each major committee staff had to keep track of so many different measures that ordinarily it could not afford to go into such detail during the formative stages of any of them.

When members of the Senate Foreign Relations and House Foreign Affairs Committees were appointed to the United States delegations to the United Nations General Assembly, aides to those committees regularly accompanied them. Inasmuch as the entire United States delegation operated under instructions from the President, the foreign affairs committee employees concerned were in effect functioning as part of the executive branch staff during such tours of duty. There they became acquainted firsthand with foreign policy problems with which they subsequently had to deal in their committee work. And they assisted the congressional delegates in presenting the legislative branch viewpoint on matters under consideration to the rest of the United States delegation.[28]

(b) Accessibility of data. During the period covered, the allegation was frequently made—generally by proponents of expanding some segment of the congressional staff—that the policies to which the President and agency heads were publicly committed imposed limitations on the availability of information in the possession of the executive branch. There were several versions of this contention, the chief difference among them being that in some the subsidiary charges were merely implied. Essentially, this argument ran as follows. The findings of fact, recommendations, and supporting presentations made by agency personnel always conformed to the policies publicly advocated by the President and/or the department heads. And the agency staffs accordingly restricted the release of information which would impugn such policies, sometimes refusing to supply any contrary data at all.

Before testing this assertion against the experience of the committee aides interviewed, notice should be taken of some common knowledge that contradicts its major postulate. The executive branch was not a monolithic structure that adhered to a presidential line throughout its manifold and often competing parts. In fact, a more typical pattern was that of fractious bureaus backed by congressional allies on the relevant legislative and appropriations committees resisting all attempts at centralizing direction of the former in the department heads or President. And at any rate, there were many struggles for control over particular programs between two or more agencies—frequently within a single department. The continuing feud between the Corps of Engineers and the Bureau of Reclamation was only one of many that might be cited.[29] Assuming for the purposes of argument that congressional committee staffs could not get any information from a department adverse to its position on a given matter, usually there would be rival agencies glad to furnish data for appraising or rebutting its proposals and supporting arguments.

Fortunately, access to information with which to evaluate or challenge an agency's program did not depend on the existence of an interdepartmental feud. Nearly all the committee aides interviewed said that they had not experienced difficulty in procuring data from an agency to oppose its recommendations or to develop alternative ones. During the 80th Congress, when the Democrats held the executive branch but the Republicans controlled Congress, the Treasury Department and Joint Tax Committee staffs ceased their previous close collaboration on major tax legislation.[30] Nevertheless, the Treasury Department technicians continued to supply basic data freely to the Joint Tax Committee staff.

Naturally, an agency would not volunteer information on the shortcomings in its proposals. It might disregard or minimize relevant factors that seriously qualified the supporting arguments. And, of course, it would not furnish competitive witnesses from its staff. Similarly, an agency could not be expected to call attention to deficiencies in its administration (unless it were seeking additional appropriations or statutory amendments to remedy them). Nor would it provide such data in response to ambiguous queries fishing for derogatory material. But almost every committee aide interviewed said that, when asked a specific question, the departments would nearly always supply the information sought even though it were adverse to bills sponsored by them, reflected on their administration, or were detrimental in other respects.[31] Although an agency might include supplementary explanatory material to present that in the most favorable possible light, it ordinarily would furnish the data requested, no matter how deleterious. To have done otherwise would have jeopardized its long-run interests of maintaining cordial relations with the committees and their staffs which were so instrumental in the enactment of any legislation it might need.

Hence, if the departments made any omissions in their presentations to a committee, whether inadvertently or intentionally, the main problem posed for its staff was to detect those gaps and to ask for the data to fill them rather than to develop substitute sources of such information.[32] Almost the only situation in which a committee aide could not go to an agency for data was where his committee did not want it to know he was working on a certain project. And sometimes even then he could call on personal acquaintances in the executive branch whom he could trust not to reveal his requests for help.

In making up staff studies. When preparing compilations of background information or other reports for Congress, departmental personnel generally consulted the appropriate committee staffs about the contents, emphases, and format. Reciprocally, committee aides sometimes discussed the organization and contents of their staff studies with executive branch personnel and frequently asked them to review those—especially any portions pertaining to agency operations and procedures—for errors of fact and occasionally of interpretation. Usually, they sought the advice and criticism of departmental experts on an individual basis. However, once in a while, a committee staff convoked a group of technicians from different agencies to go over one of its studies together. And in some cases, departmental specialists collaborated with a committee staff from the start to the completion of a study—helping to plan it, writing parts of it, and then assisting in reviewing the entire manuscript.

Joint staff subcommittees. The Treasury Department and Joint Tax Committee staffs institutionalized this process of collaboration in the form of joint staff subcommittees. Typically, those consisted of an ordinary staff subcommittee of the Joint Tax Committee[33] combined with a comparable interdisciplinary team from the Treasury Department comprised of an attorney from the staff of the Tax Legislative Counsel, an economist from the Tax Advisory Staff, and a technician from the Bureau of Internal Revenue. However, their composition was not invariable; and sometimes the Treasury Department or Joint Tax Committee staff was represented by just one member.

These joint staff subcommittees were thoroughly combined enterprises from start to finish. During the 81st and 82d Congresses, Colin Stam, chief of the Joint Tax Committee staff, and Vance Kirby, Tax Legislative Counsel of the Treasury Department, would meet periodically to decide what studies should be made by joint staff subcommittees and set them up. These joint staff subcommittees functioned exactly the same as the subcommittees comprised entirely of Joint Tax Committee employees. All the participants contributed to shaping the contents of a study, and a genuinely joint product resulted. Not only did interdisciplinary group thinking occur but also the cleavages among the members frequently were not of an interstaff nature. Rather, in many cases, coalitions of individuals from both the Treasury Department and Joint Tax Committee components of a staff subcommittee opposed each other.

After a joint staff subcommittee had completed a draft of the study with which it was satisfied, it reported back to Mr. Stam and Mr. Kirby in a meeting which other members of the Joint Tax Committee staff always—and the Director of the Tax Advisory Staff and/or other top Treasury Department officials often—attended. At these reporting sessions, Mr. Stam and Mr. Kirby reviewed the study and together with the other staff members present effected any necessary revisions in it. Once more, there was full participation by everybody in attendance, with a free and frank discussion all around. And again, there were interstaff alliances among those present. Rather frequently, a joint staff subcommittee had unanimously approved a study to which Mr. Kirby and Mr. Stam took some exceptions. For the latter regarded the matter from the broader perspective of the political considerations involved, which the technicians on the subcommittee might have overlooked. But also there sometimes were interstaff disagreements on certain proposals in a study.

Generally, they tried to compromise such points in issue. But when unable to do so, they occasionally made separate recommendations to the revenue committees. Where the differences were between subordinate personnel, Mr. Stam and Mr. Kirby would often either gavel through an enforced adjustment of those or reconstitute the joint staff subcommittee to study the whole subject anew. And in a few instances, they simply tabled the study indefinitely. However, most of the time they were able to achieve a mutually acceptable revision of the study. Then when the study was presented to one of the revenue committees in executive session—generally by Mr. Stam or one of the joint staff subcommittee members reading it—the joint staff subcommittee that prepared it, including the Treasury Department contingent, would be there.

In analyzing bills. Occasionally, when the Bureau of the Budget had been slow in clearing an agency report on a bill, a committee aide would call the agency legal staff for an "advance opinion" on the measure. Very frequently when analyzing a departmental bill, a committee staff member would contact the agency counsel who had drafted it to ascertain the policy and legal implications intended. Sometimes, committee staffs requested departmental lawyers to prepare analyses of minor and highly technical measures originating from outside sources. And throughout the consideration of an Administration bill, committee aides often asked the agency legal staffs to evaluate the effects and practicability of proposed amendments.

In bill drafting. Once in a while, during the formative stages of a major Administration measure, departmental counsel would seek suggestions from the committee aides concerned on the contents, format, and other aspects of the incipient bill for increasing its acceptability to the members of their committees. Also, in such cases, the agency legal staffs customarily submitted preliminary and intermediate drafts of the bill to them for criticism. Conversely, when a committee aide had prepared amendments to a departmental measure, he ordinarily checked with the agency lawyers to ensure that those accomplished what the committee wanted. And for the drafting of amendments and bills of a highly technical nature, a number of committee staff members usually resorted to the departmental legal staffs in lieu of the congressional legislative counsel. For where thousands of agency interpretations of laws and regulations, actuarial and other specialized skills, or extremely complicated administrative operations were involved, the congressional legislative counsel would have had to refer to the agency staffs anyway. Hence, where the departments and their committees had congenial views and especially where modifications in departmental bills were entailed, committee aides often turned directly to the agency draftsmen. And even where a congressional legislative counsel was working on a bill, departmental lawyers frequently assisted him and the committee staff in drafting it.

On reports to accompany bills. When they had prepared a bill, many agencies automatically sent along a draft of the accompanying report. Sometimes, a committee aide used that as the basis of the committee report, revising it in accordance with whatever changes the committee made in the bill. Occasionally on an understaffed committee, the clerk specifically asked departments to draft the reports to accompany minor and complex measures originating with them. Much more frequently, however, committee staff members called on agency personnel to do only portions of a report—generally the rather technical parts like the section-by-section analysis or that required by the Ramseyer or Cordon Rule. Nearly always the committee staff and/or the congressional legislative counsel carefully checked what the departmental employees had done.

Likewise, committee aides often had the executive branch staff review their reports for any errors of fact or of interpretation. In general, a committee staff member just phoned agency specialists and read them the passages in a report about which he was dubious. Sometimes, a committee aide submitted a draft of the entire report to a departmental official for criticism. And in a few cases, the committee and agency staffs reviewed a report together. For example, in the 81st Congress, after having worked out the provisions of S. 2020 (a bill to establish a General Services Administration) with representatives of affected agencies in a series of interstaff conferences, the Senate Expenditures Committee aide concerned went through a similar process in preparing the report on that bill.[34] Similarly, during the 81st and 82d Congresses, if there were sufficient time after the report to accompany a revenue bill was received back from the Government Printing Office, the Joint Tax Committee aides customarily met with members of the Treasury Department staff to go over the galley proof of it with them.

Prehearings conferences.   Almost as a routine procedure, many a committee staff would hold prehearings conferences on a major or complex bill with the executive branch personnel who had prepared it. At such conferences, the agency staff members would explain the bill in detail and answer any questions the committee staff might have about it. Sometimes, they worked out perfecting amendments to the bill there. Occasionally, the committee aides told the departmental representatives about points on which the committee members would be apt to desire additional information or more convincing justification and suggested compilations of background data, legal memoranda, and other materials the agencies could prepare that would be useful to the committee before and during the hearings. At these prehearings conferences, which ranged from half an hour to several all-day sessions in length, there was a frank and full exchange of views and information between the committee and departmental staffs.

In organizing and conducting hearings.   Sometimes, committee aides consulted an agency specialist about what nongovernmental experts to invite to testify on certain subjects in his field. For the most part, committee staffs left the selection of departmental witnesses entirely to the discretion of the agencies involved. Occasionally, in situations requiring considerable flexibility in the scheduling of executive branch witnesses and of topics for particular sessions of hearings, committee aides and departmental officials worked together closely in coordinating them. And once in a while, a committee staff would ask an agency to send up someone to assist in conducting the hearings on very technical Administration bills.

During executive sessions.[35]   The extent to which committees allowed departmental personnel into their executive sessions varied widely from committee to committee and on the same committee with different measures and agencies. Some committees rarely, if ever, let departmental staff members into their closed meetings. Others kept agency representatives waiting outside the committee rooms, called them in only to seek their views on specific matters, and after each consultation sent them back out of the room. And still others ordinarily permitted selected departmental personnel to participate in their executive sessions much as the committee aides did.

On the floor.   During the floor debate on an Administration bill, departmental representatives were almost invariably present in the gallery where they were readily available to consult with or to procure additional information for the committee aides. On occasion, agencies set up a sort of mobile "reference service" in a room in the Capitol where they assembled a collection of materials on the subjects under discussion on the floor.

In conference.   At meetings of conference committees, the status of agency staff members was almost the same as at executive sessions of the committees in either house. The only difference, if any, was one of degree. Much of the time, departmental personnel did not have as free access to conference committee sessions or did not participate to the same extent in drafting conference committee reports as they did in the case of the standing committees.

With Interest Group Staffs

For information.   Most of the relations between committee aides and the staffs of organized interest groups in their fields centered around the exchange of various kinds of information. Often they were on each other's mailing lists. Now and then, interest group representatives asked committee aides about the legislative histories and contents of certain bills.   But the prevailing flow of information was from the interest groups to the committee staffs. Most of that was volunteered by the interest group employees. But sometimes committee aides requested certain statistics or other information from them. Generally, committee staffs turned to organized interest groups for data not available elsewhere.[36] But fairly often, committee staff members secured information from them as a check on that supplied by the executive branch. In this regard, a number of committee aides observed that their efficiency was considerably increased through the operations of interest group representatives. For the latter frequently pointed out shortcomings in the statements of administrative agencies or of other opposing interests which the committee staffs might have overlooked and supplied detailed documentation for criticizing those.

On hearings.   Once in a while, committee aides asked a "peak association" like the NAM or United States Chamber of Commerce to pick out a representative sample of witnesses from its constituent organizations and to coordinate their presentations to avoid repetition and redundancy. Occasionally, when pressed for time, a committee limited the oral testimony to officials of the "peak associations" involved but allowed any of their member organizations to submit a written statement for inclusion in the record.[37]

In preparing bills and reports.   Several committee staffs frequently referred bills for comments to the affected interest groups the same as to the administrative agencies concerned.   Where a committee had under consideration a bill that had originated with an interest group, the latter's lawyers sometimes assisted the committee aides and congressional legislative counsel in drafting successive revisions of that bill and the accompanying committee report.

Overlapping memberships.   As was true throughout the entire area of interstaff relations, the dealings between the committee aides and interest group employees were highly personalized. Undoubtedly, such relationships were influenced by the fact that a number of the committee aides had previously been on the staffs of organized interest groups or were then officials of associations relating to their specialties. And, of course, nearly all the committee employees were members of the professional associations in their fields and of many other organized interest groups.

With Private Research Organizations

Several committee aides had been employees of private research organizations. For example, Dr. Charles Hardy, the first staff director of the Joint Committee on the Economic Report, had worked for Brookings Institution for a number of years.[38] In at least one case, a private research organization "loaned" a staff member to a committee for a protracted period. Herman Lazarus, top labor expert of the Public Affairs Institute, went on leave to serve as chief counsel of the Senate Labor and Public Welfare Committee from February 1, 1949 to March 18, 1951.[39]

Once in a while, a committee requested a private research organization to prepare a staff study. For example, in the 80th Congress, when the House and Senate were deadlocked over what type of agency should administer the European Recovery Program, the Senate Foreign Relations Committee asked Brookings Institution to make a study of the problem. In the 81st Congress, the Joint Committee on the Economic Report invited the National Planning Association to do a study on the effects of public and private pension programs on the national economy.[40] On very rare occasions, private research organization personnel helped to prepare committee reports. For example, in the 80th Congress, Mr. Lazarus and other staff members of the Public Affairs Institute assisted in drafting the minority report of the Joint Committee on Labor-Management Relations.[41]

The total amount of such services rendered by private research organizations to the standing committees was rather small. Further, the aides to a committee for which a private researcher was doing a job often had little contact with him because he worked directly with the chairman or other committee members.

As might be expected then, relations between the staffs of the standing committees and of private research organizations were not very extensive during the period covered. Over sixty per cent of the committee aides interviewed did not request any assistance from staff members of private research organizations. Less than a third even referred to their publications. And the committee staff members who dealt with employees of private research organizations stressed the infrequency, informality, and personalized nature of their contacts.

PART THREE

CHAPTER XI

SENATORIAL OFFICE STAFFS

Origin of Administrative Assistant Position

The authors of the Legislative Reorganization Act of 1946 wanted to provide higher-quality aides for the members as well as for the committees of Congress. The Joint Committee on the Organization of Congress recommended:

> That each senatorial and congressional office be authorized to employ a high-caliber administrative assistant at an annual salary of $8,000 to assume nonlegislative duties now interfering with the proper study and consideration of national legislation.[1]

The Legislative Reorganization Bill (S. 2177, 79th Congress) as passed by the Senate incorporated this recommendation. However, that feature was eliminated in the House, and the parliamentary situation required acceptance of the House version.[2] Shortly afterward, the Senate provided for administrative assistants to Senators by inserting the following item in the First Supplemental Appropriation Act, 1947:

> For compensation of an administrative assistant to each Senator, to be appointed by him, at a base salary of not to exceed $8,000 per year, to assist him in carrying out his departmental business and other duties, fiscal year 1947, $384,000, or so much thereof as may be necessary, to be available at the beginning of the Eightieth Congress.[3]

Jumbling of Titles and Duties

During the period covered, the senatorial office employees had almost as confusing a nomenclature as the committee staffs. The only position with a standardized title was that of "administrative assistant." In the appropriations acts, the rest of the senatorial office staff members were referred to variously as "clerical assistants," "assistant clerks," "clerks," or simply "employees other than the administrative assistants." The *Congressional Directory* listed the second-ranking member of each office staff under the heading "secretary." Moreover, the clerical assistants assumed a great diversity of honorific appellations. Clerks and assistant clerks adopted such imposing titles as: legislative counsel, legislative assistant, executive secretary, office coordinator, research assistant, chief secretary, and receptionist. And fairly often, clerical assistants were erroneously designated as "administrative assistants" in newspaper articles or in the *Congressional Record.*

To confuse matters further, there was considerable overlapping of duties among the high-level positions on the senatorial office staffs. Numerous administrative assistants were mainly occupied with legislative activities and had little to do with departmental business. Most administrative assistants did some work on legislation. And a few served principally as private secretaries. About all that could be said with certainty was that the administrative assistant was the top member of an office staff. And where he concentrated on legislative assignments, the second-ranking employee usually supervised the remainder of the clerical force in handling the bulk of the casework and other nonlegislative tasks.

With such intermingling of functions, it is not feasible to consider any of the top senatorial office staff positions separately but only to discuss the duties habitually performed by them. Hence, this chapter is focused on the types of work done by the high-ranking senatorial aides. For purposes of standardization, the following nomenclature is generally used in the rest of this chapter. Office staff members (other than administrative assistants) who were responsible for taking care of most of the departmental business and for overseeing the clerical assistants are called "executive secretaries." And the high-level senatorial aides who were chiefly concerned with work on legislation are referred to as "legislative assistants."[4]

Qualifications

Educational attainments. Of the fifty senatorial aides interviewed,[5] thirty-five had B.A.'s or B.S.'s; fifteen, LL.B.'s; two, LL.M.'s; ten, M.A.'s or M.S.'s; and two, Ph.D.'s. In addition, five had taken college courses without receiving a bachelor's degree; two were studying law; one had qualified for the bar without attending law school; and eight had done some graduate work beyond their highest degree. Two had been interns of the National Institute of Public Affairs, and another had undergone similar training in the Department of State. Ten of the B.A.'s or B.S.'s were in political science; four, in economics; four, in business administration; three, in history; two, in journalism; one each was in architectural engineering, in English, and in geology; and the rest were unspecified. Five of the M.A.'s or M.S.'s were in political science; two, in business administration; and one each was in history, in economics, and in English. One Ph.D. was in political science, and the other was in economics.

"Doctor, lawyer, Indian chief." Eight of these senatorial assistants had been newspapermen; seven, practicing lawyers; six, businessmen; five, secretaries;

three, school teachers; two, accountants; one, a professional engineer; one, a Congressman; one, Chief of the Choctaw Indian Tribe; and one, an Arkansas Circuit Court Judge. Two had held important administrative posts with universities. Three had been employees of organized interest groups. Fifteen had had experience in executive agencies.[6] Ten had occupied administrative positions in their state governments. Nineteen were career congressional employees. Seven had been on the staffs of committees. Six had worked for Representatives; three, for their present boss when he was on the House side. And one had served in another Senator's office in the same capacity.

Appraisal of training. On the whole, the academic backgrounds of these senatorial aides were creditable. As with the committee staff members, however, exaggerated significance should not be attached to their educational qualifications—particularly to their main fields of specialization in college. Rather often, their undergraduate majors did not relate very closely to their work. For example, one of the most able administrative assistants had taken his B.S. in geology. Also, for the same reasons as in the case of the committee aides, extra increments of graduate study beyond the bachelor's degree level have diminishing marginal utility in comparison with the equivalent amount of on-the-job experience. The principal exception is in the field of law. As was true with the committee staff members, a legal education is advantageous to a senatorial assistant. Besides training him to be a generalist, it is helpful in preparing legal memoranda and in handling casework involving legal technicalities. And being a lawyer is an asset in dealing with the many attorneys representing organized interest groups, executive agencies, or important constituents.

Value of previous experience. In general, there was not too much transferability of skill from positions held by individuals prior to becoming congressional employees. Nearly all the senatorial assistants interviewed emphasized the uniqueness of the "Hill" environment and the resultant need to work in it for a year or so before becoming really proficient. Nevertheless, most senatorial aides found that previous employment in the executive branch was valuable by acquainting them with how the administrative agencies operate, with where and how to obtain most readily various kinds of service, and with numerous key personnel who could greatly facilitate securing such assistance. Likewise, journalistic experience developed very useful skills not only for handling relations with the different media of communication but also for speechwriting and other office staff work.

Essential Attributes

As with the committee aides, neither educational nor experience backgrounds are as important qualifications for a senatorial assistant as the possession of certain abilities and a suitable personality. Fundamentally, a senatorial aide has to be a generalist. For he can not hope to be an expert on more than a few of the many diverse subjects with which he has to deal. Rather, he must be proficient in quickly acquiring sufficient information to handle them intelligently. He must be very adaptable. All the senatorial assistants interviewed stressed the unpredictable and erratic character of their work. They have to adjust to the irregularities in their Senators' schedules occasioned by speaking engagements, evening sessions of Congress, late committee meetings, sudden crises in governmental affairs, and personal idiosyncrasies. Standing athwart the main channels of communication to their Senators, they must be able to speak and write with facility. Nearly all the senatorial assistants interviewed were very articulate. With the objective of conserving their Senators' time ever uppermost, they must be skillful digesters.

Besides being completely loyal, a Senator's aides have to be able to regard matters from his perspective. In doing so, they must have a nice feel for the political factors involved. They have to be willing to serve anonymously. They must possess good judgment, tact, and initiative. To have the requisite detailed knowledge of the economy, geography, and political forces in a Senator's state, his top assistants—especially those taking care of casework—should be from his constituency. The heavy demands of their duties, which often entail long hours of overtime, require vigor and stamina. These qualities place the accent on youth, and a majority of the senatorial aides interviewed were between thirty and forty years old. Nearly all of them exuded enthusiasm for their work. Almost without exception, they were pleasant, friendly, and helpful. In other words, they had many of the characteristics of politicians plus a willingness to perform a supporting role.

Optimum Size

There are both philosophical and practical reasons for keeping senatorial office staffs as small as possible. As the primary representative and humanizing element in our gigantic complex of governmental institutions, members of Congress must guard against insulating themselves with successive layers of assistants and duplicating on a smaller scale the shortcomings of the administrative establishment to which they afford an essential corrective. This fundamental consideration should be constantly borne in mind, for there is an almost completely elastic demand for staff services on the part of many Congressmen. Some energetic and imaginative Senators—especially those with presidential ambitions—could keep fifty aides busy if provided with them. Others would like to try. Also, the myth of the omnipotent legislator should be reappraised against the realities of the necessary division of labor within Congress. No Representative or Senator could spread himself over every subject before Congress. And in any event, the exigencies of dispatching the program of business before his chamber would not permit him to play a major role in the consideration of every measure.

During the 80th through the 82d Congresses, a few Senators from the largest states might have needed a modest increase in their office employees to handle constituents' requests.[7] But many Senators from the small and medium-sized states, like John Williams (R.-Del.) or Mike Monroney (D.-Okla.), did not use their entire office staff allowance.[8] And most Senators had an adequate number of assistants to take care of their departmental business and to work on the legislation of greatest interest to them at any given time.[9]

General Duties

Handling the mail. In a senatorial office, handling the mail was a major operation which consumed a large proportion of the staff's time. The magnitude of the task was indicated by the fact that the staffs of some Senators from big states sent out an average of over 100,000 letters a year. Although many offices prided themselves on answering all but the obviously "inspired" mail, most of them referred a considerable number of letters over to executive agencies or committee staffs for suggested replies. And where a Senator was chairman of a committee, his office staff automatically routed all letters concerning committee matters to the clerk.

At regular intervals ranging from a week to a year in length, some offices compiled control statistics on the incoming mail. In most offices, there was a continuing effort by the administrative assistants or executive secretaries to relieve their Senators from preparing replies to any but an irreducible minimum of personal letters. And the interviewees estimated that they were able to free their Senators from seventy-five to ninety per cent of the burden of handling correspondence.

Visitors and phone calls. To increase their accessibility to visitors, a number of administrative assistants and executive secretaries had their desks in the front office. Although such an arrangement caused many interruptions in their work, they felt it paid dividends in good public relations. For the initial impression a caller received often shaped his attitude toward a Senator. If at all possible, most Senators would see their constituents for a few minutes. But after exchanging amenities, the Senators usually asked them to give the details of their problems to the administrative assistants who followed through on those. In attempting to conserve their Senators' time, many office staffs encountered more difficulty with long-distance telephone calls than with visitors. Altogether, the senatorial aides interviewed estimated that they took care of at least seventy-five per cent of the time-consuming aspects of dealing with constituents who visited or phoned their offices.

Speech, article, and book writing. Even where a Senator did not speak from a manuscript or wrote his own speeches, a considerable amount of work was entailed for his staff. One such Senator who was not very talkative by congressional standards kept his legislative assistant busy more than a quarter of the time during sessions and nearly full time during recesses gathering materials for speeches. In some offices, one staff member did all the ghost-writing. In others, the preparation of speeches was divided among the staff members in accordance with their areas of specialization.

In general, a senatorial office was only the final assembly plant for pre-fabricated speech parts obtained from various sources: administrative agencies, committee staffs, the Legislative Reference Service, and organized interest groups. Ordinarily, a senatorial assistant simply secured memoranda covering the information sought, which he reworked into the format of a speech. But fairly often, a senatorial aide requested drafts of a finished speech from several places and then synthesized the end product from the best portions of those. Senatorial assistants followed a similar procedure in writing periodical articles and books.

"Politickin." All the work done by senatorial aides was tinctured with politics. Several administrative assistants had been campaign managers for their Senators. Others had served as publicity directors in elections. Some administrative assistants frankly admitted that their primary responsibility was to advance their Senators' political fortunes. A number of senatorial assistants had had active careers in national and state politics. As previously mentioned, one administrative assistant was an ex-Congressman; another had been a Democratic state chairman for five terms; and others had held a variety of positions in political organizations and state governments. In most offices, one of the top aides acted in effect as patronage secretary. In these and many other ways, they helped their Senators to get re-elected.

Casework. The term "departmental business" comprised all the dealings of members of Congress and their staffs with the administrative establishment in behalf of constituents. Each problem of a person or subordinate unit of government was called a "case," and the aggregate efforts made in handling such matters were designated "casework." The assistance afforded ranged from merely referring a request to the appropriate department to going down to the agency concerned to argue the merits of a particular claim or complaint. Although some commentators attached invidious epithets such as "constituent errand-running" to departmental business and decried its existence, the performance of casework was firmly established as a responsibility of members of Congress in the usages which compose our "living constitution."[10]

For the most part, the senatorial aides made final disposition of the bulk of the casework. The average estimate made by the administrative assistants and executive secretaries interviewed was that they together with the other office staff members relieved their Senators from eighty-five per cent of the work on departmental business.

Legislative Activities

At hearings.   Rather often when circumstances prevented a Senator from testifying before a committee, one of his aides appeared in his stead as a witness.[11] Legislative assistants frequently accompanied their Senators to committee hearings where they located references, suggested questions, and rendered other services.   And Senators often had their legislative assistants attend committee hearings they had to miss.

At executive sessions.   There was no uniform practice among the committees about allowing senatorial assistants into executive sessions.   Some committees excluded them by standing rule; others informally discouraged their presence; but the rest admitted them freely.   At executive sessions, legislative assistants helped their Senators much the same as the committee aides did.   Besides participating in executive sessions of standing committees, some legislative assistants accompanied their Senators to conference committee meetings.

Where permitted into executive sessions, legislative assistants frequently attended as observers for their Senators.   At times when acting in that capacity, a legislative assistant in effect voted by informing the committee member to whom his Senator had given a proxy how the latter wanted it exercised. Representing their Senators in this fashion, most legislative assistants performed a valuable intelligence function.   However, the aggressive manner in which a few bumptious aides intruded into committee deliberations sometimes caused senatorial resentment.   On several occasions, committees showed their annoyance by ordering every office staff member out of the room.   And in some quarters, there was growing concern about the excessive number of senatorial assistants habitually present at closed meetings of certain committees.

On the floor.   Whenever important measures were being debated, many Senators took their legislative assistants on the floor of the Senate.   There the legislative assistants rendered generally the same kinds of services as they did at committee hearings and executive sessions.   In addition, a number of office staff members frequently went on the floor to confer with their Senators about urgent matters unrelated to the business before the Senate.   A few legislative assistants—especially the younger ones who were fascinated by parliamentary maneuvering—employed their privilege of going on the floor to secure a ringside seat at the major legislative contests.   And some legislative assistants circulated around the Senate Chamber exchanging news with other senatorial aides, endeavoring to align their principals on particular measures, and occasionally buttonholing Senators. These latter practices especially irritated some Senators.[12] Increasingly during the period covered, they manifested their resentment by ordering off the floor all office employees who were not there at the express direction of their Senators. For example, toward the close of the 82d Congress, while clearing the floor of excess senatorial assistants, a thoroughly incensed presiding officer lectured them on etiquette as follows:

> Let us have order in the Senate. The Chair is going to suspend business until we have better order, and until all the senatorial staff is cleared, except those whose presence is desired by Members of the Senate or of the House of Representatives. I do not know whether it is in the rule book, but it is the ruling of the Presiding Officer that no one may occupy chairs on the Senate floor except Members of Congress. The clerks may remain, of course, but they should sit in separate chairs. Let us have order in the Senate please. Let those who are in the Senate Chamber on missions for Members of the Senate please conduct themselves in such a way as to make it possible for the Senate to carry on its business. Whenever the present occupant of the chair sees a willful conversation or willful disregard of this statement by the Chair, whether it be by a Member of the Senate or not, the Chair will not hesitate to point the man out and let the Sergeant at Arms escort him from the Senate Chamber, even though the Chair does not want to embarrass anyone.[13]

And a few days later, Majority Leader Ernest McFarland (D.-Ariz.) complained to the chair:

> Mr. President, I merely want to request again that persons other than Senators, retire from the Senate Chamber, unless they have business requiring their attendance on the floor. It is difficult to transact business under the circumstances.[14]

Cooperation among Senatorial Aides

Among the senatorial office staffs, there were kaleidoscopic patterns of relations in exchanging information and advice, in negotiating over legislation and reports, and in planning and executing joint projects. For the most part, senatorial assistants dealt with one another individually. But during the period covered, inchoate organs of collective action were developing.

Liberal staff caucuses. During the 82d Congress, aides to Senators of the liberal bloc instituted the practice of caucusing together. The membership of their conferences varied with the matters under consideration. To a continuing core of assistants to the liberal Democratic Senators: Paul Douglas (Ill.), Theodore Green (R.I.), Hubert Humphrey (Minn.), Harley Kilgore (W.Va.), Herbert Lehman (N.Y.), Warren Magnuson (Wash.), James

Murray (Mont.), and John Pastore (R.I.) were added aides of their Democratic and Republican colleagues who were in accord with them on the particular items on the agenda of a meeting. For example, Senator Lister Hill's (D.-Ala.) administrative assistant participated in caucuses on revenue and tidelands oil bills. But, for obvious reasons, he was not included in the conferences on civil rights measures. The administrative assistants to Senators Irving Ives (R.-N.Y.) and H. Alexander Smith (R.-N.J.) were occasionally invited. And Senator Wayne Morse's (R.-Oreg.) administrative assistant attended regularly.[15]

Executive branch personnel often took part in these senatorial staff caucuses. For example, at a dinner meeting in March, 1952, the assembled senatorial aides received an advance briefing from the Assistant Director and Counsel of the Mutual Security Agency on the President's message recommending continuance of the Mutual Security Program for fiscal 1953 and consulted with the General Counsel of the Treasury Department about the imminent floor debate on Reorganization Plan Number One of 1952 for the Bureau of Internal Revenue. Representatives from the Bureau of the Budget and Council of Economic Advisers also were present at this meeting. Although in the 82d Congress these liberal staff caucuses were convened only on an *ad hoc* basis, the habitual participants made plans to hold them weekly during the 83d Congress.[16]

Republican AA's and Secretaries Association. On February 27, 1951, the Republican Administrative Assistants and Secretaries Association was founded under the aegis of the Republican Policy Committee staff. This group, which was created primarily to enable the aides to Republican Senators to become better acquainted and to exchange ideas and information, was but loosely organized. There were no written rules. A five-member steering committee was elected annually. And a special program committee was designated for each meeting. During 1951, the Association met regularly once a month while Congress was in session.

At these meetings, various Senate employees, the Director of the Legislative Reference Service, and spokesmen for other components of the congressional staff described the kinds of services they could render the senatorial aides; journalists lectured the administrative assistants and secretaries on how to improve their press relations; etc. In addition to the ordinary business meetings, the Association held a series of seminars on pending legislation. Since assistants to Senators representing every shade of opinion within the party were present, no attempt was made to reach agreement on the topics of discussion or to plan strategy as the liberal staff caucuses did.

Senate Secretaries Association. The Senate Secretaries Association was mainly a social organization comprised of administrative assistants and secretaries. Anyone who had ever occupied either of the two top positions on a Senate office staff was eligible to belong. It was absolutely nonpartisan. The officials were evenly divided between Republican and Democratic senatorial aides, and the presidency alternated between them. The group held a combined cocktail hour and dinner meeting monthly with an average attendance of about ninety persons. Although part of the members would like to have had the organization consider more serious matters, the majority felt that to do so would introduce divisive factors which would impair its major purpose of promoting friendly relations among all the Senate office staffs. Of course, the Association could give a collective voice to the group's views on any common problems about which there was unanimity. For example, in the 82d and 83d Congresses, the Association advocated more liberal retirement provisions for congressional employees.[17]

Relations with Committee Staffs

Most of the requests that senatorial aides made of committee staffs were for information on the status and contents of bills. Occasionally, a legislative assistant secured confidential committee prints or unpublished staff studies from committee aides. And once in a while, a senatorial assistant had a committee staff prepare a memorandum expressly for him. Reciprocally, committee aides sometimes asked a legislative assistant to supply further particulars on a bill introduced by his Senator or to refer them to someone who could. And there was a considerable amount of negotiation between committee and office staffs on the contents of pending legislation to resolve minor differences and facilitate compromise on major issues by their principals.

A Senator's office staff was nearly always involved in his committee activities —especially if he were a chairman or ranking minority member. Almost every legislative assistant reviewed committee publications from his Senator's perspective. Usually, a chairman's legislative assistant served as a liaison between him and his committee aides and exercised varying degrees of supervision over the latter—occasionally to the extent of being their *de facto* staff director. And Senators other than the chairmen sometimes employed their legislative assistants in effect as committee staff members.

Conversely, where a Senator was chairman or ranking minority member of a committee, its staff took care of a sizable portion of his office work pertaining to committee business.[18] Although some chairmen occasionally used employees of a committee on assignments outside its jurisdiction, there was general compliance with the requirement of the Legislative Reorganization Act that "Professional staff members shall not engage in any work other than committee business and no other duties may be assigned to them."[19]

Dealings with Policy Committee Staffs

Democratic. Assistants to Democratic Senators had very little contact with the Democratic Policy Committee staff. Over eighty-five per cent of the Democratic senatorial aides interviewed had never asked it to do any work for them.[20] The only use most of them made of that staff was to refer to the bill digests and voting records which it prepared and automatically distributed to all the Democratic Senators' offices. There was a consensus that both those services were handy. Prior to their institution, many of the requests that Democratic senatorial assistants had made of the Democratic Policy Committee staff were for voting records. Nearly all the rest of their inquiries were about the scheduling of bills for floor action.

Republican. The composition of the Republican Policy Committee staff profoundly affected the relations between it and the Republican senatorial aides. Assistants to Senators from all factions of the Republican Party agreed that it was a conservative group, comprised solely of Taft-Millikin appointees. As a consequence, aides to the middle-of-the-road and liberal Republican Senators— including two members of the Policy Committee—did not use that staff to an appreciable extent, and some of them were very distrustful of it. The few requests they made of it were for routine reference work which, they observed, they could have obtained just as readily from the Legislative Reference Service. None of these senatorial assistants employed the processed materials—which they sharply criticized for reflecting the viewpoint of only the most conservative faction of the Republican Party—prepared and distributed by the Policy Committee staff on its own initiative.[21]

As might be expected, therefore, aides to conservative Republican Senators constituted the main clientele of the Republican Policy Committee staff. They praised its bulletins and other publications, which they regularly read and filed for reference. And they had it do research and write speeches on highly partisan themes. Although very satisfied with the work received from the Policy Committee staff, over half the conservative Republican senatorial assistants interviewed remarked that they had resorted to it but infrequently.

Contacts with House Coordinator of Information

Although an instrumentality of the House of Representatives, the Office of Coordinator of Information afforded assistance to Senators and their staffs from intercameral comity. Approximately one third of the senatorial aides interviewed had called on the Coordinator's Office. Most of their requests were for spot information—usually pertaining to executive agencies. Nearly all the senatorial assistants who had used the Coordinator's Office spoke well of its celerity.

Use of the Legislative Reference Service

Senatorial aides called on the Legislative Reference Service mostly—and in some cases solely—for help on constituent inquiries. They relayed to it a large proportion of the myriad requests from constituents for information and publications readily obtainable from the LRS's files or from the Library's collections. And, of course, they used the *Digest of Public General Bills* extensively in answering correspondence from constituents about bills.[22]

In connection with work other than servicing constituents, they employed the LRS staff mainly on reference and routine research assignments much the same as the committee aides did.[23] Now and then, senatorial assistants had the American Law Section prepare briefs, opinions, and other legal memoranda. Somewhat more often, they called on other sections for nonlegal, analytical research reports—generally for incorporation in a speech, magazine article, or book.[24] Rather infrequently, they consulted with the top LRS specialists— usually about assignments the latter were performing for their Senators but sometimes for their own enlightenment.

Relations with the Executive Branch Staff

Senatorial aides obtained a wide variety of services from the executive branch staff: the provision of diverse kinds of data, preparation of analytical memoranda, speech writing, consultation, bill drafting, construction of graphs and charts, etc. Most of their requests were for information. Contrary to the prevalent supposition that minority Senators have but limited access to the facilities of the administrative establishment—usually most assiduously spread by spokesmen for alternative sources of staff assistance—aides to minority Senators representing every shade of opinion within their party averred that they had not experienced much, if any, difficulty in getting information from the departments during the 81st and 82d Congresses.

In general, senatorial office and executive branch employees dealt with each other individually. But sometimes they conferred jointly. For example, in the 81st Congress, James Webb, Under Secretary of State, and Jack McFall, Assistant Secretary of State for Congressional Relations, held a series of briefings on current world problems for Senators' administrative assistants and secretaries during luncheons at the State Department and evening meetings at Mr. McFall's home. After the State Department officials had made their presentations, the meetings were opened to questions from the senatorial aides. Approximately 150 administrative assistants and secretaries attended these quasi-social affairs.[25] And as previously mentioned, agency personnel often participated in the liberal staff caucuses during the 82d Congress.

Dealings with Interest Group Staffs

Senatorial aides often resorted to organized interest groups for both technical and political information with which to check or challenge the presentations of executive agencies, of other interests, or of Senators who were their spokesmen.[26] Occasionally, senatorial assistants called on organized interest groups for speech-writing help. And once in a while, a senatorial aide turned to association lawyers for bill drafting and other legal services.

As was the case with the committee aides, nearly all the senatorial assistants were members of the professional associations in their fields and of many other organized interest groups. And the fact that a number of the senatorial aides had been employees of organized interest groups or were then officials of associations affected their patterns of interaction.

Although not the greatest numerically, some of the most significant relations between senatorial assistants and organized interest groups occurred in connection with alerting the latter and coordinating their activities in a joint campaign to accomplish the defeat or enactment of particular legislation. After aggregating a coalition of interest groups in support of his Senator's stand on a bill, a legislative assistant frequently directed the planning and execution of their operations. Sometimes in such situations, a senatorial aide acted as an intelligence agent for his interest group allies at closed committee meetings. After each executive session, he would tell them what had taken place. And on the basis of his report, they would decide on which committee members to intensify their efforts.

Contacts with Private Research Organizations

The only use that most senatorial assistants made of private research organizations like Brookings Institution was to skim their publications. Just slightly over forty per cent of the senatorial aides interviewed had ever asked such organizations for information or to prepare anything for them. And nearly all of them emphasized that their requests for such assistance were very infrequent.

Conclusion

Evaluation. In general, the senatorial assistants interviewed had good educational and experience backgrounds. Moreover, like the committee aides, nearly all of them were well endowed with the even more essential qualifications of an appropriate personality, the ability to write and speak with facility, and the capacity to handle a wide range of complex and unrelated subjects with little prior acquaintance.

During the period covered, the administrative assistants together with the other office staff members were able to relieve their Senators of most of the burden of departmental business and other nonlegislative duties. Moreover, the high-level senatorial aides rendered valuable assistance to the Senators on their legislative work—assistance which went beyond the preparation of bills, reports, and supporting materials. Through conferring together, imaginative planning of strategy, and coordinating their efforts, the assistants to like-minded Senators often facilitated joint action by their Senators. As a frankly political component of the congressional staff, the top senatorial aides were a valuable supplement to the nonpartisan portions.

The employment of administrative assistants on legislative assignments was criticized as being contrary to the congressional intent in creating the position.[27] Though the legislative history of the act providing administrative assistants for Senators favors this contention,[28] the phraseology of the law permits assigning "other duties" to administrative assistants.[29] Anyhow, the original theory behind the law is subject to challenge as being too narrow in scope. Senators need high-caliber help in the performance of their legislative as well as their nonlegislative duties. If a Senator wants to use his top assistant mainly for that purpose, he should be free to do so.

The biggest danger for the senatorial office staffs to avoid is overexpansion. It could easily result in overinstitutionalizing the Senators. During the period covered, the problems of an excessive number of senatorial aides in the executive sessions of committees and on the floor of the Senate could be attributed partly to overstaffing. Many of the senatorial assistants involved came from the bigger office staffs. Several office forces which were supplemented from private funds showed signs of overstaffing. The official clerk hire allowance appeared to provide sufficiently large office staffs in most cases.

Provision of AA's for Representatives. In 1946, the House acted unwisely in denying administrative assistants to its members. Although Representatives obviously do not require as much staffing as Senators, their top aides should be of comparable quality; for they both perform the same legislative function. Because of the intrinsic precariousness of tenure for congressional office staffs, a large salary is the chief means of attracting and retaining the high-caliber personnel desired. Therefore, the original proposal for equipping Representatives as well as Senators with administrative assistants should have been adopted.

Since then in a series of pay acts (most of which were passed after the close of the period covered by this study), the basic clerk hire allowance for each House office has been raised from $9,500 to $17,500 a year, and the ceiling on the basic salary for the top clerk (usually called the "secretary") has been lifted to $7,000 a year.[30] Hence, in effect, the substance of the original proposal has gradually been adopted by the House. Many congressional secretaries (top office clerks) have assumed the title "administrative assistant." All that is necessary to complete the process is to raise the ceiling on the basic annual salary for the top clerk in each House office by $1,000.

PART FOUR

CHAPTER XII

THE OFFICE OF THE LEGISLATIVE COUNSEL

Origin

Joseph P. Chamberlain, Professor of Public Law at Columbia University, played an instrumental role in the creation of the Office of the Legislative Counsel. He founded and helped direct the institution which, through a demonstration project, finally persuaded Congress to establish such a facility. In 1911, Professor Chamberlain endowed the Legislative Drafting Research Fund of Columbia University and became one of its original trustees and directors.[1] In 1916, the directors of the Legislative Drafting Research Fund sent Middleton Beaman to Washington, D.C., to demonstrate to Congress the usefulness of a skilled legislative draftsman in preparing bills. Among the first to take advantage of this volunteer service was the House Ways and Means Committee. It utilized Mr. Beaman's talents to an increasing extent on the Revenue Acts of 1916, of 1917, and of 1918 and on other measures until it was preempting most of his time. Having become convinced of the value of expert assistance in drafting bills, the Ways and Means Committee decided that such aid should be provided on an official basis for any committee that desired it.[2]

Consequently, the Ways and Means Committee inserted sec. 1303 into the Revenue Act of 1918, which was approved on February 24, 1919. It created a Legislative Drafting Service to "aid in drafting public bills and resolutions or amendments thereto on the request of any committee of either House of Congress." The Service was placed under the direction of two draftsmen, one of whom was to be appointed by the Speaker of the House and the other by the President of the Senate "without reference to political affiliations and solely on the ground of fitness to perform the duties of the office." Each draftsman was authorized to employ and fix the compensation of his assistants and to make other expenditures from appropriations for the Service, subject to the approval of the Speaker of the House or the President of the Senate, as the case might be.[3] The Revenue Act of 1924 rechristened the Legislative Drafting Service as the "Office of the Legislative Counsel" and the two draftsmen as "legislative counsel."[4]   And the Revenue Act of 1941 transferred supervisory control over the Senate branch of the Office from the President of the Senate to the President *pro tem.*[5] With the exception of these two changes and several minor amendments pertaining to salary matters and the franking privilege, sec. 1303 of the Revenue Act of 1918 has remained substantially unaltered as the organic law for the Office.

In this connection, the contribution of Mr. Beaman to the establishment and successful functioning of the Office of the Legislative Counsel can hardly be overemphasized.   In fact, it might be said that the Office was an institutionalization of Mr. Beaman.   For sec. 1303 was enacted with the explicit understanding that Mr. Beaman would be the head of the House branch and that the services to be rendered by the Office would be identical with those he had been affording under the sponsorship of the Legislative Drafting Research Fund.[6] Besides playing a crucial role during the formative stages of this agency, Mr. Beaman continued as House Legislative Counsel for thirty years until January 31, 1949.

Organization and Composition

During the period covered, the Office of the Legislative Counsel was organized (as it had been from the outset in accordance with express congressional intent) into separate branches for the House and Senate, which were completely independent of each other in their direction and control.[7]   The Senate Legislative Counsel was responsible for the operation of the Senate branch to the President *pro tem.* of the Senate; the House Legislative Counsel, to the Speaker of the House.   And the lump-sum appropriation for the Office was specifically allocated between the two branches by a stipulation of the portions which should be disbursed by the Secretary of the Senate and by the Clerk of the House respectively.   Hence, for all practical purposes, there was the Office of the Senate Legislative Counsel and the Office of the House Legislative Counsel.

The two offices[8] were very similar in composition.   During the 82d Congress, there were ten lawyers and four clerks in each.   Strictly speaking, only the heads of the two offices were referred to as the "legislative counsel."   While the other attorneys were trainees, they were called "law assistants."   After they had served their apprenticeships, they bore the title of "assistant counsel."   In the House branch there was an additional position of "assistant counsel and administrative assistant."   As that designation implies, the incumbent handled many of the administrative management aspects of running that office.

Recruitment and Training

Judged by any criteria, both branches of the Office had a most effective career service during the period covered.   Customarily, initial appointments to their legal staffs were made shortly after the completion of the candidates' professional education and at a relatively low salary.   While on a probationary status, law assistants underwent a protracted period of in-service training.   After they had thoroughly demonstrated their aptitude for the work and been promoted to assistant counsel, they had in effect permanent tenure.   As they grew in experience and competence, they received periodic increases in pay.   When one of their high-ranking assistant counsel left, normally the legislative counsel did not bring in a replacement at that level.   Rather, they preferred to fill the vacancy at the bottom rung of the ladder.[9]   Finally, there was a remarkable continuity in the staffs of both branches of the Office.   In fact, during the thirty-three year span from its inception through the 82d Congress, there were but two House Legislative Counsel and seven Senate Legislative Counsel.[10]   In 1952, Allan H. Perley, House Legislative Counsel, had been on the legal staff of the House office for twenty-seven years.   C. Breck Parkman, the assistant counsel and administrative assistant, had been in the House office for thirty-one years.   John H. Simms, the Senate Legislative Counsel, had been an attorney in the Senate office for almost sixteen years.   And Charles F. Boots, an assistant counsel, had served twenty-two years in the Senate office.[11]

Selection of candidates.   Because bill drafting is such a highly-specialized occupation, virtually the only relevant experience and effective training for it must be acquired on-the-job.   Primarily for that reason, the legislative counsel generally followed the practice of appointing young men who had just graduated from law school and been admitted to the bar.   To secure the names of prospective candidates, the legislative counsel solicited suggestions from the deans of leading law schools throughout the country.[12]   Although both legislative counsel desired to maintain a broad geographic balance in their staffs, they were limited in the range of their recruiting by the distance which job applicants were willing to travel at their own expense for an interview.   For both legislative counsel considered interviewing essential in the process of selection.   They felt that only through direct observation of a candidate could they ascertain whether or not he possessed the requisite personality and temperament for success in this work. Normally each legislative counsel proceeded independently in recruiting his own staff.   However, during the 82d Congress, to save time, the House Legislative Counsel consulted the Senate Legislative Counsel about a number of job applicants the latter had just interviewed.

In accordance with the organic law of the Office, appointments were made without reference to political affiliations.   In fact, if a candidate had been prominently identified with political activities, he was automatically disqualified.[13]   Attesting to the absence of partisan considerations in the selection of his staff, Mr. Beaman said in 1945:

. . . since I was appointed, which was at the time the law was enacted some 26 years ago, I have never had anybody ask me my politics. I do not know the politics of any man in my office, and I never had anybody ask me as to their politics. I never have had any member of the House or Senate, from the Speaker down, exert any pressure on me to appoint anybody. I have had various people say that they had a good man that they would be glad to have me look at, but it has never gone beyond that. There has been no pressure of the slightest degree, as I say, to secure a job for anybody.[14]

Likewise, his successor, Mr. Perley, affirmed in 1951 that the same situation continued after he became head of the House office.[15] In the early years of the Senate office, a determined effort was made to foist a political protege on its staff. However, that attempt was frustrated by the courageous resistance of the Senate Legislative Counsel. And no further patronage pressures were brought to bear on the Senate office.

Probationary period. During the period covered, law assistants were on probation for their first year or two on the staff. About a fourth of them were eliminated at that stage. However, those who were retained were promoted rather rapidly, receiving a sizable salary increase each of their first few years of service.[16]

On-the-job instruction. A law assistant began his training by working on assignments for individual members of Congress under the supervision of the older attorneys in the office. Starting with private bills, he progressed through the more complex and difficult public bills and amendments requested by individual Congressmen. When he had developed his drafting skill sufficiently, the assistant counsel took him along on committee jobs. There he observed how the committees operated and the manner in which the assistant counsel served them. Also, he did some of the research in connection with the committee work. Then he was allowed to prepare an easily-segregated portion of a bill and to handle that before the committee. Finally, he completed his apprenticeship by taking over whole committee assignments. This entire process consumed approximately two years.[17]

Throughout, the trainee worked under the close scrutiny of the more experienced assistant counsel. At every stage, they gave him advice on how to handle various tasks. And they were constantly inculcating him with the office policies on such matters as keeping assignments confidential and avoiding pronouncements on the merits of the substantive policy in a bill, by relating those to the specific task at hand. Nothing he prepared left the office without being reviewed by at least one of the older attorneys—usually the one with the greatest knowledge of the subject matter field within which a particular job fell. When checking a new man's work, the assistant counsel "went after every comma." They stressed every conceivable item for which he should be on the lookout. For instance, they inquired if he had considered the constitutional issues involved—whether there were any or not. They pointed up all the policy questions of even the most minor magnitude and ensured that he had referred them for decision to the committee or Congressman for whom he was preparing the bill concerned. One assistant counsel likened this review procedure to the hazing upper classmen administer to a plebe at West Point. Judging by the results achieved, the system was very effective.

Ensuing repercussions. Several consequences flowed from the nature of the training necessary to produce an assistant counsel. Because under normal circumstances it required roughly two years, maintenance of the staff on a career basis was essential. Also, there was a protracted time lag before the benefits of any given addition to the staff could be fully realized. Finally, as the small number of experienced attorneys in the two offices could supervise but a limited group of trainees at any one time, the legislative counsel could not expand their staffs very rapidly.[18]

Essential Attributes

There was almost a corporate personality among the legal staff members in the two offices. Through the process of selection and training, similar personal qualities were shaped by indoctrinated attitudes into a "legislative counsel type." The legislative counsel and their assistants were highly articulate and in conversation readily divined what information was sought. They were imbued with an attitude of helpfulness and possessed a marked enthusiasm for their work. Awareness of the heavy responsibility devolved upon them was tempered by a widespread sense of humor. Their modesty and desire for anonymity were balanced by self-confidence, initiative, and adaptability. With a profound insight into the legislative process, they realistically appraised the various considerations they should take into account in their work. In brief, the personnel of the Office of the Legislative Counsel were the best explanation of the high regard in which it was held by the members of Congress and their staffs during the period covered.

Optimum Size

Neither legislative counsel contemplated expanding his staff very much in the foreseeable future. In the 82d Congress, both regarded the complement of ten attorneys in each office as the optimum size to handle the workload then. Because the flow of requests during a session was erratic, there were periods when each office fell behind in its work and had to put in considerable overtime at night and on weekends. However, if the staffs had been enlarged to accommodate the peak loads, they would have contained more personnel than was necessary to dispose of the normal volume of assignments expeditiously. During the preceding four Congresses, there was a consistent growth in the over-all workload. If that trend were to continue at the same rate during the succeeding two or three Congresses, each office might then have to add another attorney or two. Both legislative counsel had the commendable desire to keep their staffs as small as possible. They felt that a small staff could operate more efficiently than a large one and diverted proportionately less of their time from their primary duty of bill drafting to supervisory chores.[19]

Office Policies

In neither branch of the Office were the rules governing the conduct of the staff in its work or outside activities embodied in written form. Rather, the policies followed partook of the nature of "customs of the service," and all members of the staff were thoroughly familiar with them.

In regard to work. The legislative counsel and their assistants absolutely eschewed making decisions of even the most minor sort pertaining to the substantive policies in legislation on which they were working. Under no circumstances would they indicate a preference.[20] Every assignment was confidential unless the committee or member of Congress concerned authorized them to disclose it. They did not seek assistance from the executive branch staff or elsewhere without getting specific permission to do so.[21] An atmosphere of caution pervaded the staff. The legislative counsel and their assistants had an excellent feel for the bounds of propriety in their work—particularly with respect to the unpredictable and delicate situations that often arose in executive sessions of committees. No written code of conduct could possibly have covered all such contingencies or been as efficacious as the ingrained discretion of the assistant counsel.

On outside activities. Both legislative counsel had the attitude that a position on their staffs was a full time job and that anything which might interfere with that should not be permitted. The assistant counsel relied solely on their salaries as a source of income.[22] There were no express prohibitions on writing for publication, making speeches, or participating in other outside activities. However, defining the limits of allowable conduct in such areas posed no appreciable problem. For the assistant counsel were temperamentally suited for their occupation. There were no crusaders among them. Further, although bill drafting is extremely difficult work, it is highly rewarding. It is a challenge to the best talents of a lawyer, placing a premium upon ingenuity and judgment. In formulating legislative language, the assistant counsel had plentiful opportunities for the exercise of creative abilities and for professional self-realization. The significance of the work, the confidence Congress reposed in them, and the high regard in which the Office was held afforded abundant psychic income for them. In addition, they were evaluated by their superiors exclusively on the quality· of the work they did for Congress. Hence, there was no need for the assistant counsel to endeavor to build or maintain reputations as authorities through outside writing.

The Nature of Bill Drafting

The essence of bill drafting is placing a legislative proposal in the proper legal phraseology and form to achieve congressional intent. It is primarily a task of legal analysis and research rather than of composition. Rarely does the pressure of work allow time to polish grammar or rhetoric. Framing the legal language to embody congressional purpose is not as difficult as ascertaining what that purpose is in its entirety. While a committee (or individual member of Congress, as the case may be) is in the process of working out what it wants to do, the legislative counsel[23] assist it by explaining the effect of alternative proposals. Even after the committee (or Congressman) has settled upon the major outlines of a measure, subsidiary policy questions seem to unfold endlessly. The legislative counsel must point up all of those for the committee (or Congressman) to decide. To accomplish that, the legislative counsel must envisage the broad application of the proposed law in all of its ramifications. And they must consider the precise provisions for administrative structure and procedures to be specified in the statute. For policy issues—sometimes relatively major—inhere in such technical details. Until the legislative counsel have secured a determination of those by the committee (or Congressman), they cannot know the complete congressional intent.[24]

To perform their job properly, the legislative counsel have to do extensive legal research. In many cases they must check the constitutional limits on legislative authority. On occasion to anticipate presidential reaction, they have to look into a line of veto messages. To predict the legal implications of a proposed measure, they must analyze it in relation not only to the statutes on the same or cognate subjects but also to the judicial and administrative interpretations of them. Sometimes this research renders the drafting of a bill unnecessary by revealing that there already is a law covering the matter or that its objective can be achieved through complying with departmental regulations.[25]

Also, a major aspect of the legislative counsel's work is probing with questions to secure the detailed substantive knowledge of a matter necessary to draft a bill on it. They interview congressional staff members, executive branch experts, or whomever else the committee (or Congressman) authorizes them to consult. Sometimes groping with their initial queries, they learn enough about the subject as they progress to ask intelligent questions about it. The ability to elicit in this fashion requisite technical information from specialists is a crucial skill for the legislative counsel.

The Preparation of Legal Memoranda

During the period covered, both offices prepared a limited number of legal memoranda, most of which were opinions on a point of law or on the constitutionality of a measure. The Senate office bound its memoranda periodically. Once in a while, opinions prepared by the legislative counsel were inserted in the record of committee hearings, placed in the *Congressional Record,* or included in a committee report. Very infrequently, they were published as congressional documents or committee prints. In neither office was as much as a quarter—ten to fifteen per cent being a generous estimate—of the staff's time devoted to turning out such memoranda.

Although willing to write up opinions in connection with bills on which they were working, the legislative counsel preferred to render those orally. Both offices endeavored to hold the production of all other legal memoranda down to a minimum. With their primary function of bill drafting more than a full time job, they did not want to encourage this auxiliary service. If the legislative counsel had attempted to supply the potential market, they would have had to expand their staffs considerably. Finally, the legislative counsel deemed the preparation of such memoranda to be more properly the duty of the American Law Section of the LRS, which specialized in legal research and reference work.

Rendering Oral Opinions

In addition to the fact that the legislative counsel preferred to give legal opinions in oral rather than written form, there was a growing tendency among members of Congress to request "horseback" or "curbstone" opinions. Increasingly, Congressmen called up the legislative counsel to seek their impromptu judgment on a point of law or simply to inquire if there were any judicial decisions covering it. Also, rendering oral opinions is an integral part of the bill-drafting process. At all stages in the preparation of a measure, questions arise as to the legal effect of a proposed provision or the form in which it must be cast to make it constitutional or to avoid a point of order. Almost invariably the legislative counsel answered such questions orally.

Work for Committees

Patterns of committee use. As the Senate and House offices worked only upon request, there were wide variations in the extent to which different committees in the two chambers employed their services during the period covered. Although there were some fairly consistent elements in the resulting patterns of committee use, they were dissimilar in the House and Senate and changed from time to time in either house. They were affected by the shifting emphases of congressional attention and the corresponding changes in committee workloads, the preferences of the committee chairmen, and the practices of the committee staffs. Both offices experienced situations in which a committee that had been calling on them heavily ceased to do so entirely when the chairman was replaced even where the same clerk was retained. The Ways and Means Committee relied on the House branch extensively (as it had from the start), and the Finance Committee made continuing use of the Senate branch. On the other hand, neither of the appropriations committees requested major assistance from the legislative counsel in the preparation of appropriations measures. Their staffs handled the drafting of those almost exclusively. Once in a great while, they sought suggestions on the language for a legislative rider.[26]

Staff assignment. Although the legislative counsel were generalists capable of handling any bill-drafting stint, they tended to develop on-the-job specializations in the work of particular committees that were consistent customers of their offices. For instance, two of the most experienced attorneys on the staff of the House office concentrated on drafting revenue and other measures falling within the jurisdiction of the Ways and Means Committee. Of course, assignment of the legislative counsel on the basis of such specializations was always tempered by their availability, for each of them ordinarily assisted several committees. To guard against conflicts of schedule and other contingencies, both offices usually tried to have two attorneys work on every really major bill, with one of them serving primarily in the capacity of understudy.

Scope of assistance. The type of assistance sought from the legislative counsel and the stage in the proceedings at which they were called in varied from measure to measure even on the same committee. They might be asked to do anything from merely checking to ensure that a bill was in proper form to drafting it *de novo*. At any time from the inception of a measure until it had been through a conference committee, they might be requested to work on it or on the accompanying reports.[27]

Attendance at hearings. Because of their heavy workload, the legislative counsel did not have time to attend many committee hearings. Occasionally, they went to hear a particular presentation or to observe the committee's reaction. More often, they just skimmed a transcript of the testimony or received a briefing on significant items from the committee staff. However, where hearings were held on a bill on which the legislative counsel had been working for some time with the committee or subcommittee involved, they normally were present.

Role in executive sessions. On major legislation the point at which the legislative counsel were called in most frequently—certainly if they were to operate most effectively—was at the beginning of the executive sessions in which the committee (or subcommittee if there were one) afforded detailed consideration to the bill concerned. Then while the bill was being read for amendment, the legislative counsel were available to interpret the more complex provisions, to explain the effect of proposed modifications, to point up subsidiary policy issues, and sometimes to draft amendments right there. Throughout the proceedings, the legislative counsel made notes on the decisions reached by the committee. After each session, they prepared a draft in accordance with them. Then at the following meeting, they assisted the committee staff in explaining the revisions made. And either directly or through the committee staff, they called the committee's attention to any implicit policy questions which had developed in the course of drafting the new language. Finally, when a chairman was holding a press conference at the close of an executive session, he occasionally asked the legislative counsel to explain complicated provisions of the bill to the assembled newspapermen.[28]

Work on committee reports. Customarily when the legislative counsel participated in drafting a bill, they assisted the committee staff in preparing the report to accompany it. Increasingly their role in this respect was evolving into a review function. Where the committee aides or agency personnel did the section-by-section analysis in the report on a bill, the legislative counsel were usually asked to check to ensure that none of its interpretive language misconstrued the committee intent regarding the bill. About one third of the time, the legislative counsel prepared the section-by-section analyses. The House office would do that portion of the report required by the Ramseyer Rule[29] as part of a package service on a bill. In the Senate, the corresponding Cordon Rule[30] specified that the committee staff should prepare that section of the report. However, if it were especially complicated, the Senate office sometimes did it. Both offices would instruct the committee staffs how to prepare that part of a report, give them advice on handling problems encountered, and review their drafts of it. And frequently, committee aides requested the legislative counsel to look over the text, or "guff" section, of a report for any passages which might lead to a mistaken interpretation of the bill.[31]

Service on the floor. During the debate on a bill, the managers often took the legislative counsel on the floor with them to assist in explaining the measure, to advise them as to the effect of amendments offered, and sometimes to rework the language of modifications proposed there. Occasionally, while the legislative counsel were in the chamber on such an assignment, other members of Congress came over and asked them questions about the bill or requested them to draft amendments on the spot.

Work for conference committees. If there were adequate time before a committee of conference convened, the legislative counsel liked to get together with the committee staff members from both houses who were going to be present. At these intercameral staff meetings they tried to ascertain the meaning of the floor amendments adopted in the two chambers. Then they endeavored to anticipate the decisions the conferees were likely to make on the points in controversy. Sometimes they drew up alternative language for prospective compromises. Of course, only infrequently was there an opportunity for such complete staff preparation in advance. Often the legislative counsel were called into conference committee sessions at the last minute with barely time to examine copies of the Senate and House versions of the bill to become acquainted with the discrepancies between them.

Where one chamber had amended the other's bill by striking everything after the enacting clause, the conferees sometimes compromised by framing what amounted to an entirely new measure. In any event, there generally was considerable drafting to be done on a major bill in conference. Occasionally, when the conferees reached an impasse, they directed the staff to prepare language which they could use as the basis for resuming their effort to reach agreement. And as soon as the conference committee reached decisions on the various points in issue, the legislative counsel drew up amendments embodying them. Then the legislative counsel assisted in writing the conference committee report and the statement of the House managers.

Work for Individual Members

Although their organic law prescribed only the duty of assisting committees, both offices from their inception have drafted resolutions, bills, and amendments for individual members of Congress. And in 1946, the Legislative Reorganization Act recommended expansion of the Office for the express purpose of increasing its capacity to assist individual members as well as the committees of Congress.[32] The Senate office has always emphasized this category of work more than the House office has, mainly because the legislative process is more individualized in the Senate than in the House.[33] The difference in this respect is brought out by the statistics in Tables 2 and 3 on the next page. Although the requests from individual members greatly outnumbered those from committees in either chamber, committee jobs generally were of longer duration. As a result, in the 82d Congress, the total time of the staff of each office was about evenly divided between these two classes of work.

Relation to committee work. This classification of assignments between committees and individual members of Congress contained some arbitrary elements. For a committee staff might have requested a job for the chairman in his capacity as an individual legislator, or conversely, a committee might have specifically directed one of its members to have a bill or amendment drawn up expressing his ideas on a subject. Without sufficient background on the genesis or ultimate disposition of a number of requests, the legislative counsel had to guess in classifying them. Hence, it was almost impossible to separate completely the work for committees from that for individual Senators or Representatives.

TABLE 2

NUMBER OF ASSIGNMENTS PERFORMED BY THE HOUSE OFFICE, 1925-1952*

Congress	For Committees	For Members	Total
69th	69	359	428
70th	88	378	466
71st	108	442	550
72d	113	659	772
73d	152	685	837
74th	167	997	1,164
75th	169	965	1,134
76th	145	1,181	1,326
77th	112	1,056	1,168
78th	98	1,595	1,693
79th	150	2,060	2,210
80th	285	1,930	2,215
81st	302	2,702	3,004
82d	313	2,560	2,873

* From statistics supplied by the House office.

TABLE 3

NUMBER OF ASSIGNMENTS PERFORMED BY THE SENATE OFFICE, 1925-1952*

Congress	For Committees	For Members	Total
69th	72	700	772
70th	67	1,018	1,085
71st	85	1,650	1,735
72d	101	1,345	1,446
73d	165	1,022	1,187
74th	226	1,443	1,669
75th	174	1,733	1,907
76th	220	2,178	2,398
77th	275	1,676	1,951
78th	257	1,619	1,876
79th	303	2,151	2,454
80th	514	2,687	3,201
81st	643	3,801	4,444
82d	436	2,713	3,149

* From statistics supplied by the Senate office.

Moreover, during the period covered, these two categories of work were quite compatible, with the heaviest demand for each occurring at different times. Every year, assignments for individual Congressmen increased in volume during November and December, reached a peak in January or February, and tapered off before committee work approached its climax later in the spring. And performing jobs for individual members of Congress afforded excellent training for the new attorneys in each office.[34]

Assignment and scheduling of work. In both offices, the jobs for individual Congressmen that were not handled by the law assistants were distributed among the other legal staff members largely in accordance with the specializations they developed in their committee work. Of course, this method of making assignments was qualified by the availability of the attorney most conversant with the subject matter in each case. Committee jobs always took precedence over those for individual members of Congress. Requests from Congressmen were generally handled in the order in which they were received. But, for obvious reasons, top priority was given to the preparation of amendments to bills that were under consideration by a committee or on the floor of the House or Senate. Also, the drafting of simple measures that required only a little time to do was interpolated among the work on major bills that took several weeks to prepare.[35] Although the amount of service requested by different Senators and Representatives varied widely, neither office was confronted with the problem of devising a quota system.

Collaboration between the Two Offices

"Reciprocity."[36] When attorneys from both offices were assisting a conference committee, they collaborated intimately throughout—even to the extent that the Senate legislative counsel helped prepare the statement of the House managers. In addition, there were close working relations between the two offices on revenue measures. Habitually, the two attorneys from the House office who worked primarily with the Ways and Means Committee followed a tax bill over to the Senate where they assisted their opposite number fom the Senate office in handling it before the Finance Committee.[37] Whenever they were called in by the Ways and Means Committee, they notified him; and rather frequently he went over to help them draft a revenue bill from the outset. In such instances, the two staffs were completely integrated. The most experienced attorney supervised the others irrespective of which office they were from, and all participated fully in working with both committees.

Except in the field of taxation, such interchange of staff between the two offices occurred very seldom. In 1938, when the Social Security Act was being revised, there was no one with a knowledge of the subject available in the House office. So the Senate legislative counsel who specialized in social security legislation came over and assisted the Ways and Means Committee on that measure for several weeks. And in 1946, an attorney from the Senate office followed the Armed Forces Unification Act over to the House. After the expansion of both offices that occurred since 1946, there were no additional instances of this "reciprocity" other than on revenue bills.

Cooperation between opposite numbers. However, there was considerable cooperation on a continuing basis between the attorneys who handled the the same subject matter in the two offices. Although on occasion they visited each other, they ordinarily communicated over the telephone. Rather frequently, one asked the other to explain passages in a bill he had drawn or the background of changes that had been made in it by the other chamber—especially where the legislative history was not clear. When a legislative counsel encountered a novel or extra-difficult proposition, he often consulted with his opposite number in the other office on how to deal with it. In such cases, besides giving advice orally, the latter usually sent over anything relating to the subject he had in his files: legal memoranda, sections of old bills, preliminary drafts, or citations. And sometimes on rush jobs on amendments to highly complicated measures, a legislative counsel had his counterpart in the other office check the language he prepared.

Relations with Other Congressional Staffs

With committee staffs. The professional staff members of a committee facilitated the functioning of a legislative counsel in many ways. They aided him in sampling hearings by suggesting sessions he should attend to hear significant presentations and by indicating portions of the transcript he might read for the same purpose. They supplied him with background information on the context out of which a bill had arisen: the nature of the problems involved, proposed solutions, and antecedent measures. And they acquainted him with whatever action the committee already had taken on the bill. The later in the proceedings he was called in, the more extensive and essential was this briefing. Also, they explained technical substantive aspects of a proposal; e.g., how the area coverage principle is applied in planning, financing, and constructing a rural telephone system, so that he could better envision them when drafting the relevant sections of a bill.

The committee staffs greatly expedited obtaining the assistance of executive branch personnel. Where necessary, they secured the chairman's permission to contact certain agencies. Often from intimate acquaintance with the sector of the administrative establishment involved, they knew which departmental technicians to call on particular problems. And they took care of any necessary arrangements for agency experts to come up to work with the legislative counsel.

The committee staffs were most helpful in dealing with policy questions that unfolded as the drafting progressed. Many committees delegated to their staffs authority to decide minor policy issues. From familiarity with their committee's frame of reference, committee aides frequently were able to make tentative decisions of more important policy matters on the basis of which the drafting could proceed. And they often handled the reference of major policy questions to the committee for determination.

The committee staffs and legislative counsel cooperated in keeping track of committee action during executive sessions. At the close of a rapidly-moving meeting, they usually compared notes to ascertain what took place. Some committee aides prepared preliminary drafts of bills and amendments. Throughout, they transmitted—and occasionally anticipated—the requests of committee members for amendments. And the professional staffs of committees largely divested the legislative counsel of the burden of writing the reports to accompany bills.

With office staffs. Particularly on the Senate side, the office staffs rendered analogous assistance to the legislative counsel on work for individual members of Congress. They supplied background information, aided in clarifying ambiguous requests, obtained authorization to contact executive branch experts, and made minor or transmitted major policy decisions. Also, some of them prepared rough drafts of bills and amendments from which the legislative counsel could work.

With the Legislative Reference Service. Nearly all the relations between the legislative counsel and the Legislative Reference Service were with its American Law Section. Except for a few instances where senior specialists were serving on committee staffs, the two offices had practically no contact with the nonlegal researchers in the LRS. Occasionally, the legislative counsel discussed legal questions with the chief or one of the top analysts in the American Law Section. Once in a while, the legislative counsel asked them for any legal memoranda they already had made up on a particular matter—usually to relay to a Senator or Representative seeking information on the subject. Although the legislative counsel rarely, if ever, requested the American Law Section to prepare studies for their own use, sometimes they received the fruits of its work indirectly. For Congressmen occasionally included compilations and other materials from the American Law Section in the files they sent down on bills to be drafted. But for the most part, the legislative counsel called on the American Law Section for legal reference work: spot inquiries on state laws, citations, and information on the status of amendments to laws, which it could handle quickly because of the collections and indexes it maintained.

With Senate policy committee staffs. During the period covered, the Senate office received numerous requests from the Republican Calendar Committee aide. He asked the legislative counsel to explain bills they had drafted, for opinions on other measures, and to prepare amendatory language to correct mistakes or to effect other changes in bills which were likely to be disposed of during the "call of the calendar."

With the House Coordinator of Information. The House office had negligible direct contact with the House Coordinator of Information. However, when members of the Coordinator's staff received inquiries concerning points of law, they often referred the persons seeking such information to the House Legislative Counsel.[38]

Collaboration with Agency Staffs

The executive branch staff was an invaluable source of assistance to the legislative counsel. Frequently, bill drafting required knowledge not only of relevant existing statutes as interpreted by the courts but also of numerous administrative regulations and adjudications applying them. Many laws and departmental orders incorporated the highly-specialized terminology of various industries, trades, and professions. Agency personnel had a thorough grasp of the problems encountered in carrying out current governmental programs and could readily evaluate the administrative feasibility of alternative schemes for dealing with those. Naturally, the draftsman of a departmental bill knew more about its contents and phraseology than anyone else.

Through ofttimes protracted consultations with agency experts, the legislative counsel rapidly acquired sufficient understanding of the intricacies of the existing law involved and of the technical content of a proposed measure to work on it. Frequently, the legislative counsel received a detailed exposition of a departmental bill from its author.[39] When a change was to be made in a complicated administrative setup, the operating officials most conversant with it were sometimes brought up to aid the legislative counsel in formulating the language to effect the modification. Where actuarial or other highly-specialized skills were required to construct schedules of rates or of benefits included in certain bills, agency technicians normally prepared them. Throughout all phases of the consideration of a measure in either house, departmental lawyers might be present to assist in writing and criticizing portions of successive drafts and of accompanying reports. Reciprocally, before some agency legal staffs sent bills they had prepared up to be introduced, they customarily asked one of the legislative counsel to review them for technical errors in drafting.

Relations with Interest Groups

Following the principle of consulting with whomever the committees recommended, the legislative counsel occasionally worked with representatives of organized interest groups.[40] Especially when a committee was giving primary consideration to a bill written by an outside group, officials of the latter performed much the same functions as administrative agency staffs in explaining complex provisions, affording additional information, and helping prepare successive drafts of the measure and its supporting documents.

Effect of the Legislative Reorganization Act

The section on the Office of the Legislative Counsel in the Legislative Reorganization Act of 1946 consists solely of a schedule of authorizations for the fiscal years 1947 through 1950.[41] Inasmuch as Congress already could appropriate whatever amount it deemed necassary, this section is merely declaratory of the extent to which the sponsors of the Act felt the Office should be expanded. During the late 1930's and early 1940's, each branch endeavored to maintain a complement of five attorneys. With growing workloads during that period, both offices were definitely understaffed. Hence, independently of the movement that culminated in the reorganization of Congress, the legislative counsel decided to request more funds with which to enlarge their staffs.[42] The enactment of the Legislative Reorganization Act catalyzed obtaining the additional appropriations. However, as Table 4 discloses, the amount actually appropriated for each fiscal year specified in the Act was substantially less than the sum authorized.

TABLE 4

AUTHORIZATIONS COMPARED WITH APPROPRIATIONS
FOR FISCAL 1947-1952*

Fiscal Year	Authorization	Appropriation	Difference
1947	$150,000	$130,000	$20,000
1948	200,000	160,000	40,000
1949	250,000	188,950	61,050
1950	250,000	191,000	59,000
1951	Unlimited	199,500	. . . . .
1952	Unlimited	221,065	. . . . .

* Sources: Public Law 601, 79th Cong., 2d Sess., Aug. 2, 1946, sec. 204, 60 *Stat.* 837, 2 *U.S.C.* 271 note; Senate Expenditures Committee, *Hearings on the Organization and Operation of Congress,* 82d Cong., 1st Sess., June 7, 1951, p. 112; U.S., Congress, Senate, Committee on Appropriations, *Legislative Branch Appropriation Bill, 1953,* Senate Report No. 1828 (to accompany H.R. 7313), 82d Cong., 2d Sess., June 26, 1952, p. 9.

Further, for fiscal year 1948, the Senate office was allowed $20,000 less than it requested. In fiscal years 1950 and 1951, the appropriations for the House office were $4,000 and $2,000 respectively under its estimates. For fiscal years 1952 and 1953 both offices received the amounts they requested.[43]

Indirectly, the Legislative Reorganization Act enabled the legislative counsel to concentrate more on their primary function of bill drafting. As previously mentioned, the expanded committee staffs provided under it, relieved them of much auxiliary work they used to do on committee reports, prints, and statements.

Evaluation

During the period covered, the Office of the Legislative Counsel was the most thoroughly accepted segment of the congressional staff. It exemplified function admirably adapted to purpose. The first legislative counsel established, and their successors maintained, sound precedents in concept of role, in mode of operation, and in selection, training, and retention of staff. Of recognized competence, the legislative counsel and their assistants were well-suited by temperament and personality to their work. In every respect, the Office merited the esteem in which it was held by members of Congress and their staffs.

PART FIVE

CHAPTER XIII

CONCLUDING COMMENTS

Ambivalence of Congressional Staffing

With a heavy burden of legislative and nonlegislative business, Congress needs staff assistance. Yet the problem of staffing the members and committees of Congress is especially perplexing because of the diffuseness, diversity, and changeability of the internal power structures of Congress and because of the comparatively unique nature of the policy-making and representative functions of members of Congress.[1] Moreover, it is a task fraught with dangerous potentialities not only for Congress but also for the entire governmental system.

Summation

In the Legislative Reorganization Act of 1946, an ambitious attempt was made to improve the staffing of Congress by expanding the existing and introducing new elements of a professional staff. In the preceding chapters, a study has been made of the nature and functioning of the three primary components of that professional staff during the three Congresses following the institution of the Legislative Reorganization Act. Throughout the study, judgments have been made on various aspects of that staff. The job remains of summarizing those evaluations and seeing what over-all conclusions they support.

Committee staffs. In general, the principle followed in the Legislative Reorganization Act of not prescribing the internal organization of the committee staffs was sound for both tactical and practical reasons. However, during the period covered, experience graphically demonstrated that for the most effective utilization of staff personnel, for the convenience of the chairman and other committee members, and to eliminate a structural dynamic toward strife between the professional staff and chief clerk, there should be a chief of staff with real authority over both the professional and clerical components of each committee staff. Ideally, he should have a large—if not the decisive—voice in hiring and firing the rest of the staff, a distinctive title confirming his status, and a higher salary than his top-ranking subordinates.

Similarly, there was ample evidence that earmarking part of a committee staff for the minority is an undesirable practice that should be avoided wherever possible. As the provisions in sec. 202 of the Legislative Reorganization Act for assigning committee aides to the chairman and ranking minority member have occasionally been misconstrued to cause partition of committee staffs where that was not necessary, those passages might well be repealed. And the enactment of any of the increasingly numerous proposals for mandatory allocation of committee staffs in prescribed ratios between the majority and minority should be vigorously resisted. If the imposition of such statutory obstacles can be averted, the force of example of the advantages enjoyed by the committees with nonearmarked staffs and the dynamics toward nonpartisanship in the operation of the committees should ultimately bring about substantial realization of the Legislative Reorganization Act's goal of nonpartisan professional staffs for the committees.

The present provision of the law for hiring the professional staffs of the standing committees has proved admirably suited to their diverse needs. Under it during the period covered, the committees could, and some did, adopt refined recruiting techniques in accordance with sound principles of personnel administration. Among the methods of recruitment followed, the three which were best because most conducive to a homogeneous staff with a high degree of control, continuity of tenure, and willingness to serve all members of the committee alike were: (1) delegation of authority to the staff director to choose the remainder of the staff subject to the approval of the chairman and/or committee; (2) use of a staffing subcommittee in conjunction with the staff director; (3) clearance by the chairman of all prospective appointees with the ranking minority member. However, procedure as such should not be overemphasized. Where a committee genuinely wanted to obtain a qualified staff, it usually succeeded even when handicapped by faulty practices such as the allocation of staff positions among the committeemen. And a gratifying number of the committees honestly endeavored to carry out the intent of the Legislative Reorganization Act that professional staff members be selected on a nonpartisan and merit basis.

In the main, the committee aides interviewed were well fitted for their posts by education, previous employment, and aptitude. Their educational and experience backgrounds compared favorably with those of corresponding groups of governmental employees. And most of them ranked high in the possession of other qualifications even more essential to success in committee staff work: a suitable personality, the attributes of a highly adaptable generalist, and the ability to write and speak fluently. Considering the committees' need for legal services and the fact that many of the professional aides with law degrees also were well versed in other subjects, the number of lawyers on the committee staffs was not excessive during the period covered.

There are reasonable grounds for believing that the provision in S. 2177 (the Legislative Reorganization Act), 79th Congress, for using a congressional personnel director as a primary means of ensuring the quality and tenure of the committee staffs not only was politically infeasible but also was of dubious desirability. In giving him a veto power over appointments to the committee staffs, it risked building an element of unresponsiveness into them and created a potential for depriving the committees of aides most in accord with their legitimate preferences. In rejecting it and substituting the method of appointment by a majority of each committee, Congress acted wisely. Under the present system, the objective of separating the committee staffs from the chairmen's office forces can be—and to a large extent has been—achieved. And the committees can obtain as good staffs on a merit basis without incurring the dangers inherent in vesting such control over their selection in a congressional personnel director.

During the period covered, experience amply confirmed the philosophy of the Legislative Reorganization Act of having only a few highly competent professional aides for each standing committee. Keeping the committee staffs small conduced to confining them to their proper sphere and to maintaining their quality and efficiency. Most of the pathologies of staffing appeared among the inflated committee staffs. The statutory allotment of professional staff members for the standing committees seemed to be adequate for most of them.

In any event, the present practice of requiring committees to obtain special authorization for extra employees is a better approach than increasing the statutory quota. It enables the committees to accommodate more flexibly to the fluctuations in their workloads and subjects them to the check of having their requests for additional staff passed upon by their parent chamber. If anything, the House and Senate should curb their generosity in allowing extra employees, for the tendencies toward overstaffing are already discernible.

The elimination of patronage and the achievement of continuity in committee staffing are commendable objectives. However, because of the prime importance of avoiding irresponsibility in the committee staffs, the proposals for providing greater security of tenure through additional statutory or other external safeguards are undesirable. The present statement of intent in the law goes about as far as possible in promoting stability in the staffs without depriving the committees of the ability to hold them immediately accountable. Reinforced by that exhortatory language, the dynamics toward permanency in committee staffing should ultimately bring about the kind of tenure sought by the Legislative Reorganization Act without the dangers involved in any attempt to accomplish that by further legislation.

Besides handling most of the routine details in planning and conducting hearings, committee aides executed very responsible assignments in the preparation of legislation during the period covered. They acted in a liaison and mediating capacity between their committees and other elements in Congress, the executive branch staff, and interest group representatives in working out the details of bills. When drafting the reports to accompany bills, the committee staffs often had to divine the preferences of their committees and incorporate those in the reports without the benefit of a confirming check by their principals. And at conference committee sessions, the most crucial phase of the legislative process, the conferees customarily delegated a large amount of responsibility to committee aides for embodying their decisions in the conference reports. In addition to introducing new methods into their own work (for example, employing joint staff subcommittees to conduct studies), the committee staffs played an instrumental role in the development of a significant innovation in the hearings process: the use of round-table discussions.

In general, work on legislation illustrates—probably better than any of their other activities—the very complex facilitative job to be done by the professional staffs of committees, the advantages accruing from continuity of tenure in mastering the details of that job and in devising new techniques for its more effective performance, and the great trust habitually reposed in committee aides. These considerations, in turn, re-emphasize the need for having professional staff members who are well-qualified, reliable, immediately answerable to their respective committees, and imbued with the proper concept of their role.

During the period covered, much of the staff work in connection with surveillance of administration was performed by specially-authorized staffs of subcommittees and joint "watchdog" committees. The regular staffs of the standing committees did not devote a large proportion of their time to overseeing the executive branch. Nevertheless, important issues are involved in this phase of their activities.

Under the guise of supervising administration, committees and their staffs encroached on the executive branch province in a number of instances. Although some of these cases were debatable, the committees undeniably had assumed a purely administrative function where they passed upon specific administrative acts. This development was on a rather small scale. However, the requirement of ratification by the appropriate congressional committees could be extended to a large variety of administrative actions. And it was incorporated in laws with increasing frequency during the period covered. Generally, this form of legislative oversight can be exercised only with staff assistance.

Though the Legislative Reorganization Act does not empower the standing committees to ratify specific administrative acts, it has encouraged the enactment of laws that do. One of the major arguments advanced in behalf of such measures is that they would enable the standing committees to discharge better the supervisory duties imposed on them by the Legislative Reorganization Act. The underlying theory of the Legislative Reorganization Act with regard to focusing the congressional oversight function in the standing committees is faulty. It ignores the totality of the governmental process. It fails to appreciate the inevitably discontinuous nature of congressional supervision of administration. And any attempt to apply it encounters the as yet unresolved practical problem of how to divide the responsibility for supervising administration among the appropriations, expenditures, and other standing committees.

In view of these considerations, the regular staffs of the standing committees should not be enlarged in order to carry out more completely the oversight provisions of the Legislative Reorganization Act. If any increase in committee staffing for oversight purposes were deemed necessary, it would be better to confine such expansion to the specially-authorized staffs of subcommittees and/or joint "watchdog" committees. For when the missions that bring them into being are completed, they can be liquidated. Or at least their size can be adapted to the fluctuations in supervisory activities more readily than that of the permanent committee staffs.

In particular, the regular staffs of the standing committees should not be expanded in an effort to maintain continuous, detailed supervision of administration through a more or less independent staff operation. To do so could easily result in setting up a legislative bureaucracy which would aggravate extant shortcomings in our system of government and which would be self-defeating. Instead of pursuing this course, Congress would be better advised to strengthen the internal controls of the administrative establishment and to utilize legislative oversight primarily as a means of stimulating them.

Senatorial office staffs. In general, the senatorial assistants interviewed had good educational and experience backgrounds. Also, like the committee aides, nearly all of them were well endowed with the even more essential qualifications of an appropriate personality, facility of expression in writing and speaking, and the capacity to handle a wide range of complex and unrelated subjects with little prior acquaintance.

During the period covered, the administrative assistants together with the other office staff members were able to relieve their Senators of most of the burden of departmental business and other nonlegislative duties. In addition, the high-level senatorial aides gave valuable help to the Senators on their legislative work—help which went beyond the preparation of bills, reports, and supporting materials. Through conferring together, imaginative planning of strategy, and coordinating their efforts, the assistants to like-minded Senators often promoted joint action by their Senators. As a frankly political component of the congressional staff, the top senatorial aides were a valuable supplement to the nonpartisan portions.

The greatest threat in connection with the senatorial office staffs is over-expansion. It reduces a major automatic safeguard of competency and impairs efficiency. It could easily result in overinstitutionalizing the Senators. During the period covered, the problems relating to an excessive number of senatorial aides in the executive sessions of committees and on the floor of the Senate could be ascribed partly to overstaffing. Many of the senatorial assistants involved came from the bigger office staffs. Several office forces which were supplemented from private funds showed symptoms of overstaffing. The official clerk hire allowance appeared to provide sufficiently large office staffs for most Senators.

In 1946, the House acted unwisely in rejecting the original proposal for equipping Representatives as well as Senators with administrative assistants. Since then (largely after the close of the period covered by this study), however, the House has gradually adopted the substance of that recommendation by successively raising the limit on the amount of basic salary payable to the top clerk and the clerk hire allowance for each House office. All that is necessary to complete the process is to lift the ceiling on the basic annual salary for the top clerk in each House office by $1,000.

Legislative Counsel. The Office of the Legislative Counsel was a successful, going concern twenty years before the inception of the congressional reorganization movement. The Legislative Reorganization Act merely catalyzed a necessary expansion of the Office and indirectly relieved it of a large share of auxiliary duties it used to perform. Admirably suited to its function in every respect, the Office of the Legislative Counsel is truly the blue-ribbon career service of the congressional staff. Moreover, in the ingrained desire of both the House and Senate Legislative Counsel to keep their staffs as small as possible, it has an inherent protection against the "empire-building" proclivities all too apparent in other staff agencies inside and outside the legislative branch. The only conceivable danger—which is quite remote—is that overenthusiastic customers might insist upon enlarging the Office beyond its optimum size.

Conclusion

For the most part, the principles incorporated in the Legislative Reorganization Act and the other organic legislation of the three primary segments of the congressional staff covered are valid. Though some minor amendments would increase the consistency and effect other marginal improvements in the staffing provisions of the Legislative Reorganization Act, there is no pressing need for them. Rather, the major legislative task is to frustrate the growing attempts to supersede those principles in the law—especially of smallness and of nonpartisanship in committee staffs. Having built a solid statutory foundation for a staff, Congress now has mainly to protect that from erosion and to avoid erecting too large an edifice on it.

Under the extant staffing provisions, Congress has in general supplied itself with the kind of professional staff required to facilitate its functioning in relation to the other components of our governmental system. It should not build up a staff to duplicate theirs or to usurp their rightful duties. Toward the close of the period covered, Congress manifested inclinations in both these directions. Ominous tendencies toward overstaffing and using staff as an instrument to encroach on the executive branch province were developing. Only Congress can remedy this situation. The President could help somewhat by a more astute and determined defense of executive prerogatives than was made during the period covered. But fundamentally, the only corrective is congressional self-restraint based upon an awareness of the individual legislator of the danger to his vital office as well as to the constitutional balance of our governmental system from an excess or improper use of congressional staffing. Having registered a very substantial advance on the staffing front, Congress like a prudent military commander should consolidate its gains and resist the temptation to go too far.

CHAPTER XIV

POSTSCRIPT

Purpose

Because considerable time has elapsed since the close of the period covered, this postscript has been added to acquaint the reader with major trends in congressional staffing through 1961. It does not try to mention every respect in which the situation has remained the same or has changed. Rather, it focuses on significant developments concerning the three primary components of the professional staff being studied.

Majority-Minority Earmarking

Since 1953, there have been contrary tendencies with regard to dividing committee staffs between the majority and minority. The minority staff position on the Joint Economic Committee was not institutionalized. With the departure of the incumbent, Mr. Berquist, at the end of the 83d Congress, it was eliminated.[1] Moreover, through 1961, the rest of the regular staff remained immune to the growing partisanship which had rent that committee since 1955. In minority reports and individual dissents that deplored increasingly partisan action by the majority, minority members continued to extol the objectivity and accessibility of the Joint Economic Committee staff.[2] And in 1960, Senator Prescott Bush (R.-Conn.) even cited the contributions by the staff as one of the few justifications for continuing the Joint Economic Committee. He wrote:

> The majority have all but destroyed the Joint Economic Committee's usefulness by the extreme partisanship of their reports. . . . Were it not for the fact that valuable additions to economic knowledge are often made in papers prepared by contributing economists, by Government witnesses, and by the committee's able staff, I would recommend that the committee be abolished.[3]

A number of committee staffs in both chambers have continued to operate on a completely nonpartisan basis. Others have confined minority staffing to existing positions while hiring additional employees without regard to their political affiliations.

At the same time, however, there has been mounting pressure for more minority staffing. On some House committees where there had been no partisan aspect to the work of minority aides, employees have been added who devote much of their time to performing assignments for the minority membership. In the Senate, minority earmarking has spread even to the staffs of committees which had successfully resisted the practice through the 82d Congress. For example, as one of the conditions for returning to the Permanent Subcommittee on Investigations of the Senate Government Operations Committee on January 25, 1954, after their celebrated walkout six months earlier, the Democratic members insisted upon the adoption of a subcommittee rule authorizing them to select a minority counsel.[4] This rule reads:

> 2. The minority shall select for appointment to the subcommittee staff a chief counsel for the minority who shall, upon being confirmed, work under their supervision and direction; who shall be kept fully informed as to investigations and hearings, have access to all material in the files of the subcommittee, and, when not otherwise engaged, shall do other subcommittee work.[5]

In seeking additional funds for this position, Senator Joseph McCarthy (R.-Wis.) endorsed this step. Noting that his Democratic predecessor as chairman had denied a similar request from him, he said, "I feel that the minority is entitled to have someone who will work under the instructions of the minority and be available to the minority at all times."[6] A few years later one of the four positions on the professional staff of the full committee was allocated to the minority by informal agreement.

On January 30, 1957, at the instance of Senator Carl Curtis (R.-Nebr.), ranking minority member of the Committee on Rules and Administration, nearly all the resolutions providing specially-authorized staffs for committees or subcommittees were amended as follows:

> *Provided,* That the minority is authorized to select one person for appointment, and the person so selected shall be appointed and his compensation shall be so fixed that his gross rate shall not be less by more than $1,200 than the highest gross rate paid to any other employee.[7]

During the debate over the desirability of such a proviso, Senator Curtis said that he was taking this action "at the direction of my leadership and the majority of the members on the minority side."[8]

Some Senators mildly remonstrated that their committee or subcommittee staffs already contained minority employees. Others protested strenuously the application of this requirement to thoroughly nonpartisan staffs—some of which were headed by directors who had been appointed when the Republicans were the majority. A few argued that conforming with this amendment would require hiring superfluous personnel in the case of subcommittees with very small staffs.[9] To these objections, Senator Curtis blandly replied:

> We are aware that at the present time there are on many of the committees employees who have been appointed at the request of the minority, but it is done only by the grace of the majority. It is done where the majority actually makes the appointment. We have no desire to disturb those arrangements. The amendment gives the minority the selection and appointment of one employee without the concurrence of the majority, as a matter of right, if the minority so chooses him. They do not have to choose him.[10]

And even against the vigorous opposition of his fellow Republican, Senator William Langer (N.Dak.), he persisted in offering the amendment to the resolution providing funds for the Special Subcommittee on Refugees and Escapees, which was headed by Senator Langer. Apparently because of the absurdity of applying this requirement to a subcommittee with a minority chairman, the amendment was rejected.[11] With a few other exceptions, subsequent Senate resolutions authorizing special funds for committee staffs have contained the formula of the "Curtis Amendment."

The start of the 87th Congress saw the beginning of a campaign to obtain comparable action by the minority membership of the Committee on House Administration. On February 18, 1961, in his nationally-syndicated column, Roscoe Drummond deplored the lack of minority staffing for House committees, which he blamed on the House Republican leadership. He wrote:

> . . . Serving the 23 committees in the House of Representatives, the Democratic majority has a total staff of 285 professional advisers and experts, while the Republican minority has a total professional staff of 21.

> It doesn't have to be that way. But for years the House Republican leadership has done nothing about it.

> . . . .

> If the Republican members of Congress are ever to be in a position to clarify, expound, and defend their stand on the major issues presented by President Kennedy and to advance constructive alternatives of their own, they must get a steady flow of adequate, reliable, competent research and information from an adequate, reliable, and competent professional staff. This staff must be in the service of the minority, selected by the minority, and working for it.

> The Republicans have nothing approaching such a staff today. They have lost it by default. They can get such a staff only when the Republican members of the House Administration Committee realize what they are throwing away—and do something about it.

In total, the professional staffs of the House committees are 14 to 1 Democratic. Here are some samples:

Agriculture: Majority staff 8; Minority 1.
Appropriations: 21 to 2.
Government Operations: 36 to 3.
Interior and Insular Affairs: 16 to 0.

. . . .

Then he quoted this excerpt from a letter sent by Representative Thomas B. Curtis (R.-Mo.) to Minority Leader Charles Halleck (R.-Ind.) a few weeks earlier:

"I urge that the staffing of committees with adequate and objective personnel by the majority and that the providing of staff personnel for the minority be made issues for which the Republicans will fight . . . Most of the groundwork for this effort will have to be made by our minority members of the House Administration Committee."

After noting that no action had been taken on this recommendation, Mr. Drummond listed the names of the Republican members of the House Administration Committee and exhorted his Republican readers to write them.[12]

Evidently this appeal brought prompt results. Ten days later on the floor of the House, Representative Paul Schenk (R.-Ohio), ranking minority member of the Committee on House Administration, stated rather plaintively:

Mr. Speaker, some questions have been raised about the appointment of minority and majority staff members of the various House committees. May I point out that the Committee on House Administration has no discretionary power in the naming of any member of any staff. Under section 737 of the House rules the responsibility for naming members of the professional and clerical staffs of each committee is vested in the majority vote of the committee concerned. . . . Our committee, Mr. Speaker, does hold hearings on each budget request, and at each hearing the Committee on House Administration insists upon having both majority and minority members of each committee concerned testify as to the need for the requested appropriation, as to its adequacy, and whether or not the committee is in agreement as to the naming of the various professional and clerical staff members. I thought this statement should be made, Mr. Speaker, in view of some considerable correspondence that is being received by Members of the House to make it clear that the responsibility for naming the staff members rests entirely and completely within each legislative committee.[13]

During the ensuing debate over House resolutions authorizing special funds for committee staffs, Representative Clare Hoffman (R.-Mich.), ranking minority member of the House Government Operations Committee, impugned the objectivity of that committee, of its subcommittees, and of their staffs. Then he inserted a lengthy statement in the *Congressional Record* documenting his charges with a series of excerpts from minority reports of that committee. In the course of his comments, he suggested that committee employees should be allocated to the majority and minority in the same 6 to 4 ratio as their representation on the standing committees. He was joined in his complaints about the inadequacy of minority staffing by Representatives H. R. Gross (R.-Iowa) and John Kyl (R.-Iowa), a junior member of the House Administration Committee.[14]

Returning to the attack the next day, Representative Clare Hoffman repeated his charges but added somewhat querulously: ". . . if the leadership will not join in the fight, and when courageous Republicans, like the gentleman from Missouri (Mr. Curtis) and my beloved party colleague from Iowa (Mr. Gross), 'fold up their tents and silently steal away,' it would appear to be a waste of time for me to stick out like a lightening rod and attract unjustifiable criticism."[15] However, on June 1, 1961, he inserted in the *Congressional Record* another column by Roscoe Drummond castigating the failure of the Republican congressional leadership to press for minority staffs for House and Senate committees, and endorsed the sentiments expressed.[16]

Although this drive did not achieve its principal objective during the first session of the 87th Congress, it probably contributed to increased minority staffing on the House committees. At any rate, several committee and subcommittee chairmen agreed to more generous allotments of staff for the minority.[17] And the campaign for an equivalent of the "Curtis Amendment" on the House side showed no signs of abating at the end of 1961.

Several of the arguments utilized in this endeavor were based on a fallacious premise: that everybody not identified as a minority staff member was a Democratic employee. Ironically, many of the committee aides characterized as Democratic were originally appointed by Republican chairmen. For example, three of the eight members of the House Agriculture Committee staff—including the two professionals—whom Roscoe Drummond categorized as Democratic were hired by Representative Clifford Hope (R.-Kans.). And during the Democratic-controlled 81st and 82d Congresses, the two of them in the employ of the committee then were regarded as minority staff members. Similarly, Mr. Drummond listed the whole staff of the House Interior and Insular Affairs Committee as being Democratic. Yet the chief clerk, Nancy Arnold, was originally appointed in the 80th Congress, and she bore the designation "minority clerk" during the 81st and 82d Congresses.

Moreover, formal authorization for the minority to hire employees as a matter of right without concurrence by the majority, as the "Curtis Amendment" provides, goes far beyond previous arrangements informally allotting part of a committee staff to the minority. Under such agreements and even where a professional aide was allocated to the minority by a committee resolution, many of the committees continued to ratify the nominees designated by the minority. For example, the aforementioned rule of the Permanent Subcommittee on Investigations empowering the minority to select a minority counsel contained the stipulation "upon being confirmed." And an accompanying rule required that "all staff members shall be confirmed by a majority of the subcommittee."[18] In discussing the application of these rules, Chairman John McClellan (D.-Ark.) verified that this procedure was actually followed.[19]

Although practices under the "Curtis Amendment" might appear nearly the same as before, there is a significant underlying difference. Previously in theory the minority nominees remained employees of the whole committee. Now where the "Curtis Amendment" applies, they are appointees only of the minority, in theory as well as fact. Since concept of role exerts a strong influence on staff conduct, this consideration should not be lightly dismissed. More importantly, the "Curtis Amendment" removes legal control over part of the staff from the whole committee. Under its mandatory language, even a bipartisan majority of the committee cannot prevent the appointment of an objectionable candidate desired by part of the minority (usually just the ranking member). Similarly, a majority of the committee membership may not remove a minority aide or even encourage him to leave by reducing his salary below the prescribed minimum. This structures a dangerous element of irresponsibility into the committee staff. There have been enough instances where a majority of a committee had to invoke its formal power over hiring and firing to correct or prevent staffing abuses, to warrant retention of this safeguard.

What has been responsible for this formal counterattack on the basic philosophy of staffing in the Legislative Reorganization Act of 1946? A meaningful clue is afforded by the target. From the outset, specially-authorized staffs have been more prone to abuses than the regular staffs of the standing committees. The incidence of purely patronage appointments and embroilment in partisan activities has been much higher among the employees provided from special funds—although not confined to them.

During the 83d through the 86th Congresses, these tendencies flourished. Charges and countercharges of political motivation in the conduct of investigations were exchanged. Special subcommittee aides resigned or were fired because of refusal to promote the predetermined objectives of committee action. Among the most highly-publicized incidents of this sort was the acrimonious departure of Bernard Schwartz from his position as chief counsel of the Special Subcommittee on Legislative Oversight of the House Committee on Interstate and Foreign Commerce.[20] A substantial portion of the specially-authorized committee staffs was being used as a source of supplementary office employees or to pay off political debts. One of the reasons, frankly-avowed in private conversation, for introduction of the "Curtis Amendment" was to ensure a share of this spoils for the minority. More basic was a widespread sense of frustration and resentment among the Republicans at the proliferation of special staffs engaged in politically-inspired enterprises. Where investigations with political overtones were being undertaken on a multiplicity of complicated subjects, they felt minority employees with access to committee files and sessions were necessary to help them keep track of what was happening. Even advocates of nonpartisan committee staffs regarded minority earmarking as justifiable under such circumstances. In short, the intemperately partisan behavior of some committee members and their aides from both political parties operated like a sort of Gresham's law of staffing.

Besides being the most culpable, specially-authorized staffs were the most vulnerable to compensatory action. Upon becoming ranking minority member of the Senate Committee on Rules and Administration—which passes upon all money resolutions for special staffs—at the outset of the 85th Congress, Senator Carl T. Curtis (R.-Nebr.) decided to exercise the prerogatives of his position to help remedy the situation about which his colleagues were complaining. After consulting with the Minority Floor Leader, Minority Whip, and ranking minority members of the Senate committees, he initiated the amendment bearing his name.

During the 83d through the 86th Congresses, experience continued to substantiate the concept of nonpartisan committee staffs. Earmarking part of the committee aides for the minority still encountered the grave obstacle of sharp factional cleavages within either party. In fact, developments accentuated the diversity even within recognized factions. On the House side, a liberal Democratic group contained a left wing contemptuously nicknamed the "pink-clouders" or "rattleheads" by the others. They returned the compliment by referring to their more conservative brethren as "bomber liberals." Although these two subgroups concerted their efforts in institutionalized form over several years, there were genuine ideological differences as well as disputes over tactics between them. On the Senate side the liberal Democratic bloc tended to splinter into "irresponsible" and "responsible" liberals.

The existing provisions of the law allow the standing committees to accommodate demands for minority aides by informal agreement. Events have demonstrated that increasing partisanship among the committee members need not be reflected in a division of the staff between the majority and minority. On the House side where there is no legal requirement for earmarking specially-authorized staffs, some have been hired on a nonpartisan and merit basis. If further formal allocation of committee staffs to the minority can be prevented, the expansion of partisan staffing may be contained—if not reduced. For there are powerful forces conducing to objectivity in the regular staffs of the standing committees. Over the long pull, the desire of the chairman to maximize his support by the committee membership exerts a restraint on partisanship in the operation of the committee. Even when hired under minority auspices, the professional aide to a standing committee who wishes to remain in his job has a strong incentive to serve all members of the committee; and a number of such "minority" employees have become thoroughly assimilated into the committee staff. Also, committee employees recognize a collective interest in the establishment of capable, nonpartisan professional staffs. At the close of the 86th Congress, a group of them publicly attributed congressional opposition to pay raises for them to resentment toward incompetent, political hacks on committee staffs who had acted indiscreetly and displayed partisan bias. And they affirmed their belief that "the key committee staff members should be nonpolitical professionals who had the respect and confidence of Democrats and Republicans alike."[21]

Placing Chairman's "Man" on the Staff

An analogous threat to the integrity of committee staffs has come from the majority side (when either party was in control of Congress). Upon assuming the chairmanship, some Congressmen (principally Senators) have insisted on putting their "man" on the committee staff. This differs from the practice of parcelling out selection of the committee staff among the majority as well as the minority members—which was prevalent during the 80th through the 82d Congresses. Rather, this departure has occurred on homogeneous, nonpartisan, high-quality staffs unified under the control of staff directors, who usually had been instrumental in their recruitment. Moreover, at the time of such an intrusion, they had been operating with their integrity unimpaired for seven to twelve years.

For the most part, in such cases, the chairman's "man" has been used primarily on his office staff work. Generally, he has remained over in the chairman's office. Apart from handling some press releases and correspondence pertaining to committee business, he has been occupied with matters unrelated to the chairman's responsibilities to the committee—especially during years the chairman was running for re-election. And the chairman—as well as all the rest of the members—has continued to call on the regular committee staff for any assistance on committee activities.

Sometimes even the members of the chairman's own party have resented his imposing an obviously less-qualified person on the committee staff in this fashion. However, resisting a chairman's wishes in this regard is almost impossible. Such action is deemed to be within his prerogatives. There is a feeling that he is entitled to a representative on the staff who shares his views, can write like him, and will do political chores a nonpartisan career employee would be reluctant to perform.   Particularly where the chairman occupies an influential position in the power structure of Congress outside the committee, the members are reluctant to oppose him on such an issue.   Allowing the chairman this perquisite is regarded as the price of retaining his good will.

A few congressional aides opined that there is some justification for this practice.   They observed that the chairman does have a legitimate need for additional office staff to handle the increased correspondence, speaking engagements, and other demands of his station.   By taking care of such assignments, the chairman's representative has relieved the other committee employees of this more or less extraneous work.   His presence has not seriously interfered with their customary mode of functioning.   And he may have facilitated their maintaining a reputation for objectivity by shielding them from involvement in the chairman's campaigns for re-election and other duties with strong political overtones.   While containing some element of validity, these arguments appear to consist largely of "virtue of necessity" rationalizations.

Although sometimes unavoidable, this arrangement should not be deliberately perpetuated.   Even where the chairman does not funnel relations with the rest of the committee aides through his representative, the staff director's job is made more difficult.   Part of the staff is removed from his immediate direction.   Occasionally, a chairman has assignd his "man" projects concerning the committee without informing the staff director.   Once in a while, this has been embarrassing when such action has been attributed to the regular committee staff —particularly if there were adverse repercussions.   Utilizing a professional aide in effect to supplement the chairman's office force would seem to violate the legal stipulation that "Professional staff members shall not engage in any other work than committee business and no other duties may be assigned to them."[22]   A more appropriate solution to the chairmen's problem of not enough office help would be to provide an extra clerk hire allowance for them.

These instances have not constituted a trend toward greater personalization of the committee staffs.   Rather, they have represented responses to variable combinations of circumstances, and each has been somewhat unique.   Fortuity has played a role, such as the coincidence of a vacancy on a committee staff with the desire of the incoming chairman to find a place for a particular individual.   While the vulnerability of high-caliber, unified staffs to adulteration by the chairmen is dismaying, there is an encouraging consideration.   Backing by the other members of their committees has confined the extent of the damage done them.   For example, the ambition of one chairman's protege to displace the staff director was frustated by the reaction of the rest of the committee.

This development illuminates the underlying realities of committee staffing.   Much depends on the quality and perspective of the chairman, the internal power structure of the committee, and the attitude of the membership towards the staff. Exhortatory language in the law, tradition, and procedures exert at most a marginal influence. During the process of ratifying staff appointments and through institutional devices like staffing subcommittees, the rank and file members of a committee can register a protest against personnel actions initiated by the chairman. Whether or not they will invoke these procedures to oppose him depends on how fearful they are of incurring his displeasure. Conversely, the primary restraint on the chairman is his wish to maintain the good will of influential members of his committee. A patronage-minded chairman can tamper with any committee staff. How far he can go in disrupting it depends on the composition of his committee and on his willingness to upset the delicate equilibrium of relationships within the committee.

There is cause for optimism as well as despair in this situation. The major committees—particularly in the Senate—comprise powerful members (including chairmen of other committees and the majority and minority leadership of the chamber). A committee staff that enjoys a reputation among them for objectivity, competence, and accessibility has a built-in safeguard against too radical alteration by the chairman. Hence, where first-rate staffs have been established on major committees, chairmen who are spoilsmen or who honestly reject the concept of objectivity probably can do no more than build around them layers of political appointees of variable size and quality. And these can be curtailed or eliminated by succeeding chairmen of a different orientation as long as such arrangements are not sanctified by statutory provision. If the staffing principles in the organic law can just be preserved, there are good grounds for hope that a substantial core of the committee staffs will be maintained in accordance with them.

Confirmation of Worth of Staff Director

The advantages of having staff directors for committees have continued to be demonstrated. Chiefs of staff have proved a powerful force for preserving the integrity of the committees as well as of their staffs. Through sagacious counsel and suggestion of appropriate procedural devices, they have helped the chairmen resist the omnipresent drives of junior members to carve the jurisdictions of their committees among standing subcommittees with separate staffs. For example, during the 85th Congress, at the instigation of the staff director, the chairman of a Senate committee appointed a personnel subcommittee to consider a whole range of questions concerning the staff, such as size, duties, and organization. Through this device he was able to mobilize sentiment within the committee against the efforts of some (including the ranking minority member) to expand and personalize the committee staff. The resulting denial of specially-authorized staffs to the subcommittees made restraining their propensities toward autonomy and self-perpetuation much easier.   Also, by placing a layer of insulation between the chairman and the recruiting process, this arrangement was designed to discourage subsequent chairmen from placing unqualified individuals as their "men" on the committee staff.

Through persuasion and preclusive action, staff directors have frustrated patronage pressures.   Because of their prestige and the cogency of their arguments, staff directors have been able to dissuade committee or subcommittee chairmen from making patronage appointments.   On several occasions, staff directors have prevented further fragmentation of a committee staff whose homogeneity had been breached by a representative of either the chairman or ranking minority member.   When subsequent vacancies occurred, they moved swiftly to recruit replacements before demands could mount for allocation of those positions among other members of the committee.

Size of Regular Staffs

Since 1953, most of the standing committees (other than appropriations) in both chambers have not exceeded their original statutory quota of four professional aides each on their regular staffs.   For example, on February 28, 1961, only one House standing committee (Ways and Means with six) had more than four professional staff members; twelve had four; and six had less than four.[23]   In the Senate between July 1, 1960, and September 30, 1961, on the average, approximately five professional staffs of standing committees contained more than four members; five had their complement of four; and five were consistently understrength.   Moreover, the number of professionals which the five or so Senate committees added to their regular staffs (except Labor and Public Welfare which habitually had six extra) averaged less than two apiece.[24]

Specially-authorized Staffs

As during the original period covered, the principal expansion of committee staffing has occurred in the specially-authorized segments.   These have continued to proliferate.   For example, the 86th Congress expended over $11,500,000 (much of which went for staff salaries) of funds provided by special resolutions for investigations.[25]   This is slightly more than twice the amount spent for that purpose in the 82d Congress.   And there seems to be little prospect of checking this trend.   With the completion of a new Senate Office Building in 1958 and the construction of a third House Office Building well under way in 1961, the restraint imposed by lack of office space is fast disappearing.   Each year when the resolutions authorizing funds for investigations and studies are reported, members of the administration committees as well as others complain about the ever-increasing size of the requests and the apparent impossibility of reducing their volume.

With regard to the quixotic annual endeavor of Senator Allen Ellender (D.-La.) to trim the amounts authorized, Senator Everett Dirksen (R.-Ill.) sympathetically observed in January, 1961:

> But when all is said and done, what are the results, finally? I think perhaps that is what disturbs my distinguished and frugal-minded friend from Louisiana. Year after year he is here assailing these requests for money . . . but never, so far as I know, has he succeeded or chopped a nickel off them.[26]

To which Senator Ellender replied: "We were moderately successful on two or three occasions [in fifteen years]."[27]

Salaries

Since 1953, the maximum salary which a professional staff member may receive has been increased by slightly over fifty per cent. This has been accomplished by a modest raise in the ceiling on basic annual compensation and further modification of the formulas for converting base into gross salaries. Since 1958, any employee—professional or clerical—of a standing committee in the House may receive up to $8,880 basic annual compensation. For the Senate committees, there is an involved series of limitations. Of the regular employees for each standing committee, only the professional staff members, chief clerk, and assistant chief clerk are eligible for the top base salaries. One of them may receive the $8,880 maximum; two, up to $8,460; and the others, up to $8,040.[28] There are additional exceptions for employees paid from the contingent fund of the Senate. Table 5 shows the gross salaries received for these and other selected basic annual rates of pay in 1961.

TABLE 5

CORRESPONDING BASIC AND GROSS SALARIES IN 1961*

Base Pay	Gross Pay
$8,880.00	$17,649.50
8,460.00	16,911.37
8,040.00	16,173.24
7,000.00	14,345.47
6,540.00	13,537.03
5,100.00	10,988.27
3,720.00	8,239.42
3,000.00	6,781.24

*From information supplied by the Disbursing Office, U.S., House of Representatives.

Contracting Studies to Research Institutions

During the 84th Congress, a significant innovation was made in committee staff work: contracting out the preparation of studies to private research firms, universities, and other institutions. These studies were of an entirely different nature than the management surveys or audits of agencies which committees had occasionally hired management engineering or accounting firms to do. They were concerned with substantive policy issues and treated profound and forward-looking subjects, such as "Ideology and Foreign Affairs" or the "Potential Impact of Prospective Scientific Developments on U.S. Foreign Policy." The Senate Foreign Relations Committee pioneered this practice in the exhaustive review of the U.S. foreign aid programs undertaken in 1956. As the Special Committee to Study the Foreign Aid Program (which was merely the SFRC supplemented by the chairmen and ranking minority members of the Senate Committees on Appropriations and Armed Services), it let contracts for the performance of twelve research projects by private organizations, such as Brookings Institution, Center for International Affairs of Harvard University, and the National Planning Association. The twelve resulting reports submitted by the contractors had an estimated total cost of $143,300. In connection with the broad examination of U.S. foreign policy initiated during the 85th Congress, the SFRC arranged for the production of thirteen such studies on a contractual basis. Concurrently, for the closely-related inquiry into United States-Latin American relations, the Subcommittee on American Republics Affairs had private contractors do seven similar reports on selected aspects of Latin American development.[29]

In each case a similar procedure was followed. Approval was obtained of a Senate resolution authorizing the committee to enter into contracts to "use the experience, knowledge, and advice of private organizations, schools, institutions, and individuals" and providing the necessary funds.[30] After determining the problem areas to be covered, the committee publicly invited private research organizations and universities to submit proposals for studies on them. Then in consultation with the contractors selected, the committee staff developed outlines for each of the reports. Upon receipt of the studies, the committee published them separately as committee prints with an appropriate disclaimer that they constituted only background material which the committee was free to accept or reject, in whole or in part. Later, to meet the continuing public demand and to make them available in a more compact form, the committee had compilations of the studies for each of these inquiries printed as Senate documents. As soon as the legislative schedule permitted—which sometimes meant a delay of over a year—the committee held public hearings on them. Lead-off witnesses on each report were top officials of the organization that had prepared it. They were followed by executive branch officials and other interested parties.

What was responsible for the SFRC's resorting to private research firms in this fashion—particularly in view of the paucity of such relations previously? As might be expected, multiple considerations interacted. Normally, the committee staff would have prepared such studies. But increasing absorption with other duties left the committee aides less time for that purpose than before. These private research facilities afforded a fresh source of ideas which the departmental staffs were not adequately tapping. Much of the academic research currently being produced was not adapted to the needs of the committee. By making contracts specifying what was to be covered and the manner of presentation, the committee could enhance the suitability of this output.

There are several advantages in hiring organizations rather than individual specialists to do studies of this sort. The first is speed. Through the combined efforts of numerous experts within an institution, the work can be completed more rapidly. The eleven reports for the Special Committee to Study Foreign Aid, which averaged around eighty pages in length, were prepared in approximately two and one half months.[31] Secondly, many of these organizations afford an institutional safeguard against bias. Their internal procedures provide for the review of manuscripts by a board of critics with different perspectives than the authors. Thirdly, the product of an eminent research institute or university carries somewhat more weight than the handiwork of an individual expert. Finally, there are marginal economies involving routine personnel actions.

This new development has been very well received by the committee members, executive branch personnel, the academic community, and the rest of the interested public. The printed hearings on these studies are replete with testimonials from the committee members.[32] Even while taking exception to some portions of them, the departmental witnesses have lauded their quality. And at a hearing in 1959, C. Douglas Dillon, then Undersecretary of State for Economic Affairs, testified that the State Department had found a study done by the National Planning Association for the SFRC so useful that the department had the NPA bring it up to date a year later.[33] Contributing authors have expressed appreciation "for the concern that the committee has shown to obtain the views of teachers and scholars in the Nation's universities on matters of such great concern to all Americans."[34]

Compendia of Papers

The Joint Economic Committee has continued to develop refinements in the hearings process.[35] One, which was introduced in the 84th Congress, is the advance publication of papers by panelists. Originated by the Subcommittee on Tax Policy in 1955, this technique has become almost standard operating procedure for special studies done by subcommittees of the Joint Economic Committee and is used on occasion by the full committee. Though differing in details, this approach usually includes the following steps. After drawing up an outline for the study (sometimes in consultation with prospective panelists), the committee invites outstanding authorities inside and outside the government to prepare papers on each of the items covered. These are then published as committee prints—usually as compendia with the papers arranged by panel topics in the order in which they are scheduled for discussion—and distributed to the committee members, panelists, and general public several weeks before the hearings. The contributors of the papers on each major topic constitute the panel on that subject. At the start of each session, the panel members successively give five-minute summaries of their papers without interruption. Then the proceedings are thrown open to questions and comments by committeemen and panelists in regular round-table fashion.

The availability of these papers in convenient printed form enables the committee members and discussants to become conversant with the views, analyses, and findings of the panel members ahead of the hearings. As a consequence, they can exploit the unique advantages of the round-table approach more fully and rapidly. They can proceed directly to points in dispute or on which further elaboration or justification are desired. This markedly facilitates demarcation of consensuses and more complete development of the issues.

Several members of the Joint Economic Committee have become enthusiastic proponents of this device. For example, in the round tables on a policy for commercial agriculture, Representative Thomas B. Curtis (R.-Mo.) said:

> First, I want to join in the remarks of the chairman, and other members of the committee, in complimenting the gentlemen here as well as those others who have contributed papers to this compendium.
>
> Unless I miss my guess, we are going to have another best seller as we did in the studies on the economic effects of our tax structure. If that is achieved, I think one of the committee's main purposes has been achieved.[36]

And two years later in the hearings on comparisons of the United States and Soviet economies, he endorsed this technique even more strongly as follows:

> I think the technique of the panel's commenting on each other's papers is excellent and I am glad we have had the criticism and rebuttal and I hope these hearings will continue this debate and continue it in a public fashion because I think therein lies the main value of what we are trying to do here.[37]

They carefully read and dog-ear pages of the study papers for ready reference during the panel discussions. And two members, Senator John Sparkman (D.-Ala.) and Representative Wilbur Mills (D.-Ark.), have adopted the compendium-round table procedure for studies done under their supervision by the

Subcommittee on Housing of the Senate Banking and Currency Committee and by the House Ways and Means Committee respectively.

Round-Table Discussions

As indicated above, the Joint Economic Committee has remained addicted to the panel-discussion type of hearing. Because flexibility and informality have been intrinsic to this approach from the outset, generalization about round-table discussions is particularly hazardous. However, during the roughly twelve years since their inception, the procedure followed by the Joint Economic Committee has undergone some discernible changes. The committee members have largely abandoned their passive role as a sort of "studio audience" for the panelists. As their familiarity with this technique has grown, committee members—particularly when fortified in advance with a compendium of papers—have participated as fully as the panelists in the discussions. Also, the committee staff has been invited to take part in the proceedings on the same basis as the committee and panel members.

The format for the annual hearings on the President's Economic Report that appeared to be crystallizing toward the end of the 82d Congress[38] did not remain fixed for long. Within a short time, round-table discussions with spokesmen for major economic interest groups were reinstated. And governmental as well as nongovernmental technicians were included as panel members.

The Joint Economic Committee has continued imaginative experimentation with different kinds of round tables, questionnaires, commentaries on hearings and previous studies, and variable combinations of regular hearings and panel discussions. An excellent example is afforded by the study of the relationship of prices to economic stability and growth conducted in the 85th Congress. This inquiry involved two sets of compendia and hearings with the second based on the first and overlapping membership among the participants. Initially, the committee published a compendium of papers by forty-seven leading economists from universities, governmental agencies, and private research organizations on March 31, 1958. Then the committee held round-table discussions of these papers with their authors on May 12-22, 1958. The final session was devoted to a general summary of the study by an "evaluation panel." Besides the compendium of papers, these discussants had available transcripts of the preceding sessions. Next, the committee invited economists from labor and industry to submit comments on the analyses and issues raised in the first two stages of this study. The committee published these commentaries in a volume released on November 10, 1958. They also were arranged by panel topics in the order in which they were scheduled for consideration in subsequent hearings. Finally, on December 15-18, 1958, the committee conducted a series of discussions with panels consisting of the labor and industrial economists together with some of the contributors to the first compendium and set of hearings. Each panel included two economists apiece from labor, industry, and the original group.[39]

Emergence of the GAO

Since the 83d Congress, a prominent trend has been the progressively greater reliance by committees on the General Accounting Office as a supplementary source of staff assistance. For example, the number of GAO employees borrowed annually by the committees has more than quadrupled. And there has been a pronounced growth in the other services provided by the GAO to the committees.

This development reflects a transformation in the philosophy and personnel of the GAO wrought by Comptroller Generals Lindsay Warren and Joseph Campbell. Mr. Warren revolutionized the accounting and auditing methods of the Office. By adopting comprehensive and site audits, he made possible doing a better job with fewer but higher caliber personnel. While drastically reducing the number of employees (from 14,904 in April, 1946, to 6,100 in September, 1953), he strove to improve their quality. Through his auditing and investigative staffs, he examined the economy and efficiency as well as the legality of agency transactions. He initiated broad studies of programs and policies, such as foreign aid and procurement practices of the armed forces. As a former Congressman, he was constantly concerned with furnishing more and better service to the committees and members of Congress.[40] Joseph Campbell, who succeeded him as Comptroller General on December 14, 1954, has expanded and intensified these efforts.

Among their accomplishments are the following. The GAO opened a European branch with headquarters in Paris in 1951 and a Far East branch with headquarters in Tokyo five years later. Between 1952 and 1956, the GAO made substantial progress in developing personnel policies designed to attract and maintain a high quality professional staff. In 1956, the GAO underwent a basic reorganization to improve coordination among its accounting, auditing, and investigative operations and to place greater emphasis on defense activities. Also, an Office of Legislative Liaison was created then and charged with the two-fold responsibility of "seeing that the committees of Congress are kept advised of information generated through our operations which is germane to the legislative interests of the committees" and of "ascertaining the areas of interest of committees in order that such interests may be reflected in the program of the General Accounting Office."[41]

Some indication of the volume and variety of services supplied the committees by the GAO is afforded by these statistics for fiscal 1961. During that year, the GAO submitted to Congress or its committees 194 reports on audits or investigations. In many cases, copies of an additional 703 reports addressed to officials of federal agencies were furnished to committees or interested members of Congress. The GAO made 610 reports commenting on proposed legislation to fourteen Senate and fourteen House committees and seventy-five reports to the Bureau of the Budget on draft, pending, or enrolled bills. Representatives of the GAO testified on twenty-eight occasions before twenty-one committees and subcommittees. And 197 members of the GAO professional staff were detailed to one joint, seven Senate, and eight House committees to work on special studies and investigations for periods of a few days to several months.[42]

This expanded role of the GAO has evoked a mixed reaction from members of Congress and their staffs. Some have accused the GAO of being over-eager to get into policy, of being biased against foreign aid, of lacking sufficient technical background to evaluate engineering data, and so on. For the most part, however, congressional response has been favorable. Committee hearings, committee reports, the *Congressional Record,* newspapers, and periodicals have been filled with praise for help received from the GAO by members and committees of Congress.[43]

Senatorial Office Staffs

Restraint on floor access. Senatorial annoyance at the excessive number of office staff members on the Senate floor, which was becoming increasingly manifest toward the end of the 82d Congress,[44] eventuated in a measure of formal control in the 84th Congress. On January 25, 1956, the Committee on Rules and Administration adopted regulations governing the admission of senatorial assistants to the Senate floor. They require a senatorial aide to register and obtain an official pass every time he goes on the floor. Each Senator may have only two members of his office staff on the Senate floor at once. The regulations contain these significant comments:

> It is not the desire or intention of the Committee on Rules and Administration to limit assistance by staff personnel to Senators on the Floor. On the contrary, the Committee believes that these regulations will insure adequate opportunity for such assistance and, at the same time, prevent the distractions to orderly proceedings attendant upon the presence of superfluous employees in the Senate Chamber. . . . The Senators generally have expressed themselves in full accord with efforts to diminish disorder and confusion caused by the presence of unnecessary personnel on the Senate Floor. It is hoped that all Senators, especially when serving as the Presiding Officer of the Senate, will cooperate with the Sergeant at Arms and the Committee on Rules and Administration in this endeavor to control the problem.[45]

In the 87th Congress, use of the Republican Cloakroom by senatorial staffs was curtailed.   On August 11, 1961, the Secretary for the Minority circularized all Republican administrative assistants with a letter enunciating this policy.[46] These restrictive tendencies have not extended to the Senate committees.   There has not been an appreciable increase in the number of committees that exclude senatorial aides from their executive sessions.

The system of requiring a staff member to sign for a pass each time inhibited one administrative assistant from going on the floor for more than five years. He said that his presence there was "not so necessary that he was willing to register like a lobbyist." Even he finally relented in order to help his Senator during the debate on a very complicated bill.   And in the main, this registration require-ment has not seriously hampered the ability of staff members to assist their Senators on legislative assignments.   The principal effect has been to eliminate from the Senate floor the lower-ranking office employees who have no business there.

Titles and salaries.   The bewildering nomenclature unofficially adopted by senatorial aides during the original period covered has since been legalized. Merely by giving written notification to the disbursing office, a Senator may establish whatever titles he wishes for positions on his staff.   The highest-paid employee no longer has to bear the designation "administrative assistant"— although most still do.   The law now simply provides that in each Senator's office one employee may receive a basic annual compensation up to $8,880; one, to $8,460; one, to $8,040; one, to $6,540; and the rest, to $5,100.[47]   The gross salaries received for these basic rates of pay in 1961 are given in Table 5 on page 221.

Since the ceiling on annual base salaries for House office staff members re-mains at $7,000, the gap in maximum base pay between assistants to Senators and assistants to Representatives has widened to $1,880.   This amounts to a difference of $3,304.03 yearly in gross salary. Efforts to reduce this disparity continue to be made.   In 1961, several bills were introduced that would authorize each Representative to hire an administrative assistant at maximum basic salaries ranging from $7,500 to $8,500. However, they were sidetracked in favor of House Resolution 219, which merely increased the basic clerk hire allowance by $3,000 and authorized an additional clerk for each member of the House.[48] As a consequence, all Representatives now have an office staff allow-ance of $20,500 a year for basic salaries and may hire up to nine clerks apiece— except members with constituencies of over 500,000 population. The latter have a basic annual allowance of $23,000 and may employ as many as ten clerks each.[49]

Office of the Legislative Counsel

No significant changes have occurred in the operation of the Office of the Legislative Counsel. Confirming predictions, each office has expanded but slightly. The Senate branch has added one attorney; the House branch, one attorney and two clerical assistants. With the departure of the incumbent, the hybrid post of "assistant counsel and administrative assistant" was eliminated from the House office. The Legislative Branch Appropriation Act, 1958, created the position of "senior counsel" with a prescribed compensation for not more than three attorneys in the Senate office.[50] This was done solely to circumvent a salary limitation for assistant counsel that applied only on the Senate side.

In 1958, the lump sum appropriation for the Office was discontinued, and each branch began to receive a separate appropriation. Noting that the two offices were distinct in all respects, the House Subcommittee on Legislative Appropriations justified this action as being "in line with the custom of many years of omitting other appropriation requirements pertaining solely to the Senate."[51] With rather generous adjustments for salary increases steadily forthcoming, the combined appropriations for the two offices almost doubled between 1952 and 1961—being $426,950 for fiscal 1961.[52] Another obvious improvement in working conditions for the Senate branch was the provision of spacious quarters in the New Senate Office Building.

Both offices have continued to display remarkable continuity of tenure in their personnel. The two legislative counsel, fifteen of the other eighteen attorneys, and six of the eight clerical assistants in the Office in 1952 were still there nine years later.[53] And the workload has kept growing, as the statistics in Tables 6 and 7 reveal.

TABLE 6

NUMBER OF ASSIGNMENTS PERFORMED BY THE HOUSE OFFICE, 1953-1960*

Congress	For Committees	For Members	Total
83d	302	3,249	3,551
84th	452	4,265	4,717
85th	614	4,637	5,251
86th	755	4,284	5,039

* U.S., Congress, House, Committee on Appropriations, *Hearings before the Subcommittee on the Legislative Branch Appropriations for 1962*, 87th Cong., 1st Sess., May 3, 1961, p. 249.

TABLE 7

NUMBER OF ASSIGNMENTS PERFORMED BY
THE SENATE OFFICE, 1953-1960*

Congress	For Committees	For Members	Total
83d	471	3,173	3,644
84th	643	3,320	3,963
85th	612	3,871	4,483
86th	623	3,064	3,687

* From statistics supplied by the Senate office.

NOTES

Chapter I

[1] Lindsay Rogers, "The Staffing of Congress," *Political Science Quarterly*, LVI (March, 1941), 18-19.

[2] U.S., Library of Congress, *Annual Report of the Librarian of Congress for the Fiscal Year 1915* (Washington: U.S. Government Printing Office, 1915), pp. 8-9.

[3] Public Law 254, 65th Cong., 1st Sess., Feb. 24, 1919, 40 *Stat.* 1141, 2 *U.S.C.* 274.

[4] U.S., Congress, The Revenue Act of 1926, Public Law 20, 69th Cong., 1st Sess., sec. 1203, 44 *Stat.* 127, 26 *U.S.C.* 5003.

[5] Arthur W. Macmahon, "Congressional Oversight of Administration: The Power of the Purse," *Political Science Quarterly*, LVIII (June, 1943), 181-82.

This generalization is made with respect to the entire staffs of the committees concerned and hence is not qualified by the fact that several individual members of other committee staffs had established remarkable records for continuity of tenure. For instance, Joseph H. McGann, Sr., first went to work for the House River and Harbors Committee in February, 1902. He became clerk of that committee in 1920 and continued as clerk of its successor, the House Public Works Committee, through the 82d Congress. During his tenure of office, he has outlasted nine committee chairmen and more than 250 members who have served on those committees (*The Evening Star* [Washington] Feb. 1, 1952). Similarly, Elton J. Layton became a clerk of the House Interstate and Foreign Commerce Committee on April 21, 1921 and served in that capacity through the 82d Congress. Both these individuals were still in the employ of their respective committees when the data in this note was checked with them on December 7, 1954.

Also, to avoid creating a false impression by this generalization, it should be noted that a number of such committee clerks in that period were very capable persons who organized hearings, drafted committee reports, and competently performed many of the other functions which are now considered to be professional staff work.

[6] M. Nelson McGeary, *The Developments of Congressional Investigative Power* (New York: Columbia University Press, 1940), pp. 60-63. As late as 1929, however, one author listed the failure of congressional investigating committees to include technical experts among their staffs as one of their major shortcomings (Marshall E. Dimock, *Congressional Investigating Committees* [Baltimore: Johns Hopkins Press, 1929], pp. 166-67).

[7] McGeary, *The Developments of Congressional Investigative Power*, pp. 63-66; Rogers, *Political Science Quarterly*, LVI (March, 1941), 13.

[8] Rogers, *Political Science Quarterly*, LVI (March, 1941), 3-4.

[9] Based on a table in *ibid.*, p. 7.

[10] *Ibid.*, pp. 6, 9.

[11] As quoted in *ibid.*, p. 8.

[12] Frederic P. Lee, "The Office of the Legislative Counsel," *Columbia Law Review*, XXIX (April, 1929), 397-99.

[13] Kenneth Kofmehl, "The Advanced Research Section of the Legislative Reference Service; an Aspect of Congressional Staffing" (unpublished Master's essay, Dept. of Public Law and Government, Columbia University, 1949), pp. 14, 16; U.S., Congress, Joint Committee on the Organization of Congress, *Report*, Senate Report No. 1011, 79th Cong., 2d Sess., March 4, 1946, pp. 14-15.

[14] Public Law 601, 79th Cong., 2d Sess., Aug. 2, 1946, 60 *Stat.* 812.

[15] U.S., Congress, Joint Committee on the Organization of Congress, *Hearings,* 79th Cong., 1st Sess., March 13 to June 29, 1945.

The chairman and vice-chairman of the Joint Committee on the Organization of Congress were Senator Robert LaFollette, Jr. (Pro.-Wis.) and then representative Mike Monroney (D.-Okla.). Hence, the legislation embodying its recommendations, the Legislative Reorganization Act of 1946, is often referred to as the "LaFollette-Monroney Act."

[16] For typical expressions of this viewpoint, see U.S., *Congressional Record,* 82d Cong., 2d Sess., April 7, 1952, XCVIII, Part 3, pp. 3581-3610.

[17] U.S., *Congressional Record,* 82d Cong., 2d Sess., July 3, 1952, XCVIII, Part 7, pp. 9223-26, 9228, 9682-83.

[18] "Titles of Research Staff in Legislative Reference Service in Grades GS-9 and Above" (Library of Congress, 1951), pp. 1-3. (Mimeographed.)

[19] For the names of the persons interviewed from the three main components of the congressional staff covered, see pp. 269-273.

[20] (New York: Harcourt, Brace and Co., 1953).

[21] These concepts about interest groups and their role in the political process are derived from Professor David B. Truman's *The Governmental Process: Political Interests and Public Opinion* (New York: A. A. Knopf, 1951). To a large extent that book is the source of the over-all interpretation of the political process on which this study is based. The terminology relating to interest groups has been borrowed intact from that work with one exception. The phrase "concept of role" has been substituted for "influence of office" to avoid confusion with the frequent use of the word "office" in connection with office staffs.

[22] On that score, if it were possible to secure access to the requisite information without making commitments which would prevent specific disclosures based upon that, a highly illuminating study could be made of the activities of interest groups within the congressional staff—especially in the period just prior to the enactment of the Legislative Reorganization Act of 1946. For to a certain degree, the form in which that measure was finally passed reflected the outcome of contests between interest groups in the extant congressional staff. Some of those acted aggressively and exploited the congressional reorganization movement to expand themselves and their influence, whereas others engaged in a

vigorous counteroffensive against certain proposed provisions of the Legislative Reorganization Act which they felt would be inimical to their interests. Likewise, since 1946 certain components of the congressional staff have waged a continuing campaign for an ever-increasing share of the total appropriations for staffing. An account of that—especially of their efforts to work through such instrumentalities of Congress as the Subcommittee on Accounts of the House Administration Committee—would make a fascinating story. On many occasions they have displayed a skill in political manipulation and have utilized specious arguments with an effectiveness which the CIO, NAM, Anti-Saloon League, and other favorite whipping boys of the literature on "pressure politics" might well regard with envy. However, that tale must be told somewhere else; for it could not be detailed here without digressing from the main focus of the study and without compromising promises made to safeguard confidential data.

[23] For a discussion of this point with regard to congressional oversight of administration, see Macmahon, *Political Science Quarterly*, LVIII (June, 1943), 187.

[24] "Legislative Control," *Elements of Public Administration*, ed. F. M. Marx (New York: Prentice-Hall, Inc., 1946), p. 360.

[25] For a detailed portrayal of that function, see Lawrence H. Chamberlain, *The President, Congress, and Legislation* (New York: Columbia University Press, 1946).

Chapter II

[1] Prominent among the earlier works on congressional committees were: Lauros G. McConachie, *Congressional Committees* (New York: Thomas Y. Crowell Co., 1898); Eleanor E. Dennison, *The Senate Foreign Relations Committee* (Stanford University, Calif.: Stanford University Press, 1942); Albert C. F. Westphal, *The House Committee on Foreign Affairs* (New York: Columbia University Press, 1942); and August R. Ogden, *The Dies Committee* (2d ed., Washington: The Catholic University Press, 1945).

[2] Such a study is in process. Dr. George Goodwin, who generously made available some chapters of the manuscript, is at present preparing a comprehensive work on congressional committees.

Even a selected list of recent publications touching on some aspect of congressional committee operations would be excessively long for a single footnote. Besides the materials subsequently cited in this chapter, however, there is one especially noteworthy article. For very suggestive hypotheses about congressional committees, see Ralph K. Huitt, "The Congressional Committee: A Case Study," *American Political Science Review*, XLVIII (June, 1954), 340-65.

[3] Briefly, the "Johnson Rule" is that no Democratic Senator, regardless of seniority, is to receive a second top committee post until every Democratic Senator has been given at least one such assignment (George Goodwin, "The Seniority System in Congress," *American Political Science Review*, LIII [June, 1959], 416, 432).

On Jan. 12, 1965, the Republicans in the Senate adopted an analogous but more limited rule nicknamed the "Javits Rule" (*Congressional Quarterly Weekly Report*, No. 3, Jan. 15, 1965, p. 86).

4 These statistics were derived from the standing committee rosters in U.S., *Congressional Directory*, 87th Cong., 1st Sess., 1961.

5 Compiled from footnotes in U.S., Congress, *Senate Manual*, Senate Document No. 2, 87th Cong., 1st Sess., 1961, pp. 25-37, and from copies of the U.S., *Congressional Directory*, for the 83d Cong., 1st Sess., 1953, and for the 86th Cong., 1st Sess., 1959.

6 As evidenced by the fact that the Legislative Reorganization Act of 1946 permitted members in both houses to serve on them in addition to their normal quota of committee assignments. Public Law 601, 79th Cong., 2d Sess., Aug. 2, 1946, 60 *Stat.* 820, 823.

7 Goodwin, *American Political Science Review*, LIII (June, 1959), 432-34, and Donald R. Matthews, *U.S. Senators and Their World* (Chapel Hill: University of North Carolina Press, 1960), pp. 148-50.

8 Nicholas A. Masters, "House Committee Assignments," *American Political Science Review*, LV (June, 1961), 346-48.

9 *Ibid.*, p. 355.

10 *Ibid.*, p. 353; Matthews, *U.S. Senators and Their World*, pp. 152-53.

11 Joseph Young, "Murray Would Avoid Freshman Committee," *The Evening Star* (Washington), Jan. 19, 1961, p. A-2.

12 Matthews, *U.S. Senators and Their World*, p. 151.

13 Based on data compiled from standing committee rosters in copies of U.S., *Congressional Directory*, for the 82d Cong., 2d Sess., 1952, and for the 87th Cong., 1st Sess., 1961.

14 "Leaders Jolt Senate Liberals," *The Washington Post*, Jan. 11, 1961, p. A-4.

15 U.S., Congress, Senate, Special Committee on the Organization of Congress, *Legislative Reorganization Act of 1946*, Senate Report No. 1400 (to accompany S. 2177), 79th Cong., 2d Sess., May 31, 1946, p. 3.

16 Public Law 601, 79th Cong., 2d Sess., Aug. 2, 1946, 60 *Stat.* 814-30.

17 *History of the House of Representatives* (New York: Thomas Y. Crowell Co., 1961), p. 58.

18 U.S., *Congressional Record* (daily ed.), 87th Cong., 1st Sess., July 18, 1961, CVII, p. 11907. In reporting these statistics, Senator John McClellan (D.-Ark.) drew a distinction between an *ad hoc* and a special subcommittee. He applied the term *ad hoc* to the more temporary special subcommittees that considered but a single bill, nomination, or subject of inquiry.

19 Charles B. Brownson (ed.), *Congressional Staff Directory, 1961* (Washington: The Congressional Staff Directory, 1961), p. 120; *ibid., 1959*, p. 72; U.S., *Congressional Directory*, 86th Cong., 1st Sess., 1959.

20 U.S., Congress, House, *House Rules and Manual, 87th Congress*, House Document No. 459, 86th Cong., 2d Sess., p. 327.

21 Brownson, *Congressional Staff Directory, 1961*, p. 230.

22 For excellent examples, see Stephen K. Bailey, *Congress Makes a Law: The Story Behind the Employment Act of 1946* (New York: Columbia University Press, 1950); Stephen K. Bailey and Howard D. Samuel, *Congress at Work* (New York: Henry Holt, 1952); and Fred W. Riggs, *Pressures on Congress: A Study of the Repeal of Chinese Exclusion* (New York: King's Crown Press, 1950).

[23] *U.S. Senators and Their World,* pp. 168-69.

[24] John Cramer, "CSC Gets Five New Democrats," *Washington Daily News,* Feb. 3, 1961, p. 2; *Washington Daily News,* Feb. 7, 1961, p. 14.

[25] *The House of Representatives and Foreign Affairs* (Pittsburgh: University of Pittsburgh Press, 1958), pp. 27-29.

[26] *Ibid.,* p. 96.

[27] Matthews, *U.S. Senators and Their World,* p. 162, n. 16.

[28] For a discussion of the influence exerted by state party delegations, see David B. Truman, *The Congressional Party: A Case Study* (New York: John Wiley & Sons, 1959), ch. 7.

Chapter III

[1] U.S., Congress, Public Law 601, 79th Cong., 2d Sess., Aug. 2, 1946, sec. 202, 60 *Stat.* 834, 2 *U.S.C.* 72a.

[2] U.S., Congress, Public Law 4, 80th Cong., 1st Sess., Feb. 19, 1947, 61 *Stat.* 5, 2 *U.S.C.* 72a-1.

[3] Taken from the listings of committee employees in the copies of the U.S., *Congressional Directory* and in Vols. XCV-XCIX of the U.S., *Congressional Record* for the 81st Cong., 1st Sess.-83d Cong., 1st Sess., 1949-1953.

[4] *Ibid.*

[5] Interview with John Graham on July 25, 1952.

[6] See pp. 50-51.

[7] For a summary statement of Frederick W. Taylor's idea of having functional foremen, see Henry Reining, "The Art of Supervision," *Elements of Public Administration,* ed. F. M. Marx, pp. 421-22.

[8] For specific examples of such intrastaff collaboration, see pp. 106-107.

[9] For a listing of those committees and the members of their staffs interviewed, see pp. 269-70.

[10] During the 82d Congress, the Foreign Relations Committee was authorized by special resolution to hire two extra clerical employees to assist the chairman and ranking minority member with their correspondence.

[11] U.S., Congress, Senate, Committee on Expenditures in the Executive Departments, *Hearings on the Organization and Operation of Congress,* 82d Cong., 1st Sess., June 6, 1951, p. 70.

[12] This was not an honorific title for the committee clerk, because there also was a full-time chief clerk on this staff.

[13] Interview with Mrs. Curtis on Feb. 13, 1952.

[14] U.S., Congress, Senate, Committee on Expenditures in the Executive Departments, *Evaluation of Effect of Legislative Reorganization Act of 1946,* Senate Report No. 1175, 80th Cong., 2d Sess., April 28, 1948, p. 3.

[15] For a description of various kinds of intrastaff collaboration, see pp. 104-107.

[16] Of course, in making any such generalizations about the division of a staff director's time between his duties as staff director and his work as a professional aide, a problem of classification is involved. For example, when a staff director attended a hearing or committee meeting—especially one for

which he had done some of the staff work—would he be participating as staff director or as a professional aide? Similarly, when he consulted with individual members of Congress, was it in his capacity as staff director who must be informed on all aspects of the committee's work or was it as a professional staff member within whose province the particular topic of discussion happened to fall? Hence, any estimates on the division of a staff director's time between these two categories of duties are, of necessity, quite rough.

17 Senate Expenditures Committee, *Hearings on the Organization and Operation of Congress,* 82d Cong., 1st Sess., June 6, 1951, p. 69.

18 Apparently this tendency toward imperialism on the part of administrative officers is universal or at least is not confined to the experience of congressional committees. Dr. Edwin G. Nourse made the following observation about the existence of that phenomenon in the executive branch:

"The Employment Act did not specify that there should be a Secretary of the Council. My observation and the advice of friends wise in the ways of bureaucracy led me to feel that such a designation generally proves to be a means of facilitating the erection of a self-perpetuating and expanding center of authority which often comes to overshadow or even 'contain' the chairman's administrative leadership. This is true also of such titles (and job specifications) as executive director" (*Economics in the Public Service,* pp. 120-21). Copyright 1953 by and used with the permission of Dr. Edwin G. Nourse.

Chapter IV

1 For examples of such references to the committees on appropriations, armed services, interstate and foreign commerce, foreign relations, government operations, small business, the judiciary and to the Senate Special Committee on Overseas Information among others selected at random from one six-month period, see U.S., *Congressional Record,* 83d Cong., 1st Sess., Feb. 18, 1953, XCIX, Part 1, p. 1205; *ibid.,* March 18, 1953, XCIX, Part 2, p. 2061; *ibid.,* May 19, 1953, XCIX, Part 4, pp. 5140-41; *ibid.,* June 3, 1953, XCIX, Part 5, p. 6024; *ibid.,* June 15, 1953, XCIX, Part 5, p. 6465; *ibid.,* June 18, 1953, XCIX, Part 5, p. 6840; *ibid.,* July 1, 1953, XCIX, Part 6, p. 7821; *ibid.,* July 8, 1953, XCIX, Part 6, p. 8227; *ibid.,* July 11, 1953, XCIX, Part 6, p. 8555; *ibid.,* July 15, 1953, XCIX, Part 7, p. 8862; *ibid.,* July 30, 1953, XCIX, Part 8, p. 10585; and *ibid.,* Aug. 1, 1953, XCIX, Part 8, p. 10830.

2 One such study covering the 81st Congress is set forth in Ernest S. Griffith, *Congress: Its Contemporary Role* (New York: New York University Press, 1951), pp. 151-55.

3 For a systematic exposition and defense of the predominantly nonpartisan nature of our governmental process, see Arthur N. Holcombe, *Our More Perfect Union: From Eighteenth-Century Principles to Twentieth-Century Practice* (Cambridge: Harvard University Press, 1950). Also, the underlying reasons for the nonpartisan approach characteristic of most organized interest groups are discussed in Truman, *The Governmental Process,* pp. 296, 302, 304.

4 U.S., *Congressional Record,* 82d Cong., 2d Sess., April 8, 1952, XCVIII, Part 3, p. 3685.

5 *Ibid.,* p. 3693.

6 U.S., Congress, Senate, Special Committee on the Organization of Congress,

Legislative Reorganization Act of 1946, Senate Report No. 1400 (to accompany S. 2177), 79th Cong., 2d Sess., May 31, 1946.

[7] U.S., Congress, Legislative Reorganization Act of 1946, Public Law 601, 79th Cong., 2d Sess., Aug. 2, 1946, 60 *Stat.* 834, 2 *U.S.C.* 72a.

[8] In addition, clerical and professional aides were provided for the minority on many of the specially-authorized subcommittee staffs.

[9] U.S., Congress, Senate Committee on Appropriations, *Hearings before a Subcommittee on the Legislative Branch Appropriation Bill for 1952,* 82d Cong., 1st Sess., July 12, 1951, p. 79.

[10] U.S., *Congressional Record,* 81st Cong., 1st Sess., Jan. 31, 1949, XCV, Part 1, pp. 740, 743-44.

[11] *Ibid.,* July 11, 1949, XCV, Part 7, pp. 9182-83.

[12] *Ibid.,* 81st Cong., 2d Sess., Jan. 11, 1950, XCVI, Part 1, p. 290.

[13] On the staff of the full committee and on its specially-authorized subcommittee staffs between which employees were transferred back and forth in bewildering fashion.

[14] Before Senator Morse had resigned from the Republican Party and when he was still considered a bona fide, albeit unusually liberal, Republican.

[15] For a thorough description of the attitude of Senators Morse and Ives toward Mr. Shroyer's views on labor legislation and their absolute refusal to use his services during the formative stages of the Taft-Hartley Act in the 80th Congress, see Seymour Mann, "Congressional Behavior and National Labor Policy: Structural Determinants of the Taft-Hartley Act" (unpublished Ph.D. dissertation, Dept. of Political Science, University of Chicago, 1951).

[16] U.S., Congress, Senate, Committee on Agriculture and Forestry, *Report of the Subcommittee on Foot-and-Mouth Disease,* committee print, 81st Cong., 2d Sess., March 24, 1950, p. 1.

[17] Nourse, *Economics in the Public Service,* p. 254, n. 2.

[18] *Ibid.,* p. 185.

[19] *Ibid.,* p. 254.

[20] *Ibid.,* p. 254, n. 1.

[21] *Ibid.,* pp. 201, 253-54.

[22] This is not to imply that Dr. Kreps desired to be staff director himself on a permanent basis. That he did not is evidenced by his voluntarily relinquishing the position after holding it for approximately fifteen months in order to devote more time to his regular job as a professor at Stanford University. However, he was vehemently opposed to Mr. Berquist's becoming staff director or even remaining on the staff in a high-ranking capacity.

[23] At the time, Dr. Ensley was the secretary of Senator Ralph Flanders (R.-Vt.), the second-ranking minority Senator on the Joint Committee on the Economic Report, and as such served as his assistant on economic measures.

[24] Nourse, *Economics in the Public Service,* p. 254.

[25] *Ibid.,* p. 254, n. 2.

[26] *Ibid.,* p. 254.

[27] *Ibid.,* pp. 309-310.

[28] *Ibid.,* p. 309.

[29] *Ibid.*, p. 449.

[30] *Ibid.*, pp. 310, 323, 449.

[31] Interview with Senator Monroney on January 10, 1953.

[32] On some of these committees, the assistant chief clerks bore such titles as "minority clerk," "minority adviser," or simply "professional staff member," but the relationship was in essence the same. Hence, they are included in this category.

[33] Information for these classifications was obtained primarily from collation of the listings of committee employees in the copies of the U.S., *Congressional Directory* and in the semi-annual reports on committee staff members in Vols. XCVIII and XCIX of the U.S., *Congressional Record* for the 82d Cong., 2d Sess., 1952, and for the 83d Cong., 1st Sess., 1953.

[34] U.S., *Congressional Record,* 82d Cong., 2d Sess., April 8, 1952, XCVIII, Part 3, p. 3686.

[35] *Ibid.*

[36] *Ibid.*, May 22, 1952, XCVIII, Part 5, p. 5803.

[37] *Ibid.*, June 30, 1952, XCVIII, Part 7, p. 8614.

[38] Senate Expenditures Committee, *Hearings on the Organization and Operation of Congress,* 82d Cong., 1st Sess., June, 1951, p. 600.

[39] In the 80th Congress, the Senate Expenditures Committee recommended abolishing the requirements that certain staff members be assigned to the chairman and ranking minority member (U.S., Congress, Senate, Committee on Expenditures in the Executive Departments, *Evaluation of Effect of Legislative Reorganization Act of 1946,* Senate Report No. 1175, 80th Cong., 2d Sess., April 28, 1948, p. 3) and favorably reported out a bill, S. 2575, incorporating this and other changes in the Legislative Reorganization Act. But that measure was never brought to a vote in the Senate. However, serious consideration should be given to the possibility of resurrecting such a repealer any time conditions might be more propitious for its passage.

[40] For example, in the 82d Congress, Senator Styles Bridges (R.-N.H.) originally introduced an amendment to S. 913 (a bill to create a Joint Committee on the Budget) which would have divided the employees of the proposed Joint Committee on the Budget between the majority and minority in the same ratio as their representation on the Joint Committee itself and would have had each group of staff members appointed by and responsible to the majority and minority committeemen respectively (U.S., *Congressional Record,* 82d Cong., 2d Sess., April 8, 1952, XCVIII, Part 3, p. 3683). And as mentioned before, Senator James Murray (D.-Mont.) recommended prescribing by law that on every committee the minority members be permitted to select one-third of the staff personnel. Needless to say, both these schemes would not effect merely superficial modifications in but rather would subvert the basic principle of a nonpartisan staff appointed by a majority vote of the committee.

Chapter V

[1] Public Law 601, 79th Cong., 2d Sess., Aug. 2, 1946, 60 *Stat.* 834, 2 *U.S.C.* 72a(a).

[2] *Ibid.*, sec. 202(c), 60 *Stat.* 835, 2 *U.S.C.* 72a(c).

[3] In fact, subsequent events revealed that even a minority of a committee could effect the withdrawal of such authorization. After this section was

originally written in the summer of 1953, the minority membership of the Senate Permanent Subcommittee on Investigations resigned en masse in protest against a subcommittee resolution granting the chairman absolute power to hire and fire the staff, which had been passed by a straight party line vote. And they refused to rejoin the subcommittee for over six months until that obnoxious rule was rescinded on Jan. 25, 1954 (Murrey Marder, "Rules Changed to Win Democrats Back to McCarthy Group," *Washington Post,* Jan. 26, 1954, p. 10).

[4] To avoid a possible misunderstanding on this score, the distinction should be made clear between the allocation of certain staff positions to individual committeemen, who for all practical purposes filled those, and the suggestion of qualified candidates by committee members who did not bring any pressure to bear upon the chairman, staffing subcommittee, staff director, or whoever was doing the recruiting to recommend the appointment of those persons. The former not only had obvious deficiencies as a procedural device but also was contrary to the intent of the Legislative Reorganization Act. Besides being consistent with the law, the latter afforded a desirable broadening of the recruitment base.

[5] For statements to that effect by Senators Walter George (D.-Ga.), Wayne Morse (R.-Ore.), John McClellan (D.-Ark.), and George Aiken (R.-Vt.), see U.S., *Congressional Record,* 82d Cong., 2d Sess., April 8, 1952, XCVIII, Part 3, pp. 3693-94. For earlier comments of the same sort by Senator McClellan, see Senate Expenditures Committee, *Hearings on the Organization and Operation of Congress,* 82d Cong., 1st Sess., June 6, 1951, p. 69; and by Senator Eugene Millikin (R.-Colo.), see U.S., Congress, Senate, Committee on Expenditures in the Executive Departments, *Hearings on Evaluation of Legislative Reorganization Act of 1946,* 80th Cong., 2d Sess., Feb. 25, 1948, p. 221.

[6] For example, the TVA, which is renowned for its merit system, sought personnel at all levels who subscribed to the broad purposes of that organization (David Lilienthal, *TVA: Democracy on the March* [New York: Pocket Books, Inc., 1945], pp. 74, 106, 110).

[7] Through the 82d Congress only, in the pre-Cohn and Schine era.

[8] Nourse, *Economics in the Public Service,* p. 309.

[9] U.S., Congress, House, Committee on Foreign Affairs, "Report of the Subcommittee on Staffing," 82d Cong., 1st Sess., March 8, 1951. (Mimeographed.)

[10] Senate Expenditures Committee, *Hearings on the Organization and Operation of Congress,* 82d Cong., 1st Sess., June 6, 1951, pp. 65, 70.

[11] For additional information on committee staff salaries, see pp. 102-103.

[12] U.S., Congress, Senate, Committee on the Judiciary, *Report on Interlocking Subversion in Government Departments,* committee print, 83d Cong., 1st Sess., July 30, 1953, pp. 32-35.

[13] Senate Expenditures Committee, *Hearings on the Organization and Operation of Congress,* 82d Cong., 1st Sess., June 7, 1951, pp. 104-105.

[14] As finally approved by the Senate, S. Res. 16 read:

"*Resolved,* That hereafter when any person is appointed as an employee of any committee of the Senate, of any Senator, or of any office of the Senate the committee, Senator, or officer having authority to make such appointment shall transmit the name of such person to the Federal Bureau of Investigation, together with a request that such committee, Senator, or officer be informed as to any derogatory and rebutting information in the possession of such agency concerning the loyalty and reliability for security purposes of such person, and in any case in which such derogatory information is revealed such committee, Senator, or officer shall make or cause to be made such further investigation as shall have been considered necessary to determine the loyalty and reliability for security purposes of such person.

Every such committee, Senator, and officer shall promptly transmit to the Federal Bureau of Investigation a list of the names of the incumbent employees of such committee, Senator, or officer together with a request that such committee, Senator, or officer be informed of any derogatory and rebutting information contained in the files of such agency concerning the loyalty and reliability for security purposes of such employee" (U.S., *Congressional Record,* 83d Cong., 1st Sess., March 6, 1953, XCIX, Part 2, p. 1688).

[15] U.S., Congress, Senate, Committee on Rules and Administration, *Loyalty Checks of Senate Employees,* Senate Report No. 50 (to accompany S. Res. 16), 83d Cong., 1st Sess., March 2, 1953, p. 1.

Moreover, the force of S. Res. 16 was further weakened in practice by making its application optional with the Senators and committees. Almost ten months after its passage, there were indications it was not being carried out very successfully (Edwin B. Haakinson, "Security Checkup on 1800 Senate Employees Bogs Down," *Washington Post,* Dec. 29, 1953, p. 11).

[16] Public Law 601, 79th Cong., 2d Sess., Aug. 2, 1946, sec. 202(e), 60 *Stat.* 835, 2 *U.S.C.* 72a(e).

[17] U.S., Congress, Senate, A Bill to Provide for Increased Efficiency in the Legislative Branch of the Government, S. 2177, 79th Cong., 2d Sess., May 13, 1946, secs. 201, 205, pp. 34-39.

[18] For such characterizations of their opposition, see *New York Times,* June 8, 1946, p. 2; *The Washington Post,* June 11, 1946, p. 1; George B. Galloway, *Congress at the Crossroads* (New York: Thomas Y. Crowell Co., 1946), p. 344; Senate Expenditures Committee, *Hearings on Evaluation of Legislative Reorganization Act of 1946,* 80th Cong., 2d Sess., Feb., 1948, pp. 47-48, 183.

[19] See U.S., *Congressional Record,* 79th Cong., 2d Sess., June 7, 1946, XCII, Part 5, pp. 6440-42, 6444-45, 6448.

[20] See pp. 100-101.

For statements by Senator Robert LaFollette, Jr. (Pro.-Wis.) that a primary purpose of the projected personnel director was to provide security of tenure for the professional staffs of the committees, see U.S., *Congressional Record,* 79th Cong., 2d Sess., June 7, 1946, XCII, Part 5, p. 6440; *ibid.,* June 8, 1946, XCII, Part 5, p. 6518.

Chapter VI

[1] This group includes only the committee aides from whom comprehensive interview data were obtained in the 82d Congress. During the 83d Congress, several more committee staff members were asked questions about some specific aspect of their work such as processing real-estate transactions that were reviewed by their committees. However, no biographical or other information was sought from them.

[2] Exclusive of wartime uniformed service in the armed forces with the

exception of the aides to the armed services committees, which considered that a relevant criterion in the selection of staff personnel.

[3] To achieve the staffing goals of the Legislative Reorganization Act, it is essential not only to attract but also to retain high-caliber personnel. Hence, equally important as studying the experience backgrounds of committee aides is a consideration of their average length of service and the types of position for which they leave congressional employment. In particular, it would be desirable to learn if the jobs they hold before and after being committee aides form any sort of discernible career ladders. However, because of the continuity in staff during the period covered, there was insufficient data available then to support any tenable generalizations in this regard.

A large majority of the committee aides interviewed evinced interest in remaining permanently in their jobs. Nevertheless, after the terminal date of this study, a few (for example, Joe McMurray, staff director of the Senate Banking and Currency Committee) who had expressed the strongest desire to make a career of congressional staff work went elsewhere. And others who apparently had switched to a different kind of employment for good, resumed positions on committee staffs. For instance, in Dec., 1953, Robert Morris resigned as chief counsel of the Senate Internal Security Subcommittee to take a New York municipal judgeship for a ten-year term at an annual salary of $17,000. On Jan. 26, 1956, he left that position to accept reappointment as chief counsel of the Senate Internal Security Subcommittee. In doing so, he commented rather cryptically that he was reluctant to leave the court but felt obligated to come back to the Subcommittee (*The Washington Post*, Jan. 27, 1956, p. 2).

Clearly this whole question merits further investigation over a long enough time to acquire adequate information to generalize about the average length of service of committee aides and the most common reasons for their departure from or return to committee staff work.

[4] That group included the top-ranking specialists within the LRS in education, forestry, Indian affairs, and national defense and the second-highest grade specialists in all the other fields covered.

[5] Although lawyers are legal technicians, they are basically generalists in regard to the subject matter they handle. The average attorney deals with criminal and civil cases involving a wide variety of subjects. The judges in our regular court system are expected to be able to apply the law (whether statute, common, or equity) to any type of justiciable issue. The law schools are geared primarily to producing graduates capable of functioning in these two major nonspecialized capacities. Hence, the educational preparation for an LL.B. degree instills in its recipients boundless confidence in their ability to handle an assignment concerning any topic. In fact so much so, lawyers might appropriately be termed the "Marines of the intellectual disciplines." They are not afraid to wade right into any subject—no matter how complicated—learning enough about its terminology and contents as they go along to cope with it.

[6] Interview with Dr. Oakes on Sept. 15, 1952.

[7] "The Record of Congress in Committee Staffing," *American Political Science Review*, XLV (Dec., 1951), 1130. Copyright 1951 by and used with the permission of the American Political Science Association.

[8] P. 73.

[9] See the chart "Classification of Professional Staff Members of Standing Committees of the House—80th Congress," Gladys Kammerer, *The Staffing of the Committees of Congress* (Lexington, Ky.: Bureau of Govt. Research, Univ. of Kentucky, 1949), p. 45. At that time, there was only one other person, Joseph Parker, with an LL.B. besides Mr. Heimburger on the House Agriculture Committee staff.

[10] In Dec., 1954 (after the close of the period covered by this study), Mr. Fitzpatrick resigned his post, which was in Schedule C, to make way for a political appointment. Although occupying a top policy position, he had been retained for almost two years after the change in control of the executive branch, because of his outstanding qualifications (*The Evening Star* [Washington], Dec. 18, 1954, p. A-2).

[11] Kofmehl, "The Advanced Research Section of the Legislative Reference Service," pp. 46-47, 51-52.

[12] For further discussion of this point, see pp. 190-91.

[13] Mann, "Congressional Behavior and National Labor Policy," pp. 127-28, 198, 262-63, 266-72, 346-47, 398-407, 427-28. It is one of the major themes of Mann's study that Gerard Reilly was the evil genius who through his skill as a legislative draftsman shaped the Taft-Hartley Act in a much more anti-labor direction than it otherwise would have taken.

[14] For a discussion of the legal memoranda prepared by the Office of the Legislative Counsel, see p. 190.

[15] "Titles of Research Staff in Legislative Reference Service in Grades GS-9 and Above," (Library of Congress, 1951), pp. 1-3. (Mimeographed.)

[16] In fact, there is an unwritten rule that the members of the House and Senate Judiciary Committees must be lawyers themselves.

[17] Derived from Dr. Kammerer's own statistics quoted above. According to the figures she cited for 1948 and 1950, a total of 85 out of 205 professional staff members in those two years combined were lawyers. That comes to exactly 41.46%.

Chapter VII

[1] For illustrations of such invasion of the executive branch sphere, see pp. 132-33.

[2] Public Law 601, 79th Cong., 2d Sess., Aug. 2, 1946, sec. 202(a), 60 *Stat.* 834, 2 *U.S.C.* 72a(a).

[3] U.S., *Congressional Record,* 82d Cong., 2d Sess., Jan. 15, 1952, XCVIII, Part 1, pp. 165-69; *ibid.,* Jan. 21, 1952, XCVIII, Part 1, pp. 293-95; *ibid.,* Jan. 24, 1952, XCVIII, Part 1, p. 470; *ibid.,* 83d Cong., 1st Sess., Jan. 23, 1953, XCIX, Part 1, pp. 508-513.

Also, during part or all of the 82d Congress, there were specially-authorized subcommittee staffs on six of these Senate committees: Agriculture and Forestry, Armed Services, District of Columbia, Foreign Relations, Post Office and Civil Service, and Rules and Administration (*ibid*). For a discussion of the relations between the special staffs of subcommittees and the aides to their respective parent committees, see pp. 107-109.

[4] U.S., Congress, House, Committee on Appropriations, *Hearings before the Subcommittee on the Legislative Branch Appropriation Bill for 1952,* 82d

Cong., 1st Sess., June 4, 1951, p. 17; U.S., *Congressional Record*, 82d Cong., 2d Sess., Jan. 29, 1952, XCVIII, Part 1, pp. 618-24; U.S., Congress, House, Committee on Appropriations, *Hearings before the Subcommittee on the Legislative Branch Appropriation Bill for 1953*, 82d Cong., 2d Sess., March 25, 1952, p. 85; U.S., *Congressional Record*, 83d Cong., 1st Sess., Jan. 29, 1953, XCIX, Part 1, pp. 668-73.

Also, during part or all of the 82d Congress, there were specially-authorized subcommittee staffs on three of these House committees: Banking and Currency, Public Works, and Ways and Means (*ibid.*).

[5] U.S., *Congressional Record*, 83d Cong., 1st Sess., Jan. 23, 1953, XCIX, Part 1, pp. 511-12.

[6] U.S., *Congressional Record*, 83d Cong., 1st Sess., Jan. 9, 1953, XCIX, Part 1, pp. 281-82.

[7] For further discussion of ratification by congressional committees of individual administrative actions, see pp. 130-31, 133-36.

[8] For a discussion of the differential status of the standing committees, see pp. 19-21.

[9] In 1951 during hearings before the Senate Expenditures Committee, Senator Mike Monroney (D.-Okla.) stated this viewpoint very aptly as follows:

"There is always a temptation, if you write it to read not more than six or eight staff members, that most of them will try to come up to the eight, and a lot of committees, the way they work, do not need eight. We think, if they need more than four, that they should make a showing to the Rules Committee, and they can get the resolution through the House or Senate to employ extra experts to assist them" (Senate Expenditures Committee, *Hearings on the Organization and Operation of Congress*, 82d Cong., 1st Sess., June 7, 1951, p. 102).

[10] U.S., Congress, House, Committee on Appropriations, *Hearings before the Subcommittee on the Legislative Branch Appropriation Bill for 1954*, 83d Cong., 1st Sess., May 28, 1953, pp. 32-33; U.S., *Congressional Record*, 83d Cong., 1st Sess., Jan. 30, 1953, XCIX, Part 1, pp. 687-88. The House Appropriations Committee hearings list $2,296,991.63 as the total amount expended by investigating and select committees of the House to March 31, 1953 on investigations authorized during the 82d Congress. On pp. 687-88 of the *Congressional Record*, a table captioned "Expenditures Paid by the Senate from the Contingent Fund . . . for Investigations by the Standing Committees (Including Subcommittees), Special Committees, . . . and Joint Committees" lists the totals of $1,592,928.08 for fiscal 1951 and of $1,639,024.88 for fiscal 1952. When added together, these figures for the Senate and House total $5,528,944.59. Although the House and Senate statistics do not cover exactly the same period, they correspond closely enough for the purposes of the above estimate.

[11] *The Future of Government in the United States*, ed. L. D. White (Chicago: University of Chicago Press, 1942), pp. 152-53.

[12] For examples of such recommendations, see Senate Expenditures Committee, *Hearings on Evaluation of Legislative Reorganization Act of 1946*, 80th Cong., 2d Sess., Feb. 17, 1948, p. 69; *ibid.*, Feb. 18, 1948, p. 132; *ibid.*, Feb. 23, 1948, pp. 189-90; Senate Expenditures Committee, *Hearings on the Organiza-*

tion and Operation of Congress, 82d Cong., 1st Sess., June 20, 1951, pp. 404-405, 414-16; *ibid.,* June 27, 1951, p. 635.

13 Kammerer, *The Staffing of the Committees of Congress,* p. 40.

14 Public Law 601, 79th Cong., 2d Sess., Aug. 2, 1946, 60 *Stat.* 835, 2 *U.S.C.* 72a(e).

15 Public Law 271, 80th Cong., 1st Sess., July 30, 1947, 61 *Stat.* 611, 2 *U.S.C.* 72a(e).

16 U.S., Congress, Public Law 4, 80th Cong., 1st Sess., Feb. 19, 1947, 61 *Stat.* 5, 2 *U.S.C.* 72a-1.

17 U.S., Congress, Postal Rate Revision and Federal Employees' Salary Act of 1948, Public Law 900, 80th Cong., 2d Sess., July 3, 1948, sec. 301, 62 *Stat.* 1267, 5 *U.S.C.* 955; U.S., Congress, Second Supplemental Appropriation Act of 1950, Public Law 430, 81st Cong., 1st Sess., Oct. 29, 1949, sec. 101(a), 63 *Stat.* 974, 5 *U.S.C.* 932a; U.S., Congress, Classified Employees' Increase Pay Act, Public Law 201, 82d Cong., 1st Sess., Oct. 24, 1951, sec. 2(a), 65 *Stat.* 613, 5 *U.S.C.* 932b.

Moreover, this conversion system was mildly progressive, producing a relatively bigger gross salary from a small than from a large basic rate of pay—as the figures in the above table indicate. And in 1951 a ceiling of $11,646 per annum was imposed on the pay of congressional employees except for individuals specifically exempted by law (Public Law 201, 82d Cong., 1st Sess., Oct. 24, 1951, sec. 2(b), 65 *Stat.* 613-14, 5 *U.S.C.* 932b).

18 In the closing days of the 82d Congress, Senator Tom Connally (D.-Tex.) introduced an amendment to the Supplemental Appropriations Act, 1953, providing that "the compensation of the chief of staff, Foreign Relations Committee, shall be at the rate of $13,146 a year so long as the position is held by the present incumbent." This amendment, which would have granted the staff director $1,500 a year more than the other professional staff members of the Foreign Relations Committee, was defeated on the grounds it would be unfair to the staff directors of the other standing committees. Although the chief of staff of the Foreign Relations Committee, Dr. Francis O. Wilcox, was one of the most outstanding committee aides in either house, the Senate wisely rejected this approach. For it would have dealt piecemeal with the problem and involved all the shortcomings connected with prescribing individual employees' salaries in the law (U.S., *Congressional Record,* 82d Cong., 2d Sess., July 3, 1952, XCVIII, Part 7, pp. 9139-41).

19 See, for example, U.S., Congress, Joint Committee on the Economic Report, *Report on the January 1952 Economic Report of the President,* Senate Report No. 1295, 82d Cong., 2d Sess., March 12, 1952, p. 32.

20 Often one of these staff subcommittees worked in close conjunction with a corresponding group of staff personnel from the Treasury Department and Bureau of Internal Revenue. In fact, together they actually formed a joint staff subcommittee. For further discussion of such combined operations, see pp. 158-59.

21 For a more detailed description of the proceedings in these staff round tables, see pp. 116-17.

22 For example, see U.S., Congress, Senate, Committee on Armed Services,

Annual Report of the Preparedness Investigating Subcommittee, committee print, 82d Cong., 2d Sess., 1952, p. 20.

Chapter VIII

[1] For a list of the participants in these round tables and a summary of their comments, see U.S., Congress, Joint Committee on the Economic Report, *Report on the January 1949 Economic Report of the President,* Senate Report No. 88, 81st Cong., 1st Sess., March 1, 1949, pp. 84, 59-83.

[2] U.S., Congress, Joint Committee on the Economic Report, *Report on the January 1950 Economic Report of the President,* Senate Report No. 1843, 81st Cong., 2d Sess., June 16, 1950, p. 110.

[3] U.S., Congress, Joint Committee on the Economic Report, *Report on the January 1951 Economic Report of the President,* Senate Report No. 210, 82d Cong., 1st Sess., April 2, 1951, p. 118.

[4] U.S., Congress, Joint Committee on the Economic Report, *Report on the January 1952 Economic Report of the President,* Senate Report No. 1295, 82d Cong., 2d Sess., March 12, 1952, pp. 16, 130-31.

Dr. Nourse gives the Joint Economic Committee staff the main credit for introducing and refining this use of questionnaires and round tables by the Joint Economic Committee (*Economics in the Public Service,* pp. 444-45).

[5] Agreed to on Aug. 15, 1950, 81st Cong., 2d Sess.

[6] U.S., Congress, Senate, Committee on Interior and Insular Affairs, Senate Document No. 8, 82d Cong., 1st Sess., 1951.

[7] See U.S., Congress, Senate, Committee on Interior and Insular Affairs, *Hearings on National Fuel Reserves and Fuel Policy,* 82d Cong., 1st Sess., March 7-8, 1951, which are the transcripts of the proceedings at that round table, for many superb illustrations of the utility of the panel-discussion approach.

[8] For examples of round tables held by other committees, see U.S., Congress, House, Committee on Agriculture, *Report on Crop Estimating and Reporting Services of the Department of Agriculture,* committee print, 82d Cong., 2d Sess., June 16, 1952, p. viii and U.S., Congress, Senate, Committee on Banking and Currency, *Summary of Activities, Eighty-Second Congress,* committee print, 82d Cong., 2d Sess., July 25, 1952, p. v.

[9] Likewise, during this period, executive agencies and private research organizations employed ·the round-table procedure for developing the views of experts on various subjects of investigation. For example, President Truman's Commission on the Health Needs of the Nation relied extensively on this technique (U.S., President's Commission on the Health Needs of the Nation, *Building America's Health,* Vol. I: *Findings and Recommendations* [Washington: U.S. Government Printing Office, 1952], pp. x-xi). The Council of Economic Advisers held some conferences with representatives of major interest groups and planned a series of round tables with labor, business, government, and university economists. However, a cut in its budget for fiscal 1949 prevented the realization of that project (Nourse, *Economics in the Public Service,* pp. 158-160, 210, 419-422). The National Industrial Conference Board conducted a number of round-table discussions with business and academic econo-

mists, which members of the Council of Economic Advisers attended (*ibid.,* p. 161).

As with the advent of any institutional invention, it is difficult to ascribe the origin of the panel-discussion procedure in the study of economic and social problems. However, the use of this device undoubtedly was spread throughout our governmental system by professional staff members—especially by economists among whom there is a continuing exchange of ideas and strong professional bond cutting across their organizational affiliations. Obviously, Dr. Nourse was influenced by his experience with the round tables of the National Industrial Conference Board and of the Joint Committee on the Economic Report in his desire to adopt that approach in the staff work for the Council of Economic Advisers. And the staff of the Joint Economic Committee (and of other committees) played an instrumental, if largely unacknowledged, role in developing this innovation in the congressional hearings process.

[10] U.S., Congress, Joint Committee on Defense Production, *Second Annual Report of Activities,* Senate Report No. 3, 83d Cong., 1st Sess., Jan. 9, 1953, pp. 26-27. For additional examples, including some that eventuated in remedial legislation, see *ibid.,* pp. 23-28.

[11] U.S., Congress, Title V of the Revenue Act of 1951, Public Law 183, 82d Cong., 1st Sess., Oct. 20, 1951, 65 *Stat.* 541, 26 *U.S.C.* 430.

[12] For additional comments on this liaison role, see pp. 196-97.

[13] For example, see U.S., *Congressional Record,* 82d Cong., 2d Sess., May 26, 1952, XCVIII, Part 5, pp. 5938-39.

[14] For a series of illustrations in the debate over four agreements with Germany regarding settlement of external German debts, see U.S., *Congressional Record,* 83d Cong., 1st Sess., July 9, 1953, XCIX, Part 6, pp. 8322, 8324, 8335; *ibid.,* July 13, 1953, XCIX, Part 7, p. 8625.

[15] U.S., *Congressional Record,* 82d Cong., 2d Sess., May 5, 1952, XCVIII, Part 4, p. 4822.

[16] U.S., Congress, House, Committee on Foreign Affairs, *Survey of Activities, Eighty-Second Congress,* committee print, 82d Cong., 2d Sess., 1952, p. iii.

[17] The original application of this catchy term to committee reports was generally attributed to Middleton Beaman, the first House Legislative Counsel. Its usage was prevalent among the employees of both the House and Senate Legislative Counsel and of the Joint Tax Committee and was spreading rapidly among other congressional staff personnel. Some executive branch staff members adopted it. And inasmuch as Roy Blough employed it in his *The Federal Taxing Process* (New York: Prentice-Hall, Inc., 1952), it undoubtedly will gain acceptance in academic circles.

[18] U.S., Congress, House, Rule XIII, par. 2a.

[19] U.S., Congress, Senate, Rule XXIX, subsection (4).

[20] Blough uses that appellation in the *Federal Taxing Process,* p. 76.

[21] U.S., Congress, House, H.R. 7408, 82d Cong., 2d Sess., April 4, 1952.

[22] U.S., Congress, House, Committee on Education and Labor, *Prevention of Major Disasters in Coal Mines,* House Report No. 2368 (to accompany H.R. 7408), 82d Cong., 2d Sess., June 30, 1952, p. 22.

[23] For example, see U.S., Congress, House, Committee on Foreign Affairs,

Mutual Security Act of 1953, House Report No. 569 (to accompany H.R. 5710), 83d Cong., 1st Sess., June 16, 1953. Fifty of the sixty-two pages of the text of this report follow the organization of the bill and in effect constitute a greatly expanded section-by-section analysis.

24 U.S., Congress, House, *House Rules and Manual, Eighty-Second Congress,* House Document No. 739, 81st Cong. [*sic*], 2d Sess., 1951, pp. 364-65; U.S., Congress, Senate, *Senate Manual,* Senate Document No. 10, 83d Cong., 1st Sess., 1953, p. 46.

25 For a description of the varying degrees of intrastaff collaboration on different committees, see pp. 103-104.

26 Generally, the membership of a committee participated much more fully in the preparation of reports on investigations than of reports to accompany bills. Frequently, before its staff began to draft the report on an inquiry, a committee would meet to discuss the points to be covered and the treatment to be accorded them. Often, a committee marked up such a report in executive session, going over it sentence by sentence or at least scrutinizing any debatable passages very carefully. And sometimes a committee held a series of meetings in which it revised successive drafts of the report on an investigation.

27 U.S., *Congressional Record,* 82d Cong., 2d Sess., June 16, 1952, XCVIII, Part 6, p. 7299.

28 U.S., *Congressional Record,* 82d Cong., 2d Sess., June 17, 1952, XCVIII, Part 6, p. 7429.

29 Only the House managers are required to accompany a conference report with a detailed statement explaining the effects of the recommendations in that report (pursuant to House Rule XXVIII, par. 1b). A conference report may not be received by the House without such an accompanying statement (House Document No. 739, 81st Cong., 2d Sess. [*sic*], 1951, p. 473).

Chapter IX

1 In some cases, this technique of legislative oversight had explicit statutory sanction. For example, sec. 712 of the Defense Production Act of 1950, which created the Joint Committee on Defense Production, specified: "Any department, official, or agency administering any of such programs shall, at the request of the committee, consult with the committee, from time to time, with respect to their activities under this Act" (Public Law 774, 81st Cong., 2d Sess., Sept. 8, 1950, 64 *Stat.* 821, 50 *U.S.C.* 2162).

2 Two of the committees that held such consultations most frequently were Senate Foreign Relations and House Foreign Affairs. For accounts of their activities along these lines, see U.S., Congress, Senate, Committee on Foreign Relations, *Legislative History, Eighty-Second Congress,* Senate Document No. 161, 82d Cong., 2d Sess., July 2, 1952, pp. 3, 61-63; U.S., Congress, House, Committee on Foreign Affairs, *Survey of Activities, Eighty-Second Congress,* committee print, 82d Cong., 2d Sess., 1952, pp. 1-2, 8-9, 41-44.

3 Deficiency cases are the opposite of tax refund cases. A deficiency case is one in which the taxpayer has underestimated his tax liability, and the Bureau of Internal Revenue has to secure additional taxes from him. Although the Joint Committee on Internal Revenue Taxation is required by law to review tax refunds in excess of $200,000, it has no corresponding authority

over the settlement of cases of underassessment of taxes. Hence, the only tax deficiency cases that it considers are those on which the Bureau of Internal Revenue solicits its advice.

[4] U.S., *Congressional Record,* 82d Cong., 2d Sess., Jan. 21, 1952, XCVIII, Part 1, p. 292.

[5] U.S., Congress, House, Committee on Interior and Insular Affairs, *Alaska's Vanishing Frontier: A Progress Report,* committee print, 82d Cong., 1st Sess., 1951, pp. v, 1.

[6] For example, in its first progress report, the House Small Business Committee said:

"Moreover, the committee, for its part, has welcomed the opportunity to be of service to Members of the House, for it looks upon itself not only as a service organization to our small-business economy but one which stands ready to serve the constituency of the House membership.

. . . .

"The committee also has a direct responsibility to the Members of the House. It stands ready to give prompt and careful consideration to any small-business matter which a Member may wish to bring to the committee's attention. Assisting the Members in answering the appeals for help from small operators in their districts is and should be an important part of the committee's activities" (U.S., Congress, House, Select Committee on Small Business, *Progress Report— First Session,* House Report No. 1228, 82d Cong., 1st Sess., Jan. 7, 1952, pp. 2, 74).

[7] For instance, see the colloquy between Laurence Henderson, staff director of the Senate Small Business Committee, and Senator Allen Ellender (D.-La.) in Senate Appropriations Committee, *Hearings before a Subcommittee on the Legislative Branch Appropriation Bill for 1952,* July 12, 1951, pp. 95-98, and the similar exchange two years later between Senator Ellender and Senator Edward Thye (R.-Minn.) during the debate over authorizing additional funds for the Senate Small Business Committee in U.S., *Congressional Record,* 83d Cong., 1st Sess., July 8, 1953, XCIX, Part 6, p. 8190.

[8] Some indication of the volume of such casework for a "service" committee staff is afforded by the following excerpt from the first progress report of the Senate Small Business Committee:

"It is estimated that in the past 6 months your committee staff has interviewed and sought to assist some 2,100 businessmen referred in person either by members of the committee or other Members of the Senate. In this same period, the committee staff has advised and aided approximately 6,700 small-business men who have asked its assistance by letter" (U.S., Congress, Senate, Select Committee on Small Business, *Report,* Senate Report No. 2, 82d Cong., 1st Sess., Jan. 15, 1951, p. 13).

[9] For example, see U.S., Congress, Mutual Security Act of 1951, Public Law 165, 82d Cong., 1st Sess., Oct. 10, 1951, sec. 518, 65 *Stat.* 383, 22 *U.S.C.* 1669.

[10] Blough, *The Federal Taxing Process,* pp. 147-48.

[11] U.S., Congress, House Committee on Appropriations, *Hearings before the Subcommittee on the Legislative Branch Appropriation Bill for 1952,* 82d Cong., 1st Sess., June 4, 1951, p. 32.

[12] Of the 333 refunds and credits reported and allowed in fiscal 1951, the Joint Tax Committee staff criticized 17 in the first instance; of the 214 refunds and credits reported and allowed in fiscal 1952, the Joint Tax Committee staff criticized 24 in the first instance (U.S., Congress, Joint Committee on Internal Revenue Taxation, *Report Covering Refunds and Credits of Internal-Revenue Taxes for the Fiscal Years Ending June 30, 1951 and 1952,* House Document No. 286, 83d Cong., 2d Sess., Jan. 6, 1954, p. 3).

[13] Nearly all the refunds and credits were Bureau of Internal Revenue cases. For instance, only 4 of the 333 cases in fiscal 1951 and 2 of the 214 cases in fiscal 1952 were Department of Justice settlements (*ibid.*).

[14] U.S., Congress, Military and Naval Construction Act of 1951, Public Law 155, 82d Cong., 1st Sess., Sept. 28, 1951, Title VI, 65 *Stat.* 365, 40 *U.S.C.* 551. Contrary to a rather frequent misinterpretation, Title VI of this Act does not confer any substantive authority to acquire land but only imposes a procedural requirement on the classes of real estate transactions covered. The authority to acquire land for the projects concerned is provided in separate general authorization measures, which usually are enacted annually.

[15] U.S., *Congressional Record—Daily Digest,* 83d Cong., 1st Sess., May 13, 1953, XCIX, Part 14, p. D282.

[16] Among these other ways were the use of concurrent resolutions as a "legislative veto" or to terminate statutes and the requirement of periodic renewal of authorizing legislation. Because the application of the first had been so restricted in extent and because both these methods were so analogous to ordinary legislative activities of the committees, it was not deemed necessary to include them in the text.

[17] For comprehensive discussions of such supervisory activities by the appropriations committees, see Arthur W. Macmahon, "Congressional Oversight of Administration: The Power of the Purse," *Political Science Quarterly,* LVIII (June and Sept., 1943), 161-90, 380-414, and Elias Huzar, *The Purse and the Sword: Control of the Army by Congress through Military Appropriations, 1933-1950* (Ithaca, N.Y.: Cornell University Press, 1950).

[18] U.S., Congress, Senate, Committee on Expenditures in the Executive Departments, *Activities, Eightieth Congress,* Senate Document No. 4, 81st Cong., 1st Sess., Jan. 13, 1949, p. 2.

[19] U.S., Congress, Senate, Committee on Expenditures in the Executive Departments, *Activities, Eighty-First Congress,* Senate Report No. 1, 82d Cong., 1st Sess., Jan. 15, 1951, p. 47. For an earlier account of this episode, see Senate Document No. 4, 81st Cong., 1st Sess., Jan. 13, 1949, p. 5.

[20] For a summary of the recommendations made by the Wolf Company in its report on that survey, see U.S., *Congressional Record,* 83d Cong., 1st Sess., Jan. 30, 1953, XCIX, Part 1, p. 682.

[21] Senate Document No. 4, 81st Cong., 1st Sess., Jan. 13, 1949, pp. 6-7.

[22] See pp. 130-31.

[23] See p. 129.

[24] For a forceful statement of the administrative problems occasioned by subjecting individual transactions to the decision of congressional committees, see U.S., President, 1945-53 (Truman), *Message Relating to the Acquisition and Disposition of Land and Interests in Land by the Army, Navy, Air Force,*

and Federal Civil Defense Administration, House Document No. 133, 82d Cong., 1st Sess., May 15, 1951. And for a comparable enumeration of the difficulties that procedure poses for the committees, see the comments of Representative Chet Holifield (D.-Cal.) in the debate on H.R. 4323 (a bill to authorize the GSA Administrator to enter into lease-purchase agreements), U.S., *Congressional Record,* 82d Cong., 2d Sess., April 28, 1952, XCVIII, Part 4, pp. 4522, 4527

25 For illustrations of possible applications of this requirement, see comments by Senator Everett Dirksen (R.-Ill.) in the debate on H.R. 6342 (Public Buildings Purchase Contract Act of 1954 and Post Office Department Property Act of 1954), U.S., *Congressional Record,* 83d Cong., 2d Sess., April 9, 1954, C, Part 4, pp. 4954-55.

26 There were two previous unsuccessful attempts to vest in congressional committees the power to pass upon specific administrative acts. In 1920, President Wilson vetoed an appropriation bill (H.R. 12610, 66th Cong., 2d Sess.) which provided broadly that the printing of magazines by executive agencies must have the prior approval of the Joint Congressional Committee on Printing. And in 1933, President Hoover vetoed a bill (H.R. 13975, 72d Cong., 2d Sess.) which would have prohibited certain income and other tax refunds in excess of $20,000 without prior approval by the Joint Committee on Internal Revenue Taxation, which also would have been allowed to fix the amount of each refund. In both cases, the Presidents based their actions on the grounds that the bills invalidly attempted to vest executive functions in congressional committees.

Also, powers of this sort had been conferred on mixed commissions (containing Congressmen as well as executive branch officials) on several occasions extending back as early as 1920 (Robert W. Ginnane, "The Control of Federal Administration by Congressional Resolutions and Committees," *Harvard Law Review,* LXVI [Feb., 1953], 600-602).

27 U.S., Congress, Public Law 289, 78th Cong., 2d Sess., April 4, 1944, 58 *Stat.* 190, 34 *U.S.C.* 520a.

This merely wrote into the law a clearance procedure which the Navy Department had been observing voluntarily for over a year—according to John J. Courtney, original draftsman of Public Law 289, 78th Cong., who at the time was on loan from the Justice Department to the Navy Department for the express purpose of handling the latter's real-estate transactions (interview with Mr. Courtney on July 1, 1952).

28 U.S., Congress, Senate, Committee on Armed Services, *Legislative Calendar, Eighty-Second Congress,* No. 15, May 15, 1952, p. 72.

29 *Ibid.,* p. 77.

30 "SEC. 407. In the case of any public work authorized to be established or developed under the authority of section 102, 202, or 302 of this Act, the Secretary of the military department authorized to establish or develop such public work, or his designee, shall come into agreement with the Committee on Armed Services of the Senate and of the House of Representatives with respect to the cost of construction of such public work, including those real-estate actions pertaining thereto" (U.S., Congress, Military and Naval Construction Act of 1952, 82d Cong., 2d Sess., July 14, 1952, 66 *Stat.* 625).

[31] U.S., Library of Congress, Legislative Reference Service, *Digest of Public General Bills, 82d Congress, 2d Session,* No. 6, Final Issue (Washington: U.S. Government Printing Office, 1952), p. xxxv.

[32] 277 U.S. 189 at 201-202 (1928).

[33] 252 N.Y. 27 at 43 (1929).

[34] More than two years after the end of the period covered, the President did just that in connection with an analogous provision, sec. 638, in the Department of Defense Appropriation Act, 1956 (H.R. 6042, 84th Cong.). It stipulated that the Defense Department must notify the Senate and House Appropriations Committees at least ninety days before shutting down any commercial-type facilities more than three years old and that no such termination could be made if disapproved by either committee within that ninety-day interval.

In a special message to Congress on July 13, 1955, President Eisenhower stated that were it not for the urgent need for the Defense Department appropriations, he would have vetoed H.R. 6042 on the ground that sec. 638 "constitutes an unconstitutional invasion of the province of the Executive." Then he went on to say:

"I do not, by my approval of H.R. 6042, acquiesce in the provisions of section 638, and to the extent that this section seeks to give to the Appropriations Committees of the Senate and House of Representatives authority to veto or prevent Executive action, such section will be regarded as invalid by the executive branch of the Government in the administration of H.R. 6042 unless otherwise determined by a court of competent jurisdiction" (U.S., President, 1953-57 [Eisenhower], *Message Approving Appropriations for the Department of Defense, 1956,* House Document No. 218, 84th Cong., 1st Sess., July 13, 1955, pp. 1-2).

Despite this ringing declaration by the President, the Defense Department did comply with sec. 638 to the extent of notifying the appropriations committees on Aug. 8, 1955, of fourteen business enterprises it intended to close down. The Senate Appropriations Committee temporarily disapproved the termination of only one, the Boston Ropewalk (*The Washington Post,* Sept. 2, 1955, p. 2). But the House Appropriations Committee requested the Defense Department to hold in abeyance all the proposed liquidations until the appropriations committees "have an opportunity to take up these matters in orderly procedure" (as quoted in *The Washington Post,* Oct. 21, 1955, p. 21). On Nov. 3, 1955, the Defense Department announced it would defer shutting down any of the fourteen plants for another ninety days (Raymond Moley, "Bureaucracy's Nine Lives," *Newsweek,* Dec. 19, 1955, p. 100).

Meanwhile, on Aug. 20, 1955, Representative Porter Hardy (D.-Va.) disclosed he had secured a written statement from the Comptroller General that the GAO would enforce sec. 638 by disallowing any expenditures made contrary to it (*The Washington Post,* Aug. 21, 1955, p. A-2). Hence, the stage was set for initiating a series of steps that could lead to a judicial test of the constitutionality of sec. 638. However, the Defense Department continued to comply with sec. 638 until it expired at the end of fiscal year 1956.

[35] For example, see the arguments advanced by Representatives William Dawson (D.-Ill.), Porter Hardy (D.-Va.), Chet Holifield (D.-Cal.), and John McCormack (D.-Mass.) against inserting such a requirement in H.R. 4323 (a

bill to authorize the GSA Administrator to enter into lease-purchase agreements),
in U.S., *Congressional Record,* 82d Cong., 2d Sess., April 28, 1952, XCVIII, Part
4, pp. 4516, 4521, 4527, 4529-31.

[36] U.S., Congress, Joint Committee on the Organization of Congress, *Report,*
Senate Report No. 1011, 79th Cong., 2d Sess., March 4, 1946, p. 5. To avoid
offensive repetition in this section, the popular name for the Legislative Reorganization Act of 1946, the "LaFollette-Monroney Act," is sometimes used.

[37] U.S., Congress, Senate, A Bill to Provide for Increased Efficiency in the
Legislative Branch of the Government, S. 2177, 79th Cong., 2d Sess., May 13,
1946, pp. 28-30.

[38] Senate Report No. 1400, 79th Cong., 2d Sess., May 31, 1946, p. 6.

[39] U.S., *Congressional Record,* 79th Cong., 2d Sess., June 7, 1946, XCII,
Part 5, pp. 6445-47.

[40] Public Law 601, 79th Cong., 2d Sess., Aug. 2, 1946, sec. 136, 60 *Stat.* 832,
2 *U.S.C.* 190d.

[41] This contention is not completely accurate with respect to the House standing committees. Only the Senate standing committees are authorized to investigate any matters within their respective jurisdictions and are granted the
subpoena power by sec. 134(a), Public Law 601, 79th Cong., 2d Sess., Aug. 2,
1946, 60 *Stat.* 831, 2 *U.S.C.* 190b.

[42] For examples of these arguments, see Senate Expenditures Committee,
Hearings on Evaluation of Legislative Reorganization Act of 1946, 80th Cong.,
2d Sess., Feb. 17, 1948, pp. 81-82; *ibid.,* Feb. 18, 1948, p. 148; *ibid.,* Feb. 23,
1948, p. 200.

[43] "Operation of Legislative Reorganization Act of 1946," *Hearings on the
Organization and Operation of Congress,* Senate Expenditures Committee, 82d
Cong., 1st Sess., June, 1951, p. 639. This interpretation would seem somewhat
inconsistent with the recommendation of the Joint Committee on the Organization of Congress and with the provision in S. 2177 for an administrative assistant
for each member of Congress primarily to relieve him of a large share of his
departmental business. Was it contemplated that the administrative assistants
would dispose of such matters merely by referring them to the appropriate
standing committees?

[44] Macmahon, *Political Science Quarterly,* LVIII (Sept., 1943), p. 414.

[45] For example, see rules (1) and (8) of the Permanent Subcommittee on
Senate Investigations in U.S., Congress, Senate, Committee on Expenditures in
the Executive Departments, *First Annual Report of the Investigations Subcommittee,* Senate Report No. 5, 81st Cong., 1st Sess., Jan. 17, 1949, pp. 3-4.

[46] In 1952 both the expenditures committees adopted the new title "Committee on Government Operations." Hence, some of their documents cited in
the notes refer to them by that designation.

[47] Public Law 601, 79th Cong., 2d Sess., Aug. 2, 1946, sec. 102(1)(g)(2)
(B), 60 *Stat.* 816, 2 *U.S.C.* 72a note; *ibid.,* sec. 121(b)(1)(h)(2)(B), 60 *Stat.*
825, 2 *U.S.C.* 72a note.

This interpretation has generally been sustained by the presiding officers of
the two houses.

[48] Senate Expenditures Committee, *Hearings on Evaluation of Legislative
Reorganization Act of 1946,* 80th Cong., 2d Sess., Feb. 18, 1948, p. 121.

[49] For a discussion of the effects that administrative reorganization has on the substantive policies of the agencies involved, see Truman, *The Governmental Process,* pp. 431-32.

[50] For a description of the appropriations committees' supervision of management in the military establishment, see Huzar, *The Purse and the Sword.*

[51] Senate Report No. 5, 81st Cong., 1st Sess., Jan. 17, 1949, pp. 14-16, and Senate Document No. 4, 81st Cong., 1st Sess., Jan. 13, 1949, p. 30.

[52] For numerous other examples of that sort, see Senate Document No. 4, 81st Cong., 1st Sess., Jan. 13, 1949, pp. 11-12, 28-30; Senate Report No. 5, 81st Cong., 1st Sess., Jan. 17, 1949, pp. 4-7, 13-16; Senate Report No. 1, 82d Cong., 1st Sess., Jan. 15, 1951, pp. 46-47, 55; U.S., Congress, Senate, Committee on Government Operations, *Activities, Eighty-Second Congress,* Senate Report No. 5, 83d Cong., 1st Sess., Jan. 9, 1953, pp. 51-53; U.S., Congress, House, Committee on Expenditures in the Executive Departments, *Summary of Activities (82d Cong.),* committee print, 82d Cong., 2d Sess., July 7, 1952, pp. 9-10.

[53] Senate Report No. 1, 82d Cong., 1st Sess., Jan. 15, 1951, pp. 2, 46; U.S., Congress, Senate, Committee on Expenditures in the Executive Departments, *The Organization of Congress: Some Problems of Committee Jurisdiction,* Senate Document No. 51, 82d Cong., 1st Sess., July 10, 1951, pp. 34-39; Senate Report No. 5, 83d Cong., 1st Sess., Jan. 9, 1953, pp. 3-4. This was a curious argument indeed! For the staff of the Permanent Subcommittee on Investigations was itself a specially-authorized one. At the beginning of every session of Congress, the Senate Expenditures Committee had to secure the enactment of a resolution providing funds for the staff of its Permanent Subcommittee on Investigations for that year. Since nearly all such resolutions were acted upon contemporaneously—generally toward the end of January each year—it is difficult to understand how the special staff of any other Senate committee was duplicating that of the Permanent Subcommittee on Investigations or how the one was more temporary than the other. That the Senate Expenditures Committee had had the authorization for the staff of its Investigations Subcommittee renewed every year for several Congresses did not alter the fact that the latter was basically a temporary staff. Moreover, some of the other specially-authorized staffs like that of the Preparedness Subcommittee of the Senate Armed Services Committee, which the Senate Expenditures Committee categorized as temporary and duplicating the staff of its Permanent Subcommittee on Investigations, had achieved comparable continuity through several Congresses.

[54] Senate Document No. 51, 82d Cong., 1st Sess., July 10, 1951, pp. 34, 35-36.

[55] *Ibid.,* pp. 39-46.

[56] *Ibid.,* p. 45.

[57] U.S., Congress, Senate, A Resolution to Investigate Available Fuel Reserves and Formulate a National Fuel Policy of the United States, S. Res. 239, 82d Cong., 1st Sess., Aug. 15, 1950.

[58] For instance, in its activities report for the 82d Congress, the Senate Foreign Relations Committee observed with regard to the MacArthur investigation: "The inquiry had kept two of the more important committees of the Senate in almost continuous session for 2 months. Urgent legislative matters, long postponed, had to be acted upon. . . ." (Senate Document No. 161, 82d Cong., 2d Sess., July 2, 1952, p. 60).

And on this point, Dr. Francis Wilcox, chief of staff of the Senate Foreign Relations Committee, earlier had commented:

"This session is a good example of the point I am trying to make. Some members of our committee are now very much disturbed by the fact that over 5 months have passed and we have not been able to tackle what might be called the strictly legislative program of the committee. The only important exception, I believe, is the wheat-for-India legislation which was approved by the committee last month.

"The committee has been busy with very important matters—the troops-to-Europe issue, for example, and the issues stemming from the recall of General MacArthur. That means that it has not been able to devote itself to a number of significant legislative problems now before us, such as, for example, the foreign-aid programs for 1952" (Senate Expenditures Committee, *Hearings on the Organization and Operation of Congress*, 82d Cong., 1st Sess., June 6, 1951, p. 64).

[59] For examples, see Senate Expenditures Committee, *Hearings on Evaluation of Legislative Reorganization Act of 1946*, 80th Cong., 2d Sess., Feb. 18, 1948, pp. 132, 151; Senate Expenditures Committee, *Hearings on the Organization and Operation of Congress*, 82d Cong., 1st Sess., June, 1951, pp. 102, 406, 637, 639.

[60] For statements to that effect by both their proponents and opponents, see U.S., *Congressional Record*, 82d Cong., 2d Sess., April 28, 1952, XCVIII, Part 4, pp. 4513, 4516, 4522; *ibid.*, 83d Cong., 2d Sess., April 9, 1954, C, Part 4, p. 4956; *ibid.*, April 14, 1954, C, Part 4, pp. 5133-34.

[61] This and the following paragraph borrow heavily from Pendleton Herring, "Executive-Legislative Responsibilities," *American Political Science Review*, XXXVIII (Dec., 1944), 1153-1165; Key, "Legislative Control," *Elements of Public Administration*, pp. 339-362; Macmahon, *Political Science Quarterly*, LVIII (Sept., 1943), 413-414.

Chapter X

[1] Occasionally, in appropriations committee hearings or during the floor debate on an appropriation bill, reference was made to a report or other publication of a legislative committee. For examples, see U.S., Congress, Senate, Committee on Expenditures in the Executive Departments, *Activities, Eighty-First Congress*, Senate Report No. 1, 82d Cong., 1st Sess., Jan. 15, 1951, p. 59; U.S., *Congressional Record*, 82d Cong., 2d Sess., June 28, 1952, XCVIII, Part 7, pp. 8471-72; *ibid.*, July 5, 1952, XCVIII, Part 7, pp. 9504-9505.

[2] When a foreign aid measure like the Economic Cooperation Act of 1948 had been passed, the House Foreign Affairs Committee staff would lend the copies of the *Congressional Record* covering the debate on that act which it had indexed with multicolored marginal tabs to the House Appropriations Committee aides, who used those when the appropriation bill based on that authorization was under consideration on the floor of the House.

[3] U.S., Congress, Senate, *Joint Hearings before Subcommittees of the Committees on Interior and Insular Affairs, Interstate and Foreign Commerce, and Agriculture and Forestry on Weather Control and Augmented Potable Water Supply*, 82d Cong., 1st Sess., March 14, 1951, pp. 1, 10. The three bills were S. 5, S. 222, and S. 798.

4 This joint subcommittee was comprised of the Subcommittee on Public Works in Europe and Africa, House Armed Services Committee, and of the four ranking members of the Subcommittee on Government Operations, House Expenditures Committee. Representative Hardy was chairman of both these constituent groups as well as of the joint subcommittee.

5 U.S., Congress, House, Committee on Armed Services and Committee on Expenditures in the Executive Departments, *French Taxation on Military Construction,* House Report No. 1269, 82d Cong., 2d Sess., Jan. 21, 1952.

6 The troops-to-Europe resolutions were S. Res. 8, S. Res. 99, and S. Con. Res. 18, 82d Congress. S. Res. 8 was referred jointly to the Senate Foreign Relations and Armed Services Committees on Jan. 23, 1951. After holding joint hearings on this issue through Feb., 1951, the two committees together drafted a substitute resolution, which they reported in two forms as S. Res. 99 and as S. Con. Res. 18 on March 14, 1951 (U.S., Congress, Senate, Committee on Foreign Relations, *Legislative History, Eighty-Second Congress,* Senate Document No. 161, 82d Cong., 2d Sess., July 2, 1952, pp. 21-23).

7 Public Law 165, 82d Cong., 1st Sess., Oct. 10, 1951, 65 *Stat.* 373, 22 *U.S.C.* 1651. The bills concerned were S. 1762 and H.R. 5113.

8 In both these cases, however, it should be noted that the Foreign Relations Committee aides did most of the staff work in connection with the joint hearings held. Likewise, the Armed Services Committee staff assumed the main responsibility for organizing the hearings for the inquiry into the circumstances of General MacArthur's dismissal from his commands in the Far East, which also was jointly conducted by the Senate Armed Services and Foreign Relations Committees.

9 For acknowledgment of the assistance received from the Joint Tax Committee staff, see U.S., Congress, Senate, Committee on Foreign Relations, *Urging Advice and Consent to the Ratification of Certain Conventions,* Senate Executive Report No. 1, 82d Cong., 1st Sess., Aug. 6, 1951, p. 3; U.S., *Congressional Record,* 83d Cong., 1st Sess., July 9, 1953, XCIX, Part 6, p. 8300.

Of course, tax conventions did not constitute a sizable fraction of the Foreign Relations Committee's workload. From 1939 to July 9, 1953, our government concluded only twenty-six such conventions. Also, usually the committee allowed them to accumulate and then acted on a number of them at once. For example, in 1951, it handled fourteen tax conventions together and devoted but two days of hearings to them. In 1952, it considered three similar conventions en bloc without additional hearings (*ibid.;* Senate Document No. 161, 82d Cong., 2d Sess., July 2, 1952, pp. 47-49).

10 For instance, during the 81st Congress, the Senate Banking and Currency Committee had 168 bills and resolutions and 28 nominations before it for consideration. It held 145 sessions of hearings and 87 executive sessions for a total of 232 committee meetings. It reported out 51 bills and resolutions, of which 36 were enacted. And it issued 7 special reports (U.S., Congress, Senate, Committee on Banking and Currency, *Report of Activities, Eighty-First Congress,* committee print, 82d Cong., 1st Sess., Jan. 3, 1951, p. 2).

In that same Congress, the Senate Foreign Relations Committee had 150 bills and resolutions referred to it, of which it reported out 47. Thirty-six of those were enacted. Nine which were simple resolutions received the requisite approval by the Senate; and two measures were passed by the Senate but not by the House.   Sixty-seven treaties were pending before the committee, of which 7 were withdrawn at the request of the President and 25 were approved by the Senate.   The committee acted on a total of 1049 nominations, among which were 53 ambassadors, the U.S. High Commissioner to Germany, the U.S. delegations to the General Assembly of the U.N., the ECA Administrator, the Secretary of State, and other high-ranking officers in the Department of State.   The committee held 70 sessions of public hearings and 105 executive sessions for a total of 175 committee meetings.   Also, numerous subcommittees convened frequently both to conduct hearings on various measures and to consult with top executive branch officials.   In addition, there were 5 joint sessions with the House Foreign Affairs Committee and 15 meetings with conferees from that unit.   And the Senate Foreign Relations Committee issued 7 special committee prints and documents (U.S., Congress, Senate, Committee on Foreign Relations, *Legislative History, Eighty-First Congress,* Senate Document No. 247, 81st Cong., 2d Sess., Dec. 22, 1950, pp. 2, 61, 63).

And a comparable state of affairs prevailed on the House side.   These examples were selected primarily because they were major committees in the same chamber and published activity reports containing the information sought on their workloads.

[11] To recognize this condition is not to imply that the committee staffs should be expanded solely to remedy it.   Any decision on the optimum size for a committee staff entails balancing conflicting considerations.   As mentioned previously, there are cogent reasons for keeping the committee staffs small.   Besides, other more fundamental obstacles (like those described in the succeeding sentences above) probably would prevent any big increase in intracameral staff collaboration no matter how greatly the committee staffs were enlarged.

[12] Reciprocally, during the period cited in which the Joint Tax Committee staff worked closely with the Foreign Relations Committee staff on tax conventions, Senator Walter George (D.-Ga.) was chairman both of the Finance Committee (and hence part-time chairman of the Joint Tax Committee) and of the subcommittees on tax conventions of the Foreign Relations Committee. In fact, during the second session of the 82d Congress, Senator George was the one-man Subcommittee on Tax Conventions (Senate Document No. 161, 82d Cong., 2d Sess., July 2, 1952, pp. 48, 69).

[13] See pp. 124-26.

[14] Exclusive of the consultations between the legislative counsel and committee aides from both houses in preparation for conference committee sessions described on pp. 125, 192-93.

[15] For examples, see U.S., *Congressional Record—Daily Digest,* 82d Cong., 2d Sess., March 17, 1952, XCVIII, Part 13, p. D150; *ibid.,* March 19, 1952, XCVIII, Part 13, p. D156.

[16] For an instance of a Senator lauding a House committee staff study, see U.S., *Congressional Record,* 82d Cong., 2d Sess., May 28, 1952, XCVIII, Part 5, p. 6150.

[17] U.S., Congress, Staffs of Senate Committee on Foreign Relations and House Committee on Foreign Affairs, Senate Document No. 111, 80th Cong., 1st Sess., 1947.   Occasionally these and other parallel committees in the two chambers jointly published as a committee print compilations of data prepared by the executive branch.   For example, see U.S., Congress, House Committee on Foreign

Affairs and Senate Committee on Foreign Relations, *The Mutual Security Program for Fiscal Year 1953: Basic Data Supplied by the Executive Branch,* committee print, 82d Cong., 2d Sess., 1952. But Senate Document No. 111 was the only case discovered where the two committee staffs shared the writing and revision of a staff study.

[18] Public Law 601, 79th Cong., 2d Sess., Aug. 2, 1946, sec. 102(1), 60 *Stat.* 818, 2 *U.S.C.* 72a note, and sec. 121(b), 60 *Stat.* 826, 2 *U.S.C.* 72a note. For other examples of such differences, see U.S., Congress, Senate, Committee on Expenditures in the Executive Departments, *The Organization of Congress: Some Problems of Committee Jurisdiction,* Senate Document No. 51, 82d Cong., 1st Sess., July 10, 1951, pp. 5-10.

[19] Senate Expenditures Committee, *Hearings on Evaluation of Legislative Reorganization Act of 1946,* 80th Cong., 2d Sess., Feb., 1948; Senate Report No. 1175, 80th Cong., 2d Sess., April 28, 1948; and S. 2575 (a bill to amend the Legislative Reorganization Act of 1946), 80th Cong., 2d Sess., May 3, 1948.

[20] Among those was the Senate Foreign Relations Committee—according to Dr. Francis Wilcox, its chief of staff. For his comments on that and other obstacles to joint hearings by the foreign affairs committees, see Senate Expenditures Committee, *Hearings on the Organization and Operation of Congress,* 82d Cong., 1st Sess., June 6, 1951, pp. 72-73. Also, see W. Y. Elliott, "Congressional Control Over Foreign Policy Commitments," *International Commitments and National Administration* (Charlottesville, Va.: Bureau of Public Administration, University of Virginia, 1949), p. 18.

[21] The Office of Coordinator of Information for the House of Representatives was set up in May, 1947, pursuant to H. Res. 183, 80th Congress. During the period covered, it was a very small organization, consisting of but nine staff positions. The Coordinator was appointed by the Speaker of the House and was directly responsible to him for the administration of the Office. It was operated largely on a nonpartisan basis, and there was substantial continuity in its staff, most of whom had a journalistic background. For succinct descriptions of its functions by the successive Coordinators, Cecil B. Dickson and Francis M. LeMay, see U.S., Congress, House, Committee on Appropriations, *Hearings before the Subcommittee on the Legislative Branch Appropriation Bill for 1951,* 81st Cong., 2d Sess., March 6, 1950, pp. 64-71, and Senate Expenditures Committee, *Hearings on the Organization and Operation of Congress,* June 7, 1951, pp. 81-86.

In 1967, this office was abolished by the House of Representatives (Public Law 57, 90th Cong., 1st Sess., July 28, 1967, 81 *Stat.* 132).

[22] For example, see Raymond E. Manning, "Financial Capacity of Alaska to Support Statehood," Appendix D, U.S., Congress, Senate, Committee on Interior and Insular Affairs, *Providing for the Admission of Alaska into the Union,* Senate Report No. 315 (to accompany S. 50), 82d Cong., 1st Sess., May 8, 1951, pp. 36-38.

[23] For instance, see U.S., Congress, Senate, Committee on Labor and Public Welfare, *Factors in Successful Collective Bargaining,* committee print, 82d Cong., 1st Sess., 1951, 58 pp. This is an analytical survey of current literature on successful collective bargaining prepared by Dr. Gustav Peck, LRS senior specialist in labor, for the Subcommittee on Labor and Labor-Management Relations, Senate Labor and Public Welfare Committee.

[24] For examples, see U.S., Congress, Senate, Committee on Interior and Insular Affairs, *Basic Data Relating to Energy Resources,* Senate Document No. 8, 82d Cong., 1st Sess., 1951, a 222 page compilation of statistics and textual information on various kinds of fuels and electric power; and U.S., Congress, Joint Committee on the Economic Report and House Select Committee on Small Business, *Constitutional Limitation on Federal Income, Estate, and Gift Tax Rates,* joint committee print, 82d Cong., 2d Sess., 1952, 48 pp.

[25] There was an overlapping in the staffs of the House Select Committee on Foreign Aid and of the House Foreign Affairs Committee. For example, Dr. W. Y. Elliott served concurrently as staff director of both. Hence, the staff of the House Foreign Affairs Committee also was represented at these conferences.

[26] On June 22, 1947, President Truman appointed three committees—popularly known as the Harriman, Krug, and Nourse Committees—to study various aspects of the contemplated European Recovery Program. The Harriman Committee, whose official title was the "President's Committee on Foreign Aid," consisted of 19 financial, business, and farm leaders under the chairmanship of Secretary of Commerce W. A. Harriman. It was charged with determining the character and quantities of U.S. resources available for economic assistance abroad and with advising the President on the limits within which such aid might safely and wisely be extended. The Krug Committee, which was composed of governmental specialists under the direction of Secretary of Interior J. A. Krug, was to study the ability of our national resources to sustain the program. The Nourse Committee, which was comprised of personnel from the Council of Economic Advisers headed by Dr. E. G. Nourse, was to study the impact on our economy of aid to other countries (Senate Document No. 111, 80th Cong., 1st Sess., 1947, pp. 3-4, 138-39, 205-206).

[27] These conversations consisted of a series of conferences between interdepartmental commodity committees that the State Department had established to review the Report of the Committee on European Economic Cooperation and a number of European technicians who had assembled the original CEEC data. They were held for the purpose of clarifying the CEEC report and of securing some supplementary information.

[28] U.S., Congress, House, Committee on Foreign Affairs, *Sixth Session of the General Assembly of the United Nations,* House Report No. 1453, 82d Cong., 2d Sess., Feb. 29, 1952, pp. 10, 13. In 1950 the President adopted the practice of appointing two Senators (not up for re-election) in even years and two Representatives in odd years to serve on U.S. delegations to the U.N. General Assembly (*ibid.,* p. 10).

[29] For an exposition of the conglomerate nature of both the executive and legislative branches and of the crisscrossing relations between them, see Truman, *The Governmental Process,* pp. 394-438.

[30] Blough, *The Federal Taxing Process,* pp. 107-108.

[31] For further corroboration, see Huzar, *The Purse and the Sword,* pp. 100, 102-103, 384.

[32] For identical findings with respect to appropriations for the military, see *ibid.,* pp. 102-103, 384.

[33] For a description of the composition and functioning of staff subcommittees of the Joint Tax Committee, see pp. 105-106.

[34] U.S., Congress, Federal Property and Administrative Services Act of 1949,

Public Law 152, 81st Cong., 1st Sess., June 30, 1949, 63 *Stat.* 377, 5 *U.S.C.* 630. For a brief legislative history of S. 2020, see Senate Report No. 1, 82d Cong., 1st Sess., Jan. 15, 1951, pp. 11-12.

[35] Before turning to a consideration of the relations between committee and agency staffs during executive sessions, the difference between executive hearings and executive sessions should be clarified. Aside from the fact that the public is excluded, an executive hearing is identical with an open hearing. In contrast, an executive session is a closed meeting of a committee in which it reviews a report, marks up a bill, or attends to some other item of business. Loosely, both could be classified as executive sessions, and occasionally the distinction between them becomes blurred. For instance, where departmental personnel are called into an executive session to comment on proposed modifications in a measure and the committee members question them about those at some length, the procedure is analogous to that in a hearing. Conversely, where most of an executive hearing is devoted to the explanation by a committee aide of a bill which he has developed in conjunction with representatives of affected agencies and the latter—who have been invited to testify on the bill— have very little to say except that they approve of it, the proceedings approach those in a regular executive session. However, for the purposes of this study, the term "executive session" is used only in the more restricted sense to designate closed committee meetings other than hearings.

[36] For an acknowledgment of the value of the information, some of "which had heretofore never been publicly revealed," received from members of the fertilizer industry and from the two major associations representing them—the American Plant Food Council and the National Fertilizer Association, see U.S., Congress, House, Committee on Agriculture, *Nitrogen Fertilizer for American Farmers in 1949-50,* committee print, 81st Cong., 1st Sess., June 10, 1949, p. 2.

[37] For an apologetic reference to having had to do that on several occasions in the 82d Congress, see Senate Banking and Currency Committee, *Summary of Activities, Eighty-Second Congress,* committee print, 82d Cong., 2d Sess., July 25, 1952, p. vi.

[38] Nourse, *Economics in the Public Service,* pp. 116, 185.

[39] U.S., Congress, House, Select Committee on Lobbying Activities, *Hearings,* Part 7, 81st Cong., 2d Sess., July 14, 1950, pp. 34, 105; U.S., *Congressional Record,* 81st Cong., 1st Sess., July 11, 1949, XCV, Part 7, p. 9183; *ibid.,* 82d Cong., 1st Sess., July 13, 1951, XCVII, Part 7, p. 8301.

[40] U.S., Congress, Joint Committee on the Economic Report, *Report on the January 1951 Economic Report of the President,* Senate Report No. 210, 82d Cong., 1st Sess., April 2, 1951, p. 117. Also, occasionally the Joint Economic Committee was the original publisher of a study prepared by a private research organization for somebody else. For example, on July 1, 1949, the Joint Economic Committee published as a committee print a study made by the economists of the Committee of the South, National Planning Association, at the request of the Council of Economic Advisers (*ibid., Report on the January 1950 Economic Report of the President,* Senate Report No. 1843, 81st Cong., 2d Sess., June 16, 1950, p. 111). Being a study committee, the Joint Economic Committee engaged in such practices much more than the average legislative committee. However, even the Joint Economic Committee was not involved in very many instances of either sort during the period covered.

41 House Select Committee on Lobbying Activities, *Hearings*, Part 7, 81st Cong., 2d Sess., July 14, 1950, pp. 34, 75, 101.

Chapter XI

1 U.S., Congress, Joint Committee on the Organization of Congress, *Report*, Senate Report No. 1011, 79th Cong., 2d Sess., March 4, 1946, p. 15.

2 Senate Expenditures Committee, *Hearings on Evaluation of Legislative Reorganization Act of 1946*, 80th Cong., 2d Sess., Feb. 17, 1948, p. 66.

3 Public Law 663, 79th Cong., 2d Sess., Aug. 8, 1946, 60 *Stat.* 911, 2 *U.S.C.* 60a note. The Second Supplemental Appropriation Act, 1950, raised the ceiling on the basic salary rate for administrative assistants to $8,400 (Public Law 430, 81st Cong., 1st Sess., Oct. 28, 1949, 63 *Stat.* 973, 5 *U.S.C.* 932a).

4 In other words, this nomenclature refers to individuals in terms of what they really did rather than of the nominal positions they held. Under this system, administrative assistants who were primarily occupied with legislative duties are included in the category of "legislative assistants" in the general descriptive portions of this chapter. However, since "administrative assistant" was their actual title, they perforce are called "administrative assistant" in any illustrative cases where reference is made specifically to them. And in the conclusion, "administrative assistant" is used in accord with ordinary practice to refer to all persons bearing that title, irrespective of the duties they performed.

5 This group consists mostly of the first- and/or second-ranking members of the office staffs covered. For a list of their names, see pp. 271-72.

6 Exclusive of wartime uniformed service in the armed forces.

7 Subsequently, the Legislative Appropriation Act, 1954, did increase the allowance for clerk hire as follows. Three additional assistant clerks at a basic salary of not to exceed $2,700 a year were authorized for each Senator from states with a population of five million or more; two, for each Senator from states with a population of three to five million; and one, for each Senator from states with a population of less than three million (U.S., Congress, Public Law 178, 83d Cong., 1st Sess., Aug. 1, 1953, 67 *Stat.* 318, 2 *U.S.C.* 60a note).

8 U.S., *Congressional Record*, 83d Cong., 1st Sess., July 29, 1953, XCIX, Part 8, pp. 10285-86.

9 Significantly, during the debate on the Legislative Branch Appropriation Bill, 1954, several Senators from small and medium-sized states protested the provision of extra employees for any but the Senators from the large states as being unnecessary (*ibid.*, pp. 10285-87).

10 And it ought to be their duty. Far from being a pathological development, the mediation of Congressmen between the executive branch and their constituents is intrinsic to our system of government and serves very worthy purposes. For excellent justifications for doing casework, see U.S., Congress, Joint Committee on the Organization of Congress, *Report*, Senate Report No. 1011, 79th Cong., 2d Sess., March 4, 1946, pp. 15-16; U.S., Congress, Senate, Committee on Labor and Public Welfare, *Hearings before a Subcommittee on the Establishment of a Commission on Ethics in Government*, 82d Cong., 1st Sess., June, 1951, p. 560; Key, "Legislative Control," *Elements of Public Administration*, p. 354.

[11] For examples, see U.S., *Congressional Record—Daily Digest,* 82d Cong., 2d Sess., May 13, 1952, XCVIII, Part 13, p. D304; *ibid.,* May 26, 1952, p. D341; *ibid.,* May 28, 1952, p. D350; *ibid.,* June 6, 1952, p. D380.

[12] For senatorial criticisms of the presence of too many office employees on the Senate floor, see Senate Appropriations Committee, *Hearings before a Subcommittee on the Legislative Branch Appropriation Bill for 1952,* 82d Cong., 1st Sess., July 12, 1951, p. 77; U.S., *Congressional Record,* 82d Cong., 2d Sess., March 26, 1952, XCVIII, Part 3, p. 2878.

[13] U.S., *Congressional Record,* 82d Cong., 2d Sess., June 30, 1952, XCVIII, Part 7, p. 8557.

[14] *Ibid.,* July 5, 1952, XCVIII, Part 7, p. 9518.

[15] Throughout most of the 82d Congress, Senator Morse was a Republican. After his celebrated shift to an independent status in Oct., 1952, one of the administrative assistants quipped that these staff caucuses were bipartisan when no Republican senatorial assistants were present.

[16] Concurrently during the 82d Congress, the Senators constituting the liberal bloc held caucuses. This development was very similar to its staff counterpart. To some extent the purpose of a conference determined its composition. Around a nucleus of liberal Northern Democratic Senators were aggregated variable combinations of their Democratic and Republican colleagues who supported them on particular issues. Although their views on civil rights were markedly discrepant, Southern Democratic Senators Lister Hill (Ala.), Mike Monroney (Okla.), and John Sparkman (Ala.) caucused together with them on defense, foreign affairs, natural resources, and revenue legislation. Republican Senators Wayne Morse (Ore.) and Irving Ives (N.Y.) often participated in these conferences.

For example, on Dec. 30, 1952, a bipartisan group of Senators met in the office of Senator Herbert Lehman (D.-N.Y.) to plan the campaign for modifying the cloture rule at the outset of the 83d Congress. Senators Morse, Ives, and James Duff (R.-Pa.) attended. Democratic Senators present were: Clinton Anderson (N.Mex.), Paul Douglas (Ill.), Theodore Green (R.I.), Hubert Humphrey (Minn.), Lester Hunt (Wyo.), Harley Kilgore (W.Va.), Herbert Lehman (N.Y.), and Mike Mansfield (Mont.). In addition, Senators H. Alexander Smith (R.-N.J.) and Warren Magnuson (D.-Wash.) were represented by their administrative assistants (*The Washington Post,* Dec. 31, 1952, p. 1).

Although part of these conferences were restricted to Senators, their aides sometimes accompanied them and usually were allowed to attend as their stand-ins. Generally on such occasions the senatorial assistants remained pretty much in the background, serving solely as observers. However, a few of the better-known staff members participated in the discussions. From the beginning, several senatorial aides played an instrumental role in promoting these caucuses. At every opportunity they urged their Senators to meet together. And they did most of the work in organizing the conferences that were held.

During the 82d Congress, these senatorial caucuses, like their staff analogues, were convoked irregularly. But plans were made to hold them every week while the 83d Congress was in session. (The author was present at the staff conference which made the plans for holding both these senatorial and the liberal staff caucuses weekly in the 83d Congress, Jan. 9, 1953.)

[17] U.S., *Congressional Record—Daily Digest,* 83d Cong., 1st Sess., June 8, 1953, XCIX, Part 14, p. D372.

[18] Sec. 202(c) of the Legislative Reorganization Act stipulates: "The clerical staff shall handle committee correspondence and stenographic work, both for the committee staff and for the chairman and ranking minority member on matters related to committee work" (Public Law 601, 79th Cong., 2d Sess., Aug. 2, 1946, 60 *Stat.* 835, 2 *U.S.C.* 72a).

In addition, the professional aides prepared speeches, magazine articles, and other publications on subjects within the purview of a committee for the chairman.

[19] Public Law 601, 79th Cong., 2d Sess., Aug. 2, 1946, sec. 202(a), 60 *Stat.* 834, 2 *U.S.C.* 72a(a).

[20] Among these nonusers were aides to three of the nine members of the Democratic Policy Committee in the 82d Congress.

[21] Significantly, in the spring of 1952, the Republican Policy Committee staff attached the following disclaimer to its bulletins:
"NOTE: The materials presented here have been prepared by the staff of the Minority Policy Committee, except for quoted matter and official citations. Neither the Members of the Minority Policy Committee, nor other Senators or Members of Congress, are responsible for the material and views herein contained, except such as they are willing to endorse and make their own" (Senate Minority Policy Committee staff, "Republican Position on Reorganization Plan No. 1 of 1952, Reorganization of the Bureau of Internal Revenue," *Senate Minority Memo,* I, No. 10 [April 24, 1952], 1.   [Mimeographed.]).

[22] The *Digest of Public General Bills* has been prepared by the LRS regularly since the second session of the 74th Congress.   It consists of brief summaries of public bills and resolutions, with the reported measures receiving somewhat fuller treatment than the others.   Each printed issue contains a section showing the status of all bills upon which action has been taken.   All the issues for each session of Congress are cumulative.

[23] See p. 154.

[24] As of the July 1949 reorganization of the LRS, there were the following seven sections besides American Law: Senior Specialists, History and General Research, Foreign Affairs, Economics, Government, Library Services, and the Congressional Reading Room ("Manual of the Legislative Reference Service" [Library of Congress, June, 1950], pp. 19, 39.   [Mimeographed.]).

[25] For a description by Mr. McFall of the origin and scope of this experiment in improving relations with the senatorial office staffs, see U.S., Congress, House, Select Committee on Lobbying Activities, *Hearings,* Part 10, 81st Cong., 2d Sess., Aug., 1950, p. 453.

[26] For a discussion of these two types of information and the role of interest groups in supplying legislators with them, see Truman, *The Governmental Process,* pp. 332-35.

[27] Among the critics of this practice was Senator Mike Monroney (D.-Okla.), coauthor of the Legislative Reorganization Act of 1946 (interview on Jan. 10, 1953).

[28] For a number of interpretive comments to that effect in the debate on the First Supplemental Appropriation Bill, 1947, see U.S., *Congressional Record,* 79th Cong., 2d Sess., Aug. 1, 1946, XCII, Part 8, pp. 10597-98.

[29] See p. 167.

[30] During most of the period covered, each Representative had an office staff allowance of $12,500 a year for basic salaries, which would afford around $22,000 a year in gross salaries—depending on the number of employees and their salary levels. For the formulas for converting basic to gross salaries were mildly progressive. Each Representative could appoint from one to six clerks with the only restriction being that no clerk might be paid more than a $5,000 basic annual salary, which was an $8,492.02 gross annual salary in the 82d Congress.

In 1954 the basic clerk hire allowance was increased to $15,000 a year, and the ceiling on the top clerk's basic salary was raised to $6.000 a year. In 1955 the basic annual allowance was increased to $17,500, which would yield around $32,000 a year in gross salaries; each member was authorized to hire up to eight clerks; and the maximum basic annual salary allowed for any one clerk was raised to $7,000, which was a $12,131.47 gross annual salary (from information supplied by the Disbursing Office, U.S., House of Representatives).

Chapter XII

[1] Frederic P. Lee, "The Office of the Legislative Counsel," *Columbia Law Review,* XXIX (April, 1929), 381. The other two original trustees were John Bassett Moore, Hamilton Fish Professor of International Law and Diplomacy, and Harlan Fiske Stone, Dean of the Law School of Columbia University. The research activities of the Fund were directed by a staff headed by Middleton Beaman, Thomas I. Parkinson, and Professor Chamberlain (*ibid.,* p. 381, n. 2). Instituting the Legislative Drafting Research Fund was only one of many signal contributions to improving the governmental process, made by Professor Chamberlain in a lifetime dedicated to public service.

[2] *Ibid.,* pp. 385-86.

[3] *Ibid.,* p. 387; Public Law 254, 65th Cong., 1st Sess., Feb. 24, 1919, 40 *Stat.* 1141, 2 *U.S.C.* 274.

[4] Public Law 176, 68th Cong., 1st Sess., June 2, 1924, sec. 1101, 43 *Stat.* 353, 2 *U.S.C.* 271.

[5] Public Law 250, 77th Cong., 1st Sess., Sept. 20, 1941, sec. 602, 55 *Stat.* 726, 2 *U.S.C.* 272, 273, 274.

[6] Lee, *Columbia Law Review,* XXIX (April, 1929), 386.

[7] *Ibid.,* p. 387.

[8] Hereafter, to avoid the constant repetition and sometimes cumbersome use of the term "branch," the word "office" in uncapitalized form is employed to refer to the Senate or House branch of the Office considered separately. When capitalized, the term "Office" continues to be used to refer only to the two branches of the Office taken together.

[9] Joint Committee on the Organization of Congress, *Hearings,* 79th Cong., 1st Sess., April 30, 1945, pp. 423-25; *ibid.,* May 4, 1945, p. 465; Senate Expenditures Committee, *Hearings on the Organization and Operation of Congress,* 82d Cong., 1st Sess., June 7, 1951, pp. 77, 117.

[10] The names of the Senate Legislative Counsel and their respective terms of office are as follows: Thomas I. Parkinson, 1919-20; John E. Walker, 1921-22; Frederic P. Lee, 1922-30; Charles F. Boots, 1930-36; Henry G. Wood, 1936-43; Charles F. Boots, 1943-45; Stephen E. Rice, 1945-50; John H. Simms, 1950- . Mr. Boots left the office in 1936 to enter private practice. During World War II, he came back to head the office temporarily while Mr. Rice and Mr. Simms were

away in the armed forces. Upon their return, he voluntarily reverted to the status of assistant counsel, in which capacity he has continued to serve.

11 Joint Committee on the Organization of Congress, *Hearings,* 79th Cong., 1st Sess., April 30, 1945, p. 414; *ibid.,* May 4, 1945, p. 466; Senate Expenditures Committee, *Hearings on the Organization and Operation of Congress,* 82d Cong., 1st Sess., June 7, 1951, p. 75.

12 U.S., Congress, House, Committee on Appropriations, *Hearings before the Subcommittee on the Legislative Branch Appropriation Bill for 1950,* 81st Cong., 1st Sess., May 26, 1949, p. 298; U.S., Congress, House, Committee on Appropriations, *Hearings before the Subcommittee on the Legislative Branch Appropriation Bill for 1951,* 81st Cong., 2d Sess., March 6, 1950, p. 73; Senate Expenditures Committee, *Hearings on the Organization and Operation of Congress,* 82d Cong., 1st Sess., June 7, 1951, pp. 78, 113, 115-116.

13 Senate Expenditures Committee, *Hearings on the Organization and Operation of Congress,* 82d Cong., 1st Sess., June 7, 1951, pp. 79-80.

14 Joint Committee on the Organization of Congress, *Hearings,* 79th Cong., 1st Sess., April 30, 1945, p. 414.

15 Senate Expenditures Committee, *Hearings on the Organization and Operation of Congress,* 82d Cong., 1st Sess., June 7, 1951, p. 81.

16 House Committee on Appropriations, *Hearings before the Subcommittee on the Legislative Branch Appropriation Bill for 1950,* 81st Cong., 1st Sess., May 26, 1949, p. 298; House Committee on Appropriations, *Hearings before the Subcommittee on the Legislative Branch Appropriation Bill for 1951,* 81st Cong., 2d Sess., March 6, 1950, p. 74; Senate Expenditures Committee, *Hearings on the Organization and Operation of Congress,* 82d Cong., 1st Sess., June 7, 1951, pp. 78, 117.

17 Joint Committee on the Organization of Congress, *Hearings,* 79th Cong., 1st Sess., April 30, 1945, pp. 423-24; Senate Expenditures Committee, *Hearings on the Organization and Operation of Congress,* 82d Cong., 1st Sess., June 7, 1951, p. 77.

18 Joint Committee on the Organization of Congress, *Hearings,* 79th Cong., 1st Sess., April 30, 1945, pp. 423-24, 429; *ibid.,* May 4, 1945, p. 465; Senate Expenditures Committee, *Hearings on the Organization and Operation of Congress,* 82d Cong., 1st Sess., June 7, 1951, pp. 78-79, 113-114.

19 Joint Committee on the Organization of Congress, *Hearings,* 79th Cong., 1st Sess., April 30, 1945, p. 429; Senate Expenditures Committee, *Hearings on the Organization and Operation of Congress,* 82d Cong., 1st Sess., June 7, 1951, pp. 77, 80-81, 113-115.

20 Joint Committee on the Organization of Congress, *Hearings,* 79th Cong., 1st Sess., April 30, 1945, p. 416; Senate Expenditures Committee, *Hearings on the Organization and Operation of Congress,* 82d Cong., 1st Sess., June 7, 1951, p. 79.

21 House Committee on Appropriations, *Hearings before the Subcommittee on the Legislative Branch Appropriation Bill for 1951,* 81st Cong., 2d Sess., March 6, 1950, p. 76.

22 Senate Expenditures Committee, *Hearings on the Organization and Operation of Congress,* 82d Cong., 1st Sess., June 7, 1951, p. 116.

23 Hereafter when work for committees is discussed, the designation "legislative counsel" is used in a generic sense to include the assistant counsel to

avoid confusing the latter with the counsel and assistant counsel of various committees.

[24] Joint Committee on the Organization of Congress, *Hearings,* April 30, 1945, pp. 416, 418-19, 426.

[25] *Ibid.,* pp. 418-19.

[26] Joint Committee on the Organization of Congress, *Hearings,* 79th Cong., 1st Sess., April 30, 1945, p. 428.

[27] *Ibid.,* pp. 415-17.

[28] However, there was no uniform practice with regard to the services requested of the legislative counsel during executive sessions. They might be called in at any stage of the committee's deliberations and to work on but a portion of a bill. Where they were not brought in until late in the proceedings, they often were not able to do much more than the clerical job of keeping track of the committee's action and of inserting the language on which it had agreed at the proper places in the bill. And sometimes the legislative counsel were asked to draft amendments adopted at executive sessions they had not attended.

[29] U.S., Congress, House, Rule XIII, par. 2a.

[30] U.S., Senate, Rule XXIX, subsection (4).

[31] For a more complete description of the composition and preparation of committee reports to accompany bills, see pp. 119-23.

[32] For a statement to that effect by the House Legislative Counsel, see House Committee on Appropriations, *Hearings before the Subcommittee on the Legislative Branch Appropriation Bill for 1950,* 81st Cong., 1st Sess., May 26, 1949, p. 297.

[33] Lee, *Columbia Law Review,* XXIX (April, 1929), 394-95.

[34] Senate Expenditures Committee, *Hearings on the Organization and Operation of Congress,* 82d Cong., 1st Sess., June 7, 1951, p. 77.

[35] Joint Committee on the Organization of Congress, *Hearings,* 79th Cong., 1st Sess., April 30, 1945, p. 417.

[36] Term applied to the practice by Mr. Beaman, the first House Legislative Counsel (*ibid.,* p. 416).

[37] *Ibid.*

[38] The information on which these two statements are based was obtained from employees of the Office of the House Coordinator of Information, some of whom had been with that agency since its inception in 1947.

[39] For a rather picturesque description of this process in connection with the Securities Act of 1933, see Joint Committee on the Organization of Congress, *Hearings,* 79th Cong., 1st Sess., April 30, 1945, p. 422.

[40] *Ibid.,* pp. 425-26.

[41] Public Law 601, 79th Cong., 2d Sess., Aug. 2, 1946, sec. 204, 60 *Stat.* 837, 2 *U.S.C.* 271 note.

[42] Joint Committee on the Organization of Congress, *Hearings,* 79th Cong., 1st Sess., April 30, 1945, p. 415; House Committee on Appropriations, *Hearings before the Subcommittee on the Legislative Branch Appropriation Bill for 1951,* 81st Cong., 2d Sess., March 6, 1950, p. 72.

[43] U.S., Congress, House, Committee on Appropriations, *Hearings before the Subcommittee on the Legislative Branch Appropriation Bill for 1948,* 80th Cong., 1st Sess., June 6, 1947, p. 469; U.S., Congress, Legislative Branch Appro-

priation Act, 1948, Public Law 197, 80th Cong., 1st Sess., July 17, 1947, 61 *Stat.* 361, 2 *U.S.C.* 60a note; House Committee on Appropriations, *Hearings before the Subcommittee on the Legislative Branch Appropriation Bill for 1950,* 81st Cong., 1st Sess., May 26, 1949, p. 293; U.S., Congress, Legislative Branch Appropriation Act, 1950, Public Law 118, 81st Cong., 1st Sess., June 22, 1949, 63 *Stat.* 216, 2 *U.S.C.* 60a note; House Committee on Appropriations, *Hearings before the Subcommittee on the Legislative Branch Appropriation Bill for 1951,* 81st Cong., 2d Sess., March 6, 1950, pp. 71-72; U.S., Congress, Legislative Branch Appropriation Act, 1951, Public Law 759, 81st Cong., 2d Sess., Sept. 6, 1950, 64 *Stat.* 595, 2 *U.S.C.* 60a note.

Chapter XIII

[1] See pp. 14-15.

Chapter XIV

[1] For a description of the origin of that post, see pp. 61-63.

[2] For examples, see U.S., Congress, Joint Economic Committee, *Report on the January 1955 Economic Report of the President,* Senate Report No. 60, 84th Cong., 1st Sess., March 14, 1955, p. 75; *ibid., Report on the January 1956 Economic Report of the President,* Senate Report No. 1606, 84th Cong., 2d Sess., March 1, 1956, pp. 46, 76; *ibid., Report on the January 1957 Economic Report of the President,* House Report No. 175, 85th Cong., 1st Sess., Feb. 28, 1957, p. 32.

[3] *Ibid., Report on the January 1960 Economic Report of the President,* Senate Report No. 1452, 86th Cong., 2d Sess., Feb. 29, 1960, p. 53. Two months after this chapter was written, Senator Bush asked to appoint a minority staff member for the Joint Economic Committee, and his request was granted. According to Chairman Wright Patman, "Senator Bush's request was not, however, based on any plea that the minority members were not receiving services from the existing staff—indeed they were—but on the plea that the minority members now wish to have someone known and designated as minority counsel" (*The Washington Post,* March 12, 1962, p. A-16).

[4] See p. 238, ch. v, n. 3.

[5] U.S., *Congressional Record,* 83d Cong., 2d Sess., Feb. 2, 1954, C, Part 1, p. 1101.

[6] *Ibid.,* pp. 1100-1101.

[7] U.S., *Congressional Record,* 85th Cong., 1st Sess., Jan. 30, 1957, CIII, Part 1, pp. 1265, 1275-76.

[8] *Ibid.,* p. 1290.

[9] *Ibid.,* pp. 1266, 1274-75, 1278, 1282-84, 1286-87, 1290, 1297.

[10] *Ibid.,* p. 1278.

[11] *Ibid.,* pp. 1286-87.

[12] "Republicans Default: Small Staffs Limit Action," *The Washington Post,* Feb. 18, 1961, p. A-9. Quoted material copyrighted 1961 by and used with permission of the New York Herald Tribune, Inc.

[13] U.S., *Congressional Record,* 87th Cong., 1st Sess., Feb. 28, 1961, CVII (daily ed.), p. 2760.

[14] *Ibid.,* pp. 2669-76.

[15] *Ibid.,* March 1, 1961, CVII (daily ed.), p. 2760.

[16] *Ibid.,* June 1, 1961, CVII (daily ed.), p. 8734.

[17] For example, see *ibid.,* Feb. 28, 1961, CVII (daily ed.), p. 2676.

[18] *Ibid.,* 83d Cong., 2d Sess., Feb. 2, 1954, C, Part 1, p. 1101.

[19] *Ibid.,* 85th Cong., 1st Sess., Jan. 30, 1957, CIII, Part 1, p. 1266.

[20] For his account of this episode, see Bernard Schwartz, *The Professor and the Commissions* (New York: A. A. Knopf, 1959).

[21] Jerry Kluttz, "'Hill' Aides Air Pay Raise Battle," *The Washington Post,* Aug. 5, 1960, p. C-1.

[22] Public Law 601, 79th Cong., 2d Sess., Aug. 2, 1946, 60 *Stat.* 834, 2 *U.S.C.* 72a(a).

[23] U.S., Congress, House, Committee on Appropriations, *Hearings before the Subcommittee on the Legislative Branch Appropriations for 1962,* 87th Cong., 1st Sess., May 3, 1961, p. 245.

[24] Since the Senate Committee on Appropriations did not publish a comparable list of standing committee employees, these figures were derived from the quarterly reports, *Official List of Senate Officers and Employees,* issued by the Secretary of the Senate pursuant to S. Res. 139, 86th Cong.

[25] U.S., Congress, House, Committee on Appropriations, *Hearings before the Subcommittee on the Legislative Branch Appropriations for 1962,* 87th Cong., 1st Sess., May 3, 1961, pp. 258-59; U.S., *Congressional Record,* 87th Cong., 1st Sess., Jan. 31, 1961, CVII (daily ed.), p. 1464.

[26] *Ibid.,* p. 1463.

[27] *Ibid.*

[28] U.S., Congress, Federal Employees Salary Increase Act of 1958, Public Law 462, 85th Cong., 2d Sess., June 20, 1958, 72 *Stat.* 208-209, 2 *U.S.C.* 72a(e), 72a-1a.

[29] U.S., Congress, Senate, Committee on Foreign Relations, *Legislative History, Eighty-Fifth Congress,* Senate Document No. 128, 85th Cong., 2d Sess., July 28, 1958, pp. 101-102; *ibid., Legislative History, Eighty-Sixth Congress,* Senate Document No. 131, 86th Cong., 2d Sess., Aug. 31, 1960, pp. 95-97.

[30] *Ibid.,* p. 95.

[31] Derived from data in letters of transmittal for these studies published in U.S., Congress, Senate, Special Committee to Study the Foreign Aid Program, *Compilation of Studies and Surveys,* Senate Document No. 52, 85th Cong., 1st Sess., July, 1957.

[32] For examples, see U.S., Congress, Senate, Committee on Foreign Relations, *Hearings on United States Foreign Policy,* 87th Cong., 1st Sess., Jan. 27, 1961, Part 2, p. 354.

[33] *Ibid., Hearings on United States Foreign Policy,* 86th Cong., 1st Sess., Jan. 21, 1959, p. 55.

[34] *Ibid., Hearings on United States Foreign Policy,* 87th Cong., 1st Sess., Jan. 27, 1961, Part 2, p. 334.

[35] See pp. 113-15.

[36] U.S., Congress, Joint Economic Committee, *Hearings before the Subcommittee on Agricultural Policy,* 85th Cong., 1st Sess., Dec. 16, 1957, p. 26.

[37] *Ibid., Hearings on Comparisons of the United States and Soviet Economies,* 86th Cong., 1st Sess., Nov. 20, 1959, p. 223.

[38] See p. 114.

[39] U.S., Congress, Joint Economic Committee, *Report on the January 1959 Economic Report of the President,* Senate Report No. 98, 86th Cong., 1st Sess., March 9, 1959, p. 18; *ibid., Hearings on Relationship of Prices to Economic Stability and Growth,* 85th Cong., 2d Sess., Dec. 15, 1958, p. 429.

[40] U.S., Comptroller General, *Annual Report for Fiscal Year 1951* (Washington: U.S. Government Printing Office, 1951), pp. iv-v, 3-4, 22-24; *ibid., Annual Report for Fiscal Year 1952 (ibid.,* 1952), pp. iii-iv, 3; *ibid., Annual Report for Fiscal Year 1953 (ibid.,* 1953), pp. iii, 1-2, 5-6, 93; *ibid., Annual Report for Fiscal Year 1954 (ibid.,* 1954), pp. v-vi, 2-5, 7.

[41] *Ibid., Annual Report for Fiscal Year 1956 (ibid.,* 1956), pp. 1-6; *ibid., Annual Report for Fiscal Year 1957 (ibid.,* 1957), pp. 1-4, 9.

[42] *Ibid., Annual Report for Fiscal Year 1961 (ibid.,* 1961), pp. 2-4, 18, 35-38.

[43] For examples, see U.S., Congress, House, Committee on Armed Services, *Hearings of Special Subcommittee on Development and Procurement of New Combat and Tactical Vehicles by the Department of the Army,* 86th Cong., 2d Sess., June 2 to Sept 27, 1960; *ibid.,* Special Subcommittee on Procurement Practices of the Department of Defense, *Report Pursuant to Section 4, Public Law 86-89,* House Report No. 1959, 86th Cong., 2d Sess., June 23, 1960; U.S., *Congressional Record,* 87th Cong., 1st Sess., March 22, 1961, CVII (daily ed.), pp. 4284-86; *ibid.,* June 28, 1961, CVII (daily ed.), pp. 10741-42; *ibid.,* July 7, 1961, CVII (daily ed.), p. A5034; *ibid.,* July 14, 1961, CVII (daily ed.), p. 11708.

[44] See p. 174.

[45] U.S., Congress, Senate, Committee on Rules and Administration, "Regulations Controlling the Admission of Employees of Senators and Senate Committees to the Senate Floor," 84th Cong., 2d Sess., Jan. 25, 1956, pp. 1-3. (Mimeographed.) Although occasioned primarily by the activities of office staff members, this regulation applies to committee aides also. Each committee may have four staff members on the Senate floor at once.

[46] Letter from J. Mark Trice, Secretary for the Minority, "Re: Use of Republican Cloakroom," Aug. 11, 1961.

[47] U.S., Congress, Supplemental Appropriation Act, 1960, Public Law 213, 86th Cong., 1st Sess., Sept. 1, 1959, 73 *Stat.* 443-44, 2 *U.S.C.* 60f; *ibid.,* Legislative Branch Appropriation Act, 1962, Public Law 130, 87th Cong., 1st Sess., Aug. 10, 1961, 75 *Stat.* 323, 2 *U.S.C.* 60f.

[48] U.S., Congress, House, Committee on Appropriations, *Hearings before the Subcommittee on Legislative Branch Appropriations for 1962,* 87th Cong., 1st Sess., May 3, 1961, p. 249.

[49] Information supplied by Disbursing Office, U.S., House of Representatives.

[50] Public Law 75, 85th Cong., 1st Sess., July 1, 1957, 71 *Stat.* 250-51.

[51] U.S., Congress, House, Committee on Appropriations, *Legislative Branch Appropriation Bill, 1959,* House Report No. 1940 (to accompany H.R. 13066), 85th Cong., 2d Sess., June 20, 1958, p. 4.

[52] U.S., Congress, Legislative Branch Appropriation Act, 1961, Public Law 628, 86th Cong., 2d Sess., July 12, 1960, 74 *Stat.* 447, 451.

[53] On Jan. 31, 1962, Allan H. Perley, the House Legislative Counsel, retired after thirty-seven years service in the Office. His successor, Edward O. Craft, has been with the Office since Dec. 5, 1941.

APPENDIX A

COMMITTEE STAFFS COVERED

Senate Committees	Persons Interviewed
Agriculture and Forestry	Kendall, James
	Stanton, Harker
Armed Services	Mudge, Verne
	Reedy, George[1]
Banking and Currency	L'Heureux, Robert
	McMurray, Joseph
Expenditures in the Executive Departments	Flanagan, Francis[1]
	Loeffler, Herman
	Nobleman, Eli
	Reynolds, Walter
	Scull, Miles
	Shriver, Glenn
Foreign Relations	Marcy, Carl
	Wilcox, Francis
Interior and Insular Affairs	Astin, Mills
	French, Stewart
	Grorud, Albert
	Mathew, Marie
	McSherry, Nellie
	Sandusky, Arthur
Interstate and Foreign Commerce	Butz, John[1]
	Davis, Halford
	Jelsma, Edward
	Keenan, Francis
	Sweeney, Edward
Labor and Public Welfare	Barbash, Jack[1]
	Reidy, William
	Rodgers, Ray
	Shroyer, Thomas

---

[1] Members of specially-authorized staffs.

House Committees	Persons Interviewed
Agriculture	Clark, Altavene Downey, Mabel Heimburger, John
Armed Services	Blandford, John Courtney, John[1] Smart, Robert
Banking and Currency	Fink, Orman Hallahan, William
Education and Labor	Derrickson, Russell Forsythe, John Graham, John
Foreign Affairs	Crawford, Boyd Westphal, Albert
Interior and Insular Affairs	Carr, James Hackett, William Peden, Preston Ragan, Claude
Interstate and Foreign Commerce	Stockburger, Arlin
Ways and Means	Irwin, Leo
Small Business (Select)	Curtis, Jean
Joint Committees	
On the Economic Report	Ensley, Grover Lehman, John Moore, William
On Internal Revenue Taxation	Brannon, Gerard Longinotti, David Oakes, E. E.[2] Stam, Colin Train, Russell Woodworth, L. N.

[1] Members of specially-authorized staffs.

[2] When interviewed, Dr. Oakes was a former staff member who was then with the Export-Import Bank.

APPENDIX B

SENATORIAL AIDES INTERVIEWED

Senators' Offices	Persons Interviewed
Bridges, Styles (R.-N.H.)	McLeod, Scott
Dirksen, Everett (R.-Ill.)	Haller, Mabel
Douglas, Paul (D.-Ill.)	McCulloch, Frank Stern, Philip Wallace, Robert
Ellender, Allen (D.-La.)	Wurzlow, Frank
Flanders, Ralph (R.-Vt.)	Calhoun, John Eldridge, Douglas Laffin, Harry
Fulbright, J. W. (D.-Ark.)	Erickson, John Yingling, John Young, Nina
George, Walter (D.-Ga.)	George, Heard McDaniel, Thad
Humphrey, Hubert (D.-Minn.)	Kampelman, Max Simms, William
Ives, Irving (R.-N.Y.)	Shugrue, Dwyer
Johnson, Lyndon (D.-Tex.)	Woodward, Warren
Kefauver, Estes (D.-Tenn.)	Brizzi, Francis
Kerr, Robert (D.-Okla.)	Dwight, Ben McBride, Don Trask, Ralph
Lehman, Herbert (D.-N.Y.)	Brunkard, Thomas Karson, Stanley Williams, Frances

Senators' Offices	Persons Interviewed
McCarran, Pat (D.-Nev.)	McDonnell, Joseph
McClellan, John (D.-Ark.)	Matthews, Ralph Pope, Walter
McFarland, Ernest (D.-Ariz.)	Irving, Hoyt
Magnuson, Warren (D.-Wash.)	Hoff, Irvin
Malone, George (R.-Nev.)	Huffman, Hazel
Millikin, Eugene (R.-Colo.)	McRae, Dorothy
Monroney, Mike (D.-Okla.)	Yocum, Jack
Morse, Wayne (R.-Oreg.)	Adams, Harold
Murray, James (D.-Mont.)	Murray, Charles
Nixon, Richard (R.-Calif.)	Arnold, William
O'Mahoney, Joseph (D.-Wyo.)	Flannery, Leon
Russell, Richard (D.-Ga.)	Brice, Henry
Saltonstall, Leverett (R.-Mass.)	Fisher, John Minot, Henry
Smith, H. Alexander (R.-N.J.)	Guterl, C. J. Prentice, Colgate Wherry, Elizabeth
Smith, Margaret Chase (R.-Maine)	Lewis, William
Sparkman, John (D.-Ala.)	Hyde, Edd
Taft, Robert (R.-Ohio)	Lawrence, Louis Williams, James
Wiley, Alexander (R.-Wis.)	Cahn, Julius
Williams, John (R.-Del.)	Bing, Arden Williams, George

APPENDIX C[1]

INTERVIEWS WITH LEGISLATIVE COUNSEL

From the Office of the Senate Legislative Counsel

Boots, Charles F.
Pinion, Dwight J.
Simms, John H.

From the Office of the House Legislative Counsel

Cardon, Robert L.
Hussey, Ward M.
Perley, Allan H.

---

[1] The above appendixes list only the interviews with persons from the three main components of the staff covered. Over sixty additional interviews were held with personnel from other elements of the congressional staff and with members of Congress.

INDEX

Administrative assistants: 8, 167, 260n4; nature of work, 171-73, 180, 252n43; political activities, 172, 179-80, 207-208; ability to relieve Senators, 179-80, 207; proposed for Representatives, 180, 208, 228. *See also* Legislative assistants; Senatorial office staffs

Aeronautical and Space Sciences, Senate Committee on, 21, 24

Agency staffs. *See* Executive branch

Agriculture, House Committee on, 20, 43, 60, 64, 93, 98, 107, 213, 214

Agriculture and Forestry, Senate Committee on, 20, 42, 52, 54, 59, 64, 87, 97-98, 128, 148

Aiken, George, 239n5

Air Force, U.S., 130, 142

American Bar Association, 76

American Law Section. *See* Legislative Reference Service

American Plant Food Council, 259n36

American Railroads, Association of, 117

American Republics Affairs, Subcommittee on, 222

Anderson, Clinton, 261n16

Appropriations, House Committee on: 19, 20; staff, 3, 6, 8, 56, 64, 147, 213, 220, 254n2; oversight of administration, 131, 141-42, 207, 249n17, 251n34

Appropriations, Senate Committee on: 19, 20, 23, 24, 222; staff, 3, 6, 8, 64, 65, 147, 220; oversight of administration, 131, 141-42, 207, 249n17, 251n34

Arens, Richard, 65

Armed Services, House Committee on: 20, 21, 25, 26, 73, 130-31, 148; staff, 38, 39, 42, 49, 50-51, 64, 73, 85, 87-88, 109, 111, 131

Armed Services, Senate Committee on: 20, 21, 24, 130-31, 142, 148, 149, 222; staff, 64, 74, 97-98, 104, 108, 131, 148, 149. *See also* Preparedness Investigating Subcommittee, Senate

Army, U.S., 84, 130

Arnold, Nancy, 57, 58, 214

Banking and Currency, House Committee on, 24, 41, 42, 64, 98, 101

Banking and Currency, Senate Committee on, 38, 57-58, 59, 64, 66, 75, 103, 225, 255n10

Barden, Graham, 60, 71

Battle, Laurie, 77

Beaman, Middleton, 183-84, 185, 246n17, 263n1

Benson, Serge, 55, 56

Berquist, Fred, 61-63, 210, 237n22

Bill drafting: and committee staffs, 95, 103, 117-18, 124, 148-49, 196-97, 206; by the executive branch, 159-60, 178, 198; by interest groups, 162, 179, 199; and office staffs, 174, 176, 197; nature of, 185, 188-90, 198

Blair, Drury, 65

Blough, Roy, 129

Boots, Charles F., 185, 263n10

Bricker, John, 58

Bridges, Styles: 66, 238n40; quoted, 65

Brookings Institution, 163, 179, 222

Brownlow Committee, 141

Budget, Bureau of the, 87, 132-33, 159, 175, 227

Budget, Joint Committee on the, 6, 8, 53, 64-65, 238n40

Bullock, Roy, 77

Bush, Prescott: 266n3; quoted, 210

Byrd, Harry, 52

Cain, Harry, 58

Calendar Committee aide, Senate Minority (Republican), 56-57, 153, 197-98

Campbell, Joseph, 226

Capehart, Homer, 29, 57-58

Carr, James, 87

Carroll, Holbert: quoted, 29-30

Casework, 85, 128, 131, 138, 144, 169, 170, 172-73, 207, 248n6, 248n8, 252 n43, 260n10. *See also* Committee staffs; Congressional oversight of administration; Senatorial office staffs

Chamber of Commerce, U.S., 162

Chamberlain, Joseph P., 183, 263n1

Chesteen, Gaston, 129

Chicago, University of, 26

Chiefs of staff, committee. *See* Committee staff directors

Chiperfield, Robert, 30

Civil Aeronautics Authority, 87

Clark, Joseph, 22

Classification Act of 1923, 4

Classification Act of 1949, 9

Clerk hire allowance: for Representatives, 3, 180, 208, 218, 228, 263n30; for Senators, 3, 171, 180, 208, 218, 260n7. *See also* Senatorial office staffs

Cohen, Benjamin V., 94

Cohn, Roy M., 239n7

Colmer, William, 29

Columbia University, 26, 183

Commerce, Department of, 113